FROM THE FILES OF <u>TRUE DETECTIVE</u> MAGAZINE

THE MUTILATORS

Edited by
ROSE G. MANDELSBERG

PINNACLE BOOKS
WINDSOR PUBLISHING CORP.

*The editor wishes to express
her sincerest gratitude
to Stan Munro
whose help and tireless efforts
made this book possible.*

A special mention to Chris, a mutilations maven.

For more true crime reading, pick up TRUE DETEC-
TIVE, OFFICIAL DETECTIVE, MASTER DE-
TECTIVE, FRONT PAGE DETECTIVE, and INSIDE
DETECTIVE magazines on sale at newsstands every
month.

PINNACLE BOOKS are published by

Windsor Publishing Corp.
850 Third Avenue
New York, NY 10022

First Printing: November, 1993

Printed in the United States of America

10 9 8 7 6 5 4 3 2

CONTENTS

"HE DISMEMBERED 52, THEN ATE THEIR ORGANS!"

by Philip Westwood

By no stretch of the imagination could the town of Rostov-on-Don be described as attractive. Situated at the end of the mighty River Don on the coast of the Sea of Azov in southern Russia, Rostov is a sprawling city of drab factories and huge, anonymous apartment blocks. This was once the land of those brave, colorful, and much feared military horsemen of the old Russian Empire, the Cossacks. But that was long ago. The color of the region has long gone, evaporated in the Red Revolution of 1917 that turned everything a monotonous shade of gray.

The river divides the city in two. To one side are the docks and waterfront, where big freighters bringing coal and grain from the mines and communal farms of the interior tie up and unload. To the other side, just beyond the railroad station, is an area of dense, dark forest. It is a quiet spot inhabited only by small animals, deer, and lovers looking for someplace private to demonstrate their feelings for each other.

In the dying years of Soviet communism, this forest became a place of terror and death. For it was there that a man destined to become the most prolific mass murderer in the criminal history of the Soviet Union began his career. It was a career that was to plunge the man to depths of horror and depravity never before dreamed of. And yet, for all that, it

7

was a career that got started almost by chance, on a cold, rainy night just before one Christmas in the late 1970s.

Shortly before 10 o'clock on the evening of December 22, 1978, 9-year-old Lena Zakatnova was in a hurry to get home. There were several reasons why Lena was running. First, there was the rain. Lena didn't like rain. It ran down her neck, got inside her shoes, and made her uncomfortable. Then, there was the hour. It was late, too late for Lena to be out. She knew that there would be trouble from her parents when she got back home. But chiefly, there was the fact that Lena needed to go to the bathroom. She needed to go badly, but it was just too cold to go outdoors. So Lena simply had to get home. And fast.

Charging forward as fast as she could, with her head down to shield her face from the driving rain, Lena didn't notice the man coming toward her on the sidewalk.

"Hey, little girl, what's the big hurry?" the man asked as Lena, at full speed, ran straight into him.

Lena looked up at the man towering over her. She looked at his face. It was a kindly face, crinkled with a smile. Lena liked the face. It reminded her of her grandfather's.

"I'm sorry," Lena said politely. Lena's parents had taught her to always be polite to her elders.

"That's all right," said the kindly man. "Now, tell me, why are you in such a hurry? Is someone chasing you?"

Lena replied that no one was chasing her. She explained about the rain, and about the time, and because he was such a nice man, Lena told him about her need to find a toilet. She told him that she had to get home because it was too cold for her to go outside.

"Of course you can't go outside," agreed the man. He thought for a moment, and then he bent down so that his kind face was level with hers. "I know," the man said, smiling sweetly at the little girl. "You can use the toilet at my house. I live just over there."

Lena looked in the direction indicated by the man's

pointing finger. A line of illuminated windows in a row of anonymous little houses on the other side of the street was just discernible through the pouring rain.

"Come on," said the man invitingly. "It will only delay you for a minute. And, anyhow, I can drive you home in my car. You'd like that, wouldn't you?"

Lena replied, quite truthfully, that she would. So she took hold of the outstretched hand that the man offered her, and together, they made their way to a house with a front door that had once been a deep shade of brown, but had long ago lost its sparkle.

"Here we are," the man said. He unlocked and opened the door and pressed a switch that turned on a light whose power to illuminate the hallway was sadly lacking. "Come on it," he invited.

"Where's the toilet?" Lena asked as she felt her way along the walls of the dimly lit passageway.

"It's the first door on your left," replied the man. He glanced up and down the street. There was no one about. The man smiled to himself. "Have you found it?" he called out to Lena.

"Yes," the little girl replied. "I've found it."

"Good," said the man as he stepped into the hallway and gently closed the door behind him. There was a "click" as the man pushed down the button that locked the mechanism on the latch. "Good."

It was the following afternoon when Lena Zakatnova's naked body was found in the undergrowth in the forest on the edge of town. The bruising on her lower abdomen, and the blood that had oozed from between her legs and congealed on her thighs, gave some indication of the torture that she had suffered. The stab wounds in Lena's neck, chest, and back showed how her suffering had finally been brought to an end.

The killing of Lena Zakatnova sent waves of shock and horror throughout the population of Rostov. Mixed with the sense of outrage were feelings of trepidation and fear. This type of murder, the wanton and depraved sex killing of an innocent little girl, was something new to the hardworking, down-to-earth folk of the Soviet city. They wanted it sorted out and sorted out quickly, before some other little child fell prey to the monster in their midst.

The authorities sensed the mood of the people, and they pulled out all the stops in their efforts to track down the killer. Hundreds of police officers were assigned to the case. With such a huge input of manpower, it was reasoned, results must come quickly. And they did. Inside a couple of weeks, a man had been arrested and charged with Lena's murder. The man had a history of sexual assaults against children. There was jubilation when, at the man's trial, he was convicted and sentenced to death. A great sense of peace and calm returned to Rostov when the man was finally executed. Lena's murderer had paid the ultimate price, everyone said, and justice had been done. The nightmare was finally over. Or so everyone thought.

The feeling of relief that the killer had been caught so quickly did not last long. The following summer, another child's body turned up in the woods. And then another. And another. Each had been sexually assaulted, viciously and brutally. And each succeeding victim had been subjected to worse horrors than the one before. It was clear that the massive police operation in the days following Lena Zakatnova's death had not been successful. The killer had apparently not been caught. And an innocent man had been executed.

By the early 1980s, the killings were in danger of reaching epidemic proportions. Only now the murderer was not confining himself to young children. Teenagers, and even adults, were being slaughtered and dismembered by the increasingly crazed killer. And he was becoming more proficient in his work. With each murder, he gained a little more insight into the workings of the human body. And, as his knowledge increased, so did the time taken for his victims to die. Using his knife with almost surgical skill, the killer had developed his technique to the point where he was able to inflict excruciating pain on his victims while keeping them fully conscious. It is difficult to imagine the agony that his tortured victims suffered before the blessed release of death drew a veil over their torment. While still alive, boys had their sex organs sliced off and laid out neatly on the ground beside them. Young girls had their nipples cut off, and their barely developed breasts mutilated. In both sexes, the front of the body, from the chest to the abdomen, was cut open, and several internal organs were removed and laid out on the ground.

But mixed in with the examples of precision torture were elements that betrayed the killer's uncontrollably depraved motivation. For, while a victim's eyes might be gouged out with a knife held in an obviously steady hand, the tongue was removed by a far more basic method. The killer would grasp his victim's tongue between his teeth and rip it out with all the grace of a ravenous carnivore.

The killer moved around—a lot. Bodies bearing the same mutilations as those in Rostov were found in the Central Asian republic of Uzbekistan, hundreds of miles to the east. One victim was discovered in a park in Moscow, 500 miles to the north. For a time, investigating officers felt that they were dealing not with a lone killer, but with a group of satanists for whom the killings were part of some bizarre religious ritual.

They were finally dissuaded from this theory of multiple killers by forensic scientists. Most serial killers have their own trademark, some kind of sign that they leave at the scene of the crime or on their victims' bodies, to announce that the killing is their own particular handiwork. And the man who had by then become known as the "Rostov Ripper" was no exception. His trademark was his own semen, which he left, in amazingly large amounts, on the body of

11

each victim. Forensic scientists were able to show, from the semen, that all the killings were the work of the same man.

In those early days of the investigation, many subjects were pulled in for questioning and subjected to interrogation. No charges were ever brought against those questioned, but for some, the ordeal was too much. One man committed suicide after being interrogated. Another attempted to kill himself, but was discovered in time.

No matter how bad a situation might be, given time, most people can get used to it. What initially seems shocking and beyond belief eventually becomes accepted as normal. And that's how some of the people of Rostov came to look upon the Ripper. He was out there somewhere, torturing and killing. And until the police caught up with him, that was a fact they had to live—or die—with.

Ten-year-old Olga Stalmachenok knew about the Ripper. Her parents had warned her that he was out there, watching and waiting. They told her that she must never talk to strangers, and that under no circumstances should she go off with any man who offered her a bag of candy or a ride in his car. Olga knew all that, and yet, on December 11, 1982, when her school bus broke down on the way home and she was forced to walk the last half mile, she still went off with the kindly looking man who spoke to her just yards from her house. Other children watched them go off, hand in hand, in the direction of the woods. And that was the last time anyone saw Olga Stalmachenok alive.

It was four months later before Olga's body was discovered in a shallow grave in dense undergrowth in the forest. It was so badly decomposed that identification had to be made from dental records. Ascertaining the exact cause of death was impossible. In a way, that was a blessing. For it also meant that, for Olga's distraught parents, the pain of their grief was not compounded by the knowledge of precisely what had befallen their daughter before she died.

But why, after all her parents' warnings, did Olga go off

with the man who was to bring her young life to so tragic an end? Being an innocent 10-year-old, it is possible that Olga did not fully understand the danger posed by the Ripper. She would know nothing of sex, and of the perverted lust that can drive some men to commit acts of unspeakable barbarity in their quest to satisfy their desires. The same could not be said of Vera Shevkun.

Fifty miles to the northeast of Rostov is the little mining town of Shakhty. The people of Shakhty knew all about the Ripper killings. They also knew all about Vera Shevkun.

Though only 19 years old, Vera was already a hardened alcoholic. In order to get the money necessary to satisfy her craving for booze, Vera worked as a prostitute. Time had not ravaged her face. Vera was still a good-looking girl, with pale blue eyes and golden hair. So there was no shortage of men willing to pay for her favors.

On the afternoon of October 27, 1983, Vera was seen talking to a balding, middle-aged man on a street in the residential part of Shakhty. She was seen going off with the man toward the outskirts of town, just another hooker off to earn her paycheck.

The following day, Vera's body was discovered in a field close by the town. Now, she didn't look so good. Where once her pale blue eyes had been were now just two bloody red holes. Vera's golden hair was matted with the blood and brains that had spilled out when her skull had been smashed open. But the worst thing about her head was that it lay 10 feet from her body. Vera Shevkun had been decapitated.

By the start of 1984, investigators had ascribed the deaths of 31—boys, girls, and women—to the so-called Ripper. And the frenzied killer wasted no time in adding to that tally.

Seven-year-old Igor Gudkov was found in the woods, butchered like the rest of the victims. Then, on February 21st, what was left of Marta Ryabyenko was discovered under bushes in Rostov's public park. In two ways, this last killing marked a new departure for the Ripper.

First, it showed that he was supremely confident. By killing and dismembering Marta virtually in the middle of town, he was thumbing his nose at the investigating authorities. It was not as if he were just one step ahead of them; he was way out in front, and he knew it. The authorities now realized that they were dealing with a man who didn't mind who he killed. He was simply a killer who enjoyed killing. He was addicted to it in the same way that a junkie was addicted to his dope. And he had to keep killing to satisfy his addiction.

The second difference in this murder was that Marta was not like the rest of his victims. She was not a child or a teenager. She was 44 years old.

Like Vera Shevkun, Marta Ryabyenko was an alcoholic prostitute. Other call girls who worked the same beat as Marta recalled seeing her in the park on the night she was killed. She was with a man, whom they described as middle-aged and balding. But they did not remember him too clearly. He looked just like most of the men who came to the park for their services.

On March 24th, the mutilated body of 10-year-old Dima Ptashnikov was found on the outskirts of the town of Novoshaktinsk, a few miles from Shakhty, where Vera Shevkun had met her fate. A search organized by the boy's family as soon as he had failed to return home for his tea had resulted in Dima being found very quickly—though not quickly enough. But the semen that the killer had left on the little boy's body was still fresh—fresh enough to provide investigators with their first positive lead. They wasted no time in sending it to Moscow for analysis.

The hunt for the killer again intensified. Fifty detectives and 500 uniformed officers, headed up by chief State Prosecutor Vitaly Kalyukhin, were assigned to the case. A couple of days after Dima's murder, they thought they had the breakthrough they were seeking.

14

On the night of March 27th, 1984, Rostov police received several complaints concerning a man who was hanging around the railroad station. He was observed approaching a number of the young dropouts who clustered each night at the station for warmth and whatever handouts they could beg from the passengers piling out of the commuter trains that arrived at the station every few minutes. The man was heard to offer the youngsters money and vodka in exchange for sex. But it was the complainants' descriptions of the man as middle-aged and balding that really grabbed the attention of investigators. And, inside a matter of minutes, they had him in custody.

The man gave his name as Andrei Romanovich Chikatilo and his age as 50. Yes, he agreed, he had been trying to pick up youngsters at the station. But he was not the Ripper, he said. He was not a pervert. He was a happily married family man and a Communist Party official who had simply been looking for a little diversion, something different. He winked at the investigators. "You're men of the world," he said. "You know what I mean. There's no harm in it."

The investigators knew what he meant, all right. But they didn't agree that there was no harm in hanging around the railroad station trying to pick up youngsters when everyone knew that a crazed killer was on the loose and probably trying the very same thing. Prosecutor Kalyukhin had a feeling about Chikatilo. He didn't like him or his story. So he decided to hold him while they ran a few tests. "Blood tests, Mr. Chikatilo," the prosecutor explained. "Do you have any objections?"

Chikatilo said he didn't, so the tests were carried out and the results were sent to Moscow for comparison with the semen sample taken from little Dima Ptashnikov. Kalyukhin sat back to await the outcome. He was satisfied in his own mind that Chikatilo's blood group would match that of the semen sample. For two months, Kalyukhin waited for the results to come through. Chikatilo waited out the time in the confines of a cell at the Rostov Police Station. And then they arrived, Kalyukhin read the test report in disbelief. Apparently, the forensics experts had been unable to match Chikatilo's blood with the semen sample. It looked like Kalyukhin had gotten the wrong man.

The prosecutor had no alternative but to let Chikatilo go. But if the mild-mannered, well-spoken Party official was not the Ripper, who was? Kalyukhin decided to call in the Ukraine's top psychiatrist to see if he could help identify the wanted man. The psychiatrist had made a special study of the FBI's system of "psychological profiling." Using this technique, it was possible, by taking into account every detail about the killings, to build a picture of the type of man most likely to have perpetrated them.

The psychiatrist was given free access to the police files on the case. He became acquainted with the facts about the murders that had never been made public, such as how the killer was in the habit of rendering his victims deaf by puncturing their eardrums with a small, sharp-pointed knife; details of how the killer had, in the later murders of young boys, not only cut off his victims' testicles, but probably eaten them as well; details of how the Ripper had finally snuffed the life out of some of his victims by biting through their windpipes with his teeth. Most of the victims, the psychiatrist learned, had been rendered deaf, dumb, and blind by the Ripper before he started on the work of torture and mutilation.

At the end of his study, the psychiatrist deduced that the Ripper was an adult under 40 years of age who was, to all appearances, an ordinary family man. He would blend well into his surroundings and would be so ordinary as to arouse no suspicions among his neighbors.

He was articulate and intelligent. This would give him an understanding of children and the ability to talk them into going off with him. He obviously had experience with children, and so he had probably, at one time, been a teacher.

But he probably was not following that profession when he took to killing. Instead, he seemed to have a job that entailed his traveling around. Bodies had been found in various locations, so the killer was obviously mobile. He might have owned a car, something highly unusual for a Soviet citizen. More likely, he traveled by train. He was not a man who was a constant danger, such as a psychopath. The Ripper was a man who only became dangerous if a certain set of circumstances came together, though he would have the ability to engineer those circumstances. And, finally, the analyst theorized, he was impotent.

Prosecutor Kalyukhin pondered the psychiatrist's conclusions. Much of the profile fit Andrei Chikatilo. True, Chikatilo was older than the psychiatrist's idea of the killer, and he probably was not impotent. He had two grown children. But he was articulate and intelligent—he had a degree in philology—and he knew about children. After graduating, he had worked as a teacher at a school in Novoshaktinsk. He had left the teaching profession at around the same time that Lena Zakatnova, the first victim, had been murdered. Since then, he had worked for various companies as a sales representative. It was a job that entailed a great deal of traveling. So Chikatilo was mobile. He used the trains.

Scientific evidence, however, had pointed out that Chikatilo could not be the killer. His blood group did not match the blood group of the semen found on Dima Ptashnikov. However suspicious Prosecutor Kalyukhin may have been about Chikatilo, he had to accept the fact that he must look elsewhere for the notorious Rostov Ripper.

But while Kalyukhin and his huge investigative team were searching for the elusive mass murderer, the death toll continued to rise. On May 11, 1984, 32-year-old Tanya Petrosyan and her 11-year-old daughter, Sveta, were killed in the forest near Shakhty. The mother and daughter had gone to the forest to enjoy a picnic. Sveta's windpipe had been severed by the killer's teeth. Her mother's womb had been torn out of her body and thrown into nearby bushes. It seemed unlikely, given the fact that a sadistic cannibal was on the loose, that the Petrosyans would have gone to the forest without a male escort. Was that man the killer perhaps? Did they know him? Was he Andrei Chikatilo? It was possible for, Tanya and Chikatilo had, at one time, been close friends. Some people said they were more than just friends.

Two months later, on July 19th, 19-year-old Anna Lemesheva disappeared from the commuter train that brought her home from work. Six days later, her mutilated and decomposing corpse was found in the Rostov woods. On August 2nd, the body of 16-year-old Natasha Golosovskaya was found under some bushes in Aviators' Park, in the center of Rostov. Her breasts had been cut off, her eyes gouged out, her abdomen slit open, and her womb removed. And all of this had occurred in a public park in the middle of a busy town during the early-evening rush hour.

That summer was proving to be a real headache for Prosecutor Kalyukhin and his team of investigators. But it wasn't over yet. On August 26th, the ravaged body of an 11-year-old boy, Sascha Chepel, described by those who knew him as intelligent, polite, and well-behaved, was found in the forest near Rostov. Many injuries had been inflicted on the body, including the removal of Sascha's genitals. An intensive search of the area failed to locate the boy's missing sex organs. Investigators deduced—correctly, as events turned out—that the killer had eaten them.

The years passed, and the gruesome catalog of deaths continued. But these later killings seemed to follow a pattern. They appeared to center on the railroad station. Victims tended to be drawn from the young dropouts who hung around the station, or from children traveling home from school on the commuter trains. These victims also tended to be male. Female victims, such as 19-year-old Yelena Varge, who was raped and disembowelled on August 19, 1989, became increasingly rare.

In most of the male killings, the Ripper's modus operandi was the same. He would tie the victim's hands behind his back to lessen resistance, and he would bite the victim's tongue out to prevent his calling for help or screaming in agony when the pain of torture that was to come became unbearable. Then the Ripper would get to work. Anal intercourse would take place, although, in one or two cases, the Ripper waited until his victim was dead before having sex with him. The Ripper would then blind and deafen his victim, then systematically dismember him while still alive.

Internal organs would be removed. Some of them the killer would eat as he went about his hideous dissection. The victim's genitals would be removed; not crudely hacked off, but sliced away from the body with an almost professional skill. The killer would then eat the genitals. When the Ripper had satisfied his perverted desires, he would dispose of his victim by a single bite through the windpipe, a frenzied knife attack that would result in 50 or 60 stab wounds being inflicted, or by bashing in the victim's skull with a hammer. As a bizarre finishing touch, the Ripper would stand and masturbate over the corpse.

As the 1980s gave way to a new decade, Prosecutor Kalyukhin increased the scale of his already intensive manhunt and turned it into the largest police operation ever seen in the Soviet Union—or anywhere else. Thousands of questionnaires were printed and handed out to every schoolchild in the Ukraine. The questions asked were: Have you ever been approached by a stranger? Have any of your friends ever been approached? Have you seen a man hanging around your school, or the railroad station, or the bus depot, trying to stop children and talk to them? The questions went on and on, and every child had to answer every one. Police photographers, in unmarked vans parked all across the town, captured on film every instance they saw of a man walking with a child. The comings and goings at the railroad station were continuously recorded on videotape by concealed cameramen.

Inside the railroad station, policewomen posed as hookers, junkies, and runaways and mingled with the dropouts. And every day, plainclothes officers traveled in every car on every commuter train that passed through.

Throughout the spring, summer, and fall of 1990, Prosecutor Kalyukhin maintained the incredibly high level of police activity. But still the gruesome murders continued. On August 14th, the mutilated corpse of 11-year-old Vanya Fomin was found on the river beach at Rostov after his father, a guard at the nearby maximum security Novocherkassk Prison, had organized dozens of his colleagues into a search party.

On October 30th, young Viktor Tischenko disappeared from the railroad station after going to buy train tickets. His body was found, like so many others, in the Rostov woods. Kalyukhin began to despair of ever catching the Ripper. But his luck was about to change.

On the morning of November 7th, Sergeant Ivor Rybakov was standing on the edge of the woods, idly watching each man who came along the trail that led from the forest to the railroad station. There was nothing unusual in this. The trail was a shortcut from parts of the town to the station and dozens of men used it everyday. Fully grown men had never been the prey of the Ripper, so for them, the forest was pretty safe.

Quite a few men had passed by Sergeant Rybakov that morning. They were on their way to catch the trains that would take them to work. Rybakov had looked at each one in his nonchalant, but practiced manner, and had noted nothing unusual about any of them.

But then along the trail came a man who did cause the sergeant to look twice. He was a balding, middle-aged man, reasonably well dressed and apparently no different from all the others who had used the trail that morning. But to the sharp-eyed Rybakov, there was something different about this particular man. Tiny speckles of blood stained his face. Rybakov stopped the man and asked to see his identification. The man produced a card on which was printed the name "Andrei Romanovich Chikatilo."

Back at headquarters, Chikatilo was unwilling, or unable, to explain the blood spots on his face. A chilling thought crossed Prosecutor Kalyukhin's mind, and he ordered an immediate search of the forest. Inside a couple of hours, his hunch was proved depressingly correct. Lying in dense undergrowth a few yards off the trail, searchers found the body of prostitute Sveta Korostik. For her, fate had destined the dubious distinction of being the Rostov Ripper's 52nd — and final — murder and dismemberment victim.

But what about the semen that had ruled out Chikatilo as a suspect six years earlier? Chikatilo's blood group didn't match that of the semen found on the victims. That meant that he couldn't be the killer, Kalyukhin had been told. "Was that information correct?" the prosecutor asked.

"Well yes — and no," was the perplexing answer that came from scientists at Moscow's prestigious Serbsky Institute. "Back in 1984, it was correct. Indeed, until a few weeks ago, it was correct. But now it isn't."

The scientists explained that, in the summer of 1990, it had been discovered that it was possible for one man to have different blood and sperm groups. The chances were remote, about one in a million. "You appear to have that man in a million," Kalyukhin was told.

Under interrogation, Chikatilo admitted that he was the killer. "I am ready to give evidence of the crimes I have committed," he told detectives. "But please do not torment me with the details because my psyche would not cope. Everything I have done makes me tremble." He was not alone. The whole of southern Russia and Ukraine had been trembling for 12 years because of Chikatilo's crimes.

The psychiatrist was called in once more, this time to determine if Chikatilo was sane — at least in the legal sense.

No one doubted for a moment that, in the moral sense, he was a raving madman.

The psychiatrist talked for hours to the mild-mannered mass murderer. He learned that Chikatilo had a morbid fascination for cannibalism. He had grown up in the repressed and deprived era of the 1930s, when most of the population was starving under the relentless tyranny of Stalin's regime. During the famine that raged through the rural areas, starving peasants had killed and eaten Chikatilo's older brother. It was an act that had gone a long way towards shaping Chikatilo's personality and character. And then there was the war. Chikatilo's father had served in the Red Army and been captured by the Nazis. He had spent most of the war years in a prisoner-of-war camp.

When the war ended, Chikatilo's father was released. But his freedom was short-lived. On his return home, he was imprisoned again, this time by Stalin, who regarded him and thousands of his fellow Russian soldiers, as "enemies of the people who had betrayed their homeland."

So Chikatilo was raised with the memory of his brother being killed and eaten, and the knowledge that his father had been branded a traitor. It did nothing to help the development of the sensitive and intelligent adolescent.

Chikatilo also had problems with women. He had never been able to relate to them. He had been a virgin at the time of his marriage. That was in 1966, when he was 31 years old. During the first three years of marriage, his wife had produced two children. But since 1969, sex between the couple was virtually unknown.

The psychiatrist eventually decided that Chikatilo was legally sane, and in April 1992, the former school teacher stood trial in Rostov on 52 counts of murder. In the 18 months that separated his arrest and trial, Chikatilo had changed greatly. Now his head was shaved and he stared, with wild eyes, around the courtroom from the iron cage in which he was confined. Spectators in the public gallery, many of them relatives of Chikatilo's victims, jeered at the man in the cage, and called for him to be let out so that they could lynch him. "Let me tear him apart with my hands!" screamed one woman in black.

For his part, Chikatilo gripped the bars of his cage and jumped up and down like some demented ape in a circus sideshow, screaming abuse and obscenities at everyone around him.

Occasionally, armed guards, their peaked caps pulled low over their foreheads, would prod him with batons to make him desist. It was a bizarre spectacle.

At other times, Chikatilo would interrupt witnesses as they gave evidence. "I am a victim of Chernobyl," he would shout. "Why me? Show me the corpses. I am a victim of the Assyrian underworld."

During these outbursts, Chikatilo would be taken out of the courtroom by the armed guards. Thirty minutes later he would be back, bruised and subdued. This weird ritual went on throughout the six months that his trial lasted.

Finally, on October 14, 1992, the trial concluded. The verdict, contained in a document that ran to 330 pages, was read to the court by Judge Leonid Akubzhanov. In short, it said that Andrei Chikatilo was guilty on all charges. The following day, he was sentenced to death.

Andrei Chikatilo is now housed at Novocherkassk Prison. Ironically, one of his guards is the father of one of his victims. When death comes, it will be in the form of a single bullet to the back of the neck. It will be quick and clean, which is more than can be said of the many crimes of the bullet's recipient.

The innocent man executed after being wrongly convicted of the murder of Lena Zakatnova has been granted a posthumous pardon.

"BLOODY MONEY SOLVED DENA'S DECAPITATION!"

by Bruce Stockdale

BALTIMORE, MARYLAND
JANUARY 24, 1986

Until that DOA call for an address on Chauncey came over the radio at 9:02 p.m., Tuesday, April 5, 1983, it had been an unusually quiet tour of duty for Officer Jeff Fugate, Central District, Baltimore City Police Department (BCPD). Unusual because Jeff Fugate's bailiwick included that section of Baltimore most commonly referred to as "Whitelock City." It is so called by reason of nearby Whitelock Avenue which serves as the main commercial center of the neighborhood. With its motley collection of Ma-and-Pa groceries, liquor stores, dry cleaner, and bars, it is a busy place, day and night.

Once a desirable residential neighborhood by virtue of its proximity to the exclusive residential neighborhood known as Reservoir Hill, Whitelock City has become blighted.

Indeed, it is officially designated by the BCPD as a high crime area, with robberies, burglaries, drug-dealing, and even homicides providing Criminal Investigation Division detectives with a lot of work. People keep their doors locked at night in Whitelock City.

Arriving at the Chauncey Avenue address at 9:05 p.m., Officer Fugate was met by a nearly hysterical middle-aged man who directed him up a flight of stairs to a second floor apartment. As he entered, the officer readily understood why the man was upset. Lying face down on the floor under the dining room table was the body of an elderly white woman, spattered with blood. The disarray of the apartment indicated that a struggle and/or ransacking had taken place therein.

With foul play so readily apparent, the officer immediately secured the crime scene, then radioed police headquarters and requested homicide unit assistance.

Working the 3-11 shift that clear and balmy spring evening and up for new assignments were 45-year-old Detective Sergeant Ronald Lamartina and his partner, Detective Donald Steinhice, also 45. Sergeant Lamartina had just recently returned to the unit after a brief stint on the street in uniform. The good working relationship he had enjoyed with Donald Steinhice was resumed, with the result that they were chalking up an impressive string of closed homicide cases.

The two sleuths seem to complement each other well because of their special talents and capabilities. Sergeant Lamartina has acquired a reputation as an expert in that tricky area of the law which governs police handling of suspects during custodial interrogation. As a result, cases made under his supervision are seldom if ever lost as a result of the criminal's confession being ruled inadmissible as evidence in court.

For his part, the trim and boyish-looking Steinhice brings to the team a deep knowledge of people and an encyclopedic store of information about crime in Baltimore City gleaned from 20 years' experience on the street.

In what was to be dubbed by the media as "The Case of the Tell-Tale Cat Hairs," Ronald Lamartina and Donald Steinhice would find their combined skills truly put to the test.

The flashing lights of the fire department's paramedic unit and the Central District's uniformed cars told the two detectives that they had reached the right place as they pulled up to a typical two-story brick row house at the Chauncey Avenue address furnished by the central dispatcher.

9:29 p.m. Guided by Officer Fugate, the sleuths entered the second floor apartment of 76-year-old Dena Greenberg, identified as the victim by George Jenkins, who shared the apartment with her.

While Sergeant Lamartina proceeded to question Jenkins, Detective Steinhice began his examination of the body. A pull on the arm disclosed that rigor mortis had set in, indicating that the woman had been dead for several hours. Next, he proceeded to turn the body over onto its back. Dena Greenberg had been a diminutive woman (4'11", 95 pounds) in life, so this was no problem. But when he did so, even the case-hardened detective was shocked by what he saw. The victim's throat had been cut from ear to ear; indeed, the woman had been practically decapitated: Only a relatively small shred of skin connected the head to the body. Blood had rushed out of the gaping wound in such a torrent that the victim's body was now "dry" (devoid of blood). She was clad only in a housedress. No undergarments. Barefoot.

Dena Greenberg had died a horrible death. But who had done it? And why?

Sergeant Lamartina was at that point interviewing George Jenkins in a quest for answers to these questions.

The trembling, grief-stricken man related that, when he had left the apartment at nine-thirty that morning, Dena Greenberg had been alive, well, and in good spirits. Upon getting off work at four-thirty, he had gone to a friend's place of business where he had played cards until around eight o'clock. He had taken the bus home, arriving at about nine o'clock. The downstairs door was locked. He unlocked it and went up the stairs to find the door to the second floor apartment unlocked. This was strange, for Dena Greenberg

26

was a very security conscious person who always kept the doors to her apartment locked. Entering the apartment, he had found it in disarray. He had called out and gotten no response. Then he checked the cellar. Nothing. Returning to the apartment, Jenkins said he then spotted the woman's body on the floor of the dining room. When he bent down to see what was wrong, he touched her head. It was bloody and stained his hand. By now Jenkins realized that something terrible had happened and ran downstairs yelling for the occupants of the first-floor apartment to call for help.

Like many homicide sleuths today, Sergeant Lamartina is a firm believer in, and practitioner of, what is termed "the point of the circle" method of murder investigation. Accordingly, attention is initially focused on those persons closest to the victim. Investigative activity then spreads outward—until all those who have had even the most remote dealings with the victim are eliminated as suspects. Years of experience have taught BCPD homicide detectives that this is the most cost-effective way to deal with the heavy caseload of Baltimore, which sees around 250 homicides per year.

Thus, George Jenkins would first have to be eliminated as a suspect in the murder of Dena Greenberg.

He was transported to the homicide unit office to give a formal signed statement concerning the incident and to undergo a luca-malachite examination to detect the presence of blood on his person.

Meanwhile, back at the crime scene, Detective Steinhice, assisted by Ned Landigan, continued to work with the contingent of criminalistics technicians headed by Deborah Pullen.

They could all see that the task was to be a formidable and time-consuming one. Coagulated blood was sprinkled all over the dining room; the bed clothing was strewn on the floor; the dresser drawers had been pulled out, with the contents piled onto the floor.

Somebody had been searching for something, thought Donald Steinhice.

As she buckled down to the tedious and exacting job of crime scene processing, 29-year-old Deborah Pullen was spurred on by the knowledge that almost every killer leaves something of himself at the scene of the crime—something, no matter how minute—and almost always takes something with him.

The problem lay in finding it.

Also recovered for submission to the crime lab for analysis were an open jar of cold cream (which could have been used during a sexual assault) and several strips of tinfoil found littering the place. Police were to subsequently learn from George Jenkins that the victim was in the habit of using tinfoil to wrap bills of large denominations for stashing in various hiding places throughout her apartment. The spry and feisty 76-year-old grandmother did not believe in banks, having witnessed the failure of many during the Great Depression.

After two hours of painstaking work, Sergeant Lamartina returned to the scene with George Jenkins, who had been eliminated as a suspect by virtue of an airtight alibi and impeccable reputation. By now, the only thing remaining to be done was the grim task of removing the body to the M.E.'s office for autopsy.

As the morgue attendants were gently lifting the body off the floor onto a gurney, the sharp eye of Deborah Pullen was caught by two hairs which had been lying on the floor concealed by the victim's head. Her inspection of the hairs under a magnifying glass revealed that they were not gray in color but black. So they could not have come from the victim.

Did they perhaps come from the perpetrator of this atrocious crime? the law officers wondered.

As an experienced criminalist, Deborah Pullen well knew that many is the murder case that has been solved by some-

28

thing as seemingly insignificant as a hair specimen.

These hair specimens would be delivered to the Evidence Control Unit before she went off duty that night.

Detectives Lamartina and Steinhice followed the morgue van on its lonely, late-night trip through downtown Baltimore to the Office of the State Medical Examiner, a relatively small three-story brick building nestled in the University of Maryland complex in Southwest Baltimore. They needed some answers fast on the question of sexual assault so as to possibly get a better handle on the question of whether they should be looking for a sex criminal or a robber in the murder of Dena Greenberg. Perhaps the M.E. on duty could give them a tentative answer.

Meanwhile, Ned Landigan, assisted by a unit of detectives who had reported for duty on the graveyard shift, would conduct a neighborhood canvass in an effort to determine whether anyone had noticed anything suspicious that day.

Detective William Lansey hit paydirt in the form of a neighbor of Dena Greenberg. One John Morris, who lived next door and shared a party wall with the victim, told the sleuth that around noon that day he had heard a commotion in the apartment next door. He had not thought much of it at the time, figuring it was just a domestic quarrel. About 15 minutes later, Morris said, he just happened to look out the front window and spotted a black male walking away from the front of the house. The man had been carrying two shopping bags. The man had turned west and headed for Linden Avenue. Unfortunately, Morris could not positively identify the man since he had not seen his face.

While their colleagues were canvassing the victim's neighborhood, Sergeant Lamartina and Detectives Steinhice were getting some determinations from Dr. Thomas Smythe, assistant medical examiner.

Dr. Smythe said that the victim died as a result of "exsanguination caused by a radical stab wound to the neck." In other words, she had bled to death. Both arteries leading through the neck had been severed, with death virtually instantaneous.

But this was not all.

Examination of both the vaginal and rectal cavities disclosed the presence of sperm. Dena Greenberg had been both rape and sodomized before being murdered.

The lawmen were now sure of a motive in the mysterious case—Dena Greenberg had been slain to silence her as a witness to her own rape, sodomy, and robbery.

Returning to the homicide unit offices, the two detectives discovered that Bill Lansey and Ned Landigan were still working on the case. They were in the middle of taking recorded statements from the two occupants of the first-floor apartment below Dena Greenberg's.

Both these individuals denied any knowledge of the gruesome crime that had taken place that day in the upstairs apartment. The head of the household, who identified himself as William Hargrove, age 32, told investigators that he had left the house early that morning to go to his job as a cleaner at a downtown movie theater, returning around noon to get some lunch and feed his cats. This done, he had gone back downtown to do some errands and shopping. That evening had been spent at his regular hangout, a bar located downtown on Eutaw Street. Hargrove said he had neither seen nor heard anything amiss as far as the apartment upstairs was concerned.

He was shocked when he came in at 11:00 and learned what had happened. Mrs. Greenberg had been a good landlady as far as he was concerned, and he was sorry about what had happened to her.

William Hargrove's relative told the police that she had been at work all day and that she had no idea who might have killed Dena Greenberg either.

By now it was into the wee hours of the morning and

Ronald Lamartina and Donald Steinhice were two exhausted cops. They had no reason at that point to accuse anybody of the Dena Greenberg murder. Dismissing William Hargrove and his relative with the admonition to keep themselves available for further interviews, they dictated their initial investigative reports and signed off duty.

The next day, Donald Steinhice began his shift by going to the Central Records Division and looking up the record on one William Hargrove, 32-year-old black male, five-feet, ten-inches in height, about 175 pounds. Hargrove was on parole from a 1978 conviction for robbery with a deadly weapon. In 1976, he had been convicted of larceny.

As a police officer well-versed in the rules of evidence, Don Steinhice knew full well that Hargrove's record did not constitute sufficient reason to accuse him of killing Dena Greenberg, but it still was reason enough to make him a focus of investigation until such time as he could be eliminated as a suspect.

It is said that one of the best weapons possessed by the BCPD in the fight against crime is the feet of Detective Donald Steinhice. And this weapon would be put to good use on Wednesday, April 6th.

Steinhice, accompanied by Landigan, made his first stop on Eutaw Street, where Hargrove allegedly spent part of the previous day. The place was a notoriously rough joint; indeed, a Baltimore City police officer had lost his life there a few years earlier. The lawmen would have to be on their toes.

However, at that particular time of the afternoon, it seemed to be nice and quiet. The bartender was both courteous and congenial, listening attentively as Steinhice showed him a mugshot of William Hargrove and explained the purpose of his inquiry. Maybe the place is under new management, thought Donald Steinhice.

Yes, replied the bartender, he knew William Hargrove. In fact, he had been in just the day before. He remembered him well, because Hargrove had been a hail-fellow-well-met, treating everybody to drinks and paying for them with $50 bills.

Don Steinhice and Ned Landigan looked at each other. Now they were getting somewhere.

But this was not all, the bartender said. It seemed that Hargrove had once been employed at the bar as a part-time bouncer. However, management had been made nervous by the man's propensity for violence and had let him go. He explained that Hargrove had enforced demands that unruly patrons leave the premises at the point of a six-point buck knife.

Thanking the man for his help, the two sleuths continued to pound shoe leather, with their next stop a shoe repair shop just next door to the bar.

According to the proprietor, the man in the mugshot had been in just the day before to pick up a pair of shoes left for repair. He remembered him well because he had been paid with a $50 bill.

While the circumstantial evidence was beginning to pile up, the fact remained that it was still just that— circumstantial. If the police were to make a first-degree murder case, they would need a lot more evidence.

But for Donald Steinhice, the clincher came when he talked to the proprietor of a clothing store just down the street from the bar.

The store owner told the sleuths that the man in the mugshot had been in the previous day and had made a $92 purchase of designer jeans. Payment had been in the form of two $50 bills. In addition, the man asked for change for another $50 bill.

Fearing that he might be taking counterfeit bills, the owner had taken the time to examine them carefully. While they looked to be genuine, he had noticed that one of the bills was stained with some sort of reddish-colored material. Blood, perhaps? wondered Detective Steinhice.

With this in mind, the two detectives made a beeline to the bank where the clothing store made deposits. There, the manager explained that, while he wished that he could help the lawmen in their quest for the red-stained $50 bill, unfortunately, it would have already been forwarded to the Federal Reserve Bank. Thus, try to come up with it would be looking for the proverbial needle in the haystack.

Bloodstained $50 bill or no bloodstained $50 bill, it had been a good afternoon's work by Steinhice and Landigan, as far as Ronald Lamartina was concerned. In particular, he had some pointed questions to ask William Hargrove about the $50 bills that he had been spending with such abandon April 5, 1983. He was pondering the question of whether he had enough evidence to formally charge Hargrove with the murder of Dena Greenberg when he took a telephone call from criminalist Deborah Pullen. She was to help answer this question for him.

She advised that the two hairs found under the victim's head had been identified as coming not from a human being, but from a animal: *felis catus*, more commonly known as the cat. This information struck Sergeant Lamartina as peculiar since Dena Greenberg had not kept any pets. Then he remembered . . . Hargrove had told them that he had come home around noon on April 5th to get some lunch and . . . feed his cats.

With this, Sergeant Lamartina went into a hurried conference with his commander, Captain Joe Cooke, and it was decided that police now had sufficient evidence upon which to base a request for a warrant for the arrest of William Hargrove, b/m/32, for the murder, rape, robbery and sodomy of Dena Greenberg.

But serving the warrant soon proved to be a problem, when Hargrove's relative informed police that the now-wanted man had left the Chauncey Avenue address for parts unknown.

An all-points bulletin (APB) was issued for the fugitive,

who was now obviously making himself scarce.

Days turned into weeks. The sleuths were beginning to think that their suspect had somehow managed to elude their dragnet and had left town. Detective Steinhice got his lines out to his street informants in the Baltimore underworld and hoped his quarry would become careless.

Finally, during the late evening hours of April 23rd, Detective Steinhice and Lansey, acting on a tip, located William Hargrove at his old haunt—the rough bar on Eutaw Street. They took him into custody without incident.

Ronald Lamartina was anxiously awaiting him at an interrogation room at the homicide unit office.

At 11:48 p.m., the suspect was ushered into the 8' x 5' interrogation room. He readily signed BCPD Form 77-69 (Explanation of Rights), a tape recorder was switched on and the interview began.

First, Hargrove denied knowing that he had been formally charged with the Dena Greenberg murder or that he had been wanted for questioning. He claimed that he had simply moved out of the Chauncey Avenue address as a result of an argument with his relative. He denied any complicity in the crimes alleged and welcomed this opportunity to talk to the police and clear himself.

When the articulate suspect had finished with his preliminary statement, Sergeant Lamartina began his questioning in earnest.

The suspect was asked if he had spent any time in Dena Greenberg's house.

"Yes, about eight a.m."

"What happened?"

The suspect said they had engaged in sex.

"Where and when did this take place?" Sgt. Lamartina pressed.

"That morning in her bedroom," Hargrove responded.

"Did she give you money?"

"She gave me twenty dollars."

"Then what happened."

"I went to my own apartment. Then I went downtown."

Hargrove went on to deny robbing, raping, sodomizing or killing Dena Greenberg, claiming that the elderly woman had been alive and well when he had left her apartment. "I was just satisfying her nature," he claimed.

When Lamartina pointed out that, in his first statement to police, Hargrove had blanketly denied even having been in the victim's apartment on the day of her murder, the man glibly offered that he had been constrained to lie during this first interview in order to keep from becoming involved whatsoever. He had been afraid that the police might get the erroneous idea that he was guilty of the crime.

But now he was telling the truth.

With this admission, the lawmen were convinced that the Dena Greenberg case stood solved. It was now apparent what had happened: Hargrove had gained admittance to his landlady's apartment on some pretext. After raping and sodomizing the terrified woman at knifepoint, he had forced her to tell him where she had secreted her money (George Jenkins had told police that she kept her money in the form of $50 bills wrapped in tinfoil and hidden in nooks and crannies). However, once he had the money in hand, Hargrove was faced with a crucial decision. What was to be done with Dena Greenberg? Here he was, an ex-convict on parole, having just committed rape, sodomy, and robbery. If he were to be convicted of these new crimes, it would mean that he would be buried in the Maryland prison system for the rest of his life — or at least until he was too old to enjoy life.

The powerfully-built cutthroat took his razor-sharp buck knife and, as he held the tiny woman with his left arm, used his right hand to draw the weapon across her throat, slitting it from ear to ear. This was the disturbance the neighbor in the adjoining apartment had heard. Then Hargrove returned to his apartment, cleaned up, and left with the bloody clothes and murder weapon, to be disposed of when he got the chance. This explained why a search warrant executed at the Chauncey Avenue apartment of the suspect had failed to yield anything.

Hargrove, fearful that he could be placed in the victim's apartment by fingerprints (though the criminalists had failed to come up with any), had decided to walk the tightrope of admitting that he was in the apartment while denying that he committed the crimes.

Would he be able to get away with it?

Not if 50-year-old Edwin O. Wenck could help it. Wenck was assigned to represent the state in the case of Maryland v. William Hargrove.

Prosecutor Wenck is an interesting example of a preacher-turned-prosecutor. A minister for ten years in the United Church of Christ before deciding to go to law school, he was now making good use of the forensic skills developed in the pulpit in the fight against crime. As a result, he has acquired an excellent record with the Violent Crimes Unit of the Baltimore State's Attorney's Office.

He was to find his talents put to the test in the Dena Greenberg case.

He was worried about it. He had had enough experience with Baltimore City juries to know how loath they are to convict defendants of serious crimes on the basis of circumstantial evidence. And, except for Hargrove's second statement, wherein he admitted consensual sex with the victim, the case for the state rested entirely on circumstantial evidence. Indeed, it is often said that Baltimore juries don't "guess anybody into the penitentiary." As a result, Ed Wenck was sure that he was in for a hard-fought legal battle.

He was soon proved correct in this assessment. For in October, 1983, in the state's first effort to get a conviction, Judge William Murphy declared a mistrial when Defense Attorney Donna Shearer accused the State's Attorney's Office of "prosecutorial misconduct." The young defense lawyer claimed that Prosecutor Wenck had failed to abide by the rules of discovery in that she was unable to learn of the luca-malachite test administered to George Jenkins until it came out at the trial.

Prosecutor Wenck had heatedly disputed this assertion, stating that the prosecution's entire file had indeed been available for review by the defense.

In any event, the presiding judge declared a mistrial and the matter had gone up to the Maryland Court of Appeals for a decision. The matter died there due to lack of follow-up by the public defender's office, and the case was scheduled for another trial.

Finally, almost three years from the date of the crimes, on December 9, 1985 (ironically, Dena Greenberg's birthday), trial commenced again in the case of Maryland v. William Hargrove.

In the second trial, Prosecutor Wenck found himself opposed by another public defender, 39-year-old David Eaton, a subtle, low-key lawyer with an excellent track record in defending murder cases. In a number of jury trials, he had shown himself to be a master in the art of instilling the element of reasonable doubt in jurors' minds, with the result that his clients had walked out of the courtroom free.

It took two days to select a jury of seven women and five men. Ten of the jurors were black and two were white.

Judge Clifton J. Gordy gaveled for order, and Ed Wenck put on his first witness, George Jenkins. As the prosecution's case-in-chief progressed, it became evident that, in the face of the damning circumstantial evidence that was mounting, a crucial decision was looming for the defense. Would it be smart for Hargrove to get on the witness stand in his own defense to deny his guilt? If he were to do so, he would be letting himself in for a gruelling cross-examination by Ed Wenck. Or would it be best for him not to take the stand in the hope that the state's case would not be

37

strong enough to convince the jurors of his guilt "beyond a reasonable doubt unto a moral certainty."

This question was answered on December 13, 1985, when the defendant elected to take the witness stand on his own behalf.

William Hargrove was the picture of innocence, at one point breaking into tears while asserting that he was not guilty of anything but having sex with the 76-year-old grandmother who had seduced him. The sex had been completely consensual, he claimed. He had never robbed, raped, sodomized or murdered anybody. As for the $50 bills, he had come by them legitimately.

To buttress the last assertion, the defense produced one Ginger Ivey, who testified that she had given the defendant some $50 bills prior to April 5, 1983, when seized by a frenzy of generosity after a big day at Pimlico racetrack.

However, this testimony was rendered suspect when Judge Gordy, himself taking a hand in the examination of the witness, got the witness to admit that she had been the defendant's lover.

After a full week of testimony and masterful summations of their respective cases by both Prosecutor Wenck and Defense Attorney Eaton, the jury was charged by Judge Gordy and retired for deliberations.

Before dismissing the two lawyers, Judge Gordy commended them both for the very able and lawyer-like manner with which they had represented their clients. "It's been a pleasure working with you both," he said.

It was sweating-out time, thought Ed Wenck. A full day had passed and still no verdict in the Hargrove case. Prosecutors usually regard the passage of time without a verdict as an ill omen, indicating, as it does, that the jurors are in disagreement over the verdict. All it would take for a mistrial would be for one juror to hold out for acquittal.

Then the whole thing would have to be done over again.

Finally, late in the evening of December 19, 1985, the jury

38

sent word that it had reached a verdict.

Ed Wenck remembers the suspense of waiting as the jurors filed in and took their seats. The jury foreman stood up and announced the verdicts: "We, the jurors in the above titled case, find the defendant William Hargrove guilty of murder in the first-degree and robbery with a deadly weapon. We find the said William Hargrove not guilty of rape and sodomy."

Ed Wenck breathed a sigh of relief. Justice had triumphed again in Baltimore, Maryland.

All agree that, on the face of it, the jury's verdicts would seem to be illogical and inconsistent. Why would the jury find Hargrove guilty of murder and robbery but not guilty of the rape and sodomy? It just did not add up.

Veteran courthouse observers explain this simply to be the result of some horse trading which had to be accomplished before the jurors could agree on the decision. And, while the verdicts might be construed as dishonoring the memory of Dena Greenberg, they are still preferable to having her killer go free to rob and kill again.

On January 24, 1986, William Hargrove was sentenced to life imprisonment plus 20 consecutive years in the custody of the Maryland Commissioner of Correction. He is currently serving his sentence at the Maryland Penitentiary in Baltimore.

EDITOR'S NOTE

George Jenkins, John Morris and Ginger Ivey are not the real names of the persons so named in the foregoing story. Fictitious names have been used because there is no reason for public interest in the identities of these persons.

"BISEXUAL THRILL-KILLER WAS A MUTILATION FREAK!"

by Bill Cox

The grisly series of sex and mutilation murders began in the spring of 1985.

On April 17, 1985, a Denver, Colorado banker and his wife were with another couple at Lake Worth, on the outskirts of Fort Worth, Texas. They had stopped their car to visit a nature preserve and were strolling near the lake shore when a shocking sight interrupted their day's pleasant outing.

Lying on a sand bank near the lake's edge was a partially nude body. The form lay on its side in shallow water. The smell of decomposing flesh was strong in the air. The visitors came to a halt about 15 feet from the sprawled form. A glance and the nauseating odor were enough to convince the banker and his companions that the person was dead.

They hurried to a nearby residence to telephone authorities about the sickening discovery.

Fort Worth Police Officer C.D. Wilson, one of the first lawmen to respond to the found-body call, saw that the corpse was that of a young man, probably a teenager. Though some clothing was still on the body, the boy's shorts were pulled down below his knees and his shirt was pulled up around the shoulders.

Further examination disclosed that the youth had been stabbed repeatedly, but more shocking was the fact that the lad had been castrated! His throat had also been slashed, and there were other cuts. The dead boy was soon identified as 16-year-old Jeffrey Lynn Davis. He had been reported missing after he failed to return home from a fishing trip four days earlier, police records revealed.

A relative tearfully described Jeffrey as "small for his age, a sweet person who would do anything for anybody." When questioned by detectives, the victim's relatives and acquaintances were at a loss as to any possible reason for his death.

To police investigators, however, the sadistic sexual mutilation suggested that either an extremely vengeful-minded killer or a sadistic homosexual might have administered the savage stabs, slashes, and cuts. The cuts caused speculation that the boy might have been tortured before his death. There was some evidence that the victim had been killed elsewhere and dumped at the remote spot.

Investigators were aware that the boy had been living in the vicinity of Casino Beach which in earlier and better days, especially the late 1930s, had been a popular lakeside attraction for Fort Worth residents. In more recent times, Casino Beach and its dilapidated facilities were known as a trysting site for homosexuals.

But as the investigators failed to uncover any substantial leads, it appeared in the ensuing weeks, and then months, that the mystery might go unsolved.

Six months later, a sadistic sex killer struck again in the Fort Worth region. The date was October 13, 1985. This time, the location was near the little community of Boyd, in Wise County.

It's rare that a law enforcement officer discovers a murder victim. But on that warm bright autumn day, Texas Department of Public Safety Trooper Alan Troup stopped his patrol car on a bridge on Flatwood Road in Wise County, not far from the little town of Boyd. As he stepped from the unit to check something, he glanced into the creek bed below. He was startled to see the body of a nude woman laying below the bridge.

Relaying his find to the radio dispatcher in Wise County, the state trooper was soon joined by a contingent of county sheriff's officers and other area lawmen. Joining the investigation later was Texas Ranger Phil Ryan, a veteran member of Texas' elite corps of colorful lawmen, a corps dating back to the days of the Texas Republic and recognized today as one of the crack investigative agencies in the nation.

The body examined by the officers was that of a young woman, estimated to have been in her 20s or 30s. She had been stabbed repeatedly and also bludgeoned abut the head with a blunt instrument, possibly a hammer. An autopsy later would disclose 17 stab wounds and three smashing blows to her head.

Officers estimated that the woman had not been dead long. The body was in excellent condition in spite of the warm temperatures, showing no signs of decomposition.

None of the naked woman's clothing could be found when a search of the area was made. There was nothing that could identify her, except — the officers hoped — her fingerprints and some obvious scars on the body from past surgery. Since some good fingerprints were lifted from the victim's hands, Ranger Phil Ryan felt sure that a positive identification would be made within a few days.

No other evidence was located in the creek bed or surrounding terrain. Some blood spots on the concrete bannister of the bridge indicated where the killer had apparently boosted the body upon the railing before shoving it over and into the creek bed below.

Ranger Ryan and his fellow investigators compiled a detailed description of the brutally slain woman. She was believed to have been about 30 years old, stood 5 feet, 7 inches tall, weighed 135 to 140 pounds, and had curly, light brown, shoulder-length hair that had been bleached. She was wearing a full set of dentures, another item that the officers thought would help them link a name to the body.

The woman's body bore severe burn scars on the left thigh, calf, and ankle, and there was a scar on her left eyebrow area. The autopsy also disclosed that the victim had surgery scars from a Caesarean section and tubal ligation. Her blood type was A.

The officers immediately started checking out all missing persons' reports on women in the area. There are many such reports in the metroplex area of Dallas-Fort Worth and the surrounding rural counties. The victim's prints were mailed to the Texas Department of Public Safety and the FBI. But as the days passed, the woman's body, despite so many identifying marks and scars, remained unidentified. Usually, such victims are tagged "Jane Doe" on the investigative reports, but in this case, because of the evidence of a Caesarean delivery, the body was referred to as "Mama Doe."

In spite of intensive efforts made by the investigators to obtain an identification, the dead woman's identity would not be learned until nearly four years later. It wasn't because Ranger Ryan and his colleagues didn't try everything they could think of to find out who she was.

Ranger Ryan, with his wife's help, personally prepared and mailed fliers bearing a composite drawing and a full description of the victim, along with her fingerprint facts, to law enforcement agencies throughout the Texas area, as well as neighboring states. In all, more than 200 of the fliers were mailed. The officers continued to check out all reports on missing women, but it was all to no avail.

Ranger Ryan withheld one bit of information about the murder victim that he hoped would help to corroborate a confession, if one were ever obtained. It was a heinous fact: The woman's nipple had been sliced off one of the victim's breasts.

But the weeks turned into years, and the identity of the butchered woman, as well as that of her savage killer, remained an unsolved mystery.

43

A month after the sexually mutilated body of the unidentified woman was discovered, law enforcement officers in the area were confronted with another, strikingly similar murder.

The nude, stabbed, and bludgeoned body of a pretty woman estimated to be in her 20s was found by passersby in a culvert off U.S Highway 287 southeast of Wichita Falls. The site was in Clay County.

The woman had been stabbed and slashed numerous times, beaten about the head, apparently with a hammer, and mutilated, officers learned. Again, no clothing or other possible clues were found at the crime scene. It was believed the victim had been tossed from a vehicle that had stopped along the busy highway.

But the investigators were luckier this time and soon came up with identification on the victim. She was 27-year-old Sandra Lorraine Bailey of Fort Worth.

Officers learned from relatives of Sandra Bailey that she had last been seen alive on the night of November 24, 1985, at a Fort Worth nightclub located on the highway to Jacksboro, Texas. A relative told the investigators that Sandra had been at the club to help the relative celebrate her birthday.

The relative told police that Sandra had planned to meet her at another night spot and go from there to the relative's home to spend the night. But after she left the first nightclub where the birthday party had been celebrated, Sandra was never seen alive again.

There were no leads as to who had killed the woman and dumped her tortured body in the highway culvert. Officers quizzed patrons of the nightclubs and friends and acquaintances of the slain woman, but they could not find a witness who recalled seeing Sandra leave with any person. She had danced with several men during the evening, sleuths were told.

Three sadistic sex killings had occurred in the Fort Worth

44

area within eight months, the victims horribly tortured and sexually mutilated, but there were no leads to the killers or killer—*if* the three were the work of the same murderer, as the conditions of the bodies indicated.

Only 27 days after the one-year anniversary of the discovery of Sandra Bailey's body, Ripper-type sex murder No. 4 came to light in a plush Fort Worth subdivision where moderately wealthy executives and other professionals had their fashionable homes.

Steven Fefferman, an advertising executive with a Fort Worth television station, lived in a townhouse on Colony Hill Road. He was 28 years old, single, and as far as his friends and business associates knew, pretty well satisfied with his life—professionally and personally.

But on Monday, December 29, 1986, Fefferman failed to show up at the TV station. As time passed with no word from him, members of his staff became concerned. One employee called Fefferman's home several times, but each time got only the advertising man's answering machine. Later in the morning, still getting no response to his phone calls, the employee drove out to Fefferman's home. He rang the doorbell and called out his boss' name. No one answered the door.

The TV station worker noticed that Fefferman's car, a Volvo, was gone. But he knew it was unlikely that Fefferman would have gone off somewhere without notifying the station.

Still later in the day, the same employee went back to the TV executive's home, and this time, looked in a front window. His concern increased when he saw that the living room was in disarray.

Meanwhile, another TV station employee got in touch with Fefferman's landlord. The landlord drove out to the Colony Hill Road address. He and a neighbor entered the townhouse about 7:30 p.m., using the landlord's key. Immediately, they noticed that something was wrong.

With growing apprehension, the landlord walked down a hallway approaching the door of a bedroom. Looking inside, he saw a blue mound on the bed and what looked like a pair of feet sticking out. He turned and left the house, then placed a call to the Fort Worth Police Department.

The first officers to arrive at the house were Patrolman Billy Joe Cordell and Robert Cook. As the officers entered the residence, they heard music and noticed that the heat was on, and an extremely bad smell was strong in the air—a smell they recognized as something dead. Going to the bedroom, they saw the blue heap on the bed with naked feet visible.

The uniformed officers put in a call to headquarters for homicide sleuths and crime scene technicians. Within a short time, detectives and crime scene experts arrived at the house.

When the blue cover was pulled back from the form on the bed, Detective James Varnon and other homicide probers viewed a scene of bloody, sadistic carnage. Underneath was the nude body of a man, soon identified as Steven Fefferman. He was tied spread-eagled with neckties that were soaked with blood. A butcher knife was embedded in the man's genitals. The body had been stabbed, slashed, and methodically cut in what appeared to have been intentional torture. He also had been castrated.

Officer Kathy Hopson was one of three crime scene photographers recording the nightmarish scene of the body on the bed and the bedroom interior. She observed a wallet on the floor, along with three credit cards and a checkbook belonging to the murder victim.

Except for some loose change, no money was found in the house. Detective Varnon observed that dresser and chest drawers were pulled out and in disorder as if they had been rifled through and searched.

No blood was discovered outside the bedroom, but a small knife was lying on the living room floor. Cushions from a couch in the living room had been pulled off and were on the floor. A pile of men's clothing was nearby. Other items in the room were in disarray, the investigators noted.

It was the investigators' first theory that the victim and his killer had fought in the living room. But Detective A.J. Tiroff, who examined the sofa cushions pulled onto the floor and the men's clothing tossed in a heap on the living room floor, had another idea about the scene. He believed that the victim and the killer had possibly had sex on the couch.

Had the knife-wielder forced his victim to have sex on the couch before tying him spread-eagled in the bedroom and torturing him? the sleuths wondered. Or had the victim voluntarily participated in the living room sexual encounter that progressed into sadistic fury in the bedroom?

The bloody crime scene posed questions that could not be answered at the time. After obtaining a description and license number of Fefferman's missing car, police issued a bulletin for the vehicle, urging caution in approaching any driver or person who might be in the car.

Later, the victim's Volvo was found in a ditch near the community of White Settlement in the 8400 block of Interstate 30 in Fort Worth. It appeared to have been abandoned after running off the road from the westbound lane.

After the Volvo was photographed at the site, it was impounded so that a thorough search could be made of the vehicle's interior for fingerprints or other evidence.

During a search of Fefferman's home by the investigative team, detectives discovered several pornographic videos. One film included bondage scenes in which the wrists of the actors were tied.

Trying to establish Steven Fefferman's last known activities before he was slain, the homicide sleuths learned from questioning friends and associates that the TV executive was last seen alive on the afternoon of December 26th at a

Fort Worth bank.

Bank employees quizzed by a detectives recalled that Fefferman had made a deposit, purchased some Liberty coins, and placed them in his safety deposit box. He had not been seen after he conducted business at the bank, as far as the investigators could find out. Officers learned that the ad man usually carried $100 or more in cash on him. Since no money had been found in his rifled wallet or elsewhere in the house, robbery had apparently been one of the motives in the murder, detectives figured. Sex also was a factor.

As the search for clues and leads was pursued, an autopsy was performed on the victim by a Fort Worth pathologist.

The pathologist's findings reflected the horror and savagery of the murder. Even the case-hardened investigators winced at the details, Steven Fefferman had apparently been tortured and butchered and had died an agonizing death.

An assistant district attorney would later comment that "Mr. Fefferman was *slaughtered* in that room."

A deputy medical examiner reported to the detectives that Fefferman had suffered injuries all over his body—on the front, back, side, neck, torso, face, and genitals. Two of the wounds would have been "potentially fatal" by themselves, said the doctor. One was a long, very deep slash across the throat, and the other—believed to be the first major wound inflicted—was a deep stab wound in the victim's back.

The back wound indicated that the victim might have been struggling and twisting on the bed when he sustained the knife thrust in the back, the medical expert speculated. The same was true of several wounds in the victim's side.

Incredibly, the body had been sliced open in the front from the throat to the groin and had been castrated, according to the M.E.'s finding. The body also showed minor wounds that would have been painful and probably done in the act of torture, according to the pathologist's report. Fefferman had been stabbed and slashed before and after he was dead and had been killed in a slow, painstaking manner.

There was no evidence of a forced entry into the victim's townhouse. To the detectives, this indicated that the killer had been admitted, either voluntarily or after he had somehow threatened Fefferman to let him inside. Another possibility on which the sleuths speculated was that the TV executive had known the man who had so brutally murdered him.

Fingerprint technicians searched thoroughly for prints that had been left in the living room or the murder room, dusting every surface that might hold a latent print. Prints were also sought on the victim's wallet and the credit cards that had been removed and dropped on the floor.

The bloodied bedclothing, the ties, the knives, the men's clothing in the living room, and all other items that might produce a lead in the case were removed by the investigative team in the house. Detectives also canvassed the neighborhood, looking for witnesses who might have seen or heard something that could identify the killer. But the footwork turned up nothing of value to the probe.

In the next few weeks, detectives dug into Steven Fefferman's background, talking with his business associates and friends, checking all the known haunts where he ate, drank, or socialized. But the tenacious murder investigation came to a dead end.

The same discouraging results occurred in the slaying probes of Jeffrey Davis in the Lake Worth area, and the murders of Sandra Bailey and the still-unidentified woman whose bodies were found in Wise and Clay Counties, not far from the Fort Worth vicinity. Though officers could not help but note some similarities in the sadistic knife and bludgeon killings, they uncovered nothing that linked the deaths to the same killer or killers.

A veteran homicide investigator knows—after he or she has been at the job for years—that no matter how many hours you spend, how many sidewalks you pound, how

49

many doors you knock on, and how many people you quiz, a big part of solving any murder case is pure old luck. Somewhere along the seemingly endless trail of a killer, fate makes the breaks. More often than not, that long-awaited break comes in the form of someone who talks.

Sometimes it's because of conscience, sometimes for vengeance, sometimes for hopes of financial gain. For whatever reason, detectives know it happens frequently. That's why homicide detectives listen patiently and carefully when approached by someone who wants to talk about an investigation.

The approach came indirectly at first, from a counselor in a drug rehabilitation center in the Fort Worth area. The counselor who called the Fort Worth Police Department said there was a "client," a female addict who had been undergoing treatment for methamphetamine abuse for several weeks. The counselor said the addict, Arlene Douglas, wanted to talk to police about some murders which her former lover had committed more than three years before.

Police gave directions on how to get to the police department building, since the informant was unfamiliar with the Fort Worth area. The Tarrant County Sheriff's Department occupies a building next door to police headquarters, and the counselor and the addict mistakenly entered that building.

After the sheriff's deputies talked to Arlene Douglas, they learned that the murders she wanted to tell them about had occurred in locations outside the county jurisdiction—two of them within Fort Worth's city limit. The addict was then directed to the adjacent police building and began unloading her gruesome story to city detectives.

The dates was April 25, 1989, when Arlene Douglas' turgid tale of warped sex, torture, and sadistic murder began to unfold to the detectives.

The heavyset, tearful woman explained she had held her terrible secret inside all this time because she was terrified by the threats of her ex-lover that he would kill her and her baby if she didn't keep her mouth shut.

But in the next few hours, the informant gave affidavits to the detectives accusing her ex-lover, whom she identified as 28-year-old radiator repairman Ricky Lee Green, of four brutal murders that happened in 1985 and 1986.

In her statements, the distraught woman said that Green phoned her on the night of December 27, 1985 — the date of the murder of Steven Fefferman, the Fort Worth TV executive. Green told her he had done something "real bad." He didn't tell her what it was until the next morning, she said.

Arlene Douglas' story was that Green told her he met Fefferman and accompanied him to his home, where he stabbed and mutilated him and stole his Volvo and $100. Green claimed he left the knives "inside the body," the woman related. She also said that Green had admitted to killing Jeffrey Davis, the Fort Worth teenager, and two women whom he raped, mutilated, and killed in a mobile home in Boyd, where he was living at the time.

Based on the woman's affidavits, detectives and other officers drove to the little community of Azle, where Ricky Green now lived. They arrested him on the morning of April 27th at his four-room garage apartment. He was returned to Fort Worth, where questioning of the suspect was led by Detective Dana F. LaRue. LaRue had been brought into the interrogation because the Davis murder was originally his assigned case.

Checking on the suspect's background, LaRue and other detectives learned that Green's record was not the sort that would point toward a serial sex killer. In 1985, he had been given a probationary sentence for driving while intoxicated. Before that, in July 1984, Green had been placed on six months' probation for telephone harassment.

In the beginning, Ricky Greene denied being involved in any murders, but as Detective LaRue skillfully laid out details of the Fefferman death and the other homicides as reported by Arlene Douglas, Green started to waver. Finally, after the sleuths had pointed out that physical evidence, such as fingerprints found in the executive's home, would link him to the homicide, Green caved in and volunteered to make a statement.

Subsequently, Green admitted not only to the Fefferman slaying, but to the murders of the Davis boy and the two women whose bodies were found in the rural counties—Sandra Bailey and the unidentified woman. Green said he had known the latter only as "Betty Jo."

The Fort Worth investigators notified authorities in Wise and Clay Counties of the suspect's statements about the women's murders. In the following days, Green was quizzed by sheriff's investigators and Texas Rangers from Wise County.

Green had a conflicting version about the story his once-lover, Arlene Douglas, told about the sex killings of the two women. He claimed that Arlene, who was living with him during the time of the killings, had been involved with him in Steven Fefferman's death and those of Sandra Bailey and Betty Jo. Officers continued the grilling of Arlene Douglas, confronting her with Ricky Green's allegations. In her original talks with the detectives, Arlene had contended she only knew of the murders through Green. Now, she denied having had anything to do with Fefferman's slaying but said Green had forced her to watch and help him in the two women's killings.

On May 8, 1989, after she had given statements to Wise County authorities, Arlene Douglas was indicted on charges of murder and capital murder in the stabbing-bludgeoning deaths of Sandra Bailey and the woman known only as Betty Jo. She surrendered voluntarily in Decatur the next day. Green had been charged with capital murder and murder in the two Fort Worth homicides and the other killings. He subsequently was indicted on the charges in Tarrant County and Wise County. He was held in the Tarrant County Jail in Fort Worth in lieu of $1.25 million bond.

Though Arlene Douglas first said that she had only watched the murders of the two women in the mobile home in Boyd which she shared with Green, Wise County Sheriff Leroy Burch now told reporters following the sensational case that Arlene Douglas willingly helped her lover stab and bludgeon the women to death during the carefully planned "thrill killings."

And Wise County District Attorney Patrick Morris, discussing the indictments against Arlene Douglas, said both of the female victims had been beaten with a hammer and stabbed repeatedly. "In both cases, she [Arlene] is charged as acting as a partner with Ricky Green. These are capital murder cases . . . because the murders were committed during aggravated sexual assaults."

Sheriff Burch explained further: "We're finding she had a big part in it. She helped him stab them and hit them. She liked it as much as him."

The sheriff said that, based on the statements of the two suspects, the couple apparently bound and gagged both women, then murdered them as Green sexually assaulted them in the trailer home in Boyd. The women were raped and stabbed after they were forced to kneel over the rim of a bathtub "so the blood would run down the drain," the sheriff said.

"I think that's the way [Green and Douglas] got their kicks," he added.

The cold-bloodedness of the acts was reflected in another bit of information Sheriff Burch revealed: after Sandra Bailey was raped and killed, Ricky Green and Arlene Douglas covered her nude body with newspapers and went to bed, waiting until the next day to dispose of the body. Even then, they went to work the next day and did not dump the woman's body until that night, the officers said.

The suspects had told the investigators that they knew

53

little about the unidentified woman, except that she referred to herself as "Betty Jo" and apparently had mentioned that she was related to a lounge owner in Amarillo, Texas. With this meager information, the Wise County officers got in touch with Amarillo authorities, passing along what little background details they had uncovered with a set of the slain woman's fingerprints and the composite drawing.

Working on the Amarillo end was the Potter-Randall Special Crimes Unit, a special homicide unit composed of investigators from agencies of the two counties in which Amarillo overlaps.

Working with a Texas Alcoholic Beverage Commission list of lounges in Amarillo for the year of 1985—when Betty Jo was thought to have possibly lived in the Texas Panhandle city—the probers started contacting bar owners, trying to find anyone who might have known or remembered a Betty Jo.

After several futile interviews, the detectives located a lounge operator who identified Betty Jo from the composite drawing that Ranger Ryan had mailed out a few weeks after the woman's body was found. The bar owner put the officers in touch with a former friend of the murder victim, who identified her by her scars and dental characteristics.

A friend told the officers that Betty Jo had been a topless dancer in the past, using the stage name of Betty Jo Montana. She had been a drifter and had run with motorcycle gangs. It was possible the woman had been arrested and fingerprinted at some time, the detectives thought, but they could find no record for her under that name.

The sleuths learned the name of a former boyfriend of Betty Jo's. They couldn't locate him, but they did turn up an old police report under his name. It also contained the name of Betty Jo Monroe, which turned out to be the real name of "Mama Doe." The old report also had a fingerprint card for her.

Using this and the fingerprint classifications sent from

Wise County, Sergeant Modeina Holmes, who is now assistant coordinator of the Special Crimes Unit, finally made a match that confirmed the identification of the murdered Betty Jo.

In the meantime, while awaiting trial, Ricky Green granted an interview to a reporter from the *Fort Worth Star Telegram* in which he said he planned to plead guilty to the murders, although his attorneys were against it. He also implicated Arlene Douglas as an active participant in the murders and assaults of the two women.

Talking about the slayings in the trailer home in Boyd, the suspect said, "They both happened about the same way. It started in the bedroom, and the girls were tied down. Everybody had their clothes off.

"She got mad. She went into the kitchen and got a knife. She said to take her to the bathroom, so we brought her in the bathroom. We tied her hands and feet and gagged her and bent her over the bathtub. [Arlene] said she wanted to watch me have sex with her, but when I started to, she stabbed her. I [then] used my pocketknife on her. Then [Arlene] took it, and used the hammer. I never had intercourse with the women."

The story conflicted with that of Arlene Douglas, who told the investigators that Green was having sex with the women and stabbing them at the same time.

After surrendering to Wise County officers in Decatur following her indictment, Arlene Douglas remained in the county jail. At a pretrial hearing on August 30, 1989, the district attorney announced that the state would try the woman on charges of murder instead of capital murder. He said the state elected not to seek the death penalty because of some recent high court decisions.

At the hearing, defense attorneys indicated they would show at Arlene Douglas' trial that the suspect was a victim of physical and psychological abuse by her former lover. Though acknowledging that Arlene might have been

55

abused by Green, District Attorney Morris said, "You could be a battered woman and not be under duress. The real issue is duress, and that's something she has to prove."

The prosecutor added that evidence would show that Arlene regularly took part in bisexual acts while her lover Green watched. He also said that the woman helped Green kill Betty Jo Monroe after both she and Green sexually assaulted her.

Jury selection for Arlene Douglas' trial didn't begin until February 5, 1990. The site was the historic Wise County courthouse built in 1896. Designed by a famous New York architect of his day, J. Riley Gordon, the courthouse was constructed of granite. Its spires and turrets resemble a castle from another time. But what would unfold in the crowded courtroom wasn't exactly a fairy tale.

Surprisingly, although attorneys had expected the process to take several weeks, a jury of eight women and four men was chosen in four days. Testimony in the murder of Betty Jo Monroe started on February 12, 1990.

Among the first witnesses was ex-Texas Ranger Ryan, who had retired three months before the arrest of Arlene Douglas and Ricky Green. Ryan related the tenacious search he made to identify "Mama Doe." The prosecution introduced into evidence enlarged, color photographs of Betty Monroe's nude, stabbed, beaten, and sexually mutilated body after it was found underneath the bridge.

Before passing the photos among the jurors, District Attorney Morris warned, "This case is not going to be one that you're going to look back fondly on. You're definitely going to see some things you'd rather not see."

The grisly photos drew gasps from the jurors. The defendant sobbed and turned her head away as one picture of the victim's body was examined by her lawyer.

The conflicting statements made by Arlene Douglas before and after Ricky Green implicated her were introduced by the prosecution. A Tarrant County sheriff's deputy told the jury that Douglas accused Green of four murders and claimed she refused when he tried to get her to stab the two women killed in the house trailer. The investigator said Arlene Douglas repeated numerous times that she was afraid of Green. She added that he once choked her into unconsciousness, saying he didn't want her alive with knowledge of the murders.

In the statement read to the jury by the district attorney, Arlene Douglas said that Ricky Green had Betty Jo Monroe in the back of his car when he picked her up in Forth Worth on October 12, 1985. Douglas related that when she asked Green about the woman, he answered, "Just don't worry about it. I'm going to kill her."

Green, who said he had picked up Betty Jo while she was hitchhiking, brought her to the mobile home in Boyd. Douglas' statement went on to say that Green ordered the woman to undress, tied her hands and feet, then stabbed her repeatedly as he raped her in the bathroom. Then Green ordered Douglas to come look at the body.

"She had stab marks all over her," Arlene Douglas' statement said, adding that while Arlene watched, Green lifted the dead woman's hand and broke the little finger.

The second statement given by Douglas two days later to Texas Ranger Gary de los Santos, Wise County Sheriff's Captain Doug Whitehead, and District Attorney's Investigator King Barnett told a different story.

In this version, the stocky blonde admitted that she did inflict some of the stab and hammer wounds on Betty Jo Monroe. She also admitted to having helped Green dispose of both the female victims' bodies but said she did these things because she was forced to by Green.

On the witness stand, the officers testified that Arlene Douglas willingly admitted to engaging in sexually deviant conduct in her life with Ricky Green. According to the investigators, Douglas told them how Green, on at least four occasions, brought men to the trailer home for group sex.

"She advised that Ricky would have sex with them, and then she would join in," Captain Whitehead related. "She said she was not forced."

The woman also said that she had had sex with one of Green's relatives, according to witnesses.

The jury and courtroom audience listened in stunned silence to another state witness, the Tarrant County medical examiner, who had done the autopsy on Betty Jo Monroe. Questioned by Assistant District Attorney Kenneth Mahaffey, the pathologist testified that several of the 17 stab wounds in Betty Jo's body and two of the three blows to her head were done with "tremendous force." He said one stab wound in her chest was sufficient to break through a rib, and two of the blows to her head had cracked her skull.

Either the stab wounds or the head blows were enough to cause death, the witness explained. The victim probably was unconscious after being struck in the head, but it may have taken her as long as two hours to die, he added.

On two points, the medical expert's testimony contradicted that of the defendant's statements, in which she had said Green bound Betty Jo with ropes and later broke her little finger. The M.E. said he found no evidence of a fractured finger or rope burns.

Trying to show that Betty Jo's slaying fit a pattern, the defense cross-examined the medical examiner about the death of Steven Fefferman, Jeffrey Davis, and Sandra Bailey. The M.E. described the sexual mutilation of the male victims and the patterns of frenzied stabbings that marked all four homicides.

The prosecution tried to show that Arlene Douglas was a sexual deviant who willingly took part in the assaults and murder of the two women. The defense portrayed Douglas as a passive, submissive woman who watched helplessly while two women met horrifying deaths and who allowed a drunken, deranged lover to terrorize her into covering up his heinous crimes.

When Arlene Douglas was called as a witness in her own defense, the packed courtroom was a tableau of hushed, expectant spectators who leaned forward in their seats.

"I was scared to death—I didn't feel like there was anything I could do," the quiet-spoken woman testified. She repeated this statement several times during her testimony.

She calmly described three and a half years of living with Ricky Green. She said it was in 1985 that she realized she had become involved with a violent alcoholic whose favorite pastime was cruising rural roads after dark with a 12-pack of cold beer at his side.

"Ricky would get drunk every night after work and pass out," Douglas related. "It was like we weren't even living together."

Douglas testified that she discovered Ricky was bisexual and that his midnight drives frequently took him to bars and lakeside parks of sexual encounters with men. She said she didn't believe Ricky when he told her that he had murdered and mutilated a 16-year-old boy, Jeffrey Davis, after picking him up at Lake Worth in 1985. But eventually that shocking murder became just one more in a series of homicides that shocked her to numbness.

Arlene Douglas testified that she had begged Green not to harm Betty Monroe and Sandra Bailey but admitted she helped dispose of their bodies after the bloody killings because she feared she would be Green's next victim. Green also told her of the sexual mutilation murder of Steven Fefferman, she said, but by then she was relying heavily on drugs to help her forget the horrible events.

Finally, early in 1989, dragged down by her methamphetamine habit and her knowledge of the savage murders, Douglas fled from the relationship with Green, checked into a drug treatment center and eventually contacted Fort Worth authorities.

In the final stage of the trial, the jury heard two psychiatrists—one for the state and another for the defense — give conflicting opinions of Arlene's involvement in the brutal sex murders.

Said the defense doctor, "She could not stand up to Mr. Green. No question at all, he would have killed her . . . He was a killer, one of the worst type people that anyone could ever come in contact with."

Said the state psychiatrist, "She liked the drugs. I think she liked the excitement. Maybe she even liked the violence that went on." He said he doubted the battered-woman syndrome claim of the defense.

In the final arguments, the district attorney hammered away at the battered-woman theory as "a smokescreen to cloud the defendant's guilt . . . Thirty or forty years ago, when somebody committed a wrong, it was called a sin. Now it's called a syndrome."

Arlene Douglas argued that she was terrified into submission by the murders she had witnessed. Of the state's case, he said, "They were just trying to portray her as a bad girl who had bad friends — therefore, she's capable of murder."

On February 23, 1990, the jury returned a verdict finding Arlene Douglas guilty of murder but setting her punishment at 10 years' probation. The jury's findings shocked officers who had worked the case so diligently. Then the lawmen got a second jolt.

On March 1st, Douglas entered into a plea-bargain agreement in the murder of Sandra Bailey. After she pleaded guilty, the judge sentenced Douglas to another ten years' probation to run concurrently with that received in the first case. So Arlene Douglas walked away from the county jail a free woman, if she stuck with the terms of her probationary sentences.

Testimony in Ricky Green's trial for the death of Steven Fefferman, the Fort Worth TV executive, got under way in Austin in mid-September 1990 after a change of venue.

The highlight of the trial was Ricky Green's confession, read to the jury by Detective LaRue. It said, in part, referring to December 27, 1986 (which also happened to be Green's birthday):

"I was sitting in my car at Casino Beach [where he met Fefferman and agreed to go home with him after they engaged in a sex act in Green's car]. He went in and took a shower while I listened to the stereo." Green said they had another sexual encounter and then went into the bedroom.

"He wanted to tie me up to the bed," Green continued. "I saw a large butcher knife laying on the floor next to the bed. I told him no. He got mad. I told him to let me tie him up first, then he could do it to me.

"He said OK. I used his neckties to tie him. I didn't trust him anymore. I had his hands tied to the bed. He was face up. He started trying to get loose. I picked up the knife. He started kicking at me. I asked him if he had plans for me with the knife. That's when I just lost control. I cut his throat."

Green said that he thought Fefferman had intended to kill him, so he started "stabbing him all over mostly in the front." He related he then got another butcher knife from the kitchen that he used "to cut the front of him open" and to castrate him.

Green related that at Casino Beach, he had agreed to go home with Fefferman if he would buy him a 12-pack of beer, which Fefferman did. After that, Fefferman followed Green to Green's residence, where Green dropped off his car and got into Fefferman's Volvo to ride to his house.

Green described his search for money after stabbing the victim. He said he left in Fefferman's Volvo after finding about $100 in cash. He apparently ran off the road and was walking home when Arlene, with whom he was then living, happened to drive by in her car and picked him up. Green said he told her what he had done.

Another key witness in the trial was an FBI fingerprint specialist who testified that three fingerprints found in Fefferman's house were identified as those of Ricky Green.

From the beginning, the defense had indicated they would seek to prove that the defendant was insane. After the state finished their case, defense lawyers shocked the state and the courtroom observers when they announced that they would not proceed with an insanity defense because it was believed the prosecution had not proven a capital murder case.

But the jury disagreed, returning a verdict of guilty of capital murder. Now it remained for the same jury to decide whether punishment would be life imprisonment or death by lethal injection.

In testimony to determine punishment, the state introduced the confessions given by Green in the other three slayings. Again, they were read by Detective LaRue to the obviously shaken jury.

Concerning the murder of Jeffrey Davis, Green said he killed the teenager, whom he met at Casino Beach, after the two got into an argument. Before that, they had driven around, drinking beer, Green said.

"We got into an argument because he wanted to go steal something from a house," Green's statement said. "I told him I didn't want to, and he started calling me names. We got out of the car . . . I beat him up . . . Then I took out my pocketknife. It's a big one. I cut his throat pretty bad. I continued stabbing him all over. I think he was dead by then."

Green said he then castrated the boy. Then he put Davis' body in the back floorboard of his car, drove into a nearby town and bought beer. He then dumped the body at a remote site on Lake Worth, near the Nature Center.

Green's statement about the murder of Betty Jo Monroe said, in part:

"I went to the kitchen and got a butcher knife . . . I went to the bathroom and shut the door. Betty Jo was still naked. I started stabbing her because she was a whore. She was hollering, 'Why are you doing this? Why do you hate me?' "

The statement said Green left the bathroom again, got a hammer and the knife he had used to kill the Davis boy, and used them on the screaming woman. Green said that during the attack on Betty Jo Monroe, his lover Arlene warned him that he had "to quit killing people."

"I told her some people have to die," Green said in his statement.

Green made a similar chilling comment while he was stabbing Sandra Bailey. He told her he was doing it "because people like you deserve to die." He said he had picked up the woman in a highway nightclub outside of Fort Worth and took her to the mobile home in Boyd.

Some jurors wept as the horrifying confessions were read aloud by Detective LaRue. When some of the grisly photographs of the mutilated bodies were displayed, the judge, the bailiff, and some jury members turned their heads away.

Two other witnesses testified to the depravity of the accused killer.

The two young men told the jury that they were at Green's house on one occasion when he pointed a shotgun and threatened to kill them unless they performed oral sex on him. They said they managed to wrestle the weapon away from Green and ran from the trailer.

Psychiatrists and psychologists who had examined the defendant described him as a sadistic serial killer who would continue to kill if he were free. The defense called witnesses to testify that Ricky Green had become what he was because of severe child abuse that included beatings and even sexual assault by a relative.

The jury's verdict of punishment hardly surprised anyone who had listened to the shocking testimony of the trial. The jury ruled that Ricky Green should be put to death by lethal injection.

At this writing, the indictments against Green for the murders of Jeffrey Davis, Betty Jo Monroe, and Sandra Bailey were still pending. He must be presumed innocent of these crimes unless proved otherwise in a court of law. The death verdict automatically was appealed to the Texas Court of Criminal Appeals. Green, meanwhile, was transferred to the state prison system's death row.

EDITOR'S NOTE:
Arlene Douglas is not the real name of the person so named in the foregoing story. A fictitious name has been used because there is no reason for public interest in the identity of this person.

"CUFFED AND HACKED BY A 400-POUND NUDE!"

by Christofer Pierson

It was 10:00 a.m. on Thursday, February 23, 1989, and Kate Burbage was worried.

A co-worker at the Lynbrook, New York, electronics company where she worked had not shown up. It was unlike him. In his eight years with the Long Island-based company, the 42-year-old credit manager was never late. He had missed only two days of work in those eight years and had called ahead on both occasions to explain his absence. But there was no call from the conscientious credit manager this time.

Kate decided to telephone the credit manager's house. A young man answered the phone in a sleepy voice.

"Is your father there?" Kate asked.

"No, he isn't," the young man answered.

"Do you have any idea where he is?"

"I'm not sure. I think he may have gone to the doctor's."

Kate thanked the credit manager's son and hung up the phone, her uneasiness undiminished.

The day went by, and there was still no word from the credit manager. Friday morning came, and he was still inexplicably absent from work.

By Friday afternoon, the owners of the company shared in Kate Burbage's concern. The company took the unusual step of hiring a private investigator to locate their missing employee. The action was fruitless, however, and the fate of the credit manager would remain a mystery for another week.

At 8:20 a.m. on Wednesday, March 1, 1989, Jeff Ludlow left his brother's house in Far Rockaway, Queens, to go to the unemployment office and get a new card from the veteran's representative there. He was told the representative would be late that morning and was asked to come back later in the day.

Having time on his hands, Ludlow decided to go to the bottle redemption center to see if they would take Ballantine beer bottles. Ludlow had a collection of over 200 bottles and was hoping to get a little cash for them. On his way to the center, Ludlow stopped at a discount store off Rockaway Turnpike in North Lawrence, Long Island, to check the large, 30-cubic-yard dumpsters at the rear of the store for more bottles.

Ludlow gripped the cold steel rim of one of the two dumpsters and hoisted himself up and over into the recess below. Among crushed cardboard boxes, broken wood, and discarded fluorescent lights, Ludlow saw several dark green plastic garbage bags. The idea occurred to him to empty one of the bags and use it to hold any bottles and cans he might find among the rest of the trash.

Ludlow lifted one lumpy bag and spilled its contents onto the trash pile. He gasped at the sight of the released refuse: several articles of clothing and a white bedspread—all covered with blood. Ludlow dropped the bag in his hand and bent over to investigate another one. Cautiously, he squeezed the item inside the bag through the plastic. It felt heavy and gave slightly to the touch. Whatever it was, it felt more animal than mineral or vegetable. Ludlow wondered if it was a dead cat.

Curiosity got the better of Jeff Ludlow. He crouched down and tore open the bag at his feet.

Moments later, a driver from the dumpster company

66

pulled his truck behind the discount store and saw a man heading urgently toward the front of the building. The man motioned to the driver, apparently wanting to talk to him. The driver rolled down his window.

"I saw something in one of those dumpsters," Jeff Ludlow told the driver excitedly. "It was a foot. It looked like a human foot."

The driver told Ludlow to knock on a door at the rear of the store. He knew there was a security guard there who could summon the police.

Shortly after 10:45 a.m., Nassau County Police Officers Richard Prussen and John Armstrong received a call on the radio of their RMP (Radio Motor Patrol) reporting the discovery of a dead body in the vicinity. The officers sped to the discount store, swung around to the rear of the building, and spotted Jeff Ludlow and the store security guard standing by the dumpsters. Ludlow gave Officer Prussen the details of his gruesome discovery, and Prussen immediately called for homicide detectives.

At Nassau County police headquarters in Mineola, long-time partners Detectives Gary "Abby" Abbondandelo and Donald Daly were preparing to leave for a retirement banquet for a fellow detective when the call came in. Sandy-haired, brown-eyed Abbondandelo and dark-haired, blue-eyed Daly shot each other looks that said the same thing: Nothing like a dead body to put a damper on a celebration.

The detectives arrived on the scene at 12:18 p.m. Officers Prussen and Armstrong had also called in medical examiner Dr. Daniel McCarthy and Assistant District Attorney Elise McCarthy (no relation) who, having never attended a crime scene before, was being shown the ropes by Barry Grennan, chief of the Nassau County D.A.'s Major Offenses Bureau.

Detective Abbondandelo located the owner of the dumpster company and got the okay to have the contents of the receptacle removed for closer examination.

There was indeed a dead body in the dumpster, but it was no ordinary dead body. It had been hacked into pieces and stuffed into four tripled-up plastic bags. The head was in one, the arms shared another, and each leg was put in a bag of its own. That was all there was of the body in the dumpster. The torso was missing.

The detectives could tell the victim was a middle-aged, clean-shaven black man, but, given the state of the body, it was impossible to be more precise with a physical description.

A fifth bag in the pile was the one Jeff Ludlow had picked up and emptied out, the one containing the bloody clothes and bedspreads. The articles of clothing consisted of a T-shirt, boxer shorts, socks, a pair of trousers, and a shirt. Some of the items appeared to have been cut with a sharp instrument.

There was something else in the pile that the detectives knew immediately was part of the crime. A pair of handcuffs, stained with blood, lay amid the bloody articles of clothing. Their purpose in the crime was unclear at this point in the investigation.

Although the corpse's head bore a vicious-looking puncture wound on the left cheek, and although there appeared to be cuts and massive bruises on several of the body parts, it was not immediately clear exactly what had caused the victim's death.

The bags were removed just the way they were found and taken to forensics and the medical examiner's office for analysis. Detectives Abbondandelo and Daly called in a crew from the Bureau of Special Operations, an official sort of Baker Street Irregulars (plainclothes cops), to comb through the swampy area behind the discount store for clues. Several hours of searching through the icy muck failed to turn up anything of significance relating to the crime.

Once the crime scene was exhausted as a source of information, Detective Abbondandelo drove to the Nassau County Medical Center on Hempstead Turnpike in East Meadow to confer with Dr. McCarthy and Dr. Lone Thanning, who conducted the autopsy.

In an ordinary autopsy, the medical examiner opens the chest cavity and removes all organs of the body for dissection and examination. In most cases, the medical examiner scrapes select organs for tissue for microscopic and toxicological analysis to determine what foreign bodies or chemicals, if any, are present in the system.

In this case, Dr. Thanning had only one organ available for analysis: the victim's brain. There was some evidence of alcohol in the victim's bloodstream, but no sign of poisoning.

Nevertheless, Dr. Thanning was able to determine that the victim had been stabbed repeatedly. He had also been struck with a blunt object, resulting in a broken lower jaw. A fracture on one of the victim's arms proved to be an old one not suffered during the attack that killed him.

Dr. Thanning was also able to determine that the handcuffs had been put on the victim after he was dead. She could tell because there was no sign of hemorrhaging or bruising at the point on the wrists where they would be expected if the handcuffs had been put on while the victim was still alive.

Forensic analysis of the victim's clothing filled in a number of gaps in the detectives' knowledge. From the size and length of the trousers and shirt, it was determined that the victim was about 6 feet tall and weighed about 250 pounds. Rips in the shirt indicated he had been stabbed numerous times in the back and chest with a large, thin-bladed knife.

The autopsy also answered one of the primary questions in Detective Abbondandelo's mind: Was the killer a surgeon who dismembered the body with cool-headed professionalism or a butcher who hacked the body to pieces in the heat of passion?

69

The dismemberment appeared on first glance to have been carefully undertaken. The cuts were straight and neat. Dr. Thanning discovered that the killer had made two small cuts with a fine-toothed saw just above the knee on one of the victim's legs. Apparently, the saw had been unable to make much of a dent in the victim's femur at that point in the leg. The saw wounds showed no vital reaction; the killer had not attempted to saw the body until after the victim was dead. Although the killer did not seem to be a professional, he was remarkably efficient in his methods of dismemberment.

To conclude his work on the case for that day, Detective Abbondandelo had the victim's fingerprints and a dental cast taken and sent to Albany and the FBI for possible identification. Hair and blood samples were also taken for possible comparison with those from the site of the actual murder or from the vehicle that transported the body, if or when either was found.

The media were also enlisted in the task of identifying the body. On Wednesday, March 2nd, Roger Kemp, an employee of the electronics company were Kate Burbage worked, read an article in the morning's paper about the anonymous dismembered body. He immediately recognized the description of the victim as that of the missing credit manager. He called the number provided in the article, and his call was relayed to Detective Abbondandelo.

"I think I know who the body is," Kemp told the detective. "I think it's a man I work with who's been missing for a week."

"Missing for a week?" Abbondandelo asked, instantly interested. "What's his name?

"William King," came the response.

"And where does William King live?" Abbondandelo pressed.

Kemp gave Detective Abbondandelo an address on Troutville Road in St. Albans, Queens.

"Does he live alone?" Abbondandelo asked.

"He has an adult son living with him," Kemp replied.

The detective wondered aloud whether or not William King had any enemies.

"I can't believe he did," Kemp said confidently. "He was very well liked and respected. He was a good, decent man. His co-workers have been worried about him since the moment he didn't show up. I can't imagine who would have done this to him or why."

The detective wasn't absolutely positive that the victim Kemp was referring to was William King. Abbondandelo's first order of business was to contact King's 23-year-old son, William Jr., and another relative and ask them to identify the body. Both consented to be picked up by Detectives Daly and Richard Wells that afternoon and taken to the morgue.

During the drive to the morgue, Detective Daly learned that the son had contacted the 113th Precinct in Nassau County as well as local hospitals several times since February 23rd to see if officials had any information on his father's whereabouts. He had not received any news at all from any source.

Detective Daly led the two relatives to a morgue table where the victim's head lay, the point of decapitation covered discreetly with a sheet. It was not readily apparent that it was, in fact, a severed head that William King Jr. and his relative were looking at. At first, neither of the relatives was able to say positively that the head belonged to William King Sr.

"My father has a scar on his chest," William King Jr. told the detective. "Could you lower the sheet? I could tell you better if I saw the scar."

Detective Daly related that the victim's chest was not among the body parts that had been found. The relatives took in the information, then, with a little thought, concluded that the head on the table was that of William King

71

Sr. (King's dental records would confirm the identification.)

Detective Daly then brought the victim's relatives to homicide to be interviewed by Detective Abbondandelo. The detectives hoped that William King Jr., having been with the victim the night before his disappearance, would remember something that would give the detectives a lead. Nothing so concrete came from the interview; but all it would take to get on track toward a solution was one well-placed detail, and the detectives were able to assemble a few more details of William King's life.

Both William King Jr. and the other relative confirmed Roger Kemp's conviction that William King had no known enemies.

"I didn't always get along very well with my father," the victim's son said, "but I don't think he knew anyone who hated him enough to kill him."

"Why didn't you get along with your dad?" Detective Abbondandelo asked.

The portly William King Jr. frowned and said matter-of-factly, "He thought all I did was eat, play computer games, and watch TV."

The victim's son told Detective Abbondandelo what he remembered about the evening of February 22nd, the night before his father disappeared. He said his father and he had eaten a Chinese take-out meal together, then went their separate ways. William King Sr. stayed in the living room downstairs, while King Jr. watched TV and played with his computer upstairs in his room.

The next morning, William King Jr. said, he was awakened by a phone call from a friend of his father's. She always called around seven in the morning. She asked where William Sr. was. William Jr. checked his father's room. He wasn't there. He thought he was probably at work, but then at 10:00, William said, his father's co-worker Kate Burbage called wondering where he was.

Detective Abbondandelo wanted to know about the victim's habits. Perhaps by tracing his movements on a given day, it could be established when and where the victim had fatally diverged from his routine.

The detective learned that on the Saturday following his disappearance, William King Sr. was planning to drive his car to the Bedford-Stuyvesant section of Brooklyn, where he had been born and raised. King took care of an apartment house on Herkimer Street for an older relative who owned it. That Saturday he was sure to have gone there. It was rent day, and the tenants were expecting him.

Detective Abbondandelo thanked the victim's relatives and asked them to call immediately if they had any new information to volunteer.

The detectives then radioed the 81st Precinct in Brooklyn to see if officials there had information on the car described by William King Jr. — a maroon 1988 Pontiac 6000 with New York license plate WKC-824. If King had been intercepted in Brooklyn, chances were his car would still be there collecting parking tickets. It might even have been reported as suspicious.

The 81st Precinct radioed back minutes later. William King's car had, in fact, been ticketed on Herkimer Street. It was still there opposite the building owned by William King's relative.

Detectives Abbondandelo and Daly raced to the Brooklyn address with a Nassau County PD tow truck not far behind. The brick townhouse, painted a cheerful red with white frame, stood out among the row of drabber houses around it. It was evident to the detectives that William King had maintained the apartment building with a great deal of attention and care.

The detectives extensively photographed the building's exterior, the car, and the immediate vicinity before the tow truck hauled away the vehicle to forensics in Mineola, Long Island, for analysis. Then the detectives began canvassing the neighborhood to determine the earliest sighting of the car. A resident of the Herkimer Street apartment building provided them with that information. He had noticed the car at approximately 7:00 a.m. on Saturday, February 25th, two days after King's disappearance. No one had seen it earlier than that. And nobody on the Brooklyn street had seen William King himself.

"We've got a real jigsaw puzzle going here, don't we?" Abbondandelo remarked to Daly on their drive back to Mineola. "King lives in St. Albans. He works in Lynbrook. His body's found in North Lawrence. His car's found in Brooklyn. His torso's unaccounted for. He's got no known enemies. What's going on here? Was he mugged and then carved up, or what?"

A possible lead was suggested by the relative who owned the building. The detectives learned that William King had an appointment to meet with a contractor that Saturday to discuss some work being done on the building. It was known that King thought the contractor's estimate had been too high. Maybe there was bad blood between the two men. The problem was, no one knew which of the many contractors King dealt with was supposed to have met with him that morning.

The detectives had to leave that piece of the puzzle unsolved at the end of day two of the investigation. They hoped day three would clear up some of the mysteries within the puzzle.

Unfortunately, on the following morning, Thursday, March 3rd, another piece was added to the puzzle. Employees of a liquor store in St. Albans called the detectives to report having seen William King Sr. on February 23rd — the first day he'd failed to report to work. This was the first indication the detectives had that William King was still alive between the 22nd, when his son had last seen him, and the 25th, when his car was spotted on Herkimer Street.

Dutifully, the detectives looked into the liquor store lead. Within a matter of days, however, they were able to establish that the "witnesses" at the store were less than reliable. If the detectives learned anything from the contradictory statements of the store employees, it was that King had *not* gone into the liquor store on February 23rd at all.

By the following week, the fight-with-the-contractor angle had also dissolved. The contractor's identity and whereabouts were established—as was his alibi for Saturday, February 25th.

"Maybe the son did it," Abbondandelo suggested to Daly at one point during the investigation.

"He did say he and his father didn't get along," Daly mused. "He seems to be the only one who had serious problems with William King."

Abbondandelo considered the absence of solid leads pointing to King Jr., and he shook his head. "I can't see any son cutting up his father like that."

On Wednesday, March 8th, Detectives Abbondandelo and Daly and Detective Jack McHugh of the 4th Precinct in Nassau County attended a reception following William King's funeral at the Troutville Road residence. There they met several more of the victim's relatives and co-workers, who were consoling each other in the living room of the comfortable suburban home. High praise for the deceased was universal among those in attendance, but a few of the guests had their own theories about his death.

One co-worker showed the detectives a card William King had written to a female co-worker. With a little imagination, the card's message could be interpreted as being "more than friendly," the co-worker said. A jealous lover might certainly have the imagination necessary to read it that way, the detectives agreed.

The sleuths followed this lead in the next couple of days after the reception. It proved to be yet another dead end.

To make matters more confusing, a thorough search of the victim's car by forensics had turned up nothing of much interest. There were no unusual prints, no signs of a struggle, no bloodstains. It was significant, however, that some of William King's missing personal effects—his briefcase and wallet in particular—were not in the car, either.

Detective Abbondandelo had been nagged by the question, what had happened to William King's credit cards? He wondered whether or not King's killer had them, and if so, was the killer using them?

It had also occurred to the detectives that if they saw William King's financial record, they might be able to see a pattern in the victim's use of his credit cards. Perhaps King went to a restaurant regularly where he always charged his meals. Perhaps he went to a store where he regularly charged purchases. Maybe he charged a room in a hotel on a regular basis. If the pattern were suddenly broken, it might indicate where King was when he was intercepted by his killer.

Detective Abbondandelo contacted Detective Joe Mondello of the forgery squad and told him about King's missing credit cards. Mondello immediately contacted the major credit card companies and asked them to flag purchases made on cards under William King's name.

Mondello also requested and received William King's credit history. It was impossible to establish a pattern from King's random use of the cards. But the word was out to the credit companies to look for ongoing use, and Mondello was working on getting King's banks to flag uses of his ATM cards, as well. If any of the victim's plastic had been used after February 22nd, the last night he was known to be alive, Mondello would know about it—and Abbondandelo and Daly would have a solid lead pointing to the killer's location.

Two weeks had passed since the five black bags containing pieces of William King's body had been found—three weeks since King's disappearance—and the detectives were still perplexed by the lack of a solid lead.

Detectives Abbondandelo and Daly decided to call in

William King Jr. and "pick his brain." He might know about some obscure money problem his father was having or a romantic entanglement he might have been involved in. Maybe William King Jr. had seen a card like the one brought to the detectives' attention at the funeral reception. Maybe he had handled an extravagant bill addressed to his father, or overheard a heated telephone conversation.

Detective Abbondandelo phoned William King Jr. on the evening of March 15th to ask him for his help. He asked the young man if he would consent to being picked up by Detective Daly for a brainstorming session the following morning. Abbondandelo said he would be in court at 9:00 a.m., but he would join the session as soon as he was finished. William King Jr. consented to the idea.

On Thursday, March 16th, Detective Abbondandelo was at the Nassau County courthouse, two blocks from police headquarters in Mineola, when he received a telephone call from Detective Mondello of the forgery squad.

"Hey, Abby," Mondello said, barely able to contain himself. "We just got word William King's Visa was used on Thursday, February 23rd."

Abbondandelo raised his eyebrows. "The day *after* he disappeared?" The detective pondered the news and then asked, "What was the purchase?"

"A computer game," Mondello replied. "It was delivered by UPS on February 25th to — guess where."

"Troutville Road?" Detective Abbondandelo ventured. "Holy mackerel!"

Back at headquarters, Detectives Daly and McHugh had just arrived with William King Jr. when Mondello pulled Daly aside to give him the news. The detective's astonishment quickly yielded to glee when he realized he had a prime suspect literally within reach. William King Jr. was sitting in a small interrogation room only a few feet away.

If William King Jr. had not made the purchase with his father's credit card, he certainly knew who had. He had previously told detectives that he was home alone during the times the telephone order was placed and received at the Troutville Road address. If he had access to his father's credit cards after his disappearance, he very likely knew where his father was and what had become of him long before anyone else did.

Detective Daly went into the small, cramped interrogation room off the bustling main office of the homicide bureau and closed the door behind him. William King Jr. had already coaxed his 400-pound frame into the black fabric swivel chair at the small institutional desk in one corner of the room. Daly noted that the subject was wearing a white Batman T-shirt, a brown jacket, blue jeans, and white sneakers with red trim.

The detective began the interview gently, trying to elicit general background information from the subject. He was hoping to lull William into a false sense of security. If William was at ease and off guard, the detective might be able to catch him in a lie.

Detective Daly learned that William King Jr. was born in Philadelphia and lived in Brooklyn on Herkimer Street, until, early in his life, his parents moved to the house on Troutville Road. His parents had been amicably separated for about a year. William, an only child who readily admitted he loved his mother more than he did his father, nevertheless chose to stay with his father after the separation.

"I wanted to stay in the house where I was brought up," William explained. "It was my house. I didn't want to leave my friends."

William also revealed that he had dropped out of high school in the 11th grade. He later passed his GED and took general courses at a couple of New York City colleges, but he was no longer in school and had no plans of returning. He liked computers, though he never studied them. In fact, he said he spent most of his time playing with his computer. He was not employed at that time and had not been employed for two years.

William said he had two close friends but kept mostly to himself. In addition to TV and the computer games, he said, he liked listening to music and reading books — especially mysteries and true crime stories.

"Now I'm reading a book about Gary Heidnik," William said, "a guy in Philadelphia who killed people in his basement."

"Tell me more about your father," Detective Daly said. "Was it unusual for your dad to not come home?"

William shook his head and said, "I can't remember Dad staying away and not coming home the next day. There was no particular night he went out. He wasn't a party person."

"One thing's puzzling us, William. We can't find your Dad's briefcase. Do you know anything about it?" Daly asked.

"Dad's briefcase had credit cards in it," William replied. "He also had papers pertaining to work in the briefcase, but I don't know what else was in there."

"Did your Dad ever run up bills on his credit cards?"

"I don't know," William answered.

Detective Daly shifted in his chair, looked up at the ceiling and said, "Tell me more about your father, William. Was he easy to get along with?"

William hesitated, but then said, "Dad and me didn't get along at all. We disliked each other. We tolerated each other.

"One time Dad told me he was throwing me out of the house and he took my keys — this was about six months ago — but Dad gave the keys back.

"Dad was pissed off because I didn't work, didn't go to school, never got up early, didn't have any money, watched too much TV, played with my computer too much. . . ."

"Did you ever fight with your Dad, William? Did he ever hit you?"

"I had a couple of fights with Dad," William responded. "We punched each other. I would just lose it and begin

79

punching. I can't remember why or what happened. The fights were a long time ago, over a year."

The detective pressed, "Think about it, William. Why would you and your Dad have fought?"

William thought for a moment and answered, "Dad didn't give me money, but I'd steal a ten or twenty from his wallet or dresser whenever I could. A long time ago, my father caught me stealing ten dollars and he beat me up."

"Okay," Detective Daly said. "Let's go over the night of Wednesday, February 22nd. What time did your father get home that night?"

"Dad got home from work around seven-thirty. About eight-thirty, Dad went out to get Chinese food. He brought back pork for me and lobster for himself. We ate together in the dining room. There was no conversation between us. We rarely spoke to each other while we ate.

"After dinner, I went to my room and watched TV. About eleven, eleven-thirty, Dad called to me. He wasn't feeling too good. It must have been the Chinese food. So I gave him some Pepto-Bismol—he was in bed at the time—and I went back to my room, watched some more TV, and went to sleep."

William then repeated what he had already told the detectives on the second day of the investigation, about the phone calls from King Sr.'s girlfriend and Kate Burbage on the morning of the 23rd. He said he had contacted police and hospitals over the weekend of February 25th and 26th and continued contacting various authorities up until his father's body was discovered.

Detective Daly gave William a conspiratorial look and said, "Maybe you have some theories about this crime, William. Why do you think someone would have done this to your father?"

William seemed to mull over the question in his mind. "Maybe it was a case of mistaken identity," he finally postulated. "Like, someone thought he was a drug dealer or gambler or something. He wasn't into drugs or gambling, but maybe he looked like someone who was."

Detective Daly fixed the young man in his stare. "Do you have any money on you, William?"

"I don't have any money of my own. I had a bank account once, but not anymore. After Dad's funeral I got some money from my relatives. Dad never gave me any money, himself."

"How much you got on you?"

William pulled a wad of bills out of his pocket and laid it all on the desk in front of him. Daly counted $590—all $20 bills except for one $10 bill.

Outside the interrogation room, Detective Abbondandelo had just returned from the courthouse. While still in court, Abbondandelo had received a call from Sergeant Bill Cox informing him that more calls were coming in, not only from the credit card companies, but from William King Sr.'s bank. The deceased's ATM card, the detective learned, had been in constant use since the day after he disappeared, to the tune of $200 a day. The last of William King Sr.'s account had been cleared out that very morning. The forgery squad had also discovered another delivery of computer software to Troutville Road just one day earlier, on Wednesday, March 15th.

Detective Abbondandelo joined his partner and their suspect in the interrogation room. Detective Daly was in the process of questioning William King Jr. about his use of his father's credit cards.

"I haven't used them since fall of last year when I bought some computer software," William asserted. "My father was mad about that, but I paid it back doing housework."

"How did you get the card, William?" Daly asked.

"I took it from his dresser and called in the order by telephone."

"You're sure you haven't used the card since then?" Abbondandelo asked.

"Positive," William answered, but then he wavered. "I tried to use one in an automatic teller machine, but it didn't work. I didn't know the secret code for the card."

"And you haven't tried your father's credit cards or ATM card in a machine since then?"

"No," William replied. "Never. Dad wouldn't give me his cards."

"Let me get this straight, William," Detective Abbondandelo said. "You haven't used these cards since last year—correct? And you haven't had any computer games delivered to your house since then, either?"

"No. Positively not."

The detectives leaned back to prepare for another onslaught of questions. William King Jr. shifted uneasily in his chair in uncomfortable anticipation. Finally, Detective Abbondandelo leaned back in.

"William, we know someone's been using your father's cards since he was found dead," the detective said. "Who could be using those cards? Do you have any idea?"

William looked stunned. "I can't imagine who. Probably the killer."

"What about your friends, William?" Detective Daly interjected. "Could they have taken the cards?"

"No," William shot back. "They never went in his room. I'm positive."

"Well, then, who could have known the secret code if they didn't get it from your house or your father?" Abbondandelo asked.

"I don't know," William responded.

"Did you have an extra card, William? Did you find one of your father's cards lying around the house?"

"No."

"Did you ever go to the bank with your father and watch him press in his personal ID number?"

"No."

"What about UPS deliveries, William? Have there been

any deliveries to the house recently?"

"I told you—the last one was last year when I had the computer game delivered."

"You're positively sure nothing has been delivered since then?"

William nodded.

"Let's get this absolutely clear, William," Abbondandelo pressed. "Think carefully. Are you absolutely sure about your dates?"

William appeared to do some mental calculation and then said, "I'm positive. There haven't been any deliveries since last year."

"I think you're lying, William," the detective said flatly. "We know there was a delivery by UPS to your house on Wednesday, March 15th. We know it was ordered from a computer company in Michigan."

"Oh, yeah," William said. "I forgot about that!"

"Tell us about that," Abbondandelo urged. "How did you get the card to place the order?"

"Well, on Saturday after my father disappeared, I was looking through his personal papers for an appointment book to see if I could find a clue to his disappearance. I found three cards on his dresser—some credit cards and an ATM card. I also found a piece of paper in a drawer that had a secret number. I figured it belonged to one of the cards because it matched the first four numbers on the card."

The detectives asked William when he first used the credit cards after his father's disappearance. He was sure he hadn't used them before Saturday the 25th. The detectives pressed again. He was absolutely positive he hadn't used them before that Saturday.

"You're lying, William. You used them the first day your father was missing."

"No, I didn't! I told you I didn't find the cards until Saturday the 25th!"

The detectives laid out for William King Jr. the evidence pointing to his continuing use of his father's cards. They showed him the records of the credit card companies and the list of withdrawals from the bank's automatic teller machine. They reminded him there was a videocamera in the lobby of the bank, and advised him that they were waiting for the film to be developed to see who was making withdrawals on his father's cards.

Faced with this evidence, William King Jr. admitted that he had been using the cards since Thursday, February 23rd. That's when he found the cards and secret code, he said, not Saturday the 25th.

The detectives asked him what he would have told his father if he had come home the first night he was missing.

"I wasn't worried," William said, "because I did it before, and I just worked off the debt."

"Why didn't you stop using the card after you found out he was dead?" Abbondandelo wanted to know.

William paused. "If I stopped using it, you would have thought I killed him."

"Did you kill him?"

"No."

"We think you know something about your father's death, William."

"No," he said adamantly. "I don't."

The detectives told the suspect that, since he had lied about the credit cards, it would be helpful if he took a polygraph test just to make sure he wasn't lying about anything else. William King Jr. told the detectives he would be willing to take the test. He maintained that he would have no problems, because he didn't know anything about his father's death.

It was approximately 5:00 p.m. when William King Jr. began the grueling series of polygraph tests and 9:00 when he was finished. The detectives allowed the suspect a dinner break — William had three slices of pizza and a dozen chocolate chip cookies — while they waited for the results. At 11:00 p.m., the interview proceeded in a larger interrogation room.

The detectives had some bad news for William King Jr. He had failed the test miserably, they said. The only question he had answered truthfully, as far as the machine could determine, was "Do you live in the United States?"

The detectives were honest with William: They told him they were convinced he had killed his father.

"There must have been a reason for what you did," Detective Abbondandelo told the suspect. "You're the only one who can tell us."

William, now sweating and breathing hard, had his head down on his chest. He was deep in thought.

Detective Abbondandelo dangled the handcuffs found in the dumpster in front of the suspect's eyes. He told William that the police knew they were his and that he had put them on his father. The detective then took out a piece of the bloody bedspread, tossed it on the desk between him and William King Jr., and said, "We know this came from your house, too."

As William was staring at the evidence, Abbondandelo said, "Your father called you names, didn't he? How often did he belittle you, William?"

"All the time."

"How much of that could you take? Everyone has their breaking point, and you obviously reached yours. I don't think you sat around sharpening your knife, waiting for the perfect chance to kill your father. Did he do something to set you off? You're the only one who can tell us."

"I can't talk about it," William said quietly.

"You can't live with this, William. You have to get it off your chest."

"I can't."

"Do you want to pray, William?" Detective Daly asked. "It might make you feel better."

"I don't know how to pray. I don't believe in God. Maybe I should, because I know what I did was wrong."

It was now fast approaching midnight on Wednesday, March 16th, when William King Jr. finally admitted, "I killed him. I did it, and you know it."

After being advised of his Miranda rights, the suspect then told the detectives a very different story from the one he had previously told police of his father's last day alive — and of the days following when he dismembered and disposed of his father's body.

After he and his father had eaten the Chinese take-out meals, William King Jr. said, he spent the evening, as usual, in front of the television in his room, while his father spent most of the evening watching television downstairs.

At about 11:15, William heard his father calling him. William went next door into his father's room and immediately, he said, his father began yelling at him. William just "tuned him out."

"It must have been obvious that my father knew I wasn't paying attention to him," William said. "He slapped me across the face with his right hand. I knew if I stayed there I might do something that I might regret, so I immediately turned and started to leave."

William said his father grabbed him by the shoulder as he attempted to go back to his own room. William spun around and pushed his father with both hands against the wall.

"At [that] time," William told the detectives, "I realized that I had had it with him and was going to kill him."

William said he went downstairs and headed straight for the kitchen, his angry father right behind him. As William entered the kitchen, he reached with his left hand for one of the 10-inch knives in a rack on the counter. He turned and slashed at his father, striking him in the head.

William King Sr. tried to ward off the second blow by

86

grabbing his son's left wrist. William took the knife in his right hand and stabbed his father again and again in the upper body and head. He father backed up as the thrusts rained on him. He reached the open door to the basement, lost his balance, and tumbled down the stairs.

The wounded man struggled to stand up as William came down after him. William King Sr. staggered across the basement for the shelter of the laundry room door, but his son was merciless in his attack.

William King Sr. fell to his knees. William dropped the knife and picked up a baseball bat that happened to be leaning against a barbecue grill near the laundry room door.

"While my father was on his hands and knees," William told the detectives, "I swung the bat with both hands and hit him over the head. I swung several more times, not remembering exactly where I hit him. But I do recall one time hitting him on the left side of his face as he was turning and looking back at me.

"During this whole time that he was on the floor, my father kept saying, 'Why?' to me, and 'Pray for me,' and 'At least call Dial-a-Prayer.' I was probably yelling back at him at this time, but I really don't remember what I said.

"My father finally stopped talking," William continued. "He wasn't moving, but I could see that he was still breathing. . . .

"I dropped the baseball bat on the basement floor and went up to my room, where I got a pair of handcuffs that I had in my dresser. I went back to the basement where I handcuffed my father with his hands behind his back.

"I'm not sure, but I think he was dead before I cuffed him. I just didn't want any surprises. I watched my father for a while, and I realized that I had killed him."

William King Jr. decided then and there to strip naked and throw his bloodied clothes and sneakers into the washing machine. He then went upstairs and showered. After the shower, wearing only a pair of laceless black sneakers, William went back to the kitchen and began the arduous task of washing the spattered blood from the walls and floor. He used a white bedspread from the upstairs linen closet to make the job easier, but the bedspread was soon saturated with blood. He finished the job in the kitchen with a porous rag, then went down to the laundry room to wipe around his father's body. Sometime between 2:00 and 3:00 a.m., William decided the job was finished, and he shut off the lights, went upstairs, and went to bed.

The following morning, after being awakened twice by telephone calls from his father's girlfriend and Kate Burbage, William went about the house collecting items he knew his father would have taken with him to work—his briefcase, leather overcoat, gloves, hat, keys, and shoes. He put those items in a large plastic garbage bag and left it at the top of the basement stairs.

He then returned to his father's room to raid it for valuables. He turned up a couple of credit cards and a bank card as well as a personal identification number for one of them, thus enabling him to access his father's account at an automatic teller machine.

One of the first things William did after locating the cards was to place the order for the computer game—the one that led to his downfall after being discovered by Detective Mondello's forgery squad. He then went to the bank, withdrew $200, and went to the grocery store. There he bought plastic garbage bags and the book about the murderer Gary Heidnik. He returned home and spent the rest of the day there reading and waiting for darkness.

Shortly after nightfall on Thursday the 23rd, William King Jr., naked but for the laceless black shoes and a pair of gloves, went down to the basement carrying a pair of scissors. He removed the handcuffs from his father's wrists with the key, which he kept on his key ring, and began cutting the clothes from his father's body. Once the clothes were cut away, William retrieved a small, fine-toothed-wood saw from a tool closet beneath the stairs and contemplated the task of cutting up the body into more manageable pieces.

"I first tried to cut the left leg off just above the knee," William confessed. "I had trouble getting through and decided to cut the leg off at the hip so I would have fewer pieces to deal with."

William found the task upsetting. Shaken, he left the basement and went upstairs to his room. But, he told the detectives, "I calmed myself down and realized that it was something I had to do.

"I went back downstairs and cut off his left arm at the shoulder. I then cut off his other arm and leg and head, but I don't recall in what order. I do remember having difficulty with one of the limbs. I think it may have been the arm, but I'm not sure."

Once the body was dismembered, William placed the pieces into tripled-up garbage bags. He took the saw, scissors, and baseball bat upstairs and put them into the bag with his father's briefcase and other belongings. Altogether, William had assembled seven bags containing evidence of the grisly murder.

Sometime between midnight and 1:00 a.m. on Friday, February 24th, an exhausted William King Jr. went to sleep.

He was awakened the next morning by a call from one of the owners of his father's company. William told the concerned employer that he hadn't heard anything from his father. After hanging up, he decided he should call local hospitals "just to make it look good in case anyone checked" on him.

At approximately 1:00 a.m. on Saturday the 25th, William drove his father's car to the back of the house. He carried out the bag containing his father's torso and placed it on the floor behind the driver's seat. He drove to the rear of a supermarket off the Rockaway Turnpike in North Lawrence, Long Island, with the intention of putting the bag in one of the dumpsters there. He was disconcerted to discover the area behind the store well lit with floodlights and clearly visible from the turnpike. He dumped the torso, but he got scared and decided not to take the rest of the bags there. (The torso was never recovered. It is presumed to be in a landfill in Ohio where trash from that part of Long Island is carted away.)

William then returned home. He took all of the remaining bags, except the one containing his father's personal effects and the murder weapons, out of the car. He then drove to the more remote and less well-lit dumpsters behind the retail store where they would eventually be found by Jeff Ludlow.

At 3:00 a.m., William returned home for the final bag and started off for Herkimer Street. "I knew my father would normally go there," William confessed, "and figured this would throw people off [my scent]."

He parked the car across the street from his relative's house and threw the car keys into the plastic bag of evidence. He used a rag to wipe off areas of the car he thought he might have touched and tossed it into the bag. He locked the car and then put his gloves and the laceless black shoes — after changing into a pair of sneakers he'd brought along — into the bag, and discarded the evidence in a vacant lot not far from the Herkimer Street building. He then hopped on a subway for Penn Station and took a train to Jamaica Center. It was between 8:00 and 9:00 a.m. when he finally reached his house.

After getting some sleep, William decided he'd better go to the 113th Precinct to report his father as missing. "I did this just to show I was concerned," he told the detectives.

The haphazard way he had disposed of the seventh bag of evidence began to gnaw at William King Jr. He decided to return to Herkimer Street in the earliest hours of Tuesday, February 28th. Luckily for him, the bag was still where he had left it. He decided not to take any chances. He took it

90

behind a nearby bodega (a Spanish grocery) and put it in a dumpster. He returned by train to his house, arriving there just as daylight was breaking.

Later that day, William returned to the 113th Precinct to file another report on his father's disappearance, and the police decided to open an inquiry. One day later, Jeff Ludlow would discover the bags containing William King's body parts.

William King Jr. also confessed to making the telephone purchases and ATM withdrawals that eventually nailed him. He told the detectives where they could find some of the missing credit cards and a bank card — he'd disposed of the bank card he had been using only the day before, right after he cleaned out his father's account — and he gave detailed descriptions of the areas in the kitchen and basement where the murder and dismemberment had occurred.

Based on William King Jr.'s statement to Detectives Abbondandelo and Daly, a search warrant was issued the following morning, March 17, 1989, enabling the investigators to examine the suspect's Troutville Road residence. The detectives arrived at the house with a team of scientific examiners at 9:00 a.m. The detectives found the credit and bank cards on the living room table — right where William King Jr. said they would be. They also found the knife rack on the kitchen counter and photographed it. One of the 10-inch knives — the presumed murder weapon — was missing.

The detectives next turned their attention to the kitchen walls in the area where William said the attack had taken place. Though William had cleaned up as well as he could, he was, by his own admission, not the best housekeeper, and it was not difficult to find evidence of dried blood staining the walls.

The investigators then went down into the basement for luminol tests. Luminol is a chemical that reacts with traces of blood — even minute traces of dried and decomposing blood — in a startling way: Blood makes it glow in the dark.

91

The chemical is so carcinogenic that its ban from use in criminal investigations is pending.

Nevertheless, luminol has a good track record as a blood detector, and it worked well on that cold basement floor on that cold March day. When the lights were turned off, the detectives were astonished at the ghostly record of William King Jr.'s carnage. The basement walls, floor, and ceiling glowed an eerie blue like a giant Rorschach blot.

William King Jr. was arraigned in Nassau County Court that same morning and remanded to the Nassau County Correctional Center in Mineola. Bail for the first-time offender was set at $100,000. A sympathetic relative was able to raise the sum by the summer and William was freed on July 20, 1989, to wait for his trial.

During the pretrial phase, William's lawyer, Jonathan Raines, attempted to raise questions about the detectives' handling of the confession. Raines claimed that William had been starved by the investigators. A person of William's girth, the lawyer argued, requires more than the three pieces of pizza and dozen cookies William had eaten on the day of his arrest. Judge Raymond Harrington ruled against the lawyer and his client.

On March 7, 1990, William King Jr. went on trial for murder in the second degree before Judge Harrington and a jury of his peers in Nassau County Court in Mineola. The prosecutor was Assistant District Attorney Elise McCarthy, who was present when authorities first examined the body parts of the victim on March 1, 1989.

Lawyer Raines, trying for the lesser charge of first-degree manslaughter, hoped to show that his client had acted under "emotional disturbance or distress" when he killed his father. Raines put a psychiatrist on the stand to support his case. On cross-examination, A.D.A. McCarthy elicited from the doctor that he had not actually run tests on William, but had taken at face value William's claim that he "had lost control." The psychiatrist protested that he had not run tests because he did not want to upset William King Jr.

Furthermore, the A.D.A. argued, William had demonstrated enormous control over his actions in his manner of disposing of the body. The defendant had taken great pains to throw police off his scent, the prosecutor contended, and therefore seemed to know exactly what he was doing and knew it was wrong. She also argued against the psychiatrist's claim that William had suffered unusual abuse at his father's hands by posing the question, why, then, had William elected to stay with his father after his parents' separation? Wasn't it because William had it pretty good in his father's house?

Prosecutor McCarthy called Detectives Abbondandelo and Daly to the stand, as well as Assistant Medical Examiner Lone Thanning, Jeff Ludlow, and a representative from one of William King Sr.'s credit card companies. McCarthy's well-constructed case completely overwhelmed the defense. The jury took only one and a half hours on March 17, 1990, to return a guilty verdict for William King Jr.

William King Jr. was sentenced by Judge Harrington on April 30, 1990. He received the maximum penalty for second-degree murder, a 25-year-to-life sentence. William King Jr. is currently serving that sentence in Sing Sing Prison in upstate New York.

EDITOR'S NOTE:
Kate Burbage, Jeff Ludlow, and Roger Kemp are not the real names of the persons so named in the foregoing story. Fictitious names have been used because there is no reason for public interest in the identities of these persons.

"JEFFREY DAHMER: THE BUTCHER OF MILWAUKEE'S HUMAN SLAUGHTERHOUSE"

by Gary C. King

It was sultry in Milwaukee, Wisconsin, on Monday evening, July 22, 1991, as the midnight hour approached. Out on routine patrol, Police Officers Robert Rauth and Rolf Mueller had just turned onto North 25th Street on the west side of town, a tough section of the city replete with slums, drug dealers, and transients.

People were regularly assaulted and/or robbed in the neighborhood, and there were the expected bar fights that the police had to break up on a regular basis. On a more violent scale women were often raped, sometimes in the street, and there was even an occasional murder. It wasn't one of the safest beats in the city, and the acts of lawlessness that regularly occurred there had always been somewhat predictable. Until the night of July 23, that is.

Officers Rauth and Mueller weren't particularly surprised when they saw the young, good-looking black man run out of the Oxford Apartments and into the street, waving his hands and yelling for them to stop. Such a display was a common sight, and the persons seeking attention were often naked and freaked out on drugs and alcohol. But they sensed that there was something different about this incident. The man seemed sober and in control of his actions. As the two cops pulled to the side of the street to see what was amiss, they noticed something shiny dangling from the man's left wrist. When the man approached their cruiser, they saw that it was a pair of handcuffs that had been fastened around only the one wrist.

"Hey, what's the problem?" asked one of the officers as the man ran to their car.

"There's a guy in there trying to kill me!" the man gasped, as he pointed toward the Oxford Apartments. The man, in a state that seemed mixed between exhaustion and extreme fright, was placed inside the squad car.

After a few minutes, the cops were able to calm the man somewhat. He told them his name was Bruce Wilcox, and said that the man who lived in apartment 213 was trying to kill him with a large knife that he kept under his bed. Although the cops were a little skeptical due to the neighborhood and the fact that they thought they had seen everything in the course of their careers, the two officers gave Wilcox the benefit of the doubt and assured him they would check it out. They asked him to accompany them to identify the man. Still shaking from fear, Wilcox reluctantly agreed.

As they walked down the blue-carpeted hallway on the second floor of the apartment building, the officers became starkly aware of an awful, putrid stench that grew stronger with each step that took them closer to apartment 213. The smell was almost unbearable by the time they reached the door of the apartment, and when the lone occupant opened it, the odor nearly overwhelmed both lawmen.

The officers were let into the small, dingy unit by a tall, soft-spoken man with blond hair and a pale complexion. With little prompting from the cops, the man politely identified himself as 31-year-old Jeffrey L. Dahmer. His breath reeked of alcohol, and he appeared to be intoxicated. Officers Rauth and Mueller asked Dahmer what was causing the horrible stench, but he didn't reply. Instead he sat down on the couch and, with a blank look in his eyes, asked them if he could drink a beer and smoke a cigarette.

Officer Mueller headed for the bedroom while Rauth remained in the living room and attempted to learn more about Bruce Wilcox's allegations against Dahmer from the suspect himself. Rauth's efforts, however appeared futile. Dahmer was in an alcohol-induced stupor, and wasn't saying much

When Mueller reached the oppressive, fly-infested bedroom, he found a 12-inch butcher knife hidden under the bed, just as Wilcox had said he would. He also noted a Polaroid camera lying on the bed, and several photographs protruding from a drawer in a tall, 18th-century style chest of drawers.

When he viewed them, Mueller suddenly felt lightheaded and nauseous. Several of the Polaroid shots depicted nude men engaged in homosexual sex acts, and others showed numerous corpses in various stages of mutilation and dismemberment. The flesh on one of the corpses, from its chest down, had been stripped cleanly away, he guessed from some type of acid! His stomach retching, Officer Mueller could see that the grisly photos had been taken in the bedroom where he now stood.

When Mueller went into the kitchen area, Jeffrey Dahmer jumped up from the couch and began shrieking. When Mueller opened the refrigerator door, he knew why Dahmer had reacted in such a frightened manner. There, on the bottom shelf next to a box of Arm & Hammer baking soda, was a grotesquely severed human head!

Officer Mueller didn't need to see any more. He went back to the living room and handcuffed Jeffrey Dahmer, and Wilcox confirmed that Dahmer was the person who had tried to kill him. As the two officers led him out of the apartment, Dahmer began meowing like a cat.

Over the next several hours, following the issuance of a search warrant, a hazardous materials team of police officers wearing oxygen masks and protective yellow rubber suits began going through Jeffrey Dahmer's apartment. It was only then that they—and soon thereafter that the residents of Milwaukee—realized the full extent of the horrors that had occurred in Dahmer's "charnel house" of slaughter.

Three additional human heads and a human heart were recovered from a small lift-top freezer, along with a pair of lungs, a liver, a kidney, and bundles of frozen intestines. Three headless torsos were found in a 55-gallon plastic vat, or drum, submerged in unknown chemicals in Dahmer's bedroom. Nearby were bottles of formaldehyde, hydrochloric acid, and chloroform, as well as a number of hand tools and three electric saws.

As the search and seizure of evidence continued, police officers found body parts, including bones, stored in cardboard boxes around the apartment. They found a decomposed hand connected to a small piece of arm protruding from beneath the bed, and male genital organs floating in a lobster pot in the kitchen. Five male skulls, boiled and scraped clean, were seized from a box and a filing cabinet. Two more skulls were found sitting on a closet shelf, where several sets of hands and arms hung from the clothes rack.

The two skulls in the closet were painted gray, apparently to give them a plastic-like appearance, like models used by medical students and artists. The team also discovered five full skeletons at an undisclosed location inside the apartment. By their best count, at least at this point, the cops had recovered the remains of 11 victims inside Jeffrey Dahmer's apartment.

The kitchen, noted the cops, was filthy. Dirty pots and pans, crusted over with substances the investigators feared would turn out to be human leftovers, were strewn about the sink and countertop. Other dishes, also lying about, were just simply slimy. Interestingly, the cops noted, and with chilling and sickening connotations, they had not found one item of "normal" foodstuffs in the apartment—only a variety of condiments!

The investigators worked throughout the night and all through the next day, carrying box after box of body parts and other evidentiary items from Dahmer's apartment. Included in those items were several commercially successful, gruesome horror films such as *The Exorcist,* several from the *Friday the 13th* and *Nightmare on Elm Street* series, among others. A lawman close to the investigation said that, considering the grisly still photographs found inside the apartment, detectives wanted to determine if any of the videotapes had been taped over as a means of concealing live action videos of real murder and dismemberment.

Meanwhile, Milwaukee Police Chief Phillip Arreola held a new conference and announced to the nation the grim and macabre discovery his officers had made inside apartment 213. Arreola said there were many victims, all of them male as far as they could tell, and of various races. Most of the victims were black, but there were also Hispanics, whites, and an Asian, prompting some to wonder if Dahmer had prepared a smorgasbord of races and cultures as human cuisine. Arreola told reporters that it was too early to tell whether the killings were sexually motivated.

"We don't know if this individual acted alone or in concert with other individuals," said Arreola. He added that Jeffrey Dahmer had been booked into jail on suspicion of homicide, but hadn't yet been charged as of late Wednesday.

A short time later, a group of investigators converged on the Oxford Apartments and began interviewing the building's residents. They were particularly interested in what Jeffrey Dahmer's closest neighbors had to say, and wanted to know whether anyone had seen or heard anything unusual coming from Dahmer's apartment. They also wanted to know why nobody had previously reported the foul odor of the rotting corpses.

"We've been smelling odors for weeks," said one resident, "but we thought it was a dead animal or something like that. We had no idea it was humans." Many residents said that Dahmer often brought home stray cats.

Another neighbor told police that he had heard sawing noises coming from Dahmer's apartment at all hours of the day and night, and saw Dahmer take out large bags of what he thought was just garbage.

"I wondered what the hell he was building in there," said the neighbor. "I thought he was building bookcases or something. Then, when the buzzing stopped, I heard him yelling, 'Motherf---er, I told you, goddamn it.' It seemed strange because I didn't hear anyone respond or talk, except for him." Now, however, the neighbor and others in the building told police that they wished they'd taken the tell-tale signs more seriously.

One neighbor who lived down the hallway from Dahmer's apartment told investigators that she *always* smelled an oppressive odor in the corridor.

"I went sniffing at all the neighbors' doors," recalled the resident. "When I got to Jeff's, I could smell it coming out of the crack."

Having been able to see inside Dahmer's apartment on occasion, the neighbor said she had been curious about all the locks and security devices on the doors, including those to the bedroom and closet.

"I thought he was keeping burglars out," she said. "But it seems he was keeping people in."

When neighbors had complained to Dahmer about the stench coming from his apartment—some had complained as long as a year before the grisly discovery—Dahmer always had an excuse. Sometimes he said the sewage was backed up; other times he said his freezer, full of meat, was broken and his meat had spoiled. But nothing in Dahmer's demeanor, insisted neighbors, even at the time of his arrest, unveiled the dark, macabre secret he kept locked behind his door, carefully protected not only by all the locks but by an electronic security system he had devised himself.

Most of those interviewed told the police that Dahmer was quiet most of the time, that he rarely spoke to even his closest neighbors. When he did speak to them—usually when he was going to or coming from work—his comments were nearly always curt. Not surprising, most of the conversations he had with his neighbors were about the rancid smell that came from his apartment.

In the hours after Jeffrey Dahmer's arrest, detectives interviewed at length Bruce Wilcox, the man who had brought this gruesome case to light, about his nightmarish encounter with Milwaukee's cannibalistic butcher. After hearing his story, those close to the case all agreed that Wilcox was lucky he made it out alive.

Wilcox told police that he was at a Milwaukee mall when he ran into Dahmer, whom he had seen regularly in the neighborhood, at about 5:00 p.m. on July 22nd. Dahmer showed him a $100 bill and suggested they spend it on a party.

"Let's get some girls and go down to the lake and have a party," Wilcox quoted Dahmer as saying. "I'll buy the beer."

Wilcox, in apparent agreement, told the probers that he and Dahmer stopped at a store, bought some beer and liquor, then proceeded to Dahmer's apartment. Dahmer told his newfound companion that he had to stop off and change his clothes.

As soon as they entered the first floor of the building, Wilcox said he could smell the stench. When they approached Dahmer's apartment, the odor was nearly intolerable. Wilcox, feeling he was about to gag, said: "It smells like someone died in here!" Dahmer just laughed and said that the smell was caused by a problem with the sewer in the building. When Dahmer opened the door to apartment 213, Wilcox thought he would vomit.

Because of the smell, Wilcox suggested that they take some of the beer and drink it elsewhere. Dahmer, using agreement as his ruse, said: "That sounds good. I can barely stand the smell myself."

Pretending that he was going to change clothes, Dahmer opened a beer for Wilcox and motioned for him to sit on the couch. As he sipped on a Budweiser, Wilcox observed that the walls in the living room had photos and drawings of men working out on gym equipment. Dahmer's response to Wilcox's continued probing was simply that he was a member of a health club and that he took and drew the photos as a hobby. Wilcox, however, began to wonder if Dahmer was homosexual.

When Wilcox finished his beer and again protested about the smell, Dahmer brought him a hastily-made rum and coke. Although it tasted a little unusual, Wilcox went ahead and drank it anyway, thinking that it had simply been mixed too strong. However, soon after he finished it, he began to feel a little muddled and decided that his drink had been drugged, Wilcox told the investigators.

In the next few minutes, before Wilcox realized what was happening, Dahmer had retrieved a 12-inch butcher knife and shoved it in Wilcox's armpit, its deadly blade directed at his heart. "If you don't do what I say, I'm going to kill you!" Wilcox quoted Dahmer as warning him. "I've done this before. Don't make a move because I can kill you just like that," Dahmer said as he snapped his fingers. Dahmer then slapped a handcuff on Wilcox's left wrist, and tried to force Wilcox's right arm over and behind him so that he could handcuff it too. But Wilcox, although terrified, resisted, in part because he noticed that Dahmer was already intoxicated. He also knew that if he let Dahmer get the handcuff on his right hand he wouldn't stand a chance of escaping through the double-locked front door.

In an attempt to placate Dahmer until he felt the moment for escape was right, Wilcox willingly allowed Dahmer to lead him by the handcuff into the darkened bedroom. When Dahmer turned on a light in the corner next to the single bed, Wilcox said he could see that the walls were covered with photos of nude men in nearly every homosexual sex-act pose imaginable. He also noticed a large dried bloodstain on the bedsheet, and to his horror, he saw a hand protruding from beneath the bed.

"You'll never leave here," said Dahmer. "It won't be long. I'll show you things you won't believe." Dahmer then told Wilcox that he was planning to eat him! He then turned on a small television next to the bed, and placed a copy of *The Exorcist* in the VCR. "This was the best movie ever made," Dahmer said.

As Dahmer continued to babble about the movie, he walked over to a nearby filing cabinet. "I want to show you something," he said as he pulled open a drawer and removed a human skull. He rubbed the top of the skull as he fiendishly stared at Wilcox, sitting on the edge of the bed. "This is how I get people to stay with me. You'll stay with me, too."

At one point Dahmer forced Wilcox to lay on his stomach on the floor. He again attempted to pull Wilcox's right hand behind him so he could handcuff it to his left, but Wilcox continued to resist.

"I'll let you go if you just let me put your other hand in the handcuff so I can take some pictures of you," said Dahmer. "Let me be more in control. Let me take some nude pictures of you, then I'll let you go."

But Bruce Wilcox did not relent. He told the sleuths that he began to talk about anything and everything to keep Dahmer's mind off him. He also continued to get Dahmer to drink beer, and he could see that Dahmer's state of intoxication was intensifying.

Nonetheless, Dahmer's attention kept returning to Wilcox and the grisly vile plan that he was apparently intent on completing. At one point he took out several photographs of dead men in various stages of dismemberment and began showing them to Wilcox.

"You'll look real good this way," said Dahmer. "You'll

look better than they did." He also told Wilcox that he was beautiful.

Dahmer, still holding the knife to Wilcox's side, forced Wilcox to lay flat on his back on the floor. Dahmer then placed his own head firmly against his intended victim's chest.

"I can hear it beating now," said Dahmer. "Soon it will be mine . . . I'm going to cut your heart out!" Dahmer said that he wanted to see what his heart looked like, and that he was going to eat it. Based on what he had seen and heard, Wilcox had no reason to doubt Dahmer. Wilcox also believed that Jeffrey Dahmer had eaten several human hearts before he stumbled into Dahmer's debased life.

Wilcox continued to talk, and soon convinced Dahmer to take him back into the living room to drink more beer. Along the way they stopped in the kitchen, where Dahmer retrieved two beers from the refrigerator. When Dahmer opened the refrigerator door, Wilcox nearly collapsed when he saw the severed head on the bottom shelf.

As they sat on the couch, Dahmer began rocking back and forth, going deeper into his alcohol-induced stupor.

"It's time, it's time," Dahmer began chanting as he rocked back and forth. "It's time, it's time, it's time."

Sensing that his chance to escape was then or never, Bruce Wilcox stood up and landed a right-handed punch against Dahmer's jaw, hitting him with all the power he could muster. In the next instant he kicked Dahmer in the chest, knocking him to the floor, Dazed, Dahmer had difficulty getting up, giving Wilcox just enough time to open the double-locked door and flee down the stairs to safety, where he flagged down Officers Mueller and Rauth.

"At first he seemed so normal," said Wilcox. "He turned from Mr. Right to Mr. It . . . It was like I was confronting Satan himself," Wilcox told the probers.

The detectives hailed Bruce Wilcox as a hero, saying that his bravery had probably saved the lives of countless future victims that Dahmer may have killed, had his activities remained undetected. They also praised Wilcox for refusing to relinquish control, and said that that was probably what had saved his life. Serial killers, they said, thrive on being in control, and when that power is denied them, it often kills their thrill.

When Milwaukee police did a background check on Jeffrey Dahmer for priors, they learned that he was no stranger to law enforcement. He was arrested for public drunkenness on October 7, 1981, in Bath, Ohio; for disturbing the peace by dropping his pants in front of a group of onlookers on August 7, 1982, in Milwaukee; for lewd and lascivious behavior on September 8, 1986, when he deliberately exposed himself while urinating in front of a group of children, again in Milwaukee. In 1988, it was alleged that Dahmer drugged a man from Illinois in West Allis, Wisconsin, and attempted to rob him of his money. However, that charge was dropped for lack of evidence.

"I wouldn't call him a persistent law enforcement problem," said Bath Police Captain John Gardner, who had a tough time arresting Dahmer during one of Dahmer's drunken episodes in 1981. "But when he got the alcohol in him, he could become completely uncooperative." He explained how Dahmer had been thrown out of a hotel bar, but had refused to leave the parking lot. "As I drove up, he was standing in front of the doors, drinking from a liquor bottle."

Dahmer's most serious prior police record, however, showed that he was arrested in Milwaukee in 1988 for fondling a 13-year-old Laotian boy's genitals and offering him $50 cash to pose for nude photos. He pleaded guilty the following year to those charges, and at his sentencing hearing on May 23, 1989, Dahmer provided an excuse for his actions to the judge.

"I am an alcoholic," said Dahmer. "Not the sort that has to have a drink every single day. But when I do drink, I go overboard."

Dahmer served 10 months in prison for the molestation conviction. He was released on work-release in March 1990 after writing the following letter, dated December 10, 1989, to Milwaukee County Circuit Judge William D. Gardner, the same judge who had sent him to prison:

"Dear Judge Gardner,
    My name is Jeff Dahmer. On September 20, 1988, I was arrested in Milwaukee, Wisconsin for taking pictures of a 13-year-old minor. On September 27, 1988, I was released on bail from the Milwaukee County Jail. On May 24, 1989, after having entered a plea of guilty in your court, I received my sentence. It was as follows: One year of work release, and five years of probation. I have, as of this date, served six months and four days of my sentence. Sir, I have always believed that a man should be willing to assume responsibility for the mistakes that he makes in life. That is why I entered a plea of 'guilty' to the crime of which I was charged. During my stay [in prison], I have had a chance to look at my life from an angle that was never presented to me before. What I did was deplorable. The world has enough misery in it without my adding more to it. Sir, I can assure you that it will never happen again. This is why, Judge Gardner, I am requesting from you a sentence modification. So that I may be allowed to continue my life as a productive member of our society.

Respectfully yours,
Jeff Dahmer"

When his modified sentence was approved by the judge, Dahmer obtained employment as a laborer at a chocolate factory earning $8.75 an hour. He had worked there as a stock clerk, police learned, until his firing on July 14, 1991, for chronic absenteeism.

As they delved deeper into Dahmer's police record, Milwaukee homicide detectives learned that patrol officers responded to Dahmer's apartment in May 1991 as a result of a neighbor's complaint that a young Asian boy, naked and bleeding from his anus, was seen running from apartment 213. Dahmer, however, had convinced the reporting officers that the naked boy was actually 19 and was his homosexual lover. Dahmer told the cops that they had been involved in a lover's spat, nothing more, and that the "young man" was drunk. He assured the police that he would take care of his "lover."

As investigators began identifying the remains of the victims found inside Dahmer's apartment, they realized that he had taken care of his lover, all right. The lover, it turned out, had been an unwilling companion. He was identified as 14-year-old Konerak Sinthasomphone, a relative of the Laotian boy who Dahmer was sent to prison for molesting. Sinthasomphone, who looked older than his age, had been reported missing after he left home to play soccer with friends. The detectives found a photograph of Konerak among those photos seized at Dahmer's apartment, and positive identification was accomplished through dental comparisons.

In a move that would stun the world, Jeffrey Dahmer soon confessed to detectives that he had murdered the 11 people whose remains were found inside his apartment. One of the victims, he said, he picked up at a gay bar in Milwaukee. They went to a hotel, rented a room for $43, got drunk and passed out.

"When he woke up," said one of the investigators relating Dahmer's confession, "the other guy was dead and had blood coming out of his mouth."

Dahmer explained to the investigators how he left the body inside the hotel room while he walked to a nearby mall and purchased a suitcase. When he returned to the hotel, he

106

placed the body inside the suitcase, called a taxi, and took it to his grandmother's house in West Allis. It was there, he said, that he dismembered the corpse and disposed of it without ever telling anyone.

A year later he killed again, Dahmer told police, this time at his grandmother's house. He told detectives that he met the victim at the same gay bar where he met the other one, had sex with him, then gave him sleeping pills. After the man fell asleep, Dahmer strangled him. A third victim was killed in much the same way, Dahmer said, also at his grandmother's house. All were dismembered.

In 1989, Dahmer told detectives, he picked up another homosexual, had sex with him, drugged him, then stabbed him with a hunting knife. He placed the body in the bathtub, dismembered it, then used hydrochloric acid to destroy the bones. He said the killings that followed were carried out in similar fashion, but added that with practice he "began getting quicker at cutting up the bodies."

While many detectives working the case believed sexual perversity was the major factor in the killings being attributed to Dahmer, others also believed that the profound loneliness experienced by Dahmer was a major contributing factor. Dahmer told one detective that he kept his victims' body parts because he believed they would keep him company.

The detectives soon obtained all the reports of Dahmer's contacts with his probation officer from Wisconsin's Department of Corrections. Although one of the reports stated that Dahmer "appears to be depressed all the time," there was nothing to indicate his apparently ongoing murderous activities. During the interviews with his probation officer he talked about everything except the murders.

Among the subjects he discussed was his sexual orientation. He stated that he "knows he prefers male sex partners but feels guilty about it." He also said he was uncomfortable with his family because his "father is controlling," he has "nothing in common with his brother who is in college," and he expressed that he is "embarrassed by his offense" of child molestation. He was also concerned about money, and asked, "Why are people who make a lot of money so lucky?"

In an affidavit written and submitted by Police Lieutenant David Kane to the Milwaukee County Circuit Court, Dahmer "stated that he would drug these individuals and usually strangle them and then he would dismember the bodies."

Although no criminal charges were immediately filed, Circuit Judge Frank T. Crivello accepted the affidavit during a brief probable cause hearing and set Dahmer's bail at one million dollars in cash. Milwaukee lawyer Gerald Boyle was appointed as Dahmer's attorney.

"I am told by authorities and by himself that he has made many statements that inculpate him," said Boyle. "He said he has no one to blame but himself, not the police, not the courts, and not the probation department. He said there comes a time when you have to be honest, and this is the time. . . . He wants to continue to talk to the authorities, to assist the authorities in identifying the victims. The state has every right to hold him." Boyle stated publicly that Dahmer was mentally competent to participate in court proceedings.

"As to the information I can release," said Chief Arreola, "for the most part the victims are male. We have no indication up to now that we have any female victims."

Chief Arreola declined to discuss reports that Dahmer had admitted to committing acts of cannibalism, but Medical Examiner Jeffrey Jentzen told reporters that the victims' remains were "not inconsistent with cannibalism. . . . We may have opinions on that at a future time."

Dahmer's taste for human flesh was also confirmed through subsequent interviews with the suspect. He told sleuths that he once fried a victim's biceps in vegetable shortening and ate it. However, that victim's identity had not yet been determined. Many of those who heard the gruesome story wondered if Dahmer used vegetable shortening for health reasons.

"Once you've tasted human flesh," said a source who declined identification, "you'll never eat beef or pork again."

As the authorities continued to make progress in the case, another victim was identified as Oliver Lacy, 23, of Chicago.

Victim Oliver Lacy, who was positively identified from his fingerprints, had moved to Milwaukee four months earlier to be with his 2-year-old son. The former high-school track star, who was engaged to be married, disappeared shortly after he went to the Grand Avenue Mall for ice cream after work, relatives told police.

Dahmer told detectives that he put a "sleeping potion" in a drink he gave Lacy and then strangled him. He said that it was Lacy's heart that they had found in his freezer. He told sleuths that he planned to "eat the heart later," and confessed to having anal sex with Lacy's corpse.

"I don't know how this person lured [Oliver]," said one of Lacy's relatives. "He wasn't the type of person who would let someone come up to him like that."

According to Milwaukee Police Lieutenant Vincent Vitale, Dahmer worked alone. He also said that investigators had not been able, so far, to determine that a pattern of cannibalism existed despite their certainty that Dahmer had eaten at least some of his victims' remains.

"He apparently wasn't consuming every person he killed," said Vitale.

One-by-one, the identification of the victims continued to mount. Soon, as Dahmer continued to talk to the police, the remains of all 11 victims found inside Dahmer's apartment had been identified. In addition to Konerak Sinthasomphone and Oliver Lacy, the victims were:

Anthony Sears, 24, of Milwaukee. Sears was last seen on

March 25, 1989, the day before Easter. Police initially believed that Sears had been the first of the 11 killed inside Dahmer's apartment, but Dahmer told them later that Sears had actually been killed at Dahmer's grandmother's house in West Allis. Dahmer said he took Sears' skull back to his apartment to keep as a souvenir. Police believe Dahmer may have lured Sears, who aspired to be a model, to his grandmother's house for a photo session and the promise of money.

Ricky Beeks, 33, of Milwaukee, was last seen on May 29, 1990. Also known as Raymond Lamont Smith, Beeks had served time in jail.

Ernest Miller, 24, of Milwaukee, was last seen on September 2, 1990. Although Miller had been living in Chicago, a relative told police that Miller came up to Milwaukee over the Labor Day weekend to get away from all of the violence in Chicago. "He told us he was going out to eat and then back home to Chicago," said the relative. "He was a nice person. Never bothered anybody."

Curtis Straughter, 18, of Milwaukee, was last seen on March 7, 1991. A homosexual, Straughter found it difficult to come to terms with his sexuality and as a result felt estranged from some of his family members. A high-school dropout, Straughter had lost his job as a nursing assistant but had told family members that he planned to go to modeling school. Police believe Dahmer may have lured Straughter to his apartment to take photographs.

Errol Lindsey, 19, of Milwaukee, was last seen around dinner time on April 7, 1991. Like Oliver Lacy, he had been to the Grand Avenue Mall, but had returned home. However, he left again a short time later to have a key made. Police wondered if maybe Lindsey had really left to keep a rendezvous with Dahmer, a date that was perhaps made at the mall.

Tony Hughes, 31, of Madison, Wisconsin, was last seen on May 24, 1991, at a dance club for gays on Milwaukee's south side. Relatives told police that Hughes, who was deaf and unable to speak, had known Jeffrey Dahmer for about two years.

"I knew deep inside my heart that [Tony] would be one of those bodies found," said a relative of Hughes. "He was outgoing, jolly, happy. He could make friends easily. I just prayed and asked the Lord to show me where [Tony] was. I just wanted to know if he was dead or alive. The way he died, it hurts. Words can't describe it."

Matt Turner, 20, of Chicago, was last seen on June 30, 1991. He was living at a halfway house in Chicago at the time of his disappearance. When police questioned Dahmer about Turner, Dahmer told them that he had met Turner at a homosexual street rally in Chicago. Dahmer said he offered Turner money to watch videos with him in his Milwaukee apartment, and Turner agreed to ride with him to Milwaukee on a Greyhound bus. Like some of the other victims, Dahmer said he gave Turner a sleeping sedative. Turner's head had been among those found in the freezer, and his body had been stuffed inside the 55-gallon barrel.

Jeremiah Weinberger, 23, of Chicago, was last seen on July 6, 1991, at a North Side dance club in Chicago. Dahmer told detectives that he had met Weinberger at a gay bar in Chicago in early July and offered him money to pose for nude photos and to watch videos with him. He added that Weinberger stayed with him for two days, and that he had killed him when Weinberger wanted to leave. One of Weinberger's relatives told police that Weinberger had been in the wrong place at the wrong time when he met up with Dahmer. "[He] was hypnotized by a cobra," said the relative. "Unfortunately, he was bit."

Joseph Bredehoft, 25, of Milwaukee, was last seen on July 16, 1991. He had a wife and three children. Bradehoft, police learned, had recently moved in with a relative and was looking for work. Dahmer told the detectives that he met Bradehoft at a bus stop near Marquette University and offered him money to pose for photographs at his apartment. Like all the others, Bradehoft had been duped.

All of the killings attributed to Dahmer were horrible, to be sure. But the death that was felt the hardest by the police and the public was that of 14-year-old Konerak Sinthasomphone, in part because Sinthasomphone's family had been victimized twice by Jeffrey Dahmer.

"It is staggeringly hard" for a family to cope with the killing of a loved one, said a coordinator with Milwaukee County's victim-witness program. Even worse to find out that the killer was the same perpetrator of the previous attack. "I can't think of anything worse."

Sinthasomphone's family had fled Laos in 1980 to escape the repression of communism, hoping to find a better life in the U.S. Instead, they found tragedy upon tragedy was befalling them.

"It is like you are running and you think you escape but you are coming to a dangerous world in this place," said a member of the Laotian community.

"Obviously, anyone who has gone through such a tragedy as this would wonder if they've chosen the right path for their lives," said a priest and family friend. "The family is filled with a lot of different emotion. Anger is certainly one of them. They hope and pray no one else will ever have to endure such a tragedy again."

"We thought it likely that Konerak was in Dahmer's apartment," said one of Konerak's relatives when news of Konerak's positive identification was disclosed. "The whole thing is crazy. It is terrible. I don't know what to say."

While the families of Dahmer's victims mourned their dead, Jeffrey Dahmer continued to relate his grisly tale to lawmen. He admitted that he had boiled several of his victims' skulls to remove the flesh, and said that he bathed some of the skulls in acid to remove the excess flesh and to bleach or whiten them. With the admission that he'd killed three of his victims at his grandmother's house in West Allis, the death toll soared to 14. Before his wave of confessions showed any signs of receding, the death toll climbed to 16.

In addition to the initial 11 victims, Dahmer confessed to murdering David C. Thomas of Milwaukee, a father of two who was last seen on September 24, 1990; Edward W. Smith, 28, of Milwaukee, who disappeared after attending a gay pride parade in Chicago in June 1990; Richard Guerrero, 25, of Milwaukee, who disappeared in 1988; Steven W. Tuomi, 24, of Milwaukee, last seen on September 15, 1987; and Steven Mark Hicks, 19, who went missing on June 18, 1978. Dahmer then told police about killing another man, bringing the staggering death count to 17. The 17th victim, however, hasn't yet been identified. Dahmer, it seemed, recalled more abut his victims' tattoos and other physical characteristics—not to mention what he did to them—than their names.

In an interview with Detective John Karabatsos, Dahmer identified a photo of Steven Hicks. Hicks, said Dahmer, had been his first victim. Dahmer told Detective Karabatsos that he had picked up Hicks, who had been hitchhiking his way to a rock concert, and took him to his childhood home near Bath, Ohio, for a beer. The house, Dahmer said, had been left vacant after his parents divorced. Dahmer said they also engaged in sex.

When Hicks showed signs of wanting to leave, Dahmer bashed in the back of his head with a barbell, then finished Hicks off by strangling him. He dragged the body into a crawlspace beneath the house, cut it up and placed the pieces inside garbage bags. When he thought he was finished savoring his kill, he buried Hicks' body parts.

However, over a considerable period of time, Dahmer exhumed the parts for more perverted frolic, buried them again, dug them up again, and so on. Finally, when the anatomical pieces gave way to severe putrefaction, Dahmer scraped the flesh off the bones. Afterwards, he smashed the

113

bones to bits with a sledgehammer and scattered them in a ravine behind his parents' house. When Dahmer was finished telling his grisly story, he drew a detailed map of the heavily wooded, 1.7-acre property for authorities, and pinpointed locations where he believed they would find Steven Hicks' bones.

On the first day of their search at Dahmer's childhood home in Bath, an affluent Akron suburb, searchers found as many as 50 bone pieces and fragments as they raked debris from the ground where Dahmer had told them to look. Among the bones found was a pelvic bone, a long leg bone, a rib and a forearm. According to Summit County Coroner William A. Cox, as many as 70 percent of the bones were human, and some appeared to be skull fragments.

At a hastily called news conference, Cox said that investigators hoped to extract genetic material from the bones and make a positive identification utilizing DNA printing, even though they had little or no doubt that the remains were Hicks'.

"Jeffrey Dahmer has been very truthful in what he has related to us and Milwaukee police," said Summit County Sheriff David Troutman.

Although it would take some time, he said they were hopeful that they could determine Hicks' genetic "blueprint" with blood samples from his parents. They could also compare the genetic evidence with locks of Hicks' hair, which his family had saved in an album. "We may very well be able to put together who those bones belong to," said Cox.

As the search for evidence continued, the public's interest and continuously growing interest in true crime became conspicuously evident. People from the neighborhood and other parts of town stopped in front of the house in their effort to get a look at the activity. Even more shocking were the children present, who had set up a lemonade stand across the street to quench the gawkers' thirst — for a profit of course.

"I can understand why the media was here," said a neighbor, "but it's the curiosity-seekers I can't understand. It's like they're getting joy out of someone else's pain." In reality, though, the curiosity-seekers weren't reveling over the pain and suffering of others. They just wanted to know more about Jeffrey Dahmer's monstrous activities, to learn what could possibly drive a man to such violent extremes.

"There's so much we still have to learn about him," said Milwaukee Police Captain Joseph M. Purpero. "We've only been at this a few days. It seems the more we learn, the more we have to learn."

Within days after his arrest and confessions to police, investigators converged on Dahmer's grandmother's house in West Allis. Relatives told the investigators that they had discovered a vat of viscous substance in the basement of the home about three years earlier, but thought little of it when Dahmer explained to them that he was disintegrating dead animals.

During their search of the premises, investigators seized a sledgehammer, a hatchet, a sewer grate cover, and several prescription drug containers.

"He [Dahmer] said he administered some drugs [to his victims] and strangled them," said West Allis Deputy Police Chief Robert Due.

Before they were finished, according to West Allis Police Chief John Butorak, detectives recovered the remains of one man on the premises, believed to have been one of the three victims Dahmer admitted killing there. As for Dahmer's grandmother, Butorak said investigators were certain that she knew nothing of the killings.

"She's not involved in the investigation," said Chief Butorak. "She's a very elderly lady, going through a very hard time."

As the case continued to unfold and more was learned about Jeffrey Dahmer's background, it began to seem like

115

the real-life version of Hannibal "The Cannibal" Lecter, a fictional character portrayed by Anthony Hopkins in the movie thriller based on Thomas Harris' bestseller, *The Silence of the Lambs,* had jumped off the screen and taken up residence in Milwaukee. The revelations surrounding Dahmer's case also revived unpleasant memories of Chicago's homosexual killer, John Wayne Gacy, and of Wisconsin's own Ed Gein, another cannibal whose story served, albeit loosely, as the backdrop for the motion pictures *Psycho* and *The Texas Chain Saw Massacre.*

"There's no doubt he's insane," said a close family member. "But Jeffrey was not born a monster. He is not a monster."

Jeffrey L. Dahmer was born at Evangelical Deaconess Hospital in Milwaukee on May 21, 1960. Following a move to Ames, Iowa, in 1962 so that his father could attend graduate school, Dahmer moved with his parents to Doylestown, Ohio, near Akron, four years later. At age 6, following the birth of a sibling, Dahmer began to show signs that he felt neglected. The feelings intensified while he was in the first grade, in part due to an illness his mother suffered both before and after the birth of his brother.

In 1968, he and his family moved to the well-to-do community of Bath Township, where he attended elementary school. The same year, at age 8, Dahmer was sexually abused by an older neighbor boy, an incident that was not reported to the police at the time.

While still in elementary school, Dahmer received an introductory chemistry set as a present. He soon began storing animal skeletons in bottles of formaldehyde, and he "liked to use acid to scrape the meat off dead animals."

Dahmer eventually began roaming the streets in search of animals that had been killed by cars, and soon had quite a collection of bones from cats, dogs, chipmunks, raccoons, and squirrels that he kept stored in pickle jars filled with formaldehyde. Dahmer also kept spiders, praying mantises, and other pests in jars that lined his clubhouse walls. But he became cruel and mean to animals and insects, a trait that many serial killers share.

"I once watched as Jeff caught a butterfly outside his house and told his bother to take the butterfly by the wings and pull them off," said a former childhood friend. "Jeff was angry at the world, even when he was a child. He just didn't seem to fit in anywhere . . . and he later blamed this on being gay. Jeff hated himself and he hated gays. And that, I think, is the root of his problems."

While attending Revere High School in nearby Richfield, one of the most affluent and respected school districts in the state, Dahmer's grades were characterized by school officials as "unremarkable." He played tennis and clarinet, but rarely as part of any outside school activities. He was considered bright, possessing an IQ of about 145, but his grade-point average suffered because of the wide spread of his grades, which ranged from A to D. Instead of applying himself, Dahmer preferred to be known as a prankster.

"However, we had no record of disciplinary problems," said an official at Revere High. "In fact, I don't have a note of him even being brought to the principal's office."

"He had a bizarre sense of humor," remarked a former classmate. "He bleated like a sheep in class, had fake epileptic seizures in the hallways to see how people reacted. I don't remember having a normal conversation with him."

Dahmer soon began drinking heavily. He would often consume several beers before going to school, and friends frequently observed him swigging gin at his locker.

By age 16, Dahmer's taste for death and torture had intensified. A childhood friend told police that Dahmer kept chipmunk and squirrel skeletons inside a shed behind the house, and that he had an animal burial ground at the side of the house, complete with crosses and other markers.

"He had a little graveyard with animals buried in it," recalled the former friend. "There were skulls placed on top of little crosses. He had quite a collection of skeletons."

One time, another neighborhood boy encountered a mutilated dog carcass while walking through the woods near Dahmer's house. The dog's head was mounted on a stick beside a wooden cross, and the dog's body, skinned and gutted, had been nailed to a tree. After the incident was investigated, it was attributed to Dahmer.

"Whatever had gone on in Jeff's life," said another former classmate, "he couldn't talk about it. It seemed so clear that he was saying, 'Pay attention to me.' But nobody did."

Another of Dahmer's former high school friends told reporters after Dahmer's arrest that he had seen a number of stuffed animals while visiting Dahmer's home in 1978, the same year in which Dahmer said he killed Steven Hicks. He had a large collection of stuffed rabbits, owls and small birds. After having spent the afternoon drinking and smoking marijuana, the friend had asked Dahmer about the stuffed animals.

"It's taxidermy," Dahmer had responded. "I used to do taxidermy . . . I always wanted to do that to a human."

As the probers continued their search to find the key that unleashed Dahmer's bizarre and murderous actions, they kept discovering people who characterized him as an intensely troubled person from childhood to adulthood, someone who was racist and unable to cope with his sexuality. That characterization was illustrated by a minister who said he met Dahmer in a tavern about a month before his arrest. The minister told police that Dahmer was an alcoholic who hated homosexuals and blacks.

"The kid was nervous," said the minister. "He was anxious. He was, I don't know, upset all the time in the bars, like he didn't want to be there, like he was compelled to be by some inner feelings he was trying to repress and because he couldn't deal with it, he would turn around and get drunk."

By his senior year, Dahmer's parents were battling it out in bitter divorce proceedings, fighting over custody of Jeff's younger brother. Eventually his father moved out and his mother left with the younger boy, leaving Dahmer by himself, essentially deserted.

"Jeffrey was left all alone in the house with no money, no food and a broken refrigerator," recalled a family member. "The desertion really affected him." It was shortly after being deserted, Dahmer told police, that he killed Steven Hicks.

On a lighter note, before graduation Dahmer sneaked into an honor society group photo session for Revere High's yearbook. Because his grades were far from meeting honor society standards, Dahmer was not a member but sneaked into the photo as if he belonged there.

"It was a very Jeff thing to do," remembered a former teacher. "It was part of his trying to be unconventional and to mock everything around him. I think he very consciously chose the honor society because I think in some ways he was laughing at himself and us."

His picture with the honor society, however, was blotted out with a black marker before the yearbook went to press.

On another occasion, while visiting Washington, D.C., Dahmer somehow managed to talk his way into Walter F. Mondale's vice-presidential suite and humorist Art Buchwald's office, apparently as pranks or to see if he could do it.

Laura Smith, a sophomore, was Dahmer's date to the senior prom. She would exclaim after Dahmer's arrest, "My first date was with a mass murderer! I felt uncomfortable around him, because he was so weird and emotionless, and I'd heard stories about his heavy drinking. But I was lucky. As far as I know, I'm the only woman to ever date Jeff Dahmer . . . and I got away alive! I've been so upset since I saw his face on television that I haven't been able to sleep. It sends chills down my spine."

119

Dahmer did not ask Laura to go to the prom himself. Instead, he'd arranged the date by having one of Laura's friends ask her for him.

"I was told that Jeff needed a date," recalled Laura, "and a girlfriend talked me into accepting his invitation. I was excited to be going to the prom."

When Dahmer arrived to pick up Laura at her home, he was dressed in brown pants, a vest, and a tie. Most of the other boys wore tuxedos to the formal affair and, as was usual, Dahmer looked like he didn't belong.

"He was so afraid of me that he couldn't stop shaking as he tried to pin the corsage on my dress without touching me," said Laura. "But he fumbled so badly . . . it was like his hands trembled as they got near a girl. Finally, my mother did it for him."

Shortly after they arrived at the prom, recalled Laura, Dahmer hurriedly left without explanation. Laura, in the meantime, felt deserted, angry, and embarrassed.

"I was ashamed and furious," said Laura. "I had no idea where he went . . . God knows, I wonder now what he might have been doing while he was away. It makes my flesh creep . . . Finally someone told me that Jeff went to meet his best friend."

It was around 11:00 p.m. when Dahmer finally returned. He looked like he had been drinking, and he dropped Laura off in front of her house without even kissing her goodnight. He merely shook her hand. Later, he explained why he had left her alone at the prom.

"He said, 'I'm gay and I left you to go meet my boyfriend who didn't go to the prom,' " Laura quoted Dahmer as having told her. "Jeff went on to explain that his boyfriend was angry with him because he took me to the prom. And he had to make it up to him by meeting him during the dance."

A few weeks later Laura met with Dahmer again, this time at his home and in the presence of six other teenagers. With hands joined, they sat around a table that had a candle in the middle. When Laura asked what they were doing, one of the teens told her Jeff was having a seance.

"One of Jeff's friends said, 'Let's call Lucifer!' " recalled Laura. "I thought he was joking, but as he said it, the candle on the table blew out. I bolted from the room and ran across the road and waited until my girlfriend came out . . . We always saw him as the type to commit suicide, not the type who would harm somebody else."

Other former classmates apparently saw Dahmer differently. At a recent reunion, someone asked, "Remember Jeffrey Dahmer?" Another replied, "Oh, he's probably a mass murderer." The irony of it all is that the statements were made before Dahmer's now-confessed butchery had been discovered.

Following graduation from high school and the murder of Steven Hicks, Dahmer attended Ohio State University for a few months. However, his drinking increased to the point of becoming a problem. Strapped for money, he began selling his blood to get drinking money. Not surprisingly, before the academic year ended, he dropped out and enlisted in the Army.

It was in the spring of 1980 when Dahmer reported for duty at Fort McClellan, Alabama, where he began training to become a military police officer. However, for reasons that aren't clear, Dahmer never finished his MP training but was instead soon transferred to Fort Sam Houston in San Antonio, Texas, where he underwent a six-week course to become a medical specialist, a job similar to that of a nurse's aide. When his training was completed, he was sent to the 2nd Battalion, 68th Armored Regiment, 8th Infantry Division in Baumholder, West Germany.

While in West Germany, Dahmer remained a loner. His room's walls had posters of the heavy metal bands Black Sabbath and Iron Maiden. He frequently lay in bed and listened to their music with headphones as he drank himself into unconsciousness. Before passing out from drinking beer, gin, and vodka, however, Dahmer often became menacing to others living in the barracks.

"When he'd drink, he'd get real violent with me," recalled a former bunkmate. "You could tell in his face that he wasn't joking. It was for real. That's why it bothered me. It was a whole different side. His face was blank. It was kind of like he just wasn't there. I've never seen it on anyone else's face."

At other times, remembered the former bunkmate, "he talked about his dad a lot. He wanted to please his dad." The bunkmate told probers that he thought Dahmer had been an only child. "He never said anything about having a brother."

Other Army buddies who served with Dahmer in West Germany also emphasized his drinking problem. They said he frequently mixed Beefeater martinis in the barracks using shakers, stirrers, flasks, and other bar equipment that he carried in a briefcase.

"He'd be shut out from the rest of the world," said one of his former buddies. "He'd drink until he passed out, then wake up and start again. He didn't even go out for chow."

"He was smart," said another, "but he just wanted to slide by. He was just goofy. He always had that look about him, that sinisterness. He was on a steady decline in life. He was on a losing skid and didn't know how to pick himself up."

Following his honorable discharge in March 1981 (a year before his enlistment would have been completed) under Chapter 9 of the Uniform Code of Military Justice, a directive that deals administratively with alcohol and drug abuse by Army personnel, Dahmer moved to Florida where he worked in a sandwich shop and slept on the beach. A short time later he moved back to Ohio, but that didn't work out for him, either. He soon ended up moving in with his grandmother, who lived in West Allis, Wisconsin.

Then, in 1985, Dahmer went to work for a downtown Milwaukee blood bank which, considering the nature of the charges facing him, raised many macabre questions from those closely following the case. However, no improprieties or acts of wrongdoing by Dahmer have been uncovered in connection with Dahmer's position at the blood bank — so far. That same year he went to work for a chocolate factory where he remained employed until July 14, 1991.

Shy but intelligent, good-looking but having no permanent sexual relationships whether they be heterosexual, bisexual or homosexual, Jeffrey Dahmer remains a man of mystery despite his confessions to police and extensive background investigators have turned up. Why did he become an aficionado of necrophilic desire, murder, and mutilation? One can only guess. The real answers may never surface.

"At the time I knew him," said a former neighbor whose sons were playmates of Dahmer's, "there was something devastating going on in his life, and there wasn't anybody there to help him. I feel bad about that. He's done monstrous acts, yet he's a human being," she continued. "Why did he do those things? Only Jeffrey can answer that."

One state official emphasized that, while all the answers may not be readily available in a case such as Dahmer's, sex offenders tend to be the most difficult challenges for probation officers and mental health professionals.

"Our knowledge of sexuality is in the Stone Age," said the official, affiliated with the sex offender program in Milwaukee where Dahmer was supervised after his sex offense conviction. "Anyone who says they know everything about it really doesn't know." Sex offenses, according to the official, are highly recidivist crimes primarily because the offenders are compelled by deep-seated motivations that are difficult, if not impossible, to neutralize.

In Dahmer's case, the potency of his fantasies about homosexual mutilation increased to the point "where he was bursting with self-hatred and he had to relieve it."

"This kind of guy is really an aberration, even of the abnormal," said a Wisconsin psychologist. "His behavior goes one step beyond . . . Each element of the case takes you one step farther into the bizarre . . . My sense is that he hated these people. He may have befriended them, but somehow their friendship hurt. He may have experienced it as pain, not rewarding or fulfilling. When people begin to treat him with friendship, it's bewildering [to him]."

"What happened to him?" continued the mental health professional. "What was the pain? What was the alienation? Clearly he was a very alienated man personally, and socially. I don't think he felt comfortable with himself, with people."

The psychologist pointed out to police that studies have shown that most male sex offenders were sexually abused, physically abused, emotionally abused, neglected, or abandoned as children. One out of five male sex offenders has been sexually abused as a child, statistics show. However, despite the fact that a close family member reported the alleged incident of sexual abuse suffered by Dahmer when he was 8 years old to Dahmer's probation officer, Dahmer denied it. He emphatically stated that "he was never abused, sexually or physically, as a child."

The Wisconsin psychologist who assisted police in a profile of Dahmer said that existing psychological diagnoses do not fit within Dahmer's psyche. He said that if he were pressed to make a diagnosis, he would have to classify Dahmer as a paranoid personality.

"I would suspect he has a delusional system that's very peculiar," said the psychologist. "It's not that he walks around watching spaceships land, or that he can't hold a job, or that when he walks down the street he sets himself apart so that everyone stops."

Another psychologist, after pondering the extensive collection of animal remains Dahmer possessed as a youth, injected an interesting idea that might help explain Dahmer's behavior.

"His behavior didn't change," said the psychologist. "The objects changed . . . This is a person that is very deficient in some ways. His character probably wasn't very strong to begin with, and it got beaten down by ways in which he was treated throughout life. If there's anything monstrous about him, it's the monstrous lack of connection to all things we think of as being human—guilt, remorse, worry, feelings that would stop him from hurting, killing, torturing."

Another question arose: Why did Jeffrey Dahmer strangle all his victims? A forensic psychiatrist who serves as a consultant for the FBI thinks he knows the answer. Of the numerous serial killers that he has studied, the psychiatrist said that 58 percent strangled their victims.

"It's a very personal, intimate means of causing death," said the psychiatrist. "One can actually feel the victim expire." He also said that most serial killers keep a journal of their grisly handiwork, photographs of their deeds, and they keep trophies such as body parts. Most serial killers, he opined, are sexually aroused by their victims' blood because the victims are considered mere objects. "These were sexual props, not people."

Dahmer certainly fit the profile of a serial killer, as put together by Special Agent John Douglas of the FBI's Behavioral Science Unit in the 1970s. Douglas' report, in part, states that most serial killers are white males, loners from troubled homes, who possess a significant degree of intelligence but are typically underachievers. Many are often physically, sexually, or psychologically abused as children, and as adolescents are cruel to animals.

Another psychologist and author of several books on serial killers also believes that serial killers have a number of common characteristics. Most, he says, abuse alcohol and/or drugs, and have suffered from malnutrition. "All have been abused, emotionally, physically, and quite often sexually."

Many serial killers, says the psychologist, show signs of

neurological or central nervous system damage that ranges from dyslexia to epilepsy. Others have memory loss, experience deja vu often, or are sleepwalkers. Many have fantasies of killing, or experience hallucinations. Still others, like David Berkowitz, the notorious "Son of Sam" killer, play with fire and become arsonists. Most, at some point, begin to torture and mutilate animals before moving on to torturing humans. About one-third of all serial killers turn to cannibalism, and almost all keep trophies, or souvenirs, of their victims so that they can relive the killing in fantasy states.

Homophobia and racism are major factors in Jeffrey Dahmer's case, the expert says. "The victims symbolize something in the killer's past." For example, he says, "John Wayne Gacy killed male prostitutes because he was extremely homophobic, and he was killing the hated homosexual part of himself. Most serial killers believe that they are doing good for society by killing certain types." An example is the common prostitute killer.

"Part of their frustration is that they have high ability and potential but they can never realize that potential." As a result, they focus their intelligence toward killing.

"The more people know about Mr. Dahmer, the better chance they have for recognizing others like him," says the psychologist. "And I guarantee you that right now there are at least two more like him out there, waiting to be discovered."

Milwaukee police and residents alike hoped that those serial killers weren't residing in their city. They'd had almost more than they could handle dealing with Dahmer. Milwaukee County District Attorney E. Michael McCann even went so far as to consult with William Kunkle, a Chicago lawyer who helped put John Wayne Gacy on death row in the 1970s. Gacy was responsible for murdering 33 young men and boys between 1972 and 1978. Most of Gacy's victims were found in the crawlspace beneath his house.

Others were found in nearby rivers.

"We had a meeting and we're providing Mr. McCann with some of the transcripts involved in the Gacy case, some of the motions that were filed and what our responses were, some of the legal research that was done before on some of the same questions that he's presented with," said Kunkle. While he would not divulge the contents of the conversations he had with D.A. McCann, Kunkle said that he "didn't know enough about the Milwaukee case to talk about the similarity of the people or the crimes. Obviously, they're multiple homicides; they're situations where there may be unidentified remains. Those things are exact similarities" to Gacy, he said.

"We're dealing with some of the same dynamics that we can see in Gacy," said an author of a book on the Gacy case. "The dysfunctional family, a guy who denies his homosexual feelings to erase whatever shame he might feel in committing these acts, who destroys the people who attracted him in the first place. He's punishing himself and punishing them at the same time."

There is little doubt that Jeffrey Dahmer's horrifying revelations sent the country, if not the world, reeling. Paramount Pictures Corporation immediately pulled ads for their new horror movie, *Body Parts,* throughout the Milwaukee area because of the pain and suffering the victims' families were experiencing, and Wisconsin's largest movie theater chain pulled the film completely from their schedule.

"We pulled our TV ads out of sensitivity to the tragedy in Milwaukee, even though the storyline is not related at all to what happened," said a spokesman for Paramount. The movie, based on the novel *Choice Cuts,* is the story of a criminal psychologist who loses an arm in an automobile accident but receives a new arm after undergoing an experimental procedure. The new arm was that of a murderer.

"There is some concern, naturally, over the subject," said

127

an executive of the National Association of Theater Owners, who suggested that theater operators in Milwaukee feared a negative reaction from the public if the film opened there. "It's unfortunate, but it's really bad timing."

Also, investigators from as far away as California and Germany are looking at Jeffrey Dahmer as a possible suspect for unsolved slayings in those locales. California's interest stems from the discovery of a human foot near Fresno, the town where a relative of Dahmer's lives. Fresno authorities believe the foot may have belonged to Patrick Lawrence VanZant, 31, who disappeared on May 4, 1990. Homicide investigators are trying to determine if Dahmer made any trips to California within the time frame in which they are interested.

Authorities in Germany also want to question Dahmer regarding five mutilation slayings that occurred near the Army base where Dahmer served on active duty. One of those slayings involved the death of a young woman, Erika Hansthuh, 22, whose body was found in snow approximately 50 miles from the Army base at Baumholder. She was found stabbed and strangled on November 30, 1980, within days after hitchhiking from Heidelberg.

Dahmer, however, emphatically denied any involvement in any deaths other than those he has already confessed to police.

"I have told the police everything I have done relative to the homicides," said Dahmer in a statement released through his attorney. "I have not committed any such crimes anywhere in the world other than this state, except I have admitted an incident in Ohio. I have not committed any homicide in any foreign country or in any other state. I have been totally cooperative and would have admitted other crimes if I did them. I did not. Hopefully, this will serve to put rumors to rest."

Despite Dahmer's statement, U.S. Attorney General Dick Thornburgh pledged that the Justice Department and the

look like a human head." Metz made sure the girls were separated so they would have less chance of conferring on their stories while he enlisted investigative personnel to interview them. Metz and two other officers, Detectives John Uritescu and Randall Willms, left for the second-floor crime lab while the interviews began.

A cursory examination in the crime lab revealed that the object in question was in all probability a human head. Recognizing the magnitude of what they might be dealing with, Sergeant Metz contacted the Macomb County District Attorney's Office. The man he spoke with was Assistant District Attorney William Dardy, a 20-year veteran prosecutor.

At the Macomb County Medical Examiner's Office, Dr. Dee Folkman, an assistant medical examiner, was also contacted. Sensing the urgency of the investigation, he rushed over to the station where he would conduct a more thorough examination of the head.

It was at this point that Sergeant Metz was informed by the officers interviewing the young girls that they had an address for the crime scene: a house on Jean Street in Warren, another suburb of Detroit. A computer check revealed several complaints against the house for loud parties in the normally quiet neighborhood. Sergeant Metz quickly got officers from Road Patrol to keep the house under constant surveillance to prevent potential suspects from escaping.

Dr. Fulkman arrived at the Warren Police Station the same time officers were busy securing the Jean Street property. He began the grisly task of examining the object in the plastic bag. In the event of a trial, Sergeant Metz videotaped the doctor's entire examination. It didn't take long for Dr. Fulkman to arrive at the same conclusion as the officers.

Sergeant Metz called upon Detective Mark Christian to begin completing the affidavits necessary to serve a search warrant. Without a warrant, any evidence discovered at the suspected scene of the crime would be rendered useless.

District Court Judge Dawn Grunnenberg received the affidavit. At approximately 5:45 p.m., she authorized the execution of the search warrant. With this action, the officers were free to work toward making arrests.

Sergeant Michael Metz, Detectives Jim Larroway, Randall Willms, Mark Christian, John Uritescu, and Mark Fontaine, along with two identification technicians and two evidence technicians, proceeded to the house. Unfortunately, a short time before the detail of officers could secure the house, they received bad news. Noticing the police activity, a neighbor had informed one of the officers at the scene that two men matching the suspects' descriptions had left the premises in a black Fiero. The search team was disappointed by this development, but they still hoped to find helpful clues at the Jean Street house.

Warren is a middle-class residential area with three-bedroom brick ranch houses valued at slightly under $100,000. Crime in the suburb is limited and minor. Homicide is so rare as to be nonexistent, and on Jean Street, only one house had proven to present problems to the police prior to July 11, 1990. Since September of 1989, the house had logged eight reports against it for disturbances ranging from loud music to fighting. It was the same house where the three girls found the severed head, the same house officers had kept surrounded for the past two hours.

Sergeant Metz and the other lawmen were prepared to find the house vacant. But when they acted under the authority of their warrant and broke through the front door, they discovered that the helpful neighbor had been wrong. The house wasn't vacant after all.

Directly in line with the front door, lying prone on the kitchen floor apparently in hopes of avoiding detection, was a 5-foot-10, 175 pound male who nervously identified himself as Jaime Rodriguez Jr. The officers quickly cuffed the dark-haired, 21-year-old suspect, read him his rights, and began to carefully search the first floor. Rodriguez proved helpful to probers when he asked, "What about the other guy?"

132

A more thorough search was then initiated. Prepared for anything, the officers moved from room to room, trying to locate the other suspect. They didn't have any luck. When the officers had covered every visible area, they began to worry that perhaps the suspect had gotten away. Had he been one of the men in the Fiero?

The hallway closet revealed the answer to that question. Along its roof was a barely visible trapdoor that appeared to lead to an attic. If the second suspect was up there, capturing him would take ingenuity and patience. Sleuths knew that brashly ascending a ladder in hopes of capturing the fugitive could prove dangerous if he were armed.

Sergeant Metz had an idea. He instructed an officer to open the trapdoor and place a mirror through the space. The reflection revealed that a teenage boy with long, unkempt hair and a mustache was crouched in a corner, holding a cordless phone.

After being discovered, Agustin Todd Pena, 15, descended the ladder and allowed himself to be placed under arrest. Detective John Uritescu would recall that Pena wore a look on his face that seemed to say "he hated the world."

A phone records search revealed that Pena had been calling friends since the surveillance officers had arrived to encircle the house. Police interviews with those friends revealed that Pena had already told them he would be away for a while. The story he told them was that he'd been present when Jaime Rodriguez had killed a local homeless man. Afterward, Pena had assisted Rodriguez with disposing the body inside a drainage ditch. Pena claimed that Rodriguez forced him to help.

Opening the garbage bags immediately was problematic. To do so would risk destroying any fingerprints that could potentially link the killers to the crime. Fortunately, modern technology offered the officers a solution.

An expensive laser amplification device, owned by a consortium of law enforcement officers in Macomb County, was stored at the public safety office of a local college. It would enable the detectives to computer-enhance any latent fingerprints on the garbage bags.

The sophisticated technology offered hindrance along with help. Because of the enormous power it required, every time the laser amplification device was plugged in, it blew a fuse. So officers were forced to stand around and wait for the arrival of an auxiliary generator. Many of the lawmen had already been working for close to 16 hours.

Finally, at around 10 p.m. the evidence technicians were able to find several usable prints on the outside of the garbage bags.

It was well past midnight when Jaime Rodriguez offered probers his own form of assistance. Hours had already been spent interviewing Agustin Pena and the friends he'd called prior to his capture. But it was Jaime Rodriguez who gave police the most help.

Sergeant Metz was one of those who interrogated Jaime Rodriguez. Rodriguez's attitude throughout his confession that night was, "real cold . . . no emotion. He didn't think it was a big deal. It was kind of scary. No admission that he, maybe, didn't do things the right way," Metz would later say.

What Rodriguez did do, according to his confession, was participate in a cold-blooded killing. A young runaway had come to the house, which was owned by a relative of Rodriguez and Pena (who, police had discovered, were cousins). In Rodriguez's own words, the girl was killed because "she was a pest."

The house contained other secrets nearly as dark as the murder itself. Lawmen uncovered books on black magic and various charms and crystals in the house. Apparently, black magic had fascinated Rodriguez, and his younger cousin, Pena, had apparently followed along in a kind of twisted hero worship. A few of the boy's friends believed that the suspects may have used the young female victim's budding curiosity about black magic to do her in.

To the girl, Satan was probably little more than a character from Halloween. "Based on statements given to us," Sergeant Metz would later say, "Jaime and Augie [Pena] had lured her down to the basement on the premise that they were going to do some black magic incantation or something. As she was sitting on this stool, Jaime was standing there facing her. He had his hands on her shoulders, and Augie came up and stabbed her in the back."

Pena them came around and sliced his young victim from crotch to stomach. Then the two killers began the grisly task of tearing the body apart.

But whose body was it?

The story was played up in the national media. Worried parents of missing children began to phone in from across the country. During the 36 hours following the discovery of the corpse, police scrambled to ascertain the identity of the victim the suspects had killed. Friends of Pena and Rodriguez, including the three teenage girls who'd brought the head into the station, were able to give a description of the girl. She was blonde, blue-eyed, about 5-foot-7 and weighing 180 pounds. But they knew her only as "Stephanie." It was as if she'd appeared out of thin air.

Finally, a computer check on missing persons' reports hit paydirt. Stephanie Dubay, 15, matched the description given to the officers. She'd been reported missing a few weeks earlier by relatives when she didn't return to the trailer park she lived in. Officers quickly notified Stephanie's family that she had apparently been found murdered.

Knowing who she was helped. But police needed more than an identity and Jaime Rodriguez's confession. If convicting Agustin Pena was to become a certainty, the lawmen knew they needed hard physical evidence. They had to connect Pena directly to the crime. Otherwise, the police case they were building ran the risk of falling apart in court.

On the Friday afternoon of July 14th, evidence technicians had nearly completed their thorough search of the house on Jean Street. They were in the basement, the room where, according to Jaime Rodriguez, the heinous crime had occurred. "They found a hammer hidden behind a bunch of boxes with some bloody latent fingerprints on it which later matched those of Pena," Sergeant Metz would later explain. "The medical examiner's speculation was that the hammer was used to pound knives through the victim's joints to dismember the body.

"That obviously became a crucial piece of evidence as far as his [Pena's] participation," Metz said. In a few short days, police had collected enough incriminating evidence to feel confidently prepared for the trial.

In June 1991, the trial of Jaime Rodriguez, who gave his occupation as tattoo artist, began. A self-described satanist, Rodriguez sported tattoos of a pentagram and a goat's head across his chest. His lawyer, Timothy Barkovic, entered a plea of not guilty by reason of insanity on his client's behalf.

"There is an undertone in this whole thing concerning devil worship," Assistant D.A. William Dardy explained. "It appears that Jaime Rodriguez was an overt devil worshipper, meaning that he read certain books on satanism. There's no indication that he conducted worship services or performed rituals or did anything like that at the house on Jean Street," Dardy said.

"To what extent satanism was an underlying motive of the crime is not completely clear. . . . We know that Jaime Rodriguez was driven by an evil force. Of course we maintain that that evil was that he was simply an evil man, not that he was controlled by outside circumstances or a reified devil or anything like that. It was just his personality to be evil."

Circuit Judge Fredrick Balkwill evidently agreed with this assessment. The insanity plea was summarily dismissed by him.

Rodriguez's confession was played for the jury. Both the officers present and the reporter who received an exclusive interview with Jaime Rodriguez were called on to testify. The reporter's interview contained within it word-for-word copy of the confession Rodriguez had offered the police on the night of his arrest.

"The confession is made inherently reliable," D.A. Dardy explained, "because it's been made to two different sources as well as the fact that it is thoroughly corroborated by other evidence within the trial."

In the end, the case presented against Jaime Rodriguez was overwhelming. It took a jury of his peers a mere 41 minutes of deliberation before they returned a guilty verdict.

On July 18, 1991, a little over a year since he killed young Stephanie Dubay, Rodriguez appeared before Judge Balkwill for sentencing. The judge minced no words. Stressing that he was horrified by the "depth and depravity" of the crime, Judge Balkwill was quoted as saying, "If the court was empowered to impose a more extreme and final sanction for your act, I would not hesitate to impose that punishment on you." Jaime Rodriguez was then sentenced to life imprisonment without possibility of parole. The death penalty is banned by the Michigan constitution.

The case against Agustin Pena waited. In the mid-August heat, Pena began his trial as an adult. Assistant D.A. Dardy offered jurors photos that captured the menacing appearance Pena had affected on the day of his arrest. Pena's court appearance was drastically different. Although Pena now had short hair, neat clothes, and a meek manner, his lawyer, Dennis Johnston, would later tell the press, "It's not a calculated move to improve his appearance for trial."

Sergeant Metz disagreed with this, however. He said, "I think Pena became quite the actor when it came to his courtroom appearances, but the minute he stepped out of the courtroom he was laughing and joking [as if] this was all a big joke. But in court he'd break down and cry; he was always terribly sorry for what he did."

As evidence, jurors were shown the police video tape taken by Sergeant Metz during Dr. Fulkman's examination of the head. They were also offered the hammer that contained Pena's prints, as well as the garbage bags, which also had Pena's prints on them. And as Assistant D.A. Dardy said, "One person could not have stabbed her to death. She had to be restrained. Pena viciously stabbed her, inflicting at least ten stab wounds."

The tape made of Jaime Rodriguez's confession was again played, this time for Pena's jury to hear. "On the morning of Stephanie Dubay's death, the two got out of bed in the morning and they, according to Jaime Rodriguez's report, were sitting at the breakfast table and . . . Pena said, 'Let's kill Stephanie,' " D.A. Dardy explained in recalling the portion of Rodriguez's confession that was used to link Agustin Pena to the premeditation of the crime.

During the course of the trial, Dardy also quoted a former cellmate of Pena's. According to this witness, when he asked Pena why he killed Stephanie Dubay, Pena's reply was that he wanted to see "what the inside of a girl looked like."

On September 6, 1991, the jury deliberated for four hours before finding Agustin Pena guilty of first-degree murder. In December, Pena was sentenced to life in prison.

"I think, because of the dismemberment of the body, it was probably the single most gruesome case that I've been involved in," said D.A. Dardy after the verdict. "I've been involved in a lot of murder prosecutions, and people have died in terrible ways, with a lot of blood and gore. But I have to say that this is the most gruesome homicide case in my career of twenty years of being a prosecutor in Macomb County."

Sergeant Michael Metz had similar recollections. "I've been playing cops and robbers for a long time," he says, "and I have obviously, in twenty years, seen a lot of bad accident scenes. I've been to homicides and suicides. I've seen real gory things. But I think this upset me the most because it was so callous and so cold. It's probably the coldest thing I've ever experienced as far as one person to another, man's inhumanity to man."

"THE BARFLY LOST HER HEAD TO A NINJA NUT!"

by Barbara Malenky

The morning of August 18, 1989 dawned hazy and promised to be another scorcher for the Jacksonville, North Carolina, area. By 10:25 that morning, the temperature reached 75 degrees with 93 percent humidity.

Two U.S. Marines assigned to the Motor Transport School at Camp Johnson were beginning a routine exercise in the backwoods area of the Knox Mobile Home Park located on Marine Corps Base Camp LeJeune. This abandoned section of the trailer park was overgrown, deserted and ideal for the men to test-drive a tactical five-ton vehicle.

As the vehicle was guided onto the old stretch of asphalt, the marines spotted what at first appeared to be a pile of garbage lying in the middle of the road. As they drew nearer, they realized they were viewing the body of a woman. Driving to within five yards, they could see a dark pool of blood and a large gaping wound between the victim's neck and shoulder.

The marines rushed to a nearby store and notified military police.

The victim was Caucasian with reddish-brown hair. She appeared to be in her mid-30s. She was lying on her right side and except for high-top jogging shoes and two pairs of socks, she was nude. A large tattoo was etched on her left shoulder. Her head lay on a black tank-top shirt soaking in a pool of blood that spiraled away from the body across 20 feet of asphalt and off the roadway. A large cutting wound started at the base of the victim's neck and continued over the left shoulder. The woman's head was nearly severed from her body.

Arriving military police (MP), Criminal Investigative Division (CID) agents, and Naval Investigative Service (NIS) agents roped off the area, forming an orange triangle with nylon tape. Personal items were scattered in a row next to the victim: a blue denim purse, a small plastic cup containing a white liquid, a plastic salad dish cover, a yellow elastic eyeglass restrainer, a pair of brown sunglasses, a pair of black gym shorts, and a black collar line from the tank top.

A Navy pathologist arrived and examined the body at the crime scene. He found lividity fixed on the right side of the victim's body and rigor mortis in her hands, arms, and shoulder. After the crime scene photographs were taken, the victim was rolled over and wrapped in a white sheet. She was placed in a body bag before being transported to the Naval Hospital Morgue.

A preliminary autopsy revealed that the victim had been severely beaten about her face and head prior to receiving on the base of her neck a single incised wound that severed large vessels, the trachea, the spinal column and cord, and three ribs. There was no evidence of sexual assault. The approximate time of death was placed as the early morning hours of August 18, 1989.

Special Agent Tony Titra had been with the Naval Investigative Services for two and a half years. Recruited by the agency from Florida, he'd spent 11 years as a policeman and three years as an MP in the U.S. Army before that. A highly respected NIS agent, Tony Titra was put in charge of the murder investigation. From information in the blue denim purse found near the body, the victim was identified as Brenda Lee Salomon.

Under Agent Titra's supervision, between 20 and 30 NIS agents were brought into the case. They would work 20 hours a day, seven days a week if needed, to find out who had killed Brenda Salomon.

Meanwhile, Brenda Salomon's husband woke at his usual time of 5:00 a.m., on the morning of August 18, 1989 to prepare for work at Camp LeJeune where he was a staff sergeant in the U.S. Marine Corps.

His wife Brenda was not in the bed and it soon became obvious to him that Brenda hadn't returned home at all from the night before.

Although annoyed, Brenda's husband wasn't unduly concerned. He was getting used to Brenda's behavior. In the last four years of their 11-year marriage, Brenda would sometimes stay out for a couple of days at a time. An alcoholic, Brenda was a regular fixture at a line of area bars every day, leaving their three children with babysitters until her husband came home from work. He'd encouraged Brenda to seek help for her drinking only to have deaf ears turned to his pleas.

It was barely a month since he'd returned home from a six-month deployment in Okinawa to find his family on the edge of calamity. The mortgage payments on their modest house were months behind, the utilities were on the verge of being disconnected, and Brenda had been convicted for drunk driving and sentenced to serve seven consecutive weekends in the county jail, to begin the very weekend he returned. He didn't have to ask where the money he'd sent home regularly had gone. He knew.

The morning of August 18th, Brenda's husband was filled with discouragement and resignation. The time had passed when he believed his marriage could be salvaged, but he loved his kids and because they loved their mother, he could continue to put up with a lot for their sakes. At least he was there to watch over them. But some day, some day . . .

Brenda would show up later, he reasoned that morning. She always did.

Before leaving, Brenda's husband looked in on his two

small daughters. His 10-year-old son was away visiting his grandparents. A friend of Brenda's, a young woman who danced at a bar was also living in the house with them, but her door was closed. Leaving the house at 6:15 a.m., Brenda's husband stopped to pick up another marine and together they arrived at the company office. He then changed into his uniform and reported for work. Sometime later that morning, he left the base without reporting out, a violation of rules, and was not seen again until 11:00 a.m.

Sometime after 4:00 p.m., two NIS agents drove to Sandy Drive. They had the unpleasant job of informing Brenda's husband of his wife's murder and driving him to the morgue to identify the body. Finding him working under the hood of his car, the agents quietly informed him of his wife's death. The fact that he didn't seem surprised or especially grieved at the news, shrugging his shoulders and insisting he be allowed to finish up the mechanical work on his car, left the bitter taste of suspicion in the agents' mouths.

He was driven to the morgue, where he identified his wife's body, then taken to NIS headquarters for questioning. It would be the first of several times he'd be interviewed over the next week.

Brenda's husband was very cooperative. He spoke freely, giving the agents permission to search his car and house. He allowed them to take into evidence the clothes he'd worn that day and personal items from his home, including several knives and ornamental swords he'd collected.

Through interviews with him and the woman living with the Salomons, agents learned about Brenda's alcoholism and daily jaunts to the local bars.

Brenda's husband was allowed to leave. He went home to his children, who had not been told of their mother's death.

The strip of bars located along Highway 17—from the Triangle Motor Inn down to the entrance of the New River Air Station—is referred to as the "Second Front." The bars sit side by side, so close that a patron wanders from one to another scarcely realizing the change of establishment. Aside from the fact that some provide topless dancing or a pool table, there is little to differentiate them. The bars all serve the same basic human needs: a place to drink a beer, shoot a little pool, play the video game machines, or shoot the breeze over the pounding vibrations of a jukebox.

Although the Second Front is off-limits to military officers, it draws a large rowdy crowd of young enlisted marines who rub elbows with bikers, drug pushers and the fast women who also frequent the bars. The Second Front earned a wild, rough reputation where drug busts, murders and prostitution arrests are numerous. A person seeking trouble doesn't have far to go.

The bars open early and close late to satisfy customer demand. The owners work long and hard, barely making ends meet. Their employees are rough, street-wise and conditioned to handle almost anything that happens. The Second Front provides something of a home for its group of regular patrons and through that "family" network, NIS agents hoped to find the link to Brenda Salomon's murder.

Agents began arriving late that August 18th, interviewing every employee, owner and customer they came in contact with. People were more than willing to talk. After all, Brenda Salomon had been one of them, and they wanted the person responsible for the murder to be caught. Next time, it may just be another member of their "family."

Agents began piecing together a disturbing picture of the victim. A known alcoholic, Brenda Salomon was "generous and well liked" when sober, but she wasn't often. Intoxicated, she was another person altogether, often becoming loud, belligerent and abusive. At 5 feet 8 inches tall and 155 pounds, Brenda was seldom intimidated by anyone and constantly engaged in verbal, sometimes even physical confrontations, agents were told. Spending almost all day and night on the Second Front, Brenda would often beg for money, a meal, another drink or a ride to somewhere else from strangers and friends alike. She was known to go off with anybody and willing to do anything for another drink.

Although few could glorify Brenda's reputation, no one could name someone angry enough to kill her.

Several theories were developed by NIS, with a team of agents assigned to prove or disprove each one. The theory that Brenda had been picked up on the Second Front and taken off to her death was substantiated by witnesses who claimed to have seen Brenda with several different men during the evening of August 17th. The strongest theory, however, was fueled with motivation. The victim's husband was a strong suspect.

Things were looking grim for him. Authorities were looking closely at him as they investigated his wife's death. Over and over the agents were told that Brenda Salomon was frightened of only one person, her husband. Numerous witnesses claimed to have seen bruises on the victim's neck and arms after her husband's return from Okinawa the month before. When asked about them, Brenda would say, "Me and my old man had it out." A friend reported that Brenda had repeatedly said her husband was planning to divorce her when he came home in order to marry an Oriental woman he'd met while on deployment.

The son of a Second Front bar owner told agents he'd witnessed the victim's husband drag Brenda from the bar one night, threatening to kill her. A co-worker of the husband stated that he'd heard him arguing with Brenda over the telephone on the afternoon of August 17th. Second Front friends recalled Brenda's excitement because her husband had promised to meet her after work for a rare evening out together. They remembered the disappointment in Brenda's face when he didn't show up, sending her money through a friend instead. Brenda continued to drink that night.

The officer who'd arrested Brenda for drunk driving earlier that year claimed she'd appeared sincerely frightened when told that her husband would have to be notified of her arrest. Breaking down and sobbing, she'd said he would kill her this time. The officer thought then it was a plea for sympathy; now, he wasn't so sure.

When co-workers who were interviewed couldn't confirm the victim's husband's alibi between 7:45 and 11:00 on the morning of August 18th, he was brought back into NIS headquarters on August 21st. He was read his rights, but declined the aid of a lawyer. For the first time he was interrogated as a suspect. He issued a sworn statement of his activities on the 17th and 18th of August. Explaining his absence at work the morning of August 18th, the suspect said he'd left the base to drive home. He wanted to see whether Brenda had come home. He'd left a note there to remind her that she was to begin serving her jail sentence and to call him as soon as she came home.

On August 22nd, still refusing to have an attorney, the suspect voluntarily took a polygraph examination. He answered the examiner's questions calmly.

"Did you strike your wife on 18 August 1989?"

"No."

"Did you strike your wife with a sharp object on 18 August 1989?"

"No."

"Do you know the name of the person who caused your wife's death?"

"No."

After the questioning was finished, the suspect sat alone, drinking a cup of coffee, while NIS agents conferred with the polygraph examiner. Agent Tony Titra brought him the news. He'd failed the test. The party was over. Why didn't he put the pieces of the puzzle together? Why didn't he confess? He would feel better. They understood. He certainly had the motive. Brenda had put him in serious debt, over $20,000. She was an alcoholic, hard to handle, leaving him with all the problems. Probably unfaithful. It was a lot for one man to bear. It was understandable the way he felt.

Looking into Agent Titra's serious but kind face, the suspect saw the future. He asked for a lawyer.

A second autopsy was conducted by Dr. Edward Kilbane, deputy chief medical examiner for the Armed Forces Institute of Pathology. Dr. Kilbane reached the same conclusion as to the victim's cause of death—but with one important difference. He placed the time of death at a little past midnight of August 18, 1989, not the early morning hours.

He advised NIS to look for an extremely strong individual. It is almost impossible to decapitate a human being with a single blow—yet the blow Brenda Salomon had suffered almost severed her head from her body. The doctor said the most likely weapon used was a big ax, something with a four-foot handle and a very heavy, large blade, because of the tremendous amount of carnage done to the victim.

When the woman living with the Salomons was interviewed, she confirmed the husband's alibi that he'd spent the night of August 17th in front of the television. His four-year-old daughter produced the note he claimed he drove home to leave for Brenda on the morning of August 18th. The NIS agents were back to square one. Their number-one suspect had an alibi.

On August 23rd, while interviewing Knox Trailer Park residents, NIS got a break. While fishing close to midnight on August 17th, off a bridge leading to Camp Johnson, a man spotted a light-colored, two-tone truck with a camper top pull up to the bridge. The fisherman felt uneasy as the truck sat with its motor running and bright lights fixed on him. Then to his relief, after a few minutes, the truck turned around and sped off. NIS requested a list of trucks matching that description and registered at Camp LeJeune.

In all murder investigations, leads take valued time to check out, most ending in frustration and dead ends. This investigation was no different. Composite drawings were made from descriptions by cab drivers of strange-acting men they claimed to have picked up on August 17th and 18th.

Employees of a logging company discovered working in

the area, had to be interviewed. Agents even confiscated a bush ax as the possible murder weapon.

Three anonymous calls were phoned into the Jacksonville Police Department, alleging that a Puerto Rican female was with Brenda Salomon on the night of her death and may have witnessed the murder. After hours of investigation, the story turned out to be a hoax.

On Thursday evening, August 24, 1989, one week after Brenda Salomon's death, NIS agents grouped together in five teams. They planned to survey the Second Front bar area one last time. The idea was to find people who had not been interviewed over the past week, someone who could provide witness information not heard yet, or an individual who perhaps only went out on Thursday nights.

From past interviews, the agents had narrowed down the last sighting of Brenda Salomon to 9:30 p.m. at a topless dance bar. At 9:00 p.m., Agent Tony Titra and John Michaud pulled into the lounge parking lot. Parked out front was a blue-over-white Nissan truck. The tag number was jotted down for a routine check later; Agent Titra glanced inside the cab. He saw part of a sword sheath sticking out from behind the seat.

A few minutes after entering the bar and conducting some brief interviews, Agent Titra followed as a tall, well-built young marine left the bar and headed for the truck. Titra introduced himself and the other agent and told him they wanted to talk with him. The marine was friendly and cooperative. He identified himself as Lance Corporal Curtis Gibbs. He told the agents he came to this bar four nights a week and, yes, he'd been there the night of August 17th, but had never seen the woman whose photo he was shown. He gave the agents permission to look inside his truck. Agent Titra found a variety of weapons behind the seat, including Ninja climbing claws, an encased 10-inch knife known in the military as a "K-bar," and a 24-inch sheathed sword.

Agent Titra asked for permission to take the sword. He

147

wanted to show it to other agents to study as a possible weapon used in the murder. As he wrote out a receipt, Gibbs spelled out the name of the sword. It was Ninja-To, and it seemed important to the marine that it be spelled correctly. He mentioned that he was leaving for a new assignment in California in a few days.

As Curtis Gibbs drove away, the two agents continued screening interviews at a neighboring bar. The owner was standing outside his club. He'd been interviewed earlier by agents, but agreed to talk again with Agent Titra.

Because of severe respiratory problems that were aggravated by tobacco smoke, the bar owner spent a good deal of time outside his club. On the night of August 17th, he had witnessed Brenda Salomon holding hands with a man and he saw her enter his truck. When asked what kind of truck, the bar owner replied, "Well, if I'm no fool, it looked a lot like that truck," referring to Curtis Gibbs' vehicle. Titra asked if he could recall what the man looked like. The bar owner replied, "Well, if I'm no fool, it looked a lot like that guy," again referring to Curtis Gibbs.

The agents looked at each other. A sheer piece of luck!

On the 25th of August, Agent Titra requested that Curtis Gibbs come to his office. At the time, he only suspected him of lying about whether or not he knew Brenda Salomon. The feeling was that Gibbs perhaps had picked her up and driven her somewhere else or had even seen her leave with someone but didn't want to get involved.

When Curtis Gibbs walked into the office, his face was red; he was visibly nervous and breathing heavily. As Agent Titra filled out a log sheet for identification purposes, Gibbs became noticeably more nervous, his face grew redder and a vein stuck out on his neck. Titra asked about Gibbs' parents, and the marine's eyes filled with tears. Although Titra still did not suspect he was looking at the murderer, he felt at that point something wasn't right and decided to read Gibbs his Miranda warnings.

At first, Curtis Gibbs admitted to picking Brenda up, but

claimed he'd dropped her off at a phone booth. He admitted it had been his truck that the fisherman had seen on the bridge, but said he'd driven there alone "to think."

Hearing this, Agent Titra realized he was face to face with Brenda Salomon's killer. Taking Gibbs into an interrogation room, he called in another agent. After a few minutes with the seasoned agents, Gibbs admitted he had killed Brenda Salomon.

In a chilling, precise eight-page confession, Curtis Gibbs described the night of August 17, 1989. He related how he had picked up the victim at a bar, promising to buy Brenda dinner and drive her home. He stopped by a bank automatic teller machine near the base to withdraw cash, then drove through a restaurant drive-in window, where Brenda asked for a taco salad. Gibbs was sober, but the victim was so intoxicated she passed out after eating. Gibbs said he wanted to get rid of her and claimed that when he tried to put her out, Brenda became belligerent and physically abusive, slapping the 6-foot-4-inch, 225-pound man and calling him names. He became enraged and a fight ensued.

"I hit her face about eight to ten times. I then kicked her in the side of the jaw. I felt like I stepped outside my body, like I was watching myself kicking her four or five more times in the face. I then walked to the truck, removed the Ninja-To. I was in a rage. I then stood over her in a stance like you would chop wood. I then raised the sword above my head with both hands on the handle. I then came down with all I had. I was extremely pumped. A gush of blood shot out over her head."

Gibbs told the agents he returned to the bar for another soft drink and played video games until closing time.

There was no doubt that Curtis Gibbs was the murderer. He provided accurate details on what Brenda Salomon was wearing that night. In addition, the items he had thrown from his truck matched the evidence found around the body. He drew the exact location where the body was found. NIS agents obtained copies of the photos made by the ATM bank camera and the restaurant's register tape. The time on the cash-withdrawal photos and the sale of the taco salad were only minutes apart. Interestingly, in one bank photo, Gibbs could be seen looking back at his truck, which was backed away from its parking spot, indicating he was not alone.

Agents searched Gibbs' barracks room. Clothes and tennis shoes were confiscated as evidence and sent to the U.S. Army Criminal Investigation lab in Fort Gillem, Georgia. Human blood found inside the scabbard of the sword matched the victim's blood type. Traces of Brenda's blood were found on the right tennis shoe. The stitching on the shoe matched up perfectly to a line of bruising on the victim's face.

Although most would be inadmissible in court, the chapters of Gibbs' grisly past had been collected by top-notch Prosecutor Captain Guy Womack into a veritable small book.

Born March 3, 1963, Gibbs had been brought up in La-Grande, Oregon. He promised early on to be a giant of a man, towering over the other kids in school at a young age. Gibbs was slow moving, and as a result he was the butt of cruel practical jokes and teasing nicknames by schoolmates.

A loner, he was considered "different." Considered volatile, Gibbs was viewed as an individual who could blow up without warning, like a live volcano lying dormant. He had a photographic memory, yet was only an average student. No one could remember Curtis Gibbs ever having a girlfriend. He couldn't be called handsome. His staring eyes were diminished behind thick glasses and, with his slow smile and bulbous nose, he appeared slightly retarded.

From an early age, Curtis had a military fixation. He wore military-type clothing throughout his school years. He collected Ninja paraphernalia, Ninja throwing stars, clothing, and a long and a short Ninja sword. In 1980, he joined the LaGrande High School Military Career Education program. He was looking forward to a future in military service.

One night in early 1982, a woman neighbor, aroused from sleep by a noise, flipped on the lamp to discover Gibbs crawling across her bedroom floor. He panicked and jumped on top of the terrified woman. Twisting her head until her neck bones popped, he then fled the house.

Police found the woman's jewelry and checks in his possession. Curtis Gibbs was charged with burglary, forgery and two counts of theft. He entered a guilty plea pursuant to plea negotiation and several of the charges were dismissed. Because it was his first offense, the 19-year-old Gibbs was sentenced to remain in custody in the county corrections facility for three months and receive six months of treatment at the county mental health clinic.

In September 1982, Gibbs took part in a search team that was looking for a missing 43-year-old woman. His team found the body, weighted down in a stream by large rocks. The victim had been shot in the head, but the cause of death was deemed to be drowning. The woman had literally been buried alive in water. Although her murder remains unsolved, a military-type boot print was found on the creek bank near her body.

In January 1984, Gibbs was caught and arrested in a "Peeping Tom" incident involving a young girl. He was charged only with carrying a concealed weapon, five Ninja throwing stars. He was sentenced to five days in jail.

Curtis Gibbs held several jobs before becoming a marine. Working as a lifeguard in 1986, Gibbs arrived one afternoon dressed in military attire and wearing a Ninja fighting sword. He walked into the swimming pool area, pulled out the sword and began cleaning it. It was not the first time he'd done this sort of thing, and staff and pool visitors were frightened by his actions. They had complained before to the supervisor, who had warned Gibbs not to bring the sword to the pool again. On this afternoon, she confronted him.

"Why do you need a sword for anyhow?"

Gibbs eyed her seriously before replying, "I use it to cut people up."

The supervisor had Gibbs fired.

On January 2, 1990, a military jury of seven men heard opening statements as the court-martial of Curtis Gibbs began.

Prosecutor Captain Guy Womack informed the members of what was to come. He told them the history of the case. He discussed briefly what the 17 witnesses he would call to the stand would offer. He explained why the corroboration of evidence expected to be presented was necessary.

He described Curtis Gibbs as "harmless looking" and "cold stone sober" during the murder. He felt confident the jury members would realize the elements of the crime and reach the only correct verdict: premeditated murder, which in this case could result in a death sentence.

Major Bob Chester, Gibbs' defense attorney, suggested the jury try hard to understand the rage and provocation his client felt that night. Given the evidence he would present of the victim's aggressive nature and drunkenness, exemplified by her actions on August 17th, he felt certain the jurors would find Curtis Gibbs guilty only of aggravated manslaughter or unpremeditated murder.

On Saturday, January 6, 1990, the jury deliberated for 70 minutes, then found Curtis Gibbs guilty of premeditated first-degree murder. They recessed for the weekend and would report back two days later to hear additional evidence and arguments before sentencing.

On Monday, January 8, 1990, Lance Corporal Curtis A. Gibbs and his tearful family pleaded for mercy for his life. In an unsworn statement to the jury, Gibbs apologized to the jury, the Marine Corps and the victim's husband. He said, "If I had the ability to turn the clock back in time, I would.

"I still think I have something else to give. I still have nightmares about what I've done. I'll have them the rest of my life, however long it may be."

The prosecution called to the stand the Oregon woman who was Gibbs' next-door neighbor in 1982. She told the jury of the night Gibbs broke into her house, twisted her neck until bones snapped and placed a pillow over her face. Prosecutor Captain Guy Womack reminded the members of the kick marks "etched in her (Brenda Salomon's) skin forever." He told how Gibbs, with a choice of weapons in his truck, including his own hands, deliberately chose the Ninja-To sword as the murder weapon. He told them that the evidence presented showed "cold reflection, as cold as the blood in a murderer's heart, and he should pay for that."

On January 9, 1990, the members of the seven-man jury took only one hour and 45 minutes to sentence Curtis A. Gibbs to death by lethal injection.

The sentence will be reviewed by two military appellate courts, a process that could take several years. The death warrant must be signed by the President of the United States before Gibbs will die by lethal injection at Fort Leavenworth, Kansas.

Curtis Gibbs is currently on Death Row pending his appeal.

"BUTCHERED NUDE IN THE BATHTUB!"

by Bob Carlsen

MULTNOMAH COUNTY, OR.
MARCH 8, 1985

The call came in at 10:51 p.m. on July 7, 1984. The caller reported that a woman was being attacked in her apartment and that there was blood on the front door. The door was locked and they couldn't get in to help her.

Field officers of the Gresham Police Department in Gresham, Oregon immediately were notified. Several rushed to the apartment complex near the Gresham Golf Course.

Sergeant James Kalbasky and Officers Rick Rivera, Michael McGowan, Cindy Sprague and Tom Walker headed for the scene. Sergeant Kalbasky was one of the first to arrive, and he radioed to other officers that neighbors had heard a lot of screaming and had seen a bloody arm reach through the open front door before it had been slammed shut. Sergeant Kalbasky told the officers enroute to look for anybody running from the scene.

As Officer Stuart Eisenmeyer left another fight call at 11:00 p.m. and headed for the apartment, he spotted a white male running westbound from where the assault had been reported. Officer Eisenmeyer made a U-turn and pulled up behind the runner. He told the man to stop before putting his spotlight on the possible suspect. The man was a Californian who'd moved to the area just a short time before, Eisenmeyer learned.

The officer noticed that the man appeared to be clean. There wasn't a trace of blood on his clothing. The initial report to field officers had stated that the suspect might be bloody. Officer Eisenmeyer jotted down some notes about the possible suspect and then let him go. He had no reason to hold the man. Even if the Californian had assaulted or killed somebody, Eisenmeyer had no probable cause to hold him at that time. To place him under arrest could jeopardize the case, if it turned out the guy was the suspect. However, Eisenmeyer could demonstrate in a court hearing that he did have probable cause to stop the man, because he was seen running from the scene.

Officer Eisenmeyer had the Californian's Troutdale address. If the police needed to contact him, they'd know where to get a hold of him.

By the time Eisenmeyer got to the apartments near the Gresham Golf Course, other lawmen already were at the scene.

Officers Rick Rivera, Mike McGowan and Cindy Sprague stationed themselves at the front door as Sergeant Kalbasky went to the patio on the opposite side of the building. Rivera knocked loudly on the front door. There was no answer. Being careful not to smear any prints, he used a handkerchief and daintily tried to turn the knob. The deadbolt lock prevented entry via the front door.

They heard Sergeant Kalbasky call them on the portable radio to come to the patio sliding glass door. They obliged. At 11:01 p.m. the officers entered the apartment via the patio door. The first thing they spotted was a bloody saber saw on the floor and a thong nearby. There were several spots in the kitchen where drops of blood had fallen. As the officers progressed toward the bedroom and bathroom of the apartment, their flashlights piercing the darkness, more evidence of a struggle and more blood could be seen all over the place.

A cursory search of the apartment revealed ample evidence of a fight, but no body was found. Sergeant Kalbasky ordered everyone out of the apartment to await the detectives and crime scene technicians. At that point, it was still unclear who lived in the apartment.

Sergeant Craig Walliker arrived with his police dog and made a second walk-through of the apartment. He, like his predecessors, made certain that he didn't disturb any of the evidence. The others had told Walliker that they hadn't turned on the bathroom light when they made their search. They'd relied on their flashlights. When Walliker arrived at the bathroom, he used the butt of his flashlight to flick on the switch. The shower curtain was closed. He used the flashlight to move it aside.

Lying in a fetal position in the bathtub was the naked body of a once-beautiful woman.

"She's in here," Sergeant Walliker called to the others. "She's in the bathroom." He sighed deeply.

The victim had no pulse. The lawmen cleared out of the apartment to await the arrival of superiors and homicide experts.

The front door area, and the entire rear yard area behind the apartment building to the nearby fence, were secured by police officers who put up ribbon lines.

The apartment manager told Sergeant Kalbasky that the girl who lived in the apartment was named Judith Ann Gracia, 20. Kalbasky asked to see her application for tenancy. The apartment manager fetched it. She had moved into the apartment June 15, 1984, just a few weeks before her brutal murder, Kalbasky learned. She owned a Datsun 510, according to the application.

Sergeant Kalbasky told Eisenmeyer and Rivera to start diagramming the apartment complex's parking lot, to write down all the license plate numbers and types of cars for future use, and particularly to be on the look-out for the victim's Datsun.

Kalbasky ordered that a check be made on the Datsun with police department records. It was learned that, though Judi Gracia had listed the Datsun as being her own on the application which she'd filled out, the Datsun actually was registered to somebody else. Eisenmeyer traced the owner to Portland, Oregon. The registered owner said he'd sold the Datsun to another man, who apparently had given the Datsun to Judi Garcia before he moved to California. The man was Judi's estranged husband, Eisenmeyer learned. Furthermore, Judi had returned from a trip to California the previous weekend.

After diagramming the parking lot, Officer Rivera was stationed at the front door of the apartment. While there, he spotted a .44-caliber shell casing lodged in some rocks near the front of the apartment.

At five minutes after midnight, Captain Jack Cunningham arrived at the scene and took charge of the case, which eventually became the responsibility of Gresham Police Department Detectives Robert J. Peterson and Eldon Long.

The two sleuths questioned each of the officers who had initially responded to the call. They learned that the first officers were on the scene within five minutes. The body wasn't found in the bathtub for about a half hour, but in this situation it didn't make much difference, the autopsy would later reveal. Some of the many wounds were so severe they would have been fatal within a minute or two.

Sergeant Craig Walliker told the detectives that he hadn't noticed any blood outside of the apartment. There was no trail for the police to follow. This indicated that the assailant had not been injured seriously.

Walliker explained that he thought it was odd that no victim was found inside the apartment during the first search. If the victim had been removed from the scene, there should have been blood outside the apartment, at least on the walkways, he explained to detectives. It was sound reasoning. That's why he went into the apartment to search a second time.

In the darkness of the bathroom, using his flashlight, he noticed some bloodstains on the bathtub. He turned on the

157

overhead light with the butt of his flashlight and found the body, he told Detectives Long and Peterson.

Sergeant James Kalbasky told the detectives that he was the first to arrive. He recalled how he had spotted a man running across the parking lot and had given chase. But the apartment manager, who had been standing guard at the front of the apartment with two other men, yelled that the man had just come from upstairs and wasn't involved. The sergeant didn't chase him very far.

"The patio door was open eight to twelve inches," Kalbasky told the detectives. "Two tenants had heard her screams and stood at the front door to make sure nobody entered or left. The way I see it, the guy left through the patio door while they were at the front door."

"That seems to be the only possible explanation, assuming the tenants and apartment manager are all telling the truth about their actions," Peterson said.

"When I got here and looked in the patio door and saw the blood, I had the officers perform a quick search for a victim," Kalbasky said. "We didn't see or hear anybody and wanted to preserve the scene, so I ordered them out. I thought perhaps the victim had been forcibly removed or maybe had been taken to the hospital. I had the officers check that out, but she hadn't been admitted anywhere. Then Walliker found her in the tub."

Kalbasky explained how he'd assigned tasks to various officers to conduct an area search and how he then notified the chain of command and secured the area.

Kalbasky had assigned Officers Michael McGowan and Cindy Sprague the job of interviewing tenants in the apartment complex.

The resident of number 73 told McGowan that he was asleep when the murder occurred. McGowan noticed that the man's apartment was a shambles. Papers and magazines were strewn everywhere and it was sparsely furnished.

"I went to bed about 9:00," the man told Officer McGowan. "I didn't see anything or hear anything until you woke me."

Apartment seventy-four was vacant. Seventy-five was occupied by a woman who wasn't home at the time the murder occurred. She told McGowan that she'd been getting obscene telephone calls from a man for four to six weeks. Sometimes he'd call as often as 20 times in one night. The problem had been reported to police on June 18, 1984. McGowan noted the date was just three days after the murder victim moved into the apartment.

Officer McGowan found another witness who lived down the hall from the murder victim. This woman said that about a week after the victim moved into the apartment complex, somebody tried to break into her (the witness's) apartment.

"My husband was here at the time," the witness recalled. "Somebody was trying to open the front door with a key. When my husband opened the door, the stranger said, 'Excuse me, I must have the wrong apartment.' Then he walked down to Judi's apartment."

The witness described the man as about 20 to 25 years old, 5 ft. 10 in. tall, weighing 160 to 170 pounds. He had light brown hair to his collar. "I haven't seen him since," the witness said.

The bachelor living in apartment number 80 claimed he was at work, and his story checked out.

The witness who first heard Judi Gracia's screams lived down the hall, Officer McGowan determined. He'd been watching the movie *Animal House* on television when he heard the screams. He looked out his door and saw Judi's front door open. She was lying on the floor inside her apartment. Her arm reached out the open door for the knob. A male's hand grabbed hers and yanked it back inside the apartment. Before her assailant slammed the door shut, she pleaded to the witness, "Help, help, he's trying to rape me! Oh, God! Not again." Before the witness could even get to her door and force his way in, it had been slammed shut and the deadbolt thrown.

By that time a second man had arrived at the front door. While one stood guard, the second ran to the apartment manager and told him what was happening. The police were called.

Detectives questioned the apartment manager and the two men thoroughly and determined that the story was true. Judging from the condition of the victim's body, her assailant must have had blood on himself. None was found on any of the three men who had been at the scene moments after her screams were heard. And there was no reason to think they would all lie for one another or would have cooperated in such a grisly crime.

Officer McGowan told detectives that a witness had spotted a man driving out of the parking lot on a motorcycle shortly after the attacker must have left the apartment. The witness hadn't gotten the license number, nor had the witness gotten a good look.

But as luck would have it, the motorcyclist returned to the scene while the detectives were still there. He was questioned and found lacking a decent alibi. However, he was wearing the same clothes the witness had described. Close examination of that clothing revealed not a trace of blood on him.

If he'd fled the murder scene on his motorcycle, and returned later wearing the same clothes, blood would naturally have been on his clothing. Because none was found on him, he was dismissed.

Shortly after one o'clock on July 8, 1984, crime scene experts from the Department of State Police arrived at the apartment complex to conduct the interior search.

The murder scene apartment was located on the ground level of one of the several apartment buildings in the complex and was on the south side. The building was divided into north and south structures with a courtyard walkway between. The buildings consisted of three levels and were connected on all floors by supported walkways.

The victim was found naked except for a blue and white

cloth slipper on her left foot. She was lying in the bathtub on her right side, with her head near the drain and her feet pointed south. Her left arm was lying over her chest, hand lying palm up on the bottom of the tub. The right arm was bent at the elbow, with the hand palm up near the drain. The left knee was lying over the calf of the right leg, and the right knee was bent adjacent to the right elbow. The face, arms and torso were heavily bloodstained, and no recognizable latent prints in blood were noted on the body at the scene or prior to the autopsy.

Crime scene technicians found that the front door dead bolt was in a half-bolted position, which effectively prevented the door from being opened. The dead bolt knob on the inside was bloodstained. Blood smears were found on the outside of the front door below the level of the doorknob and predominantly along the opening edge. Blood smears were also found around the inside handle of the patio glass door.

The living room failed to reveal signs of a struggle other than bloodstains. On the coffee table near the center of the room was a fork and a plate with some food residue. A drinking glass with milk residue was also found near the plate. On the opposite corner from the plate and glass was an empty pot pie tin with crumbs surrounding it.

Blood smears and drops were found on the living room carpet between the dining area and the bathroom dressing area. On the left edge of the drapes were blood smears. The drape cord located in the corner of the living room was bloodstained. The blood on the cord was located on the lower portion near the floor and in the floor pulley, indicating the cord had been moved after the blood was deposited.

The dining area was located north of the living room, and the front entrance to the apartment was in the corner of this area. The kitchen was located to the east of the dining area. Numerous blood drops and smears were found predominantly in the area in front of the entrance door, and several smears of blood were found in the area between the front door and living room. A right rubber thong was noted approximately six inches from the door and approximately two and one-half feet from the east wall. A matching left rubber thong was found in front of a bench chest. A blood-stained saber saw was found on the floor approximately two feet from the front door.

At the kitchen entrance sleuths found a blood smear approximately four and one-half feet above the floor. To the west of the front door was a window with a lightly blood-smeared drape. The drape was in a closed position. No blood was found in the area of the kitchen sink.

The bathroom dressing area had numerous bloodstains and smears. The floor revealed several partial footwear prints in blood with a pattern of parallel wavy ridges. Crime scene technicians observed the shoes of police officers who had reportedly entered the area and found none with a tread pattern similar to the bloody prints. Blood spatters were on the walls, cupboards and sink. The sink had not been used after blood had been splattered into it.

A short carpeted entryway led from the bathroom dressing area to the bedroom. A bloody footwear print with a pattern similar to those on the floor in the bathroom dressing area was noted leading into the bedroom. The bedroom contained an unmade bed with bloodstains on the pillows, sheets and blankets. At the foot of the bed on the floor was an unfolded robe with blood drops. The positions of these blood drops indicated that the drops had been deposited on the robe while it was on the floor, technicians noted. Partially under the pink robe was a folded pair of blue pants. Near the open closet door, and with a portion lying over part of the pink robe, was a white bra. A pair of folded white socks was discovered on the floor between the open closet door and the blue pants. In front of the closed closet doors in the bedroom was an open blue suitcase with some folded clothing.

In the bedroom they found one of the two murder weapons. A paring knife was on the carpet under the extended side of the waterbed. The blade of the knife was bent at a right angle.

A cursory examination of the body revealed to the medical examiner that the cause of death had been multiple stab wounds. Although a bullet shell was found outside the front door of the apartment, it was not believed to be germane to the crime. It was seized as evidence just in case it turned out to be important.

Fingerprints were taken of bloody palmprints on the saber saw, the front door and the bathtub. Shoe print photographs were taken from the floor of the bathroom and entryway into the bedroom. Whoever committed the brutal murder left his calling card in the form of prints. Find a suspect, and detectives would be able to determine if he was the killer simply because of the numerous prints.

The search for evidence expanded to the Gresham Golf Course, where the second murder weapon, a kitchen butcher knife, was found.

Meanwhile, detectives learned that Judi's divorce was amicable. Detectives contacted police in California. Rather than the Gresham authorities' telling Judi's ex-husband of her murder over the phone, the California authorities did so in person, so that a reaction could be noted. The report came back that, although the ex-husband didn't appear to be very grieved about Judi's death, his whereabouts in California could be verified for the time of the murder.

Probers checked out several suspects in the Gresham area. The Troutdale resident, formerly from California, seen running from the area of the crime, the motorcyclist leaving the parking lot and others were again questioned by the many officers and detectives working on the case. Nothing of significance could be turned up, though.

The detectives questioned persons in other buildings of the apartment complex, employees who worked at the nearby golf course, and the assistant manager of the apartment complex. The assistant manager, Randy Denton Fisher, 21,

163

told detectives he'd been out picking strawberries in the daytime on July 7th. He'd also shampooed his carpets that day. Others living near the murder scene also had accounts of their activities. Most involved being at work and could be easily verified. For the evening hour in which the murder occurred, many of the tenants could account for their whereabouts, but others could not.

As the investigation progressed, detectives learned that Randy Fisher had been in the victim's apartment prior to July 7th to do some maintenance work. A work order on file with the manager indicated that on June 25th, Fisher connected the victim's cable on her television and put up the patio screen door. There was nothing unusual about that, except that it was about the time when a young man had tried to gain entry to the apartment next door to Judi's. Furthermore, the description of the man who tried to get into the neighbor's apartment matched Fisher's features.

Detectives investigated further and learned that on the weekend the murder occurred, Fisher's family had been visiting relatives. Nobody could verify that Fisher had been in his apartment when the murder occurred.

As part of the investigation, detectives had been requesting tenants to come in to be fingerprinted. Most agreed. Some were disgruntled by the idea. The sleuths naturally would focus on anybody who refused. On July 18th, Fisher and others arrived at headquarters for the routine printing. They were all thanked for their cooperation, and they left.

Fingerprint experts had been carefully comparing all the prints found in the apartment with the bloody fingerprints there. The bloody prints were not the victim's. They had to belong to the killer. But fingerprints were lifted from other objects as well in the apartment.

Evidence prints had been taken from the television selector knob (because the television had been on when the victim was found), the telephone receiver, the white plate found on the coffee table, the fork, glass and pot pie tin, the hot water handle on the kitchen sink, a water glass on the bedroom dresser, the telephone on the dresser, coffee mugs, spatulas, the pot pie box found in the garbage, bowls in the kitchen, and of course the two murder weapons that had been found.

Fingerprint experts found something quite interesting. One fingerprint (not bloody) found on the patio screen door matched a bloody print found in the bathroom. Detectives gave the print experts Fisher's prints because he had been the one who had fixed the patio screen door. When the experts compared the bloody prints to those of Fisher, they hit paydirt.

On July 23, 1984, at 4:05 p.m. Randy Denton Fisher sat before Detectives Eldon Long and Robert Peterson in the Gresham Police Department's interrogation room.

The detectives knew they had their killer. They merely wanted to give him the opportunity to admit to the crime.

Fisher said he'd replaced the victim's patio screen door and hooked up her cable television in the latter part of June. He'd seen her sunbathing in a two-piece bathing suit while he mowed the lawn on the terrace above her patio. He described her as attractive, soft-spoken and having a nice personality. She never tried to put the make on him. He last saw her on July 2nd, while he was mowing the lawn.

On the night of the murder, Fisher said he took a shower at 10:45 p.m. He said that every night either the apartment manager or he would do what is called a "walk-through." One of them would walk around all the buildings to make certain everything was secure. He did the walk through on the night of the murder, even though the apartment manager was on duty that day and scheduled to do it.

When asked why he did this, Fisher replied, "Well, just boredom."

On past occasions Fisher had declined to tell detectives that he'd done the walk through. This was the first time he mentioned it. Detective Long thought that was quite suspicious.

"Another thing, Randy," Long said. "You're assistant manager, right. So you see all these lights, you see an ambulance coming from a building that you just walked through. You weren't curious to go over and say, 'Hey what happened? Maybe I missed something.' "

Detective Long accused Fisher of being in Judith Gracia's apartment that night.

"I wasn't in that apartment," Fisher responded.

"How did your bloody fingerprints get inside this girl's apartment?" Long asked.

"I don't know. I wasn't in her apartment."

Detective Long told Fisher that they knew the killer used the saber saw to knock the victim on the side of her head. Randy's bloody palmprint was on the saber saw and his fingerprints were on the front door, bathtub and elsewhere. Fisher again denied being in the apartment.

"Somebody was real busy with your hand, buddy," Detective Long said.

Long told Fisher about the man who tried to get into the apartment next door to the victim's. "You tried the key in there and the guy opened the door, and you know you said, 'Excuse me, I've got the wrong apartment.' Do you remember that?" Long asked. Fisher didn't.

"We know you were at her apartment the seventh, the night she was killed. We know you went to her apartment and that's important. You left that out (of previous conversations with police) and we need to know stuff like that," Long said.

"No, I don't think I was."

"Well, yes, we know you were. I would not make that statement, if I did not know it was true. And if you start leaving stuff like this out, it is going to come back and haunt us later. You walked over to her apartment that night."

"I did walk around the apartments," Fisher admitted.

"Well, you walked into the inside part," Long continued.

"What?"

"What do you call it, the breezeway? Is that what you call it?"

"The walkways."

"The walkways, yes."

"Yeah, well, when we do our walk around, we walk around each building."

"This was about 10:30 at night? You should have told us, you know, that you were walking in there."

"I didn't know anything about this until the next morning," Fisher said.

"So you did walk over there around 10:30 at night?"

"Yeah, well, I walked around each building."

Fisher stuck by his story of having done the walk-through but not going into the apartment. Later in the interview, Long asked Fisher why he wasn't curious about the police and ambulance at the apartment complex. Since he was the assistant manager, it was only natural that Fisher would be concerned.

"I'd seen the ambulance there so I figured that if somebody got hurt they are better qualified taking care of whatever it is," he explained.

"Wouldn't you be curious which one of the tenants got hurt, since you just walked through there? Weren't you worried about that?"

"Well, not really."

"I would have worried about it. Another thing you are leaving out. You were inside Judi's apartment that night."

Fisher denied it twice; then Long asked, "Why would you leave something like that out?"

"I wasn't in that apartment."

"Did you go over there to find out if the screen door worked okay, or why did you go over to her apartment?"

"I walked by it, that was it."

"No, you entered the apartment."

"No."

"Randy, don't mess with us," Long admonished.

"I'm not," Fisher said.

"Okay. I want you to explain one thing to me if you can."

"Okay."

167

"How did your bloody fingerprints get inside this girl's apartment? How did that happen?"

"I don't know. I wasn't in her apartment."

"Somebody must have taken your hand and gone into the apartment and put your hand all over things?"

"I don't think that's possible," Fisher conceded.

"No, it's not possible," Detective Long said. "So don't lie to me and say you weren't in her apartment. Why do you think we wanted you to come down here and do all these fingerprints? You never thought that that was curious?"

"No," Fisher responded.

"Your palmprints? How did your prints get on that little jigsaw inside her apartment? Bloody ones. Can you explain that to us?"

"No."

"The inside of the front door, Randy, your bloody fingerprints, palmprint on the saber saw that was found laying on the floor, bloody, bloody prints on the inside of the screen door."

"I was not in the apartment."

"Somebody put those fingerprints in there, and there are no two identical fingerprints on the face of this earth. You had to be in that apartment to put your own prints on that. You probably never did it on purpose, we know, but you were excited, you left fingerprints. And they are bloody fingerprints. And it had to be you. Nobody else in this whole world," Long said.

Detective Peterson then said, "And in an investigation as serious as this, we don't make these accusations without the power to back them up. Believe me. You can be guaranteed, we're not out here wasting your time, and we hope you are not here wasting ours."

But Randy Fisher was wasting their time. The transcript of the interview, when typed, would run more than 35 pages. Fisher repeatedly denied being in the apartment.

Once he slipped up and said, "I've got a very nice looking wife and I don't need to go out and rape and kill somebody."

Detective Long seized the opportunity: "Did I say you raped her?"

"No."

"Then why did you say that?"

Fisher pinned it back onto the detective: "Because of what you said earlier."

"What did I say earlier?"

"You said you didn't know if I went over there and raped her or tried to get a little."

"I didn't know that. I still don't know why you went over there. I do know you went over there. By your own admission you were over there at 10:30 that night."

For a second in the interview, Detective Long believed that Fisher had finally tripped himself up by broaching the subject of rape. But Fisher was smooth as glass and covered it well. Finally, the detectives realized Fisher wasn't going to admit being in the apartment, so they concluded the interview.

Randy Denton Fisher was placed under arrest for the brutal murder of Judith Gracia.

The final step in the case was to get somebody to identify the murder weapon as belonging to Fisher. The logical choice was Fisher's family, who had nothing to do with the crime or subsequent cover-up attempted by Randy.

When detectives interviewed one close relative, she was cooperative, but defended Fisher. She truly believed he couldn't commit such a ghastly crime.

She told detectives that upon returning home on July 9, 1984, from visiting relatives, she found Randy doing laundry, something that he rarely did. But she wasn't suspicious.

Officer Mike McGowan, who had been assigned the task of interviewing her, asked if she had noticed a paring knife missing from her apartment. At that point the woman realized that perhaps Randy was more deeply involved than she could have believed.

"I'm not liking this," she said as the realization hit home.

"I'm missing a knife."

Later, Officer McGowan returned to question her some more. This time he brought the paring knife, one of two murder weapons. When shown the knife with the brown wooden handle, the woman collapsed and said she couldn't continue. Her grief was genuine. Later she would identify the knife for the police.

The evidence against Randy Denton Fisher was overwhelming and conclusive. He was charged with burglary, attempted rape, rape, murder and aggravated felony murder. Under Oregon law, prosecutors can file a variety of charges against a suspect in connection with a crime, and it is up to a jury or judge to determine if the suspect is guilty of one or all the charges.

In January of 1985, the case went to trial. Oregon State Police Sergeant Coleen Has presented the most damning testimony. She was the fingerprint expert who had nailed Fisher.

As part of the prosecution's evidence, the detectives' interview with Randy Fisher, in which he repeatedly denied entering Judith Gracia's apartment, was submitted into evidence, and the jury listened to the tape recording and read the transcript of the interview.

But for his defense in the trial, Fisher changed his story. He said that he had entered the apartment and discovered the body, and accidentally got his hands in the blood and his bloody fingerprints around the apartment.

The footprints also matched a pair of his athletic shoes.

The jury didn't buy his story. On January 29, 1985, a Multnomah County jury found Randy Denton Fisher guilty of aggravated felony murder, murder, first-degree rape, attempted rape and first-degree burglary.

On March 8, 1985, Fisher was sentenced by Judge James Ellis to life plus 20 years in prison. Fisher is currently serving his sentence.

"HE LEFT JULIE HACKED UP AND 'HEART-LESS'!"

by Bill Henry

Eric Wolf had taken his two little dogs for a romp and a swim in Ft. Lauderdale's New River many a time before. Poochie and Reagan would chase each other along the riverbank under the Interstate-95 highway bridge, and when Eric threw a stick into the river, they would race to get it and bring it back. Poochie usually reached the stick first. Eric was not surprised when Reagan ignored the challenge to race Poochie for the stick and instead swam off to get a red and blue beach bag that was floating further away. It was too heavy for a small dog to drag up the riverbank, so Eric went down to see what treasure his dog had found. Reagan was reluctant to surrender it, but finally let his master have it.

Eric could see that the beach bag was in good condition, but it contained no treasure. Whatever was in it had an awful odor. Curious about its contents, Eric opened the beach bag. To his horror, he saw that the bag contained a partly decomposed woman's head together with her hands and forearms.

Even Eric's dogs seemed to sense that the discovery put an end to their romp and swim in the river.

The medical examiner would subsequently determine that the woman had been killed by a small-caliber bullet that had penetrated her skull about one and a half inches

171

above the left eye. X-ray examination showed that the bullet was still lodged in her head. In addition, the examiner found another small bullet in the right side of the victim's skull, apparently an old wound, the bullet having been enclosed by a growth of bone around it.

The woman was estimated to be between 25 and 30 years old. She had shoulder-length brown hair. Her fingertips had been cut off to prevent finger-print identification. Her teeth had received regular dental care, but her killer had chipped away at her teeth to make such identification difficult or impossible. Even her eyes had been punctured to prevent their use in identifying her. Until she could be identified, sleuths knew there was no hope of knowing how she may have died and who had killed her.

Tuesday, May 8, 1990, the day after the victim's head and hands were found, the Fort Lauderdale police had their skin divers explore the river bottom where the head and hands had surfaced. But no other parts of the body were recovered. Other police departments were contacted to check their records for missing persons of the same age, hair, and skin description who had disappeared within the past week or 10 days.

The police, hoping someone would recognize the beach bag and lead them to the identification of the victim, made copies of the crime scene photographs and took them door to door in their canvass of residences on the south side of the river.

Three days after Eric Wolf's dog found the unknown victim's head and hands, another resident, while walking her dog about a quarter-mile south of the river close to I-95, found a single human foot. Police were called to search the area again and found another foot and the two legs of the dismembered victim, who was now believed to be 5 foot 1 or 2 inches tall.

After the first newspaper account about the severed head appeared, almost daily news items reported the progress, or lack of progress, in the investigation to determine who the victim and her murderer were. The police still hoped to hear from some witness about a missing person with a prior gunshot head injury, or to find someone who recognized the beach bag. A list of women who had such head injuries was compiled, and each was found to be alive and well.

Sergeant Richard Hoffman of the Homicide Bureau obtained the assistance of the entire class of police cadets to search the area south of the river for other missing parts of the woman's body, but nothing was found.

As time passed, the police theorized that the killer had gotten rid of the missing torso by leaving it in a dumpster. They reasoned it had probably been picked up in the trash collection and buried in some landfill. The first parts that were found were partly decomposed. Those found later were in worse condition. The medical examiner had estimated the death to have occurred two or three days before the head was found, which would have been on May 3rd or 4th. Two weeks after the beach bag was found, the police called off their search for more body parts.

Enough was known about the slain woman to assure some families that the dismembered victim was not their missing wife or daughter. Police knew that the victim had an old bullet wound, possibly due to a suicide attempt, wore a size six-and-a-half or seven shoe, and had three holes for earrings in each ear.

The police were convinced that the killer and victim knew each other very well. That was the reason the killer had worked so hard to conceal her identity, sleuths reasoned: Dr. Ronald Keith Wright, the chief medical examiner, would subsequently say that he never saw a body so badly mutilated in order to hide its identity.

The police had not neglected the fatal bullet in their efforts to find the killer. Every .25-caliber gun found or confiscated since May 1, 1990, was test-fired to compare its bullet with the one recovered from the victim's brain. The chance of finding the killer by matching the test bullet from his gun with the fatal bullet extracted from the victim's brain depended upon the killer being foolish enough to keep the weapon and to do something foolish enough to be caught with it.

Detective Mike Walley suggested other possibilities to find the killer. Walley wanted the chairman of the anthropology department at the Florida Atlantic University, in conjunction with the Broward County Medical Examiner's Office, to use the victim's skull as a frame on which to sculpt a reconstruction of her head as it probably appeared in life.

"I am concerned that no one came forward to identify and claim the body by this time," Detective Walley said. "Whoever the killer is, he has probably been able to assure her friends and relatives that she is all right and need not be reported to the Missing Persons Unit."

The Homicide Detective Unit asked the Sheriff's Crime Laboratory to make a DNA analysis of the victim's remains and verify that all the parts came from the same woman.

Meanwhile, on Monday, May 21st, a Hollywood, Florida, police officer was patrolling an alley behind a barber shop on State Road 7 when he noticed a light coming from a partly open door behind the shop. The door led to a meter room for all the shops in the project. The officer approached cautiously, not knowing whether the trespasser was a burglar or some homeless vagrant. He observed a hand reach for the door handle and quietly close it. When the officer opened it, he saw a short, clean-shaven man stooping to slip a pistol into a sleeping bag in order to hide it.

Before the short man could stop him, the officer reached for the pistol and held it in one hand, his service revolver in the other. "What are you doing in here?" the officer demanded.

"I ain't done nothing," the man answered. "I'm just staying until I can get a place for myself."

The officer looked around the brightly lit room. The man had a television set hooked up and operating in one part of the room. A telephone had been tapped into the telephone cable. The short man sure knew how to take possession of a place.

"I'm arresting you for trespassing," the officer said. "And for having a concealed gun on you."

The officer read the man his rights and ignored the suspect's protests that he had done nothing wrong. The man claimed to have worked as a computer technician and more recently as a security officer. Unemployed for a short period of time, he could not pay his rent, he said. He had been living in a one-room efficiency apartment in Fort Lauderdale. The address he gave was for a rental complex close to I-95 and a half-mile south of the bridge crossing the New River, on S.W. 18th Terrace.

The suspect was in custody the rest of that night and until the afternoon of the next day, when he was released on a bail of $100 posted by a friend. The Hollywood police kept the suspect's gun, a .25-caliber Raven pistol.

Fort Lauderdale police should have been notified immediately about the .25-caliber pistol. Instead, the notification was delayed. However, the Fort Lauderdale police were making progress on their dismembered victim by other means.

On Friday, May 18th, three days before the trespasser's arrest, the father of a missing woman called the police to say the dismembered body might be that of his daughter, Julie Murphy. Her age was 29 and the estimated weight and height supplied by the medical examiner matched Julie's, the father said. He agreed to obtain her dental records for the medical examiner the following day. Julie's last address was on 18th Terrace, a short walk to the river where the victim's head and hands were found.

Julie's father said she usually visited or phoned her parents once or twice each week. Her last visit had been on May 3rd. Two weeks later, on Mother's Day, her family received no call from Julie, who had never before failed to call or visit on Mother's Day.

175

The father considered Julie a responsible person. She earned her living as a waitress, owned her own car, a Pontiac Firebird, and had her own apartment until recently, when irregular employment forced her to move in with friends. Julie lived with various friends until mid-April, when she had to move again and arranged to share an efficiency apartment with a young man who had similar difficulty in paying his rent. This man was named Charles Commander. He was a computer expert who sometimes worked as a security guard.

Before going to the Fort Lauderdale police the next day, Julie's father went to Commander's apartment. He found it vacant. There was a notice pasted to the door stating that Julie's Firebird had been towed away. A neighbor told the father that Charles Commander had been evicted for failing to pay his rent.

Homicide Unit detectives went back to the neighborhood south of the New River to ask more questions. They asked residents, "Can you tell us where to find Charles Commander? And tell us what you know about him and Julie Murphy. And where can we find the landlord of this building?"

The neighbors knew Julie Murphy as a good-natured young woman who frequently needed help because she had lost her job. She was too trusting with strangers and generous to a fault when she had money, they told police. She had not been seen for two weeks, not since someone heard her and Commander quarreling about money to pay the rent.

The police persuaded the landlord to let them inspect Charles Commander's apartment. It had already been scrubbed clean to be rented again. Lawmen checked for fingerprints but found none. They cut off a part of the carpet that looked bloodstained. Analysis would subsequently show it was stained with human blood, but it had been too well washed for detectives to determine the blood type. Sleuths had heard that Commander had fired a bullet into a neighbor's ceiling, and they recovered the slug. The crime laboratory later found the slug to have been fired from the same gun that fired the bullet into the head of the dismembered victim.

The neighbors referred sleuths to a relative of Commander's. He told them that Charles had been arrested by the Hollywood police but was released on bail posted by a friend. Detectives wanted Charles Commander, and they wasted no time trying to find him. Several officers were sent out to look for him at hangouts he was known to frequent. By eight o'clock that night, Charles Commander was found and brought down to the police station. He was booked and charged with first-degree murder.

Meanwhile, Julie Murphy's dental records were obtained and checked against the teeth in the skull of the victim. The match was perfect. It was now a certainty that Julie Murphy was the victim whose dismembered body had been found in the New River. But what sleuths still had to prove was that Charles Commander was her killer.

Among the things the police learned by questioning the suspect's neighbors was that two shots had been heard coming from the Commander apartment about midnight of May 3rd to 4th. At that time and for about two weeks before that night, Julie Murphy and another man were sharing Commander's apartment with him, probers were told. The man, known as Tom Clark, was arrested for burglary about May 7th and was probably still in jail. In that incident, Clark, with his girlfriend, went to a music store and threw a paving block through a plate-glass window. In spite of a loud burglar alarm rousing the neighborhood, Clark climbed into the store window to steal a guitar and other musical instruments. Clark was apprehended soon after he climbed out and ran away from the display window. The newspaper account of the crime disclosed Clark's extensive criminal record and said he'd used several aliases.

When the police interviewed Clark in the county jail, they found him to be unusually candid. He admitted to the burglary and to others for which he had been arrested. He rarely soiled his hands in honest employment, he said. He'd moved into Commander's apartment five or six weeks earlier. He claimed he gave his host $300 at that time but nothing since then because he had so little money. However, he said he often bought beer and crack because he found both to be indispensable. He knew Julie Murphy only a week before she moved in with him and Commander. She bought some food while she stayed there, but she paid no rent. That disturbed Charles Commander very much, Clark said.

Julie slept in the only bed, Commander slept on a couch, and Clark slept on a mat on the floor. They spent most of the time partying, drinking beer or wine and smoking crack.

"Who killed Julie?" one sleuth asked.

Without hesitation, Clark replied, "Charlie."

Clark was asked why and how it happened.

"Julie was out all day. Charlie was uptight about the rent. The landlord said he would evict us. She came in about ten-thirty or eleven. She had a big bag of steaks, eight or ten of them in a bag from a supermarket. But no money, and Charlie wanted some money. They didn't want me to listen, as if I gave a damn about it. They went into the bathroom. It was the only place they could be alone. Then all of a sudden I heard, 'Bang—bang.' "

"You mean you heard two shots?" Clark was asked.

"Yeah, two shots. Then Charlie came out, looking wild-eyed, the gun in his hand. I asked him, what did he do?

"He got a knife from the kitchen and went back to the bathroom. I heard him stab her—thump, thump, thump—over and over. He wouldn't stop. Then he came out, and I took a look to see her. She was in the bathtub, and she looked dead. I asked him why he did it.

" 'The bitch slapped me,' he said bitterly, 'and I shot her.'

"I asked him what he would do now. He said it was his problem and [that] I shouldn't worry about it. He could deal with it.

"Later he said, 'She slapped me, and I pulled out my gun

178

to scare her. She grabbed for it, and we struggled until it went off and killed her. It was an accident. I'll say that.'

" 'But you fired two shots,' I said. 'How can you call it an accident?' "

"I know that. It's difficult, but I can deal with it," Commander told Clark sternly. "Don't worry. I'll manage."

Clark continued, "Then [Commander] went back to the bathroom with his knife and a saw blade, closed the door, and I could hear him working on the body, cutting it up."

"What did you do?" a sleuth asked Clark.

"I just smoked crack and drank the beer," he replied. "I was too uptight and drank the beer to steady my nerves. After midnight, I left to take a walk and returned about two. Commander had left the bathroom to drink some beer and smoke some crack, so we just talked for a while. I got the idea he had decided to get rid of the body, but he didn't explain how.

"I fell asleep about five a.m. and didn't awake until one in the afternoon. I didn't want to look at the body so I went to the toilet in [a nearby market] and bought some beer."

The police gave Tom Clark a lie detector test. He failed it, but much of what he told them rang true. No lawman could guess what Clark was hiding from them, but they nevertheless continued with their questioning. Clark told them how Commander regularly returned to the bathroom to work on the corpse, then rejoined Clark in the living room to drink beer and smoke crack.

That evening, Saturday, May 5th, Commander asked Clark to help him get rid of some of Julie's things. He had filled her red and blue beach bag with the stuff; he only wanted Clark to drive her car and take him to the closed marina next to the I-95 bridge over New River. Although it wasn't far away, Commander feared being seen with the bag before he reached the darkness of the waterfront. Clark had no problem starting the car since Julie had left the car keys on the kitchen table. It was three in the morning when Clark left Commander at the marina. As they planned,

Clark drove back to the apartment without waiting for Commander to return to the car. Later, Commander said he threw the bag in the river.

When Clark used the bathroom that Sunday morning, he was surprised to see Julie's body had no head.

At last Commander confided in Clark that he intended to cut up the body into little pieces and leave them where they would not be found. Commander said he had put some rocks in the beach bag. He seemed not to know that flesh becomes more buoyant as it decomposes. He complained that cutting up the body was a tougher job than he expected and he needed a sharper hacksaw. Clark agreed to get one for him. Later that morning Clark stole one from a store in the Southland Mall.

That same afternoon, Clark helped Commander carry Julie Murphy's legs and feet to a suitable hiding place, but the two men were too tired to go as far as the river. So they visited a friend in the neighborhood. Clark's ex-girlfriend was there, and they partied for a while, dulling their senses with beer and crack.

When they returned to the apartment and Commander resumed cutting up the victim's body, Clark, still drinking beer in the living room, decided he had to leave town before the murder was discovered. He had only $25 left so he decided that stealing musical instruments, which could be readily sold, was the quickest way to raise cash.

By this time, the smell of the decomposing body was sickening. Commander went to a local store for cleaning materials, which he hoped would eliminate the stench. He also bought some more beer. Commander interrupted his work to party with his friends. Actually, there were three at this party, but Clark withheld from the police the name—or even the existence—of the third man until some weeks later. By that time, both Tom Clark and Charles Commander were in jail and the third man was long gone, not to be found by the police for questioning. The third man knew of the murder just minutes after it occurred, the investigation would subsequently reveal.

Apparently, the man just happened to call on Charles Commander while he was stabbing Julie's dead body. Commander was making sure that he had finished off Julie in case the bullet in her head had failed to do it. Clark had opened the door and told the man to go away because Commander was busy killing Julie. The man had called on them twice since then and urged Commander to get rid of the body—but he was shocked when told how Commander was cutting it up. Nonetheless, he went with Clark to the store to buy detergents and beer. He helped them try to dispel the odor, and they partied together after the futile attempt.

It was the last time the three men would party together. A few hours later, Tom Clark would be caught in the music store—a burglar caught in the act. And when questioned by the police, he would eventually tell them everything he knew about Julie Murphy's murder. He would get his reward. Charged with burglary and with being an accessory to murder after the fact, as well as with a violation of probation charge, Clark agreed to cooperate with the police in every way he could on the promise that for all these crimes he would serve no more than three years in prison. Clark was satisfied that his state-appointed lawyer got him as good a deal as he could realistically expect. His lawyer was a conscientious criminal attorney. He persuaded his client to list every crime he ever committed and to plead guilty to them all. The lawyer explained that if all Clark's crimes were included in the deal, then when Clark got out of prison, no remaining charges could be brought against him. The state supplied the lawyer to protect Clark from any law enforcement units trying to punish him for his many crimes.

Charles Commander, who had been held without bail, appeared in court on May 22, 1990, charged with the murder of Julie Murphy. His lawyer told him to speak to no one about the case unless his lawyer was present. Charles was never inclined to accept advice. He talked with newspaper reporters whenever he could.

181

He admitted knowing Julie Murphy and said he did not kill her. "I'm innocent," he declared. "I'd never do anything like that."

The reporter who interviewed Commander for the *Sun Sentinel* of Fort Lauderdale wrote that in his baggy jailhouse uniform, Commander looked more like a 15-year-old who should still be fighting acne than a 22-year-old fighting a murder charge. Commander said, "I guess I'm a regular guy. I've never been in trouble in my life. I'm not a violent person."

Commander told the reporter he was 5 feet 3 inches tall, not 5 feet 7 inches. He leaned closer to the glass to whisper to her, "It's a hell of an experience. There's people in here who committed crimes and stuff. I don't belong in here."

It was Commander's idea to talk to reporters, speaking against the advice of lawyers. He said he needed to correct the public's impression of him. He saw the reporter many times.

However, Commander's future was much more endangered by what he said and would say in the future to prisoners in the Broward County Jail. His face turned white when he heard what Tom Clark told the police about the murder and dismemberment of Julie Murphy.

Yet, while the papers reported the doubts by police that Murphy's torso would ever be found, Commander boasted that he knew where it was. He finally told Dennis Hogan, a fellow prisoner, that he killed Julie Murphy by shooting her twice and that he had cut up her body except for her torso. He said he had no one to help him get rid of it, but he wrapped it in a plastic bag, stuffed it into a green suitcase of Julie's and carried it to a spot not far from the house. He dumped the torso next to a pile of trash that he used to cover it. He returned with the suitcase, which he felt was worth saving.

The inmate Hogan knew the value of such information. When he had all the details needed to find the torso, which the police search had thus far failed to uncover, Hogan told his lawyer. Police found the torso on May 29th, exactly where Charles Commander told Dennis Hogan he had left it.

Although the case against Charles Commander was complete, witnesses could forget, change their stories, or disappear before the trial. Moreover, Commander had no criminal record, yet both Hogan and Clark could be made to look untrustworthy when cross-examined by a clever defense attorney. Furthermore, some jurors would not believe that a sane man could live with a dead body while cutting it up day after day. No prosecutor could ever be certain that even the strongest case would end in a conviction.

The trial began on May 15, 1991, almost a year after Charles Commander was arrested with the murder weapon in his possession. Assistant State Attorney Peter LaPorte had lost his skirmish with the defense counsel, Michael Dutko, who moved that the death penalty be excluded as a possible penalty for the defendant since the victim had been killed instantly by a bullet that was fired into her brain. Normally, the death penalty can be imposed if the defendant killed his victim in some unusually cruel and painful manner. The defendant's subsequent frenzied stabbing of the victim's breast some 30 to 40 times — one medical examiner gave up counting when he reached 25 — could not be considered. Judge Leroy H. Moe granted the defense motion.

In their opening statement, both lawyers mentioned the three things that must be proved to convict someone of first-degree murder. First, the supposed victim must be dead. There was no dispute about that, nor that the dismembered remains were all that was left of Julie Murphy. The second was that the defendant had caused the death. Defense Attorney Michael Dutko said his client informed him that Tom Clark had killed Julie Murphy and Commander had cut up the body, partly as a favor to a friend and partly because he feared Clark. But then Dutko continued, saying that even if jurors believed Commander had

183

killed Julie Murphy, it was impossible to believe that he planned to kill her—that this was, in fact, a premeditated murder, the essential third requirement to charge someone with murder in the first degree. If his client was guilty of anything, said Dutko, it could only be manslaughter or, at most, murder in the second degree.

Such would be the real objective of the defense. They wanted to prevent a conviction of Commander for first-degree murder, which would result in a 25-year sentence before he would be eligible for parole. There was no minimum term that must be served if convicted of murder in the second degree or for manslaughter. Commander could serve as little as five years if convicted of either. And there was always the chance that a jury might acquit him because he looked young and lovable.

The mass of evidence shown to the jury seemed overwhelming. The jurors lost count of the color photos showing the victim's bloody arms, legs, and feet. Each was shown to a technician who had taken the photos. He told the jury how he was called to the places where each limb was found.

The man who cleaned up Commander's apartment when he was evicted told how he was sickened by the stench of the place and saw Commander sitting outside with his few belongings. Commander stank as much as the apartment. The man found that the dumpster outside contained a variety of women's clothing and some cheap jewelry. The man had no use for ladies' panties, dresses, or sneakers. He did save some rings and bracelets.

Later, the police interviewed the man and he showed them the jewelry. They took the items from him. Most of the things were recognized by members of Julie Murphy's family—a ring and one bracelet had been gifts from one of Julie's relatives within the past year. Commander had sold the ring, as well as a watch and a pocket calculator, to a pawn-shop owner for five dollars. Julie's family had recognized them. The fact that Commander hid her things showed how completely Commander took possession of Julie's property as well as her naked, dismembered body.

Defense Attorney Dutko had little opportunity to discredit the state's best witness, Tom Clark.

Prosecutor LaPorte began his questioning by obtaining from the witness all the aliases he had used in the past 10 years and the crimes he had committed. With each new alias, Clark assumed a new birthdate and Social Security number. He never paid any income tax, was never true to any woman he lived with, and was never loyal to a friend if he could gain something by being a snitch. But he had not volunteered to testify against Charles Commander. Instead, the police had found out that Clark had lived with the defendant, must have known about the murder, and may even have helped dispose of the body parts. Why should Clark accept the blame for Commander's crime? When it paid to tell the truth, Clark was all for doing it. And he was a convincing witness.

Next to testify was Chief Medical Examiner Ronald Keith Wright, one of the county's most admired coroners. In this case, Wright's testimony was as useful to the defense as to the prosecution. When Julie's head and hands were found, judging by the progress of decomposition, Wright estimated her death to have been two to three days earlier. Later testimony by Tom Clark that the murder occurred about midnight on May 3rd to 4th placed it two and a half days before Dr. Wright had examined the remains.

Wright testified that the bullet to the victim's brain had caused death instantly, although the heart could beat about a minute longer. This testimony persuaded the judge to exclude the death penalty if Commander was found guilty of first-degree murder.

When asked if Julie was high on cocaine or alcohol, Dr. Wright was positive that she had no more than two or three beers. Since he found no residue in her brain, he doubted she had used crack shortly before her death.

It was Dr. Wright who had recovered the bullet from Julie

Murphy's brain that was proved to have been fired from Charles Commander's .25-caliber pistol. Wright's study of the saw cuts inflicted on Julie's body showed that Commander's saw was the most likely tool used to dismember her body. Wright was intrigued by the amount of bone Commander had removed to take out the woman's heart. The victim's heart was never recovered. Why did the murderer want it?

Dr. Wright said he never had a case in which a criminal had worked so hard to prevent the identification of a body. If a body is left to decompose naturally, he explained, only the teeth and some surgically implanted metal replacement, such as a stainless-steel pin and socket with a serial number on it, can make identification possible. Dr. Wright said the work of maggots can be especially destructive to a corpse. Maggots can eat everything on a corpse except for the teeth and bones.

The jurors were especially attentive while Dr. Wright testified. At no time did they appear more interested than when the chief medical examiner spoke. His evidence was so scholarly and objective that the cruel reality of Julie Murphy's death faded into the background. That may have had an important effect upon the verdict they would reach later.

The testimony of Dennis Hogan, the informer—Defense Attorney Dutko always referred to him as a snitch—brought them back to the defendant's reckless confession to a fellow prisoner. Hogan had been arrested for robbery on March 23, 1990, and came into contact with Commander when they were both inmates on the sixth floor of the jail. Still concerned about his image at the prison, Commander had admitted to Hogan that he shot Julie, but claimed he had not intended to kill her. He claimed they had been arguing about the rent money she had not given him, and he threatened her with the gun. She grabbed for it, and while they struggled for it, the gun went off.

Commander claimed he told Tom Clark that this was the way it happened and asked for his help in getting rid of the body. Commander seemed to think that cutting up the body to conceal his responsibility for the crime was a reasonable thing to do. He said he made all those stab wounds in the abdomen to drain the blood. And he was making good progress with it, although he stopped many times to relax with his friend and drink beer. But three days after the killing, his friend was arrested for burglary, and he had no one to help him get rid of the victim's torso.

Dennis Hogan said he felt he should cooperate with the police. He gave a detailed statement of Commander's confession to Detectives Vicki Russo and Mike Walley. Commander continued to confide in Hogan. He seemed proud of his success in hiding the victim's torso. He belittled the police efforts to find it. Finally, he told how he managed to fit the torso into a large green suitcase and carry it to an abandoned gas station. There was a pile of trash behind the station, so he used some of that trash and some palm fronds to hide it. Hogan gave all this information to the police, and the body was found a couple of hours later.

In subsequent questioning by Prosecutor LaPorte and in cross-examination by Defense Attorney Dutko, it was established that Hogan, a huge man who had earned his income from doing strong-arm robberies for many years, was released from jail in June 1990. He resumed his normal way of life until arrested again for several more robberies.

The next day, Prosecutor LaPorte called another "jailhouse witness" for the state. The defense attorney protested. It was an unusual situation since the witness, Ronald Hightower, had been a defense witness whose testimony could discredit a witness used by the state, Dennis Hogan. Hogan had already testified that Commander had admitted to him that he killed Julie Murphy. To discredit Hogan, Commander wanted his new friend, Ronald Hightower, to say that he was present when Hogan threatened "to do a number" on Commander and to say that Commander admitted he planned to kill Julie Murphy before he took her into the bathroom and shot her. Hightower had promised to perjure himself to help his friend. He'd lied to Defense Attorney Dutko that Commander was being abused by the big man. Hogan was reported to have said that his testimony would ensure that Commander be convicted of first-degree murder.

As required by law, Dutko notified LaPorte that he was calling Hightower as a witness and LaPorte interviewed the man. Unexpectedly, Hightower broke down and told how he planned to lie to discredit Dennis Hogan. He agreed to tell the jury how the defendant had urged him to perjure himself to discredit Hogan. Prosecutor LaPorte wanted to use Hightower as a witness.

Judge Leroy H. Moe ruled that LaPorte had a right to do it, so Dutko's objection was overruled.

In spite of Dutko's concern about the testimony of the witness who accused Commander of asking him to lie for the defense, no lawyer can be certain of the influence such testimony may have on the jury's verdict. Hightower's offer to lie for the defense and his betrayal of the defense to the state attorney no doubt made some jurors suspicious of the testimony he gave against Charles Commander. The state always had the liability in that they were using disreputable witnesses whom the defendant referred to as friends and companions.

Late that afternoon, the state rested their case. Dutko decided to call no witnesses for the defense. He was ready with his closing statement, which Prosecutor LaPorte would later describe as a three-headed snake. The first head said Commander didn't do it; Tom Clark was the killer. The second head said that even if Commander did it, it was an accident. The third head said if it wasn't an accident, the state failed to prove it was premeditated so the jury must find Commander guilty of either manslaughter or second-degree murder.

LaPorte reviewed the evidence he had presented in detail to convince the jury of Charles Commander's responsibility for Julie Murphy's death. He insisted that a killer who fires two bullets into a victim and then stabs her more than 30 times was seriously trying to cause her death.

Defense Attorney Dutko still said that none of the state's evidence supported that claim.

Judge Moe gave the jurors the required instructions and sent them into the jury room to deliberate. They thought about the problem for three hours and returned with their verdict. They found Charles Commander guilty of murder in the second degree.

Judge Moe was limited by guidelines in imposing sentence. For a defendant with no prior conviction, he could sentence Commander to as little as 12 or as much as 22 years. Judge Moe sentenced Charles Commander to serve 22 years in prison.

Florida prisons are so crowded now that almost all inmates are paroled when they have served a third of their sentence. It is doubtful the judge was pleased with his sentence, but he did the best he could under the Florida penal code.

EDITOR'S NOTE:
Poochie, Reagan, Eric Wolf, Tom Clark, Dennis Hogan, and Ronald Hightower are not the real names of the persons so named in the foregoing story. Fictitious names have been used because there is no reason for public interest in the identities of these persons.

"HE SAWED OFF HER PELVIS AND BUTTOCKS!"

by Billie Taylor

Norfolk Lake is a vast expanse of beautiful blue waters in northern Arkansas. Its shoreline extends several hundred miles through several counties. It attracts thousands of tourists annually as well as local folks who try their luck at dragging in the bass and crappie that fill the lake.

About 8:00 a.m. on August 23, 1990, two local fishermen were drowning bait near Arkansas Bridge 101. They spotted a big red and white cooler floating in the water. Its top was popped half-open.

The fishermen paddled closer to pull in their catch. A foul, noxious odor emanated from the cooler. When the anglers looked inside the ice chest, they saw what looked like human body parts.

They towed the cooler to a tree at the shoreline and tied it up. From the nearby Corps of Engineers office, they called the Baxter County Sheriff's Department. Chief Criminal Investigator Phil Frame responded. His inspection of the chest verified the stunned fishermen's guess. The water-soaked remains were indeed human.

Sheriff Joe Edmonds and Sergeant Robert Alman soon arrived at the crime scene, followed by the coroner, Arkansas State Police Investigator Bill Beach, and several other officials.

The body part looked like a large buttocks and a partial

190

pelvis. At this point, of course, it was impossible to determine the identity or anything else about the victim. The cooler was dispatched to the Arkansas State Crime lab for analysis by State Medical Examiner Fahmy Malak and other specialists.

In the meantime, officers began an immediate search of the area for other body parts. They searched the wooded shoreline, coves, and caves — but their efforts were all to no avail.

Sheriff Edmonds commented, "Whoever cut the victim up and put it in the cooler meant for it to stay at the bottom of the lake. But once the body started decomposing, the gases that escaped popped the lid open and the cooler rose to the top." The killer had apparently poured several pounds of concrete into the cooler, but had miscalculated the amount necessary to make it sink. Thus, the partial corpse had risen from its watery grave.

"If the other parts are chopped like the one we found, I estimate there are three or four more coolers somewhere. We will still keep looking," Sheriff Edmonds informed the searchers.

The Arkansas State Police sent in a team of divers equipped with underwater television cameras. They searched the vast lake as thoroughly as possible. But it was like looking for a specific shell in the Pacific Ocean. Hopes were raised high at one point when cameras spotted what the divers thought was the upper torso of a body. But it turned out to be only a limb sticking out of the mud.

As the shoreline search proved fruitless and the divers couldn't find a body on the bottom of the lake, the innovative investigators tried another method.

The cooler, concrete, and remains had weighed a total of 95 pounds. The sheriff obtained a cooler of the same size and filled it with concrete to make it the same weight. The sleuths found an appropriate spot on the bridge and threw the cooler into the lake.

"We were trying to see if it would float or sink," Edmonds explained. "It never sank. So now we will stop searching the lake bottom."

Meanwhile, Dr. Malak's preliminary medical report had given strong new leads toward identifying the victim. He had determined that the pelvic structure was that of a white female of large build, weighing about 200 pounds, and in her late 40s or early 50s. The woman had been dead two to three weeks, he speculated in making his report.

The torso had been cut at the second lumbar vertebra in the spine. The legs had been cut off at the upper thigh. The remains had weighed about 24 pounds.

The cut had been made by a fairly common type of handsaw. A tiny blue fleck of paint had been removed from the torso. This fleck was sent for trace analysis.

The tissue contained no trace of drugs. The alcohol content was .04.

Sheriff Edmonds' crew had been working diligently on missing-person reports that were coming in from all over the Southwest. The bizarre case was already drawing national media attention.

Fifteen females who fit the meager description of the victim were all traced, but fortunately were found alive.

Then, on September 10th, another woman was reported missing by a relative. The woman, 50-year-old Lou Alice Brenk, had last been seen by her relative in early August.

The missing woman had last lived near the lake in a trailer park. The relative told Investigator Beach that Mrs. Brenk had had surgery in West Palms, Missouri, a few months earlier. Beach flew to Missouri, picked up the X-rays of Lou Alice Brenk and took them, along with Dr. Malak's X-rays of the victim, to a doctor who was the chairman of the University of Arkansas' anthropology department in Fayetteville, Arkansas.

This doctor had at his disposal very sophisticated equipment for bone identification. He and a colleague studied the two sets of X-rays. Based on a 14-point identification similarity, they concluded that the gruesome remains found floating in the lake were those of Lou Alice Brenk.

Investigator Frame and Sergeant Alman broke the news

to the victim's relative, with whom they had a long and serious talk. After several hours of interviewing the relative, the officers went to visit the victim's husband. He wasn't hard to find.

Herbert F. Brenk, 52, was in the Fulton County Jail. He was serving time for failure to pay a DWI fine from 1988.

But the officers were not at the jail to offer Brenk their condolences. Instead, they arrested and charged him with capital murder. Brenk pleaded not guilty. He was held without bail.

Under persistent questioning, Herbert Brenk denied knowledge about his wife's death. He told officers that his wife was visiting neighbors in southern Arkansas. When this story was proven false, Brenk said he had lied because his wife of three years had left him for another man and he was ashamed.

Brenk vowed he had never seen the cooler that Sheriff Edmonds showed him a picture of, but later he recanted that statement. The cooler had unique stains, either from paint or epoxy glue, that set it apart from all others. Brenk said he had once owned the ice chest. But he claimed he'd sold it at a flea market to an unidentified man.

Brenk declared himself indigent. He got two court-appointed defense attorneys, Larry Kissee and Tom Garner. The prosecutor was Gordon Webb. Webb made his intentions of seeking the death penalty clear to all.

Lawmen learned that the Brenks had two homes. One was in Salem. It was a small wooden frame house that was little more than a cabin, about 40 miles from the crime scene. Their second home was a recreational vehicle parked in a mobile home park near Norfolk Lake. They were living in the RV at the time of Lou Alice's disappearance.

Search warrants gave officers and crime lab personnel access to both homes, Lou Alice's car, and a communal bathroom at the trailer park. Probers also searched the yards and wooded area around the park.

They amassed evidence that included the following items: a key ring with nine keys, two golden wedding rings, Lou

Alice's eyeglasses, bloody sheets, and a pair of Brenk's jeans. But no body parts were found anywhere.

Officers also searched the home of Brenk's friend whom he stayed with after Lou Alice left and before his arrest. Six handsaws were among the items seized there.

The bizarre case of the mutilated lady in the lake had received national publicity. It had also aroused harsh feelings against the accused. Herbert Brenk was shuffled from one jail to another, trying to keep his whereabouts as secret as possible. He had several cellmates between September and his June trial.

Herbert Brenk was given the usual mental competency test, which he passed. At his attorneys' request, he was given a second test by a professional of their choosing. Brenk also passed this test.

The trial was moved to Boone County on a change of venue request. The jury panel was almost exhausted by the time six men and six women were finally chosen.

Prosecutor Webb kept his vow to ask for the death penalty. He told the jury that he would show a pattern of violence that led to the discovery of the lady in the lake.

Defense Attorneys Kissee and Garner told the jury and the packed courtroom that they intended to prove that the remains found in the cooler had not been conclusively identified as Lou Alice Brenk. And even if she was the victim, the state could not prove how she had died or who had done it, the defense contended quite emphatically.

The state had a long line of witnesses whom they intended to call and an impressive array of evidence.

One witness was the owner of a small general store that the Brenks visited often. The man identified the cooler as one which he had in the store for almost a year. He remembered the distinctive stains on the lid. He couldn't sell it, so he moved it to the back of the store near the back door. It was also near the store bathroom that the Brenks often used.

When Investigator Beach had shown him a picture, the shopkeeper was surprised because he hadn't realized the cooler was gone. After seeing the picture, he checked and found that it really was gone.

The clerk testified that the last time he saw the Brenks together was in early August. The next time he saw Herbert, he was alone. Brenk had explained that his wife had gone to south Arkansas to visit friends. The witness said he never heard Brenk threaten his wife.

But another store clerk in Missouri had a different tale. He was called to testify and related what Brenk once asked the clerk, when referring to his wife, "Could I leave the bitch here?"

When Herbert left, Lou Alice began to cry. She pulled her collar back and showed the clerk bruises on her neck. The witness said she told him, "He's gonna kill me."

Lou Alice had at least one friend, a neighbor who gave her refuge from her battering husband. Lou Alice would visit the friend and her husband and listen as they read the Bible. She told these neighbors that her husband wouldn't let her have a Bible in their home.

One night, Lou Alice fell asleep during their Bible study. This surprised her friend because she knew how important that time was to her.

Lou Alice confessed to the friend that she was afraid to fall asleep at home because she feared her husband would kill her while she was asleep. She frequently slept outside the neighbors' trailer on the hood of her car, she said, because she was afraid of snakes.

Her friend testified that she urged Lou Alice to leave her husband. Lou Alice told her in late July or early August that she was going to leave Herbert. Records showed that Lou Alice made a call to a home for battered women shortly before she disappeared.

Salem City Police Chief Albert Roork had arrested Herbert Brenk at least once for wife-beating. He testified, "Herbert beat [Lou] Alice up pretty bad, even blackened her eye a couple of times. In fact a felony charge was filed against him for beating her. But she dropped the charges later. He could sweet-talk her or something."

More damaging testimony against the defendant came from the postmistress at Salem. The state had maintained that the motive for Lou Alice's murder was that she intended to leave Herbert and take her income with her.

Lou Alice drew a Social Security check of $368 per month. Herbert, an unemployed plumber, used as much of this money as he could get to buy beer and cigarettes. The postmistress testified that the Brenks always came in together. At least once Lou Alice looked like she had been beaten up.

But on August 3rd, Herbert had come in alone to pick up the mail that contained Lou Alice's Social Security check. He told the mail clerk that his wife had gone to visit a relative.

Linda Taylor, a questioned documents examiner, testified that the signature on the August check was forged and did not match known samples of Lou Alice's handwriting.

Testimony also revealed that on September 12th, Herbert Brenk had turned up alone at the home of a friend and former cellmate, driving Lou Alice's car. The friend thought this was strange because Lou Alice never let Herbert have the car without her.

Brenk at the time told his friend that he was lonesome, that Lou Alice had gone to visit some friends. He was welcomed by his friend and stayed for a week. Lou Alice never contacted Herbert while he was there. Herbert left once and went to the trailer. He returned and told his host that Lou Alice had returned only to leave him for another man.

Brenk had visited his friend's house several times and was very familiar with it. In fact, this was the house he was at when he was arrested and taken to Fulton County on the failure to pay the fine for DWI.

This friend testified that Herbert always referred to his wife as "it" or "bitch," never as a human being.

The friend told the court that while Brenk stayed with him, Brenk followed the story of the torso in the cooler closely in the newspapers and on television. Once when a newscaster said the authorities were searching the lake,

Brenk laughed and said, "They will have hell finding her there!"

Officers had taken six handsaws from this witness' residence for testing. One had blue paint on it. It was tempera paint, and the fleck matched the blue fleck that had been found on the victim's pelvis.

The witness had told officers that he didn't know if the saw had ever been moved.

Brenk had brought his small poodle dog, Boomer, with him. Once, when the dog barked too loud, Brenk told Boomer that he had better shut up, that "they make coolers in six-pack size."

A very devastating blow to the defense's case came from another acquaintance of Herbert Brenk. The man stated, "He actually solicited my help in murdering her."

Herbert Brenk had told this witness that he had married Lou Alice for her check and that now she was leaving him. "He said he couldn't stand it any more, he had to get rid of her by any means," the witness testified.

"He planned to knock her in the head, but he needed help throwing her off the bridge." He said the woman was too big to handle, that she weighed 200 pounds. "He asked once if he could borrow my two-wheeled dolly," the man's testimony continued. "He said he would have to get her down to a size he could handle."

The man never went to the authorities even though Brenk had mentioned doing away with Lou Alice 20 or 30 times. He said he didn't think Brenk was serious about it.

When defense attorneys asked if Brenk was drinking at the time of the alleged plotting, the man replied that yes, he was. Then he added, "I never saw him when he wasn't drinking."

Criminologist Donald Smith had made comparison tests between the suspect saw blade and the sawtooth marks on the corpse's torso. The fine-toothed saw had cut clean through the bone. It had left a tiny fleck of blue paint on it. Smith brought the femur to the courtroom and demonstrated the cut.

The teeth of the saw and its length were consistent with cut marks on the victim's bones. "If this saw didn't do it, then one just like it did," the expert swore. He said the five other saws taken from the residence tested negative.

Another item confiscated from the Brenks' trailer was a videotape of *Scarface*. One of the scenes in the movie depicts a man being murdered with a chainsaw.

Criminologist Smith said he had dissolved the concrete, which he characterized as poorly mixed, and found bone and hair fragments.

Although he had no known samples of Alice's hair, tests showed that the hair was not Herbert's.

Smith testified that he returned to the scene of the crime for further searching. But he admitted under defense questioning that he found no hair in sink traps.

Smith testified that he had used a fairly new testing method called luminol for detecting blood. Luminol detects the presence of blood after visible blood has been cleaned from the surface. The expert testified that it takes 15 gallons of water to one drop of blood to remove it so thoroughly that luminol testing won't reveal it.

Luminol is applied to a suspect surface in total darkness. If blood is present, the area begins to glow.

The test showed that blood was likely on the sink, floor, and walls of the communal bathroom in the park where the Brenks lived. The tests also showed blood in Lou Alice's car on the driver's side and the armrest.

The courtroom darkened and Criminologist Smith presented a dramatic display of photos glowing with an eerie light.

The defense dismissed the luminol test as "science fiction" and forced Smith to admit that the test can't show if the blood is human. But another test on Brenk's jeans showed that spot to be human blood.

Other officers testified that they had found burned cloth, rivets, and snaps in a trash pile near the trailer.

Medical Examiner Malak testified that his equipment was not the right kind to make the tests he needed on the remains in his possession. So he contacted the chairman of the anthropology department and requested his assistance. The chairman confirmed 14 identification points on the two sets of X-rays. The defense questioned the chairman's accuracy and his credentials.

When questioned about how many points made a positive identification, the chairman said he didn't know, but he thought 14 was adequate.

Dr. Malak had also testified that there were no drugs and only a small amount of alcohol in the torso's tissues. Lou Alice Brenk was a known nondrinker.

But a doctor testified that he had regularly given prescription drugs to Lou Alice. She had been his patient from October 1984 to August 1990, he said.

The lady was a chronic dieter, he said, whose weight fluctuated from 200 to 250 pounds. He had last seen her in August in his office. At the time, she weighted in at 203 pounds. He had given her a routine checkup and found nothing that would make him think she would die anytime soon. The doctor had also documented one instance of bruises on Lou Alice's body.

The defense argued that the torso found in the lake couldn't be Lou Alice's because it didn't have drugs in it. But it did contain alcohol, which it should not have. A pathologist said that decomposition could have masked the presence of drugs and could have formed alcohol.

Herbert Brenk was in several area jails and detention centers during the 10 months he was in custody. He visited with a cellmate casually at one of them, trading milk for honey buns.

On November 13th, that man, now out of jail and seeing newspapers, called his lawyer, who in turn called the prosecutor.

The stoolie told Prosecutor Webb that Brenk had said he stole the cooler and "if he had done with the part of her body in the cooler what he had done with the rest of her, he wouldn't be in this situation and they'd [have] never found out."

The informant was allowed to testify over strenuous objections by the defense, who said he shouldn't be allowed to testify since the trail had already started.

When this cellmate started talking, officers started checking records of inmates who had served time with Brenk in earlier years.

One of these cons told Investigator Beach that Lou Alice had once brought cigarettes to Brenk in jail. She had a black eye and a split lip, he recalled. Brenk told the man that Lou Alice had gotten the marks because she hadn't moved fast enough when he had ordered her to bring him his cigarettes and beer. He bragged about how he controlled her and that he only kept her around for her check.

Brenk and Lou Alice had only been married for about three years. Before that he had been married to another woman from 1965 to 1984.

During their marriage, this lady said under oath, Herbert had abused her frequently. Once, he had strangled her into unconsciousness and threatened to "scatter pieces of me from Arkansas to Louisiana," she testified.

She divorced him then and, she declared, "I made sure I was never alone with him again."

A relative of Lou Alice's testified that Lou Alice got her Social Security check because she was "a little slow." Lou Alice also had a history of accepting abuse from the men in her life. She seemed to need attention, even of a destructive kind, the witness said.

The trial lasted for six days. The state had presented 98 pieces of evidence and 47 witnesses.

The defense had fought hard for Herbert Brenk. They had filed numerous motions. Most of them had been dismissed. Twice they had asked for a mistrial. One reason was because of the surprise witness. Another motion was made because the X-rays of the torso and of Lou Alice had been lost for a period of time, and they argued that they hadn't had enough time to study them. Both of these motions failed.

Every day from the onset, the courtroom was packed

with spectators. The judge had allowed television cameras in. As the sensational trial progressed, the crowd grew and the members of the news media multiplied.

The defense took 40 minutes to present their case. They presented three pieces of evidence and three witnesses. Brenk did not testify in his own behalf. Throughout the trial, the bespectacled and balding defendant showed no emotion.

The jury was out for two hours. They judged Herbert F. Brenk guilty and passed a sentence of death by lethal injection. There will be a mandatory review of the case.

Herbert Brenk had shown no emotion throughout the trial, nor did he blink when he heard his death sentence announced. He had no family visitors or friends during his incarceration.

Shortly before he was taken to state prison, Brenk asked to see his pet poodle, Boomer, saying he was the only friend he had in the world. Sheriff Edmonds granted the request.

Despite constant searching throughout the entire investigative period, no other traces of human body parts were ever found. Lou Alice Brenk's family held a private memorial service for her.

"CAROL WAS CUT UP INTO 200 PIECES — GROUND UP, THEN COOKED!"

by Barry Bowe

Easter Sunday 1990 in Bensalem, Pennsylvania, won't be remembered for chocolate bunnies, egg hunts, fancy bonnets, parades, or jelly beans. Instead, the locals will always remember it for one of the grisliest crimes ever committed in Bucks County, a killing that some likened to Gary Heidnik's "House of Horrors," which had been discovered three years earlier in nearby Philadelphia.

Buck County starts where the northeast edge of Philadelphia ends. Bensalem hugs the city limits, following the contours of the serpentine Delaware River, Interstate 95, and the Amtrak right-of-way. Bristol Pike, paralleling I-95 and the train tracks, is a commercial strip domesticated with the occasional three-story brick apartment complex.

The Colonial Park Apartments, pinched between the highway and the tracks, lay in the 900 block of Bristol Pike. It was there that John Vincent DiGregorio, 60, and his divorced daughter Carol, 38, shared a two-bedroom unit.

For 10 years, bespectacled, white-haired John had worked as a printer in the local offices of a North Carolina-based film processing center. But life had rarely run smoothly for him.

When he was six years old, John DiGregorio's mother suffered a nervous breakdown. As a result, John and two siblings were placed in an orphanage, where they spent the next five years. At 16, near the end of World War II, John dropped out of school and joined the Marines. Three years later, he was discharged. The year was 1949. John got married the same year, and the marriage bore two children, Carol and a younger daughter. But in the late 1960s, John's wife left him and their two children. Divorce followed in 1970.

Carol was a teenager when her parents' matrimonial problems began. She was already somewhat disturbed because she believed that her mother loved her sibling more than she loved her. Her parents' divorce emotionally devastated her, and she soon required psychiatric attention.

By the time Carol reached her early 20s, her condition seemed to have stabilized. She married a New Jersey state trooper, and the newlyweds had one child. But in 1983, Carol's marriage ended in divorce, and Carol, who was 30 at the time, moved into the Colonial Park apartment with her father.

"[John] believed [Carol] needed love and kindness, and that would be enough to cure her," said someone close to the family. "He always seemed to think that love was the answer." But Carol remained a puzzle throughout the years.

On the one hand, Carol attended church regularly at St. Charles Boromeo Roman Catholic Church. During the fall semester of 1987, she attended classes at Holy Family College in Philadelphia. In the summers, Carol sunned herself at the apartment complex swimming pool and attended aerobics classes with a neighbor at a local gym. At times, she was witty and charming. But Carol had a bizarre side, as well.

Carol had been diagnosed as a paranoid-schizophrenic, which meant that she suffered delusions. She fantasized that she was the Virgin Mary, was married to God, and that her child had been conceived by immaculate conception. She scribbled graffiti on the apartment walls. Some of her scrawlings were extensions of her religious obsessions, such as the 10 commandments. But these were peppered with more profane and obscene scribblings, too.

There were times when Carol called her father Satan and locked him out of the apartment. Many nights, Carol would awaken during the height of the witching hours and scream out or bang on the walls. Sometimes, Carol would put pots on her head and say that aliens from outer space were attacking her. She once smeared cigarette ashes on her face and ate the butts.

Three times, police officers had been summoned to the DiGregorios' apartment to quell disturbances. The most serious incident took place in June 1988 when Carol ran to one of the neighboring apartments, banged on the door, and screamed, "Lady, lady, help me!" When the neighbor saw Carol's bloody head, she called the police.

Officers responded and were told that Carol had tried to attack her father with a knife. John said he'd hit her in the head with a hammer in self-defense. The officers were skeptical of the story. While no arrests were made, the incident resulted in Carol being committed to a psychiatric hospital, a recurring pattern that had existed for most of the eight years that father and daughter had been living together after Carol's divorce.

Carol would always return home after a short confinement and everything would be fine for a while. But eventually, Carol would stop taking her medication, all hell would break loose, and she'd be recommitted to the hospital for another short period of treatment, only to be released shortly thereafter.

The first four months of 1990 had seen a dramatic deterioration in Carol's condition. She never left the apartment. She rarely left her bedroom. She refused to bathe, and she changed her clothes only two or three times during those four months. She defecated in her bedroom, into pots and tin cans, and kept the containers of excrement in her room. Conditions were perfect for a major blowup as Easter Sunday morning dawned.

Carol's father woke up on Easter Sunday around 6:00 a.m., hoping to drive to New Jersey for a round of golf. John played golf almost every Saturday and Sunday, weather permitting. But when he saw that it was raining much too hard to play golf, he cancelled his game.

Around 8:30, John was in the kitchen standing at the sink. He turned on the faucet, but the water backed up. Something was clogging the drain. Upon inspection, John found a huge pile of coffee grounds. He knew *he* wasn't responsible for the blockage. Carol was the culprit, John thought. He began to yell at Carol as he tried to unclog the drain. It was a banal beginning to what would be a lethal argument between father and daughter.

At 52 minutes after midnight on Tuesday morning, 36 hours later, the phone rang at the Bucks County Police Department. Dispatcher Robin Shero took the call. The voice on the other end claimed to be a New Jersey resident who had some information about a homicide that had taken place on Easter Sunday morning in Bensalem.

Officers Kyle Sheluga, Fred Harran, Chris Barry, Dan Schwab, and Sergeant James Murphy responded to the Colonial Park Apartments. A few ticks before 1:00 a.m., the officers knocked on the door. Moments later, the door opened and the lawmen entered the apartment. Ironically, one of the first things they noticed were some huge letters Carol had written on one of the walls: THOU SHALT NOT KILL.

In the kitchen, the policemen observed three large pots sitting on the stove. Inside the cooking vessels, they saw what appeared to be small chunks of human body parts submerged in water, apparently cooked. Part of a human arm was sticking out of the garbage disposal and suspicious drippings coated the inside of the microwave oven. On the counters, the policemen found evidence of foul play; rubber gloves, a carving knife, a hacksaw, a knife sharpener, a keyhole saw, a razor knife, and a food processor.

Sergeant Murphy opened the refrigerator door. A severed human head rested on a top shelf, next to a container of milk. More body parts lined the other shelves. Bones were everywhere in the apartment, but there was not one sign of blood.

Reinforcements were called to the scene. Bensalem Detectives Terry Lachman and Bruce Van Sant were the first investigators to arrive, followed closely by District Attorney Paul Rubenstein.

"It certainly has to mark as one of the most bizarre results of a murder in Bucks County," the district attorney said. "I've never seen anything like this in over seventeen years as a prosecutor. It was one of the most hideous crimes [the officers will] ever see."

Frank Friel, Bensalem's director of public safety and a career law enforcement professional who'd handled more than 2,000 homicides for the Philadelphia Police Department, described the scene as "a horrific display of human suffering. I think this case rivals that of the Heidnik murders."

In 1988, Gary Heidnik was convicted for the murder, kidnapping, and rape of two women whom he'd imprisoned and tortured in his north Philadelphia basement. A Wall Street financial wizard, Heidnik's exploits were partially responsible for the story-line of the Academy Award-winning movie *The Silence of the Lambs*.

The investigators began an around-the-clock search, locating family members, interviewing friends, workmates, and neighbors, and trying to piece together the crime. In this manner, sketchy news of a mutilation passed from mouth to ear throughout Bensalem. One of John DiGregorio's co-workers heard that something had happened at his apartment and said, "I thought, my God, his daughter killed him!"

The Bucks County authorities called National Medical Services of Willow Grove to help with the collection of the body parts. Technicians spent the next 12 hours packing the pieces into containers. Before they finished their ghoulish task, they loaded assorted parts, skin, and body fluids into several large plastic garbage bags, four five-gallon containers, and two 55-gallon drums. The remains were then transported to a local funeral parlor which was specifically equipped to handle the autopsy of mutilated cadavers.

There, Coroner Thomas Rosko and Chief Deputy Coroner Halbert Fillinger sorted out the pieces.

"I am satisfied that there was one and only one victim," Rosko said after the gory postmortem. "Based on police evidence and the general circumstances of the case, I would say this was the daughter of [John DiGregorio]." The coroner ruled that the cause of death was massive hemorrhaging caused by several blunt instrument traumas to the head. Later that night, the pathologists positively identified the remains by matching fingerprints taken from the uncooked right hand.

Before Tuesday ended, a tearful John DiGregorio stood before District Justice Catharine Ritter and was charged with murder and abuse of a corpse at a 45-minute preliminary hearing. To the court, Officer Schwab described his arrival at the DiGregorio apartment earlier that morning.

"Where is she?" Officer Schwab asked DiGregorio.

"You're going to lock me up," DiGregorio answered.

"Where is she?" the policeman demanded.

"I cut her up and I'm cooking her," DiGregorio said.

Officer Schwab and Detective Lachman told the court that they'd found body parts in the hamper, inside three pots on the stove, in trash bags, and in the refrigerator. They found a torn sweatshirt and a torn blue shirt, which they believed had been worn by the victim, and they found several tools that had apparently been used in the dismemberment.

"[John DiGregorio] said he wanted to cut up [the body], cook it, grind it up, and get rid of the pieces," Detective Lachman told the district justice.

When Justice Ritter bound over John DiGregorio for trial in Bucks County Court without bail, Defense Attorneys Salvatore Averna and John Klamo alluded to an insanity defense. As DiGregorio was being led out of the courtroom reporters shouted questions at him.

"Did you love your daughter?"

"Oh, very much," DiGregorio answered.

"Are you sorry for what you did to her?"

"Yes, I am," he replied, unable to hold back a flow of tears. When his attorneys advised him not to make any more statements, he was led away. But reporters obtained comments from friends and neighbors who'd attended the hearing.

"He was the sweetest guy you ever wanted to know," said a neighbor.

"He wouldn't hurt a fly," said a close female friend. "John is a very kind, quiet, giving person, and I have nothing bad to say about him. It's very hard for me. I never turn my back on a friend. He's my friend and he doesn't have anybody."

But not everyone described the accused murderer in glowing terms.

"It's gruesome, yet fascinating," said District Attorney Paul Rubenstein. "You ask why someone would do this to his own child and what caused that. That's the compelling question." In fact, the district attorney found the question so fascinating and compelling that he decided to personally try the case himself, his first trial since convicting a pair of killers two years earlier.

DiGregorio's trial began on September 6th, before Judge Ward F. Clark in Doylestown. Hoping to catch a glimpse of the county's top prosecutor in action, more than two dozen lawyers swelled the gallery in the packed courtroom where John DiGregorio faced life imprisonment. Stacked against the prosecution was the claim that the defendant had acted in self-defense when he killed his daughter. There were no eyewitnesses.

"She'd been dismembered, hacked up and chopped up onto hundreds of pieces, and neatly wrapped in bags," the district attorney said in his opening remarks. "Does someone acting in self-defense put a child in a meat grinder? Does someone acting in self-defense put any portion of his child in a microwave oven?"

When his turn came, Defense Attorney Klamo said that "on the fifteenth, a murder was going to happen. Either to DiGregorio or to Carol. Carol came at her father with a

208

knife, as she had done many times in the past, and Mr. DiGregorio defended himself. The defendant is not a cold killer. He regrets everything that has happened and is in total disarray."

The case for the prosecution began with policemen painting a scenario of the crime based on their observations at the crime scene and on statements made by the defendant.

According to the official scenario, John DiGregorio woke up around 6:00 a.m. on Easter Sunday, planning to go golfing, but bad weather cancelled his outing. Around 8:30 he was using a pickle fork rod—a two-and-a-half-pound tool used to knock tie-rods out of automobile suspension systems—to unclog the garbage disposal. Earlier, Carol had dumped coffee grounds into the disposal but had failed to flush the grounds through the system. Soon John and Carol were arguing.

According to the defendant's statement at the time of his arrest, Carol cursed him, grabbed a carving knife, and threatened to slash him. John claimed that Carol had pulled a knife on him at least 10 times in the past. So that morning, when she came at him with the knife, he cold-cocked her with the pickle fork rod five or six times. Carol screamed twice, then fell backwards and landed on the living-room couch.

"I cried so much," John had told the officers at the time, "I can't cry anymore." When the policemen asked him why he hadn't called them to report the self-defense incident, DiGregorio replied, "I figured she was dead and all I thought about was the last incident when the police wouldn't believe me. I didn't know what to do, so I decided to cut her up and get rid of the body. I was afraid for my life and was frightened to death. I'm not glad Carol is dead, but I realize her suffering is over."

With his dead daughter lying on the couch, John cut off Carol's clothes with a pair of scissors. Then he carried her naked body into the bathroom and laid it in the tub. Three hours later, the butchery began.

Using a hacksaw and the same knife that John claimed

his daughter had threatened to use against him, he dismembered Carol's body. According to the arresting officer, John DiGregorio "fileted her and washed each piece under the water and put them in the [kitchen] pots."

For two hours, Dr. Fillinger described for the court the autopsy of Carol's remains. The deputy coroner said he counted 11 deep cuts to the front, back, and sides of Carol's skull, at least one of which caused her death.

"Carol was then cut up into well over two hundred pieces," Dr. Fillinger told the court, adding that some of the pieces were as small as half-an-inch by half-an-inch. "Frankly, I gave up counting pieces. There were a great number."

But the pathologist said he'd been unable to find some of the victim's parts: Carol's uterus, her vagina, her left ear, and her right nipple. Aside from the nipple, both of Carol's breasts had been found intact, uncooked, along with her heart, which was also raw. But most of the rest of her parts had been cooked in pots on the stove and in the microwave oven, including her head, which had been found in the refrigerator with the left side of the face sawed off. Traces of human blood, skin, and other tissue had been found on the microwave tray. In the medical examiner's opinion, the mutilations had all taken place postmortem.

On Monday morning, John DiGregorio awoke early once again. He cleaned the apartment, then left for work at 6:45. Co-workers said he appeared to be normal that day. He played cards at lunch time, as usual. That afternoon, he left for a few minutes to mail his income tax return. According to his boss, John asked for Tuesday off, saying that on Easter Sunday, Carol had run away again.

John left work at 4:45 Monday afternoon and returned to his apartment to see if anyone had discovered what had happened the previous day. From there, he visited a nearby discount store and bought a food processor, a knife sharpener, a keyhole saw, and some hacksaw blades. That evening, in his own words, John began "cooking more stuff for a couple of hours." Around seven o'clock, he called his other daughter, who lived in New Jersey.

John drove to Atco, New Jersey, later on. There, over coffee, he told his daughter and son-in-law that he'd killed Carol. He asked them not to mention anything about the crime to anyone. But at 12:52 Tuesday morning, the son-in-law called the Bucks County police to report the homicide.

Before he concluded the prosecution's case, District Attorney Rubenstein called three FBI forensic experts to ID fingerprints, hairs, and blood samples, which tightened the case circumstantially. Then the defense took over by calling character witnesses.

Many of John's friends, neighbors, and co-workers cried while describing him as a devoted father who deeply loved Carol. "His hope was she'd always get better," said one witness, "but the man when through living hell."

A psychiatrist testified that DiGregorio "felt like he was on fire" after he killed his daughter and he experienced a panic-anxiety attack, with effects similar to what someone would experience during a heart attack. The psychiatrist said that John had trouble remembering some of the details of the mutilation. For instance, he remembered Carol's nude body lying in the bathtub, but he couldn't recall ever seeing a drop of blood.

A psychologist said that John had ignored Carol's behavior through the years as long as she talked to herself in a conversational tone. But when she acted out and started screaming, he feared for his own life.

"He said he knew he'd die by his daughter's hand and [he'd] told others about it," the psychologist told the court. He said John cared for his daughter at home, rather than committing her permanently to a mental institution, because he denied that she had mental problems. However, when his denial weakened, due to her periodic violent flare-ups, he'd have Carol temporarily admitted to a psychiatric facility. After her treatment and for as long as she took her medication, Carol would behave in a normal manner. But in time, she would stop taking her medicine and her problems would begin anew.

"[John] felt like he was a prisoner in his own home," the psychologist said, "but he also felt sorry for her and he loved her."

The psychologist testified that, on the morning of the killing, John believed he could talk Carol into putting down the knife when she threatened him. But he was mistaken, and he wound up killing her. Then, a flood of anxiety, fear, shame, and guilt unnerved him.

"When all of those feelings come together," the psychologist told the court, "people do bizarre and strange things that they would never think of doing if they were in their right mind." The psychologist said John may have been mentally disturbed when he killed Carol, but he was not insane. Then the defense rested their case.

With his case looking tenuous, the district attorney called a surprise witness as the case wound down on Friday, September 17th, the ninth day of the trial. The name the bailiff called was that of John DiGregorio's other daughter.

"I had a hard time living with my conscience, and I thought the jury should know what's right," she said. To begin with, her father drove to her home in Atco on the night after the killing. At the time, he told her he couldn't report the incident to the police because he'd "go to the electric chair."

"I love my father," she told the court.

"Why did you lie?" John called out in a weak, quivering voice. "You liar. You liar," he repeated, before covering his face with his hands and sobbing uncontrollably.

"Oh, Daddy, I'm not lying," the witness answered. "I love my father and I love my sister." Stunned by the intense emotional exchange, the audience and jurors alike hung on every word of the young woman's testimony.

She said that in February 1989, her father had told her that Carol was not doing very well, and he mentioned that he was thinking about killing her. Several months later, he told her that Carol had painted the apartment walls with a chocolate cake.

"Oh, Daddy, I'd kill her," the witness had said at the time.

212

"I'm thinking of that," was his response. In March 1990, a month before Carol was killed, the witness met her father at the Sands Casino in Atlantic City. They were shooting dice at a five-dollar craps table when the daughter asked: "Daddy, how's Carol?"

"I'm thinking of killing her," he answered.

"I said, 'Daddy, you're losing your mind.'" But a few hours later, John repeated his desire to kill Carol.

On Easter Sunday night, when her father described how he'd dismembered her sister's body, the daughter started gagging and left the room. Later, he asked if he could use a trailer on her property to grind up Carol's bones.

"My sister did not want to get help," the witness told the court. "She didn't think she was sick, and my father didn't think she was sick."

"Can you at least tell the truth," John said to his daughter.

"You know I'm telling the truth, Daddy," she responded.

During the next recess, the defense attorney complained to the press. "Her testimony was for shock value," Defense Attorney Klamo said. "The prosecution saw its case was weak."

On Monday, the defense attorney was forced to call John DiGregorio to the witness stand to refute his daughter's testimony, a strategy he'd been trying to avoid.

"Every time I came to my senses," John told the packed courtroom, "there was another piece gone. It was like a bad dream to me. Just let me say, I don't remember a lot of things." Twisting a handkerchief and crying, the grandfatherly-looking defendant continued, "I don't know whether I was a very good father or wasn't a very good father. I tried my best. I love my children. I couldn't believe what I'd done."

With the verdict prepared to swing in either direction, the attorneys made their closing arguments on September 19, 1990. Defense Attorney Klamo quoted from Shakespeare's *King Lear*. "How sharper than a serpent's tooth it is to have a thankless child," the defense attorney intoned, referring to the defendant's daughter's damning testimony given the preceding Friday. "The commonwealth wants to make him out to be a cold, calculated killer giving a confession without remorse. He is going to go through life punished, tortured by this situation."

"Maybe your heart goes out to him on some level," said District Attorney Rubenstein as he began his summation. "Then close your eyes and think about what happened in that apartment. In her madness, in her mental illness, [Carol] wrote something on the wall that her father did not bother to read: 'Thou shalt not kill.'

"You don't cover up if it's in self-defense.

"Could you do this to your child, dismember your child while looking at her face? Could you do this to your worst enemy?"

The judge then charged and sequestered the jury for the night. They had five options for conviction: first-degree murder—that is, intentional, premeditated killing with malice, which carried a penalty of life imprisonment; third-degree murder—killing with malice but without a specific intent to kill, which carried a penalty of 10 to 20 years; voluntary manslaughter—unlawful killing without malice but with sudden passion after intense provocation from the victim, which carried a penalty of 5 to 10 years; involuntary manslaughter—unintentional killing by a reckless act, which carried a penalty of up to five years; and, finally, abuse of a corpse—intentional treatment of a corpse that would outrage ordinary family sensibilities, which carried a penalty of one to two years.

After nearly eight hours of deliberation, the eight-man, four-woman jury reached their decision around 3:45 the next afternoon. The foreman stood and announced the verdict: On the charge of first-degree murder: not guilty.

John DiGregorio sighed, his head dropping noticeably toward his chest.

On the charge of third-degree murder: not guilty.

John DiGregorio cried out loud and started wringing his hands as he awaited the remaining pronouncements.

On the charge of voluntary manslaughter: guilty.

"I am not happy with the verdict," John DiGregorio said after hearing that he'd also been found guilty of abuse of a corpse. Slowly, three sheriff's deputies escorted him out of the courtroom, past a gaggle of TV cameramen and reporters.

"If it wasn't for the mutilation," Defense Attorney Klamo said afterwards, "I think the jury would have come back with a not-guilty verdict. But it was just too much to get over the mutilation. It was just too much to get over."

"There was some sympathy for Mr. DiGregorio," the district attorney admitted, "but clearly he had no right to murder her. This case makes Hamlet look like the Bobbsey Twins. I've always had confidence in a Bucks County jury to separate fact from fiction, and there was no way this killing was in self-defense."

John DiGregorio is currently serving 6 to 12 years in the Pennsylvania penal system.

"WOLFMAN'S BIZARRE MUTILATIONS OF 3 GAYS!"

by Philip Westwood

KENSINGTON, ENGLAND
JULY 10, 1987

Jimmy Burns was feeling pretty low. It had been two weeks since the doctor had given him the news that he was suffering from AIDS. It was news that did not come as any great surprise to Jimmy. He was well aware that his life-style as an active and promiscuous homosexual meant that he stood a better than average chance of contracting the dreaded disease. But to be told officially by his doctor that he was probably going to die gave the stamp of finality to something that had previously been little more than a passing thought.

During those two weeks, Jimmy's moods had fluctuated between mild gloom and absolute depression. But by that particular evening of March 15, 1986, he had settled into a sort of fatal resignation as to his doomed future. If, however, Jimmy had been blessed with clairvoyant powers, his fear of AIDS would have melted away. Death resulting from AIDS is a slow process. It stretches over many months, even years. Fate had something much quicker in store for Jimmy Burns.

The rain beat drearily on the window of his even drearier basement apartment in the west London district of Kensington. But a wet night was not going to keep Jimmy Burns at home. He needed to go out. He needed his friends now more than he had ever needed them. The time he had left, he determined, was going to be spent in seeking out new experiences, new thrills. Jimmy was not concerned that he would, in all probability, pass on his killer disease to those with whom he came into contact. Why should he be concerned? It had not bothered the man who had given it to him.

Changing out of the uniform he wore for his job, the 37-year-old railroad conductor put on the uniform he wore for seeking out his pleasure. The black leather jacket was a perfect match for the tight black leather trousers and the tan, high-heeled cowboy boots. Burns looked at himself in the mirror. Despite the advancing years, he was still in fine shape. He could still pull the younger men and boys. He smiled with satisfaction at his reflection. The killer disease had not yet taken its hold. Just one last touch. In the top pocket of his jacket, Jimmy carefully placed a black handkerchief; a sure sign to those of his kind that he was seeking violent sex.

Jimmy closed his apartment door and set off down the road. His high-heeled boots clicked on the wet sidewalk. A few passersby stared momentarily at him, but took little notice.

Jimmy walked the short distance to the Earls Court District. He walked into a few pubs, but there was little action. The rain had kept most of his friends indoors. So he made his way back to Kensington and stopped in at a pub where he felt things might be more lively. He was not wrong.

Leaning against the bar was a young man Jimmy had not seen before. But he knew right away that the man was a kindred spirit. He wore blue jeans that were almost slashed to ribbons, a sign that, like Jimmy's black handkerchief, showed the man wanted gay sex that was both bizarre and violent. Jimmy and the man talked for a while, and then left the pub, smiling, arm in arm.

Early the next morning, two hobos were searching through the basement of a derelict house in Warwick Road, Kensington. They had spent the previous rainy night in a shop doorway, and now they were looking for somewhere a little more comfortable where they might be able to get the sleep that the rain had denied them. The basement seemed an ideal spot—apart from an unpleasant and pungent odor.

The men settled themselves down in a corner and closed their eyes. But that smell was really bad. Even though they were very tired, they couldn't get to sleep until they got rid of it. It seemed to be coming from something in the darkness on the other side of the basement.

Muttering under his breath, one of the men struck a match and shuffled off in the direction of the smell. His friend stayed where he was and continued with his efforts to get to sleep. A startled cry soon put a stop to that.

"Get the police!" shouted the man with a match. His friend sat bolt upright. The police were usually the last people these men wanted to see.

"What is it?" demanded the man in the corner.

"Come and see for yourself," invited the first man.

The first man struck another match. The second man looked at the sight revealed by the flickering light. "I'll get the police," he whispered.

Detective Chief Superintendent Jim Begg looked down at Jimmy Burns' body as it lay against the wall of the basement. The cause of death was strangulation which, forensic experts would later establish, had been carried out with a black silk scarf. But, for the moment, it was the other things that had been done to Jimmy Burns that interested Begg.

The dead man's leather trousers had been removed, and homosexual intercourse had taken place. That did not surprise Jim Begg. What attracted the detective's attention was that Burns' jacket and shirt had been removed and his

218

Andrei Chikatilo, the world's worst serial killer,
yawns during his trial.

Ricky Green, who confessed
to four grisly slayings.

William King.

William King, Jr., his father's murderer.

Jeffrey Dahmer.

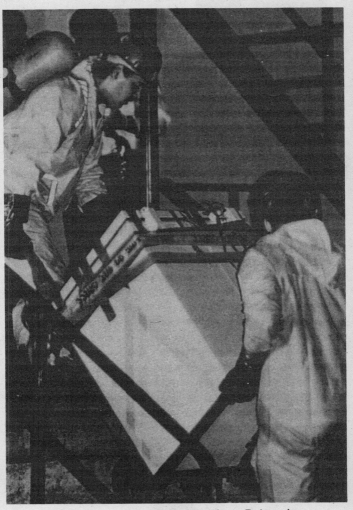

The freezer being removed from Dahmer's
apartment contained three heads, a heart, two
lungs and various internal organs.

Judith Garcia
in happier days.
Garcia was stabbed
so many times,
the knife bent.

Garcia's killer,
Randy Denton Fisher.

A man walking along the riverbank under this highway bridge discovered Julie Murphy's head in a beach bag.

Charles Commander killed his roommate Julie Murphy in a dispute over the rent on this apartment.

Herbert Brenk (*left*) is on death row for dismembering his wife with this saw.

Cooler containing the buttocks of Lou Alice Brenk.

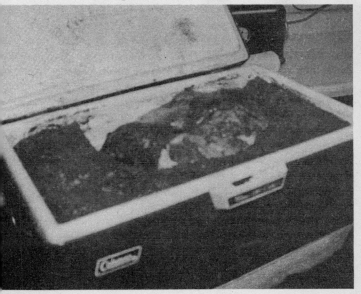

The unremarkable apartment complex where Carol DiGregorio was hideously murdered by her father, John.

Parts of DiGregorio's remains were gathered up and carried out in several large garbage bags, four five-gallon containers, and two of these 55-gallon drums.

Larry Duane White. A homeless man found White's legs in a dumpster.

Robert Eugene Bennett pleaded guilty to White's murder, and remains a suspect in the disappearance of his own wife.

Malcolm Green was on parole from a murder conviction when he killed Clive Tully.

This stretch of road can be busy, but it wasn't when Tully's body was dumped.

naked body had been slashed with a rusty razor blade. Burns' body had then been smeared with excrement; and it was the smell of this that had prevented the two hobos from getting to sleep.

But the most bizarre thing about Burns was that his tongue was missing. Apparently, his killer had bitten it off!

The murder of Jimmy Burns quickly became the sole topic of conversation among those who frequented London's gay pubs and clubs. The killer, who was dubbed the "Wolfman" because of the strange mutilation he had performed on Jimmy, became an object of fear, and even panic. Begg had warned that this killer could strike again, and had advised those who dwelt in the twilight world of sleazy nightclubs and backstreet bars to be constantly on their guard. Homosexuals on the north side of the River Thames ensured that they sought only the company of friends whom they had known for a long time and whom they could trust. That way, they felt reasonably safe.

On the south side of the Thames, however, the feelings of fear were at a much lower level. In some places they did not exist at all.

On the evening of Friday, April 4th, Anthony Connolly left his apartment on the Crowley Estate, in the south London district of Brixton, and made his way to the area's best known homosexual pub in search of his weekend excitement. Twelve months earlier, the 26-year-old waiter had arrived in Brixton from a town in the north of England. He had hoped that his peculiar tendencies would find a more ready acceptability in London than they had in his hometown. The British, in general, find homosexuality difficult to come to terms with. They tolerate it because the law says that they must. But they don't like it. In many provincial towns, a favorite pastime among adolescents on Saturday nights is to seek out anyone who looks remotely like a gay and beat them up—a quaint old British custom known as "queer bashing." Anthony Connolly had suffered many such beatings back home.

But in London things had been much better. Connolly had experienced no difficulty in finding men like himself; during his year in the English capital, he had a steady succession of boyfriends.

But on that evening of April 4th, Connolly was footloose and fancy-free. His last regular boyfriend had contracted AIDS, and Connolly had decided that was a good time to put an end to their relationship.

After spending a pleasant evening in the pub, Connolly left to make his way home. He was seen walking towards his apartment at around one o'clock on the morning of Saturday, April 5th. At the time, he was alone. But, before he reached home, he met a man. That man was to have a profound effect on Anthony Connolly's life. He ended it!

At 5:15 P.M. on that Saturday afternoon, three children were playing near the railroad tracks outside Brixton. Running and chasing each other in the way that children do, they had soon crossed the tracks and made their way into a train yard where hundreds of wagons were stacked waiting to be loaded. Since it was Saturday afternoon, there was nobody around. The children's happy laughter echoed around the deserted yard as they ran in and out between the empty wagons.

Suddenly, they spotted a shed at the end of the yard. It looked like a good place to play, so they ran towards it. The children were still laughing and shouting as they went in. But their laughter ended abruptly. There was a momentary silence, and then a piercing scream.

The children had been laughing as they entered the shed. But when they left it, they were crying and almost hysterical. They ran blindly out of the yard and back across the tracks. When they reached the street, they were stopped by a couple of passersby and taken to a nearby police station.

At the station, the desk sergeant had difficulty in

making out what the children were saying. They rambled on incoherently about "a dirty man with no clothes on," a terrible smell and blood.

It was a little while before officers could persuade the children to take them and show them the cause of their hysteria. But, eventually, the children agreed to accompany the officers to the shed in the train yard, though they steadfastly refused to enter the small wooden building. The detectives who did go in were not surprised at the children's reluctance.

Anthony Connolly lay on his back. He was quite naked; his studded, black leather jacket, his jeans, his green T-shirt, and his socks, underclothes, and boots were liberally scattered around the confines of the tiny shed.

Connolly's body bore the marks of several dozen razor slashes, though they were initially difficult to see beneath the excrement that covered him from head to toe.

But one thing about Connolly was plain to see. His mouth was wide open. At first sight, it appeared to detectives that the dead man's mouth was abnormally large. Then they realized why. Connolly's tongue was missing. Whoever had killed him had bitten it off.

Anthony Connolly's body was taken to Southward mortuary, where an autopsy revealed the cause of death to be strangulation.

Police set up an incident room at Brixton. A similar incident room investigating the death of Jimmy Burns had been set up in Kensington. Though the killings were remarkably similar, detectives could not assume a definite connection at that early stage. Copycat killings — particularly where such perverse elements are involved — are not unknown. So the sleuths decided to keep an open mind.

Like all major cities throughout the world, London has its share of hobos; homeless drifters who stagger through one day at a time with little thought of what tomorrow will bring, because they know that it will in all probability

221

bring just another 24 hours of misery and hopelessness. With a shop doorway for a home and the bottle for a friend, these pathetic creatures shuffle like zombies through the darkened city streets; forgetful of the past that brought them to their present circumstances and mindless of the future.

At two o'clock on the morning of Friday, April 18th, one such pitiful specimen leaned against a lamp post on the Hungerford Bridge, which crosses the River Thames. He had a problem.

In the course of his nocturnal wanderings, the hobo had come across a real treasure. Lying in the gutter was a cigarette that was only half-smoked. He'd picked it up, and, with some careful manipulation of his hands—not easy when the brain is befuddled by methylated spirits—he had managed to return the flattened object to its original tubular shape.

Cackling with delight at this achievement, he stuck the half-smoked cigarette between his lips. It was then that his problem dawned on him. The hobo didn't have a match—or anything else with which he could light the cigarette. What was he going to do?

He was still pondering the problem when a young man came strolling towards him across the bridge. The hobo probably didn't notice the young man's slashed jeans and black leather jacket. All that concerned him was whether the young man might have the means to enable him to enjoy his cigarette.

"Got a light, mate?" the hobo asked as the young man approached.

The young man stopped, felt in a pocket of his leather jacket and took out a lighter. He flicked the catch on top of the lighter, and a flame appeared. Cupping a hand around the flame, the young man pushed it towards the hobo who aimed the end of his cigarette at the tiny fire. Blue smoke curled upwards into the night air.

"Thanks, mate," said the hobo as he turned and walked

away, puffing contentedly on his cigarette.

The hobo had gone a matter of only a few yards when it suddenly seemed as if the world was falling apart around him. A hand gripped his shoulder and spun him around. He saw the young man's face, but only for a moment. A knee in the groin sent the old hobo crashing to the ground. The cigarette fell from his lips and rolled away along the sidewalk. The hobo could see it and tried to make his way towards it. He could not afford to lose such a treasure. The hobo stretched out his hand to try and retrieve the cigarette. It was the only thing that mattered to him. But something was holding him back.

He lay facedown on the sidewalk. Someone was kneeling on him, preventing him from reaching the cigarette. Why should they be doing that? Did they also want the cigarette?

From somewhere behind him, a hand came forward across his nose and mouth. The hand was holding something. It looked like a stocking. Another hand appeared around the other side of his face and took hold of the free end of the stocking. The hobo could feel it drawn tight across his nose. Then he felt it move downwards across his mouth and onto his neck. The knee in his back was pushing him forward, but the stocking around his neck was pulling him back. He could still see the cigarette. It was only a few feet away. Maybe he could reach it. He stretched out his hand towards it. The stocking around his neck was getting tighter. He could not breathe. Why was the young man doing this to him? The hobo had done nothing. He had only asked for a light for his cigarette. He could still see the cigarette, glowing on the sidewalk. It was tantalizingly close. He looked at the glow. It was not so bright and it seemed strangely blurred. Breathing was impossible now. The hobo looked at the cigarette and knew that he would never reach it. Someone else would get it. As he watched, the glow grew dimmer and dimmer until it finally disappeared altogether. . . .

The hobo's body was found on the bridge. He was never identified and his body now lies in an unmarked grave somewhere in London.

A little less than a week after the nameless hobo was killed, a young hospital orderly entered a club in Kensington. It was around eight o'clock on the evening of Thursday, April 24th, and 22-year-old Damien McCluskey was in need of company.

Being on your own in a big city full of people can be the most depressing kind of loneliness. If that city happens to be in a foreign land and many miles from your own home, then those feelings of desolation can really start to hurt until the pain becomes almost physical.

In the few months since he had arrived from his native Ireland, Damien McCluskey had experienced friendlessness and isolation. It had gotten so bad that he was prepared to speak to anyone who gave him just the hint of a friendly smile.

Damien looked at the people gathered in the club. They were talking and drinking happily among themselves. Most of them seemed to be in groups. It would be difficult for him to break in.

Then, at the end of the bar, he noticed a young man who, like himself, was alone. The man smiled at Damien. He returned the smile, and went over to him. He may not have noticed the unusual way the man was dressed—a black leather jacket, slashed blue jeans, and expensive brown leather, Spanish riding boots. If he did notice, then he was not bothered. The two men talked for about an hour, about what is not recorded. But they seemed to get on well. When they left the club at around 9:30 p.m., the man had his arm around Damien's shoulder.

Damien's body was found the next morning in a basement apartment in Cromwell Road, Earls Court.

Like Jimmy Burns and Anthony Connolly, Damien McCluskey had been strangled and subjected to a frenzied razor attack before being covered with excrement. His

224

tongue had also been bitten off.

By the beginning of May, police at Kensington and Brixton had coordinated their efforts to track down the Wolfman. A special squad under the command of Detective Superintendent John Shoemaker had been set up, and was based at Croydon, a town some 10 miles to the south of London.

The 20 detectives making up the squad were all volunteers. The work they were to undertake was both difficult and dangerous in that they had to infiltrate — and become part of — the twilight world of the sadomasochistic homosexuals who frequented the bars and clubs of the seamier side of London.

The first thing they had to do was to make themselves as familiar as possible with the type of people with whom they would be dealing. They had no direct experience regarding the workings of the community of which they had to become a part. But they had to learn — and learn fast.

Initially, they spent hour upon hour watching the movie *Cruising* in which Al Pacino played a cop tracking down a sadistic killer in the homosexual community of New York. The movie taught the sleuths a lot, including the system of color-coded handkerchiefs that the gays used as an indication of the particular type of sex they were seeking. They learned what movements and gestures to use, and the special meaning of certain words and phrases.

With their "training" completed, the detectives set to work. In teams of four, they toured the bars and clubs that were the known haunts of the more bizarre and outlandish types of homosexuals. Each night, they hoped that a chance encounter would bring them into contact with the Wolfman, and so enable them to put an end to his nefarious activities forever. But luck eluded them. All they got were some of the most unusual suggestions of ways to spend an evening. A number of detectives had to

225

do some pretty fast talking to extricate themselves from situations that promised experiences that were both undreamed of and unwanted.

But then the undercover men got a break. It came in the unlikely form of Billy Allen.

Billy was a 30-year-old homosexual who liked to have casual relationships with men — nothing too heavy, just one-nighters. He was not into violence.

On the evening of May 7th, Billy was leaving a pub in south London's Nine Elms district when he encountered a handsome young man standing outside the door. They got to talking; one thing led to another, and they agreed to go to a nearby truck yard for sex. After finding a dark, quiet corner well away from prying eyes, they started to undress. The young stranger produced a small bottle from his jacket pocket, and offered it to Billy.

"Sniff this," invited the stranger.

On asking what the bottle contained, Billy was told that it was amyl-nitrate — a substance used by homosexuals as an aphrodisiac.

So Billy took a sniff. The substance had an immediate effect. Billy felt high. Any inhibitions that he had just disappeared. He wanted to make love — to anyone.

Billy passed the bottle back to the stranger, who also took a sniff. He seemed to be affected in the same way as Billy. So, with their mutual passions aroused, they started rolling around in the quiet corner of the truck yard. Soon, both were oblivious to the sound of their grunts and groans. Billy no longer cared whether anyone could see or hear them.

Billy turned and lay facedown on the ground. He spread his legs apart, anticipating the stranger's next move. But what actually happened was something that Billy was not expecting.

The stranger pulled Billy's head back. In his hand he held what Billy thought to be a black stocking. He was trying to get the stocking around Billy's neck. To Jimmy

226

Burns and Anthony Connolly, such a move would not have come as a surprise. Being into masochistic sex, they would have expected to be half-strangled during a love-making session. But Billy Allen, in that respect at least, was straight. Whatever the circumstances, if someone tried to put a stocking around his neck it meant only one thing—and it had nothing to do with sex.

With his other hand, the stranger tried to grab the free end of the stocking which dangled so menacingly before Billy's startled eyes. He felt the stranger's arm roughly brush the side of his face. He saw the stranger's hand shoot towards the stocking—and miss!

That was enough for Billy. All thought of passion left him in an instant. Uppermost in his mind at that moment was how to get away.

In one swift movement, Billy Allen got to his knees and swung his left arm backwards. His elbow connected with something soft, and the stranger let out a shriek of pain. Gathering up whatever clothes he could, Billy sprang to his feet and started to run. He didn't stop running until he had reached the front door of his apartment.

Once inside his apartment, Billy flopped down on his bed and stayed there until he had gotten his breath back. When he had recovered, he started to think about what he should do next.

He was hesitant about reporting the matter to the police. Publicity was the last thing he wanted. Colleagues at work didn't know about his homosexuality, and he was fearful of their reactions should they find out. Maybe he should keep quiet and forget all about it, he thought to himself.

But then he remembered reading the newspaper reports about the murders of Jimmy Burns and Anthony Connolly. It gradually dawned upon him that the man with whom he had gone to the truck yard was in all probability the murderer who the police were seeking. Billy got a strange feeling in the pit of his stomach when he realized just how close he had come to being another statistic on the roster of the Wolfman; another unsolved homicide in the files of the London police. That settled it. He had to report the matter; publicity or no publicity.

So Billy Allen contacted the police at Brixton, and they put him in touch with the special squad at Croydon.

The squad welcomed Billy with open arms. He was their first positive lead, and they would do everything they could to protect him. He had committed no crime, they told him, and so he needn't fear. They would ensure his anonymity. Even at any subsequent court hearing, his real identity would not be revealed.

Billy felt relieved, and offered to help the squad in any way he could. There was only one way and it would not be easy. Billy would have to visit all of the pubs likely to be frequented by the Wolfman, in the hope that he would be able to make a positive identification. Billy was not too happy about that, even when he was assured that officers would be with him and would not let him out of their sight. But he agreed.

So at nine o'clock on the evening of Thursday, May 15, 1986, Billy Allen set out on the quest for the Wolfman. Four undercover detectives followed at a discreet distance, ready to move in immediately should trouble arise. They visited pubs in Kensington, Earls Court, Nine Elms and Charing Cross, but without success. There was no sign of the man who had attacked Billy in the truck yard.

Shortly after midnight, they were in Brixton. This was to be their last round of pubs before they called it a night. The first two pubs they tried were quiet. No sign of the Wolfman anywhere. So they moved on to the third. It happened to be the pub in which Anthony Connolly had been drinking on the night he was murdered; though the detectives thought it best to keep that piece of information from Billy.

Billy opened the pub door and went in. It was full of men laughing and talking. Some were dancing together to the sounds of music coming from a battered old jukebox that stood in the corner.

Billy peered through the heavy, smoke-laden atmosphere. Most of the men were in couples or in groups. Gradually, Billy's eyes became accustomed to the subdued light. He noticed that one man was alone at the bar. Billy froze. He recognized the man. The four detectives noticed the sudden fear that had come over their star witness. They moved closer.

"What is it?" whispered Detective Sergeant Denis Gregory.

Billy started to shake. "Over by the bar," he told the officer. "It's him!"

"Right," said Gregory in a matter-of-fact tone. "Go over and confront him."

"What!" shrieked Billy in utter disbelief.

"We must have a positive identification," explained Gregory. "Don't worry. We'll be right with you."

Trembling with fear, Billy made his way over to the man at the bar. The man looked up and obviously recognized Billy. Billy wondered what the man would do. Would he attack him? Or would he simply try to run? He did neither. What he did do took both Billy and the detectives completely by surprise.

The man smiled warmly at Billy. "Hello," he said, as if he were greeting a friend he had not seen for many years. "How are you? Keeping well, I trust."

Billy looked at the man. "You tried to kill me," he said sharply.

Detective Gregory then stepped forward, produced his identification, stated the nature of the investigation, and asked the man to accompany himself and his colleagues to their headquarters in Croydon. The man willingly agreed, which came as something of a surprise to the detectives. They had expected at least a token resistance. But there was none.

Back at Croydon, the man was only too happy to

cooperate. His name was Michael Lupo and he was 34 years old. Quite freely and without any prompting, he confessed to the murders of Jimmy Burns and Anthony Connolly, as well as those of Damien McCluskey and the hobo; though he didn't really know why he killed the hobo. "It just came over me," he said. "Something inside me told me I had to do it."

But that was far from the end of the story. The case of Michael Lupo was to involve many more people before it was finished. It was to reach into the world of the rich and the famous, and to touch those at the very top of the social ladder.

Michael Lupo was the son of a bricklayer. He had been born Michele de Marco Lupo in the small town of Genzano di Lucavia, in the south of Italy. As a boy, he had been blessed with a singing voice of great beauty and pureness of tone. So good was his voice that he became a choirboy in the great cathedral of Bologna. He was also highly intelligent, and his future seemed assured when, on leaving school, he went to college to study languages. His studies went well.

Things started to go wrong for Michael in 1972 when he was drafted into the 22nd Commando Unit of the Italian Army, to do his military service.

Since his early teens, he had been aware of feelings that drew him towards members of his own sex. Yet he had always managed to suppress them. He had liaisons with girls, but they were only superficial and meant nothing to him. In fact, he only went out with girls because it was the expected thing to do, and he was anxious that his family did not discover his homosexual trait.

But in the army he met men who, although only the same age as himself, were nevertheless experienced in most aspects of homosexual sex. Soon, Michael had been initiated and had become a willing participant in nightly sex sessions.

But though his new-found experiences gave him the

230

satisfaction he had denied himself for so long, they also left him with feelings of doubt and degradation. At the end of each session, Michael felt dirty and ashamed. What he was doing was against the teachings of his strict Catholic upbringing.

So he decided that, when his military service was finished, he would make a fresh start in a new country. That was how, in 1975, he came to be in London and working in a boutique.

He had a real flair for the work, and before long he had a boutique of his own. It was a great success, and within a couple of years he had a chain of such establishments scattered throughout London's fashionable and prosperous West End.

His clientele consisted of those with plenty of disposable income; television and movie personalities, political figures, and those in positions of power and influence.

Being fluent in five languages, and a witty and charming conversationalist, soon led to Michael being invited to all of the high-society parties and dinners. The bricklayer's son from southern Italy had come a long way. He moved easily through a world where social position is everything, and the only god is money.

But, in such a world, there is inevitably a darker side. To some people, sex in all of its perverted forms becomes a top priority. They actively seek out new ways to pep up their jaded appetites. It was all too easy for Michael Lupo—who already had male lovers from the fashion world in Berlin, Amsterdam, New York and San Francisco—to become enmeshed in the seamier side of his new life-style.

Detectives who searched his $500,000 home in the Chelsea district of London found one room outfitted in the style of a medieval torture chamber. Whips, chains, and other instruments for inflicting pain on his more than willing partners were there in abundance.

But it was a set of seven innocent-looking, leather-bound books that were found locked in a safe that caused the officers most concern. The books contained the names and addresses of 700 rich and famous people. Although it was quickly established that none of them were connected with the Wolfman's killings, the question of just how far these people were involved in Lupo's world of perverted sex was not so easily answered.

Some of the names in the books were of so sensitive a nature that their investigation was passed on to the government intelligence agency, M15. Others were deemed to be of a different type of sensitivity. Probing their involvement with Michael Lupo became the task of officers of the Royal and Diplomatic Protection Squads. The results of investigations by officers of these squads, and of those by agents of M15, are not a matter of public record.

In the 12 months between his arrest and his trial, Michael Lupo was examined regularly by a team of three psychiatrists. They probed his mind, trying to find evidence of insanity. After all, anyone who did what Lupo had done must be insane, musn't they? It was too frightening to contemplate that the killings were the work of a rational human being.

But after a year of constant examination, the psychiatrists were forced to conclude that Lupo was perfectly sane. It came as something of a surprise to these experts. But it was no surprise to Lupo himself.

Early in the investigation he had told detectives, "I could say that I'm sorry for what I did, but I'm not. I knew exactly what I was doing. I was not drunk—and I'm certainly not mad!"

At Lupo's trial at the Old Bailey in the summer of 1987, Prosecutor Julian Bevan told the jury that the killings were Lupo's way of obtaining sexual satisfaction. "In other words," the prosecutor concluded, "he enjoyed it."

On Friday, July 10, 1987, Michael Lupo was convicted of four counts of murder. He showed no emotions as the verdicts were announced.

The judge, Sir James Miskin, sentenced Lupo to four terms of life imprisonment, plus seven years for attempting to murder Billy Allen.

In cases where a prisoner receives multiple life sentences, it is usual for the judge to make a recommendation regarding the minimum number of years that must be served before parole is considered. But in Lupo's case, Judge Miskin decided to make no such recommendation. Explaining why, the judge said that he was confident that, in this particular instance, life meant exactly what it said.

After many years of debauched living, Michael Lupo has contracted AIDS. He will, in all probability, die in prison within the next few years.

EDITOR'S NOTE:
Billy Allen is not the real name of the person so named in the foregoing story. A fictitious name has been used because there is no reason for public interest in the identity of this person.

"BLONDE'S BODY WASHED ASHORE — BIT BY BIT!"

by Dr. Clarence Miller

VENTNOR, NEW JERSEY
OCTOBER 7, 1983

For many months, sounds of strife had been coming from a townhouse on Marshal Court, in Ventnor, New Jersey. Then, early in the evening of February 17, 1981, neighbors heard a shrill female voice shrieking in terror. They called the police.

Upon entering the residence, lawmen confronted Brewster Bart, a tall and hairy faced former green beret who was threatening to kill Keerans Carter, his live-in girlfriend. Bart's powerful muscles were trembling from the effort of restraining his rage over an alleged affair between pert little Keerans and a slightly built young man who was also living in the apartment. Though the conflict revolved around the young man, Angelo D'Amato, he was standing nonchalantly off to the side, his cherubic face expressionless under its mop of dark brown hair.

The officers restored calm. Then, after determining that Keerans had not been harmed and no one wanted to press charges, the lawmen left.

Thereafter, the calls to police about the strife at the townhouse ceased. But neighbors were now voicing another concern: Where, they asked, was Keerans Carter?

How had she vanished so suddenly? One persistent young woman insisted Keerans would not have willingly left town without letting her know.

In response to the community's concern, detectives visited Bart in the evening, upon his return from work. The probers found D'Amato also present. They took each man aside to be questioned separately.

Bart told the probers he did not know anything about Keerans's present whereabouts. However, he added, he could supply them with some names and addresses of her friends and relatives.

"You were living together, weren't you?" sleuths asked.

"Yes," he responded. "We were living as man and wife for two years. Then my love was gone, and I wanted her out of the apartment, so she left."

"Just like that?" the prober pressed.

"What else could she do? Only my name is on the lease. She knew I could just pick her up and throw her out, so she left," Bart explained.

The lawmen questioning D'Amato in the adjoining room, then brought in their report. The probers found the young man's answers agreed completely with those given by Bart.

"This could mean both men rehearsed the story," reasoned one detective. "Then they must both be involved in her disappearance," he added, following this line of thought.

"For what possible reason?" another investigator wondered aloud. "Maybe the answers both men gave were the same only because they were telling the truth?" he continued. Then he added hopefully, "The girl could be somewhere safe and sound. She could have gone without saying anything because of the fight."

"She was vulnerable, leaving like that," a lawmen suggested, "and could have gotten hurt somewhere else."

The probers decided to press on with the investigation while the case was still fresh. "Because too many missing persons cases are never solved," said a veteran on the force, speaking for the rest of the staff.

The detectives then canvassed neighbors, transit workers, cab drivers and others who Keerans could have met along routes used to leave town, but no one recalled seeing any young, blonde haired girl fitting her description recently.

Investigators checking Bart's past found out he had earned the reputation of being resourceful and cunning while in the service, and since getting out, he had gotten into trouble for drug possession. His recent lifestyle, however, was characterized by uninterrupted daily work in his own auto body shop, and this pattern had not changed at the time of Carter's disappearance around the 18th of February.

Because there was no hard evidence of any actual crime, the active investigation by the lawmen ceased. But they were kept alert by the continuing mystery of Carter's disappearance.

Then, in November of 1981, there was a startling development. Ventnor police headquarters received a call from Captain Daniel Bloom of Yardville prison. It was about an inmate who claimed to know of "a very serious crime committed somewhere in the state of New Jersey." The inmate claimed that a new prisoner, who had recently arrived from Ventnor, had confessed to this crime.

Convict Stewart Lee, who had the reputation of a braggart and a liar, said that the new prisoner, who could also be creative with the truth, had told him that he strangled a girl and cut up her corpse, then threw it "in or near a body of water."

Atlantic County Investigator Thomas Prendergast recalled that among the many missing persons cases not yet solved, there was the case involving Keerans Carter from Ventnor who had not yet been heard from. He immediately returned the call and requested a meeting with the prisoner.

Investigator Porcelli was also concerned with the Carter case, and so he joined Prendergast in the trip to Yardville. On arriving, the detectives learned that Lee had first approached a social worker, who arranged a meeting with Capt. Daniel Bloom of Internal Affairs. The social worker and Bloom then became convinced that Lee was telling the truth, because he wanted nothing but protection for the information. His life depended on the authorities believing him, he said.

Prendergast and Porcelli then proceeded to question Lee. The convict said he began living in terror during the summer of 1981. It was soon after he became friends with a recent arrival who was sentenced to Yardville for cashing checks of fictitious employees created on a company's payroll. The new prisoner's powers of invention excited Lee's admiration, until it became evident that one of the stories related by his new friend was true and that it was dangerous for him to know about it.

It happened during one particularly boring day, said Lee. His new friend, Angelo D'Amato, suggested they pass the time by having a bragging contest. The winner was to be the one who could describe the worst crime. But it also had to be a crime that he had actually committed.

The contest began with D'Amato describing a crime he had been convicted of in 1977, when he bludgeoned and stabbed a young man to death, then cut a leg off the body—allegedly because the victim made homosexual advances. And then D'Amato bragged that he had also done something even worse which no one even knew about. He said he had strangled a girl, and had cut her up into pieces, then stuffed the parts in trash bags and threw them in garbage bins and waterways in the Atlantic City area.

To check on the possibility that this was just an attempt to obtain a lighter sentence, a lawman asked Lee why be believed a story which was obviously an exaggerated version of D'Amato's earlier crime, and apparently invented for the occasion only to win the contest.

Lee admitted he didn't believe the story when he first heard it. That was during the summer. But since early November, D'Amato had been threatening him and his family, warning Lee he would suffer if anything was revealed. Then to show he could actually carry out his threat, D'Amato produced the address of Lee's sister. And when asked how he got it, D'Amato explained, "The same way I'll get you if you say anything about the girl." Then he bragged about his underworld connections.

The probers considered it possible the crime had indeed occurred, for that would explain the sudden disappearance of Keerans Carter. So they arranged to speak to D'Amato.

Upon being questioned, D'Amato said he could add nothing to what he had told detectives when they first investigated Keerans' disappearance. Also, what possible motive could he have to kill her? No, Bart did not murder Keerans either, said D'Amato. Bart did want her out of the house, but didn't have to resort to murder in order to have her leave. Then D'Amato added that he wouldn't be stupid enough to make believe he committed a crime someone else was guilty of just in order to win a contest. As to why Lee would invent such a story, it was the detectives' job to figure that out, D'Amato told them.

The investigators then arranged to reinterview Bart, and to have D'Amato closely observed, and also to have those areas searched where Lee had said trash bags filled with body parts had been dropped.

The close observation of D'Amato by the probers produced immediate results when a phone call from D'Amato to Bart had been recorded. Detectives had D'Amato on tape telling Bart they should stick to their original story about Keerans leaving without telling anyone where she went. As a matter of fact, before D'Amato had an opportunity to make the call Bart had already been reinterviewed and had not altered his story.

D'Amato was then reinterviewed by the lawmen and

asked to explain the call. It was an act of friendship, he said. D'Amato went on to explain that after the detectives spoke to him he began worrying about his friend Bart possibly panicking and making things worse. So D'Amato said he called to reassure Bart, to let him know he had a friend who would back him up with the truth.

Though Keerans' disappearance remained a mystery, detectives did not have any actual evidence that a crime had occurred, so the case of Keerans Carter was at a dead end. All the lawmen could do was wait and keep alert.

Then five months later, on May 28, 1982, Inv. Prendergast received a call about someone finding skeletal remains. The first call was recorded at 10:50 a.m. The location was a strip of township between Somers Point and Longport, where salt marshes border the road. A plastic trash bag had been found far from the side of the road, near a closed bar. The bag appeared to have washed up out of the water, off the Longport-Somers Point Boulevard. It was blown up like a balloon and was dripping wet. Upon ripping it open, noxious gases escaped and dry bones spilled out.

Reporters, smelling a sensational story, managed to surround one of the officers.

"The bag contained bones," he said. "They were pretty clean, and there was something that looked like a small rib cage, but no skull. If they are human, I don't see how they could ever identify who it was."

Then there was the arrival of Lieutenant (now captain) James Barber, the Atlantic County Major Crimes Squad commander. After examining the material, he judged it to be possibly human and had it sent over to the New Jersey medical examiner.

"We really don't know what kind of bones they were," Barber said, "and it would be premature to speculate at this point." Because there was no skull in the bag, he explained, a quick determination was difficult. Then he assured the press that an investigator from the squad

239

would meet with the medical examiner as soon as possible.

Prendergast also arranged to meet the medical examiner, Dr. Geetha Natarajn. The sleuth was told the bones did come from a human being, but medical records were required to establish the identity of the corpse.

The first records provided by probers to pathologist Natarajn were those of Keerans Carter. Dr. Natarajn then reported to the lawmen on the relationship she found between these medical records and the data obtained by examining the torso.

Keerans had undergone surgery to enlarge her breasts, said Dr. Natarajn. The torso included breast-enlarging insertions—plastic bags filled with a saline solution, Natarajn explained. The measurements of the insertions found in the torso, Natarajn added, were identical to those Keerans had had implanted, according to her medical records. Also, X-rays from Keerans' 1979 automobile accident, Natarajn continued, also indicated that it was her torso.

Asked by probers if it was possible to determine the cause of death, Natarajn said there was no evidence of anything other than the dismemberment. On the other hand, the examination of the torso did reveal Keerans had been taking drugs.

Asked if she could definitely state that this was murder and not possibly death due to natural causes, Dr. Natarajn replied, "If a person died as a result of a natural disease, one would not go to the extent of chopping up the body and putting it in plastic trash bags. Clearly there was evidence of dismemberment . . . The manner—the way of disposal—indicates this was not a natural death and that includes death from an overdose of medication from drugs."

The lawmen returned to D'Amato and confronted him with the fact of Keerans' death, and of her remains being found in plastic trash bags exactly where he had told Lee he dropped them.

"I didn't do it," he said, "I knew about it but was afraid to say anything. Now I have nothing to lose and can tell you the truth. Bart called me at home around 2 a.m. on February the 17th. He wanted me to go to the auto body shop he owned. When I arrived, he came out with a mask on and took me to the paint booth. The odor was so foul and I looked down and Kerry was down on the floor. She was on a blanket. There were no arms, no legs. Her head was there . . . I was in shock. He said to me, 'I didn't kill her. I didn't kill her. I'll take care of this but I need you to take care of the apartment and get rid of all her things."

"Are you saying you just went ahead and did everything he asked you to do?" the investigators asked incredulously.

"Yes, I was afraid of him and I was afraid the police wouldn't believe me because of the manslaughter thing."

"Why didn't you make an anonymous call?" the lawmen persisted.

"Bart would find out. He could turn me in or something."

"All right now, how is it that Lee heard about the murder, and with you as the killer? The last time you knew nothing. But now we have the body parts where Lee said you had told him you threw them."

"We were talking about the worst and dumbest thing we ever did. I told him the worst and dumbest thing I ever did was selling Kerry's furs."

"Worse than the manslaughter charge?"

"The worst thing I ever done was the manslaughter charge. We were talking about the worst and the dumbest. The dumbest thing I ever did was selling her furs 'cause I could get jammed up," D'Amato explained.

"We heard you did the whole thing," detectives retorted.

I told Lee about it, but was afraid to name Bart. Lee probably said I did it to get a lighter sentence, 'cause he needed to name somebody."

"He didn't want anything."

"I told you who did it. Why should I do it? She was nothing to me. The cops saw Bart trying to hurt her. Why don't you look at that?"

Meanwhile, other lawmen were questioning Bart.

"I had been having arguments with Carter for months," he said. "You know we were living together a few years. The arguments began before Angelo came. He came to stay with us a few months before the murder. That's when it got worse. I knew they were carrying on with each other, and I asked her to leave."

"And what about D'Amato?"

"What?"

"Did you ask him to leave?"

"No. It was her. My love was gone already, and things were getting worse. Two days before the murder it got really bad. I kept asking her to leave, then police came while I was threatening her. Police came the next day when it got really bad."

"D'Amato was present both times?"

"Yes."

"Was D'Amato ever involved?"

"No, it was her. My love was gone. I wanted her out. Kept asking her to leave. Things got so bad the night of the murder, I slept on the couch in the living room downstairs and she slept in the master bedroom upstairs. Then, around seven in the morning D'Amato woke me up. He said he killed Carter."

Asked by sleuths if he knew why D'Amato had killed her, Bart explained that D'Amato had become very angry at Keerans a few days before. At that time D'Amato had tried to sell Keerans three television sets he had stolen, Bart continued. She had agreed to pay $200 for each set. But she paid him only $200 for all three. Then she found a secret compartment in D'Amato's wallet and took the $200 back when he was asleep.

Then, becoming highly excited, Bart said, "So she got all the televisions for nothing. But to me that was no reason to kill her. That was no reason to kill anybody. Even now I still don't believe it. There had to be something more. I know it was my responsibility to turn him in to the cops, but I couldn't because I thought they'd arrest me."

"You said D'Amato awoke you and told you about killing Carter," the detectives quickly interjected.

"He brought me upstairs," Bart said, speaking very rapidly, "and he showed me Carter's body under my bed."

"Then what?" the sleuths prodded, noticing that Bart was hesitating.

"We left her body under my bed for two whole days. It was really getting bad. We definitely had to do something. Then, D'Amato suggested we bury Kerry under the apartment. After digging a while we hit water. It was about one and a half feet down. Then D'Amato suggested cutting her up. I suggested using the hacksaws which were in my auto body shop. We brought her to the shop in my car. When we got there we carried her into the paint booth. D'Amato started cutting one leg, and I went to my office to wait for the job to be finished."

Bart then said that about two and a half to three hours passed before D'Amato returned. They both then took the plastic trash bag containing the torso and threw it into the water below the Margate Bridge. After that D'Amato, himself, got rid of the rest of the body parts.

"Let's back up a bit," said a sleuth. "You said D'Amato killed Carter because of some television sets?"

"Yes," Bart replied. "He killed her because she ripped him off for the sets. You might not feel that's important enough to kill her for. But you have to remember what kind of person Angelo D'Amato is. He's a braggart, a person who's used to getting anything he wants."

The deposition having been completely taken, Inv. Prendergast called for a meeting to evaluate the information compiled on the case so far and to provide the probers with an opportunity to toss ideas around.

One investigator observed that Bart seemed to have a believable motive to kill Carter, while the motive ascribed to D'Amato, seemed highly questionable.

"The M.O. of the crime clearly fits D'Amato's past record," retorted another detective. "And, after all, what motive ever really does make sense?" He added, "It's all relative."

"The M.O. fits too clearly," observed another sleuth. "Perhaps Bart arranged things to look that way. He had a reputation for being resourceful and cunning. He could have set things up to point suspicion at D'Amato, and then used D'Amato's record to force him into becoming involved."

"That doesn't fit his character," argued one investigator. "The police had come to his apartment several times during domestic disputes, and the whole town knew it, so why would he kill her in his own apartment. And being a resourceful green beret, why wouldn't he act alone, and why call someone he suspected of having an affair with Carter?"

"The crime might not fit Bart's character," a detective reasoned, "but it fits his motive. And acting out of character under such circumstances is not surprising. After all, how many people are capable of acting with forethought and reason while in the throes of passion?"

A prober concluded by noting that as soon as the murder took place, it didn't take much intelligence for each suspect to know suspicion would be cast almost equally on both of them, no matter who actually committed the crime. He then explained that the reason they probably united in covering up the murder was because they had this hold on each other. He added that perhaps an investigation of D'Amato's alleged motive, the stolen television sets, might disclose the actual murderer.

The meeting broke up on that note.

The sleuths checked on robbery records in Bart's neighborhood and learned that the television sets in question were stolen shortly before the murder. Further, the thief left a cigarette behind which was the same brand smoked by Angelo D'Amato. And, in combing through the records of both suspects, detectives discovered that a cigarette of the same brand smoked by D'Amato was found near the body of the young man he was convicted of killing in 1977.

The combination of evidence and witnesses against D'Amato finally became much stronger than against Bart. Indeed, the evidence seemed sufficient to charge D'Amato and only D'Amato with murder. The authorities became convinced that Bart only became involved with disposing of the body but was never involved in the actual murder.

But Bart suddenly became difficult. He demanded certain guarantees before he would testify. The lawmen agreed to take his statement at headquarters, with his lawyer present and the guarantees arranged. During the meeting set up at headquarters, Bart received limited-use immunity. This prevented law enforcement authorities from using anything against him which he found necessary to speak about in order to give a full account of the murder. However, he could be prosecuted for possessing and receiving stolen property because evidence of these crimes was obtained independent of his statement. Also, any evidence uncovered linking him to the actual murder, which he denied having committed, could be used to prosecute him. As part of the agreement, lawmen stated they did not believe he was the murderer.

Almost at the same time, Stewart Lee presented a problem. He also refused to testify. For after the body was discovered, D'Amato began to be too closely guarded to be of any danger. But D'Amato's alleged underworld connections began to appear dangerous to witnesses against him. A fire broke out in Bart's house, and there was speculation it could have been arson. Lawmen, however, still had Lee's recorded statements about the murder, including where the body parts in plastic trash bags would be found. But finally the problem of Lee's refusal to testify was overcome. Through a compromise arrangement, Lee received a slightly more lenient sentence, and then he agreed to take the stand.

The trial was set for June 1983. The case was heard for three weeks without the jury able to reach a unanimous verdict. On June 24th, a mistrial was declared. This decision was reached after 17 fruitless hours over a three-day period. Superior Court Judge Manuel Greenberg ordered a second trial for September. Excusing the jury, he said, "We know you did your job conscientiously and to the best of your ability, and it just happens sometimes that 12 people cannot come to an agreement. You are certainly not to be faulted."

Public Defender Barry Cooper requested that charges be dropped, because the defense was not informed of a lenient sentence granted to Lee for his testimony by the Atlantic County prosecutor. During this trial, D'Amato admitted to, and was found guilty of, stealing and selling some of Carter's jewelry and furs.

The second trial began on Monday at 10:00 a.m., September 6, 1983. It was characterized by a lot of fireworks from Defense Attorneys Robert Moran and Barry Cooper on one side and from First Assistant Prosecutor Steven E. Rosenfeld on the other.

Defense attorneys first objected to the bones being shown because they were "highly inflammatory and prejudicial." Then they suddenly reversed themselves. They just made certain the jury understood that Pros. Rosenfeld was known for doing things to create excitement.

Rosenfeld took advantage of the freedom granted, making certain to attain the desired effect despite defense counsel's warnings. He showed pictures of Keerans as she looked before the killing and then as she was reduced to bones in trash bags. Then, by way of illustration, he held up a clear plastic bag with the bones visible. Then Rosenfeld held up the hacksaws allegedly used to dismember

Keerans, saying, "These are the flashy things, the artful things I'm supposed to do—the things Mr. Moran has accused me of in his closing. But if I'm really after justice, it's not the flash that should convince you of Angelo D'Amato's guilt—it's the case."

Defense Attorney Moran kept trying to create reasonable doubt in the jury's mind by showing that Bart could be the murderer, but because of D'Amato's record, he was the only one who was charged with the crime.

Pros. Rosenfeld presented the logic of his case, showing how unreasonable it would be to assume that Bart and not D'Amato was the murderer. "Why would he (Bart) kill her in his apartment? If he was as resourceful as Mr. Robert Moran says he is, why would he kill her someplace where he would have to get rid of the body? Why not kill her in a place where he could kill her and leave her?" Finally completing this line of argument, Rosenfeld showed that Bart would have to be "so stupid that he killed her in his apartment and also was stupid enough to dial the telephone and call Angelo D'Amato." He then emphasized the fact that D'Amato was the cause of domestic friction between Bart and Keerans Carter.

Moran also tried to create reasonable doubt by his closing argument. "Why would Angelo D'Amato make up a story?" he asked. "Is there proof beyond a reasonable doubt? Would you convict anyone or just Angelo D'Amato on the basis of the evidence you have before you?"

But Pros. Rosenfeld's arguments prevailed with the jury. On Wednesday, September 21, 1983, in less than four hours, the Superior Court jury convicted Angelo D'Amato, 25, of the strangulation death and dismemberment of Keerans Carter. In consequence of the conviction, D'Amato faced a life sentence, to which Judge Greenberg could add the stipulation that he serve as much as 25 years before becoming eligible for parole. On October 7, 1983, D'Amato received a life sentence and must serve

$27^1/_2$ years before he is eligible for parole.

Commenting on the trial, a close relative who had come from Atlanta, Georgia, philosophized, "I feel like maybe it was Kerry's destiny to put this guy away." And another relative enthused, "I feel good."

EDITOR'S NOTE:
Brewster Bart and Stewart Lee are not the real names of the persons so named in the foregoing story. Fictitious names have been used because there is no reason for public interest in the identities of these persons.

"SHOT, CHAINSAWED, CREMATED, AND FED TO THE DOGS!"

by David N. Benson

Kimberly Knight's relatives were planning to celebrate her 19th birthday on July 14, 1990, with a party in their home. But as the hours unfolded, Kimberly's relatives slowly began to realize that they weren't going to be singing "Happy Birthday" that evening, for their guest of honor had apparently stood them up.

This wasn't like Kimberly, who was the type of girl who always called home every two or three days. A pretty young woman with blonde hair and blue eyes, Kimberly had just started working as a waitress in Jonesville, Michigan, about 20 miles away from her relatives' home. She took adult education courses on the side, and when she wasn't working or studying, she indulged herself in her hobby of collecting glass and ceramic unicorns. Kimberly had hundreds of these figurines on the shelves of her mobile home, which she shared with her boyfriend.

It had already been a week since Kimberly last called her family. That in itself was cause for worry. But why would Kimberly miss her own birthday party? her relatives wondered. And why wouldn't she have called?

Kimberly's relatives decided to call her in Jonesville. No one was home. All they could do was leave a message on her answering machine. Maybe Kimberly had made other plans, the relatives guessed. Maybe she was celebrating with her boyfriend and friends.

As the days passed, however, cause for concern over Kimberly's welfare only grew. The phone at Kimberly's mobile home was not being answered, and her relatives had to keep leaving messages on the machine.

By July 20, 1990, four days after the failed birthday party and the 11th day since relatives had heard from Kimberly one relative started calling Kimberly's close friends in Jonesville. Information was scarce. No one had seen Kimberly in the past 10 days.

On the 20th, the relative finally had a call back. It was not from Kimberly, but from her boyfriend who had lived with her for the past two years. He told the family member that Kimberly had walked out on him after an argument 10 days earlier. He hadn't seen her since, he said.

The next call the relative made was to the Michigan State Police post in Jonesville.

Jonesville is a quiet town in southern Michigan, where the shops close early. The main street is U.S. Route 12, a busy highway that gives the small town a hustle-and-bustle it wouldn't otherwise have. Also known as the Chicago Road, the highway links Chicago and Detroit. Jonesville is slightly closer to Detroit, but in spirit it is much further away from the two crime-plagued metropolises than mileage might indicate.

Kimberly's relative told State Police troopers the details of Kimberly's disappearance, and the case was assigned to Detective-Sergeant Curtis E. Robertson.

"I believed it was foul play from the first day," Robertson would later recall. "Kim had always called home, and now she missed her birthday. That's unusual for a girl that age, especially if she was expecting presents."

As her boyfriend was the last known person to see

250

Kimberly alive, he was invited in for an interview. He was interviewed on three separate occasions at the state police post, including once by Sergeant Robertson.

The first impression 32-year-old Jeff Van Patten made on Robertson and other investigators was that he was a man of contradictions. He stood 6 foot 4 and weighed 200 pounds, but his forbidding size seemed at odds with his soft-spoken nature. He answered questions calmly, as if he were discussing the weather or making small talk. He was always willing to cooperate with authorities.

Van Patten ran an auto repair shop from the house he shared with Kimberly about two and a half miles north of town. He said he last saw Kimberly between 2:00 a.m. and 3:00 a.m. on the morning of Wednesday, July 11th. She had walked out on him because of an argument they were having, he said.

Jeff said Kimberly had wanted to buy the restaurant where she had just started working. She thought it would be a good idea, he with his garage and she with her restaurant. The problem was the price. The owner wanted $200,000, and Kimberly didn't have that kind of money. She suggested that they ask one of Jeff's relatives, who happened to be a banker, for financial assistance.

The couple went to Jeff's relative's home to discuss their business proposition. But the banker said they couldn't get a down payment for a loan that large and the interest payments would be too high.

After returning home, Jeff and Kimberly called the owner of the restaurant and asked if he would accept a land contract in lieu of cash. He declined. Jeff said Kimberly had a temper and was becoming upset.

That night the couple decided to tear down their waterbed. It had been leaking for some time and they hoped to replace it with another waterbed they had on the premises. After tearing the waterbed down, they decided it would be best to repair the rotted floor before putting up the new bed.

Around midnight, Jeff was tired and wanted to go to bed. He suggested they sleep on the sofa bed. According to Jeff, that made Kimberly even angrier. She liked to finish what she started, he explained. After a few words passed between them, Kimberly grabbed a box, put in some blue jeans and shirts, some of her treasured unicorn figurines and possibly some undergarments. Kimberly put the box under her arm and left. She started walking south on Michigan Highway 99. It was raining off and on that night, so Jeff followed Kimberly in his car and tried to talk her into going back to the house at least until morning.

Despite his pleadings, Kimberly turned him down twice. He last saw her walking over a hill on M-99, heading toward Jonesville. She would have been carrying approximately $100 in cash. Jeff told Sergeant Robertson that Kimberly talked about hitching a ride on a semi-truck and seeing old boyfriends in Texas and Virginia. Jeff recalled she was wearing blue jeans and a T-shirt bearing the logo of the restaurant she wanted to buy.

There was one other thing Kimberly had been angry about, Jeff said. A couple of her relatives took their car to Jeff to be looked over. Since the relatives were going on vacation, Jeff gave the car more than just the once-over and corrected a few things he had found wrong with the vehicle. His diligence had run the bill up to $200. Kimberly seemed to think he was padding the bill, Jeff said.

In those early interviews, Sergeant Robertson paid more attention to how Jeff Van Patten answered his questions than to the answers themselves.

"When I first interviewed him, I couldn't call it," Robertson recalled later. "I didn't think he was telling

252

me the absolute truth, but I couldn't say he was a total liar, either. It was a middle-line call, but I'd say leaning toward deception."

Scientific evidence to substantiate the detective's hunch came a few days later. At Robertson's invitation, Van Patten agreed to take a polygraph test. The test was given at the Michigan State Police post in Paw Paw. The results were inconclusive.

Robertson reasoned that if Kimberly Knight had indeed walked out on Van Patten that night, she might have stopped at one of the 24-hour restaurant or gas stations along the way, especially since it was raining. Or she might have made a telephone call from one of the pay phones there. Or if she had hitched a ride to Texas with a trucker, maybe someone would remember her, Robertson speculated.

Robertson attempted to get the records of calls made from pay telephones. He also had the name of Kimberly's former boyfriend in Texas and his hometown. Robertson contacted the police department in Texas and asked for lawmen to make contact with the old boyfriend.

Troopers armed with photographs of Kimberly Knight started asking questions of third-shift waitresses, gas station night managers, and truck drivers who might have seen her that night. It would take a few days for troopers to find all the people who had worked that night. Most knew who Kimberly Knight was and where she lived. But none could remember seeing her that night.

Robertson wasn't having much better luck with the telephone records. The telephone company routinely destroyed the records after seven days, so it would be up to other witnesses to corroborate Jeff Van Patten's story.

The restaurant owner told Sergeant Robertson that he remembered Kimberly asking how much he wanted for the establishment. Two hundred thousand dollars, he had replied. That night, Kimberly called to ask if he would accept a land contract instead of cash, but the owner wasn't interested in such a deal. Kimberly didn't seem angry or upset on the telephone, the man said, but she didn't come back to work again, either. However, he did get a call from Jeff Van Patten a few days later. Kimberly wouldn't be coming back to work because she had left town, the restaurant owner remembered Jeff telling him. In a voice that sounded nervous and worried Jeff said he could come up with a replacement waitress for Kimberly.

Jeff's banker-relative told Sergeant Robertson that he remembered Jeff calling at about 5:00 p.m. on July 10th and asking if he and Kimberly could come over to discuss a business proposition. The tan Lincoln drove up to the banker's house two hours later.

The banker remembered Kimberly as being impressed with the amount of money the restaurant was taking in—$400 on her shift alone. The banker said he tried to tell the couple that the down payment on the loan would be large and the interest payments would be high. He further tried to explain that the money that came into a restaurant had to be used to pay expenses.

Kimberly didn't seem to understand these fundamental business practices. She seemed to think the money that went into the cash register was pure profit. Still, she hadn't behaved abnormally after being told she would be unable to buy the restaurant.

He didn't remember the next time he saw Jeff after Kimberly disappeared. But he did see Jeff on a Thursday at a theater. Kimberly wasn't there and Jeff didn't say why. Perhaps he didn't have to since it wasn't unusual to see Jeff without Kimberly. The couple didn't always get along.

Sergeant Robertson talked with Van Patten again and

asked for permission to look around his place. Van Patten agreed and gave Robertson a house tour.

The place he and Kimberly had lived in for the past two years was a double-wide mobile home on Borden Road near M-99, north of town. Entry into the basement was possible only from the outside. Jeff had a garage and shop building for his auto repair work.

Once inside the house, Robertson could see that the front living area was clean while the rest of the house was sloppy and dirty.

Jeff showed the detective two T-shirts from the restaurant where Kimberly worked. In the bedroom, Robertson observed a spent pack of cigarettes of the brand Kimberly smoked. He also noticed that on a windowsill was an ashtray full of marijuana roaches.

Van Patten pointed out empty shelves where Kimberly had once kept her unicorns. It was obvious that someone had removed *something* from the shelves because of the absence of dust on them. There was still a large collection of unicorn figurines and other unicorn items throughout the house.

The outside of the house was littered with junk cars, which wasn't surprising, given Van Patten's occupation as a mechanic. There were no recent digging sites to indicate a burial site, Robertson noticed.

So perhaps the theory that Van Patten had somehow done Kimberly in was wrong. People who knew the couple told probers that Van Patten had a nonviolent nature. He had a reputation of walking away from fights. Many said he had never struck Kimberly. He denied having another girlfriend on the side, and other witnesses backed him up. Even investigators were surprised by his calm demeanor.

As lawmen dug deeper, they learned that Jeff and Kimberly were not alone, at least for part of the night Kimberly disappeared. Sleuths found out that Gloria

Quemar, who was described as Kimberly Knight's best friend, visited the residence that night as well.

When Gloria left at 9:30 p.m., she noticed that Kimberly and Jeff were arguing about something. She didn't quite catch it, but she thought Kimberly wanted something for which Jeff didn't have the money.

The next morning, Gloria returned to the couple's mobile home. Jeff was outside tending a still-smoldering burn pile. Gloria recalled that Jeff told her that Kimberly was inside sleeping. Usually Jeff would invite Gloria inside the home and awaken Kimberly. This time, all Jeff told her was that Kimberly wouldn't be getting up for a while—even though she was supposed to have walked out on him. Gloria remembered Jeff saying that Kimberly had made him burn a waterbed he and Kim had dismantled the previous night.

Gloria returned at 10:10 a.m., and Lester Nye, an employee of Jeff's, was there. Jeff told Gloria that Kimberly had walked out on him.

Sergeant Robertson interviewed Lester Nye, who said he didn't see Jeff and Kimberly fight the night before because he worked mornings. When Nye arrived for work at 9:00 a.m., the morning after Kimberly disappeared, Jeff told him that Kimberly had taken off. Nye remembered Gloria arriving an hour later and also being told by Jeff that Kimberly had left him.

There was another thing Lester Nye remembered: Jeff had seemed depressed at the time, but lately Jeff's mood seemed to have improved. Within two weeks, Jeff was in the best mood he had ever been in.

Investigators learned that Jeff and Kimberly hadn't been getting along for the past year. Some thought they were falling behind in bills.

Sleuths also learned that Kimberly and Jeff used marijuana. Jeff apparently was trying to quit. Kimberly's attempts to quit never lasted more than a couple of days. If she went more than a couple of days, she became irrational.

Another piece of information developed: Jeff was becoming more religious. A sporadic churchgoer in the past, Jeff had converted to an austere Christian sect and was going to church virtually every Sunday.

With all the information sleuths learned, there was still no sign of Kimberly. If she was alive, why hadn't she called her relatives? And if she was dead, where was the body?

On July 26th, detectives ran a check on Kimberly's driver's license to see if the missing girl had been given a ticket. Detectives also ran a check on the criminal history of the missing waitress. Kimberly Knight had never been arrested, they learned.

On July 27th, based on the statements from witnesses, Sergeant Robertson obtained a warrant entitling him to search the buildings, the residence, the business garage, the basement, and the grounds of Jeff Van Patten's home. Robertson didn't have to execute it; Van Patten gave his permission.

Robertson led a delegation of detectives, troopers, and a K-9 team into the mobile home. They found a large stain on the carpet in one of the rooms. Van Patten claimed he had dyed it. Samples were removed anyway, although it would turn out that Van Patten's explanation was correct.

Nothing more was found on the property or in the cars. But on top of the burn barrel furthest from the dog pens was a broken unicorn. Also found were some marijuana pipes, a jewelry container, and an eye-makeup tool—all burnt.

Probers took these items into evidence. "At that point we figured Van Patten had killed her and had burnt the evidence. What we needed to know was what he did with the body," Robertson would later explain.

Dog teams were brought in to search for a cadaver. Different hunches were tried out every couple of days. One team wandered the banks of a river near Van Patten's place. Others searched nearby farms and gravel pits. One time, a dog indicated the presence of a recent gravesite. But the dog outsmarted itself. After troopers dug out the grave, they discovered the corpse of a dead dog.

For their part, Kimberly's relatives never gave up. They would spend many hours scouring the Hillsdale County countryside looking for some sign of Kimberly. They made up a missing poster with Kimberly's picture and the Jonesville State Police post's telephone number and circulated it far and wide. Copies would turn up on highway rest areas hundreds of miles from Jonesville.

"She's never gone more than three or four days without calling me," said one relative of Kimberly's. "She would know what I'm going through."

A few improbable tips came in. On July 30th, a 19-year-old man who claimed to be a former high school classmate of Kimberly's said he saw the missing blonde five days earlier at a large department store in Jackson. She was alone and carried no packages. He waved to her, but she didn't wave back because she was looking the other way. Later, he saw the poster listing Kimberly as missing and reported it to authorities.

The next day, two tips came in. A law student called the state police to report that he saw the missing blonde in Lansing. She was riding in a cab with a black male.

An unidentified call told an official of the Hillsdale County Sheriff's Department that a hidden lane existed behind a certain house on M-99. The lane led directly to a river, and a car was seen driving down the lane at the time Kimberly Knight disappeared. A dog team canvassed the site, but didn't discover anything.

On August 2nd, Sergeant Robertson contacted a ma-

258

jor banking institution in Lansing. He asked an official to run a credit check on Kimberly Knight to see if she had applied for credit anywhere. The results were negative, although Robertson's contact agreed to run Kimberly's name again at a later date.

A few days later, a waitress reported that a truck driver told her he overheard on the CB that a woman in the Toledo area was asking for a ride to Texas. This would have been about the time Kimberly disappeared.

It would take a few more weeks for the police department in Texas to find Kimberly's former boyfriend. When they found him, he had no relevant information to offer.

In the meantime, Kimberly's relatives thought they had discovered a hidden road that belonged to a church. It was marked with a "No Trespassing" sign and appeared as if it might offer a clue. Robertson checked it out on August 2nd with negative results. The road led to a municipal building and was securely locked after business hours.

Robertson decided it was time to question Jeff Van Patten again.

"Our plan was to interrogate him thoroughly about what happened that night," Robertson later explained.

Robertson solicited the aid of the post commander, Lieutenant Thomas G. Finco. Finco had 19 years of experience and had spent nine years as a detective, rising to the rank of detective-lieutenant. He was eager to see Van Patten, whom he had never met.

Van Patten was invited back to another interview at the post. He arrived bright and early on August 28th. He was told that it was just a routine re-interview. This time, however, the scenario was different. Sergeant Robertson decorated his office with aerial photographs of the area around Van Patten's home. The case file sat on his desk, fattened with several sheets of worthless papers to make it look more impressive. As a final touch, one of Kimberly's missing posters was taped to the wall.

Van Patten was led upstairs to the office where he was left to cool his heels. He was there long enough for him to stare at the materials, long enough for him to sit and think, and long enough for his conscience to go to work.

When Lieutenant Finco and Sergeant Robertson arrived, they took him out of Robertson's office and moved him next door to the interrogation room. Unlike Robertson's office, the walls in the small room were barren and the windows were draped off. The only thing for Van Patten to pay attention to was the two lawmen. Robertson informed him that although the door to the small room was closed it wasn't locked. He could leave at any time.

"I started doing the talking. I wanted to know what happened from day one in his own words, rather than in report form," Finco would later recall.

As the questions unfolded, however, Van Patten betrayed a pattern. He would direct his answer to Robertson and then look away. Robertson figured he was disturbing the suspect somehow and excused himself from the room to go downstairs for a cup of coffee. He would later call his departure a "tactical exit."

With Robertson gone, Lieutenant Finco steered the conversation away from Van Patten's possible involvement to the desire of the state police to recover Kimberly's body. "You could really see something was eating him up," Finco said. "He wanted some water so I went downstairs to get him a glass of water. He drank his water and he said how we could never find the body," Finco recalled.

Finally, Jeff Van Patten began to tell Finco what happened. Finco stopped him and brought Sergeant Robertson back into the room. After Van Patten recited the details, the two detectives asked him to agree to a tape-recorded interview. Van Patten consented.

He talked about how Kimberly wanted to buy the restaurant and about her relative's car. But what really ticked her off, the suspect said, was not having any marijuana. "She could smoke an ounce a week, if it was there, a whole ounce," Van Patten said. "She kept looking to find marijuana and she couldn't find any. She was really mad because she couldn't get any."

What she did find were a couple of kitchen knives at least seven inches long. "She said she was going to have my heart hanging on the end of the knife before she was done—that she was going to kill me."

Van Patten's story had Kimberly chasing him around and outside the house. The chase led into a spare bedroom where Van Patten kept a 12-gauge shotgun. He got the shotgun and some slugs but didn't immediately load it, hoping Kimberly would back off. But she kept coming at him, even as he loaded the gun.

"She snapped, and she was acting really crazy," Van Patten said. Van Patten moved in the master bedroom. He found himself in the doorway of the room's bathroom. Kimberly stood near the foot of the bed.

"All of a sudden she came at me and I pushed her back. I was trying to get her to stay away from me and she kept swinging the knives and she was really getting serious about coming at me with those knives."

"Well I kind of had the gun in my hand, and I just kind of, with the gun, shoved her back, and she just kept coming at me. And I do not know why, but I shot her."

The bullet struck Kimberly in the right shoulder. She fell backward and landed on the bed. Van Patten said he then pulled the trigger once more.

The second shot struck Kimberly and may have punctured the waterbed. Van Patten realized he had more work to do. He began draining the water mattress. While the water gushed out and began rotting the floorboards, Van Patten went outside and built a fire with some wood.

Returning to the house, Van Patten wrapped Kimberly's corpse in the mattress and threw the package on the fire. To get the fire even hotter, he added the wood frame from the waterbed and some tires he had.

When morning approached, he pulled the corpse out of the fire. Kimberly's head, legs, and arms were missing, but her torso remained so he took out his chainsaw, cut the torso into four pieces and fed it to his great danes. He then began to clean up the burn pile. He dumped the debris near a fence row. He was in the middle of cleaning up the hot coals when Gloria Quemar came by and asked where Kimberly was.

Later on, Van Patten removed the debris to a township dump. He took some of Kimberly's unicorns off the shelves and put them in a box, which he hid in his shop.

"Is there a reason, Jeff, when you were outside, that you did not take off running through the field until she calmed down?" asked Sergeant Robertson.

"No," replied Van Patten.

The interview ended at 11:20 a.m. Robertson next summoned technicians from the Michigan State Police Crime Lab in Lansing to examine the crime scene. Then, Van Patten requested to see a minister. The minister and the suspect spoke alone in the detective's office for 30 minutes.

"He found religion sometime after he killed her. Maybe it was his guilt that led him to confess," Robertson would later say. In any event, Van Patten seemed relieved after confessing. As Finco remembered, "He said he felt a lot better. He wanted to shake my hand."

The detectives next called the prosecutor's office. A search warrant was drafted for Van Patten's property and Van Patten was arrested on charges of open murder, mutilation of a corpse, and the use of a firearm in the commission of a felony. He was taken to the Hillsdale County Jail.

The crime lab arrived at the Van Patten residence at 2:45 p.m. and began collecting evidence, the most grisly being the bones from the doghouse. At 4:50 p.m., some of the murdered waitress' relatives walked into the police post after an afternoon of searching for her body. It was only then that they learned the bad news.

The next day, Jeff Van Patten was taken to Jackson for a polygraph examination. He passed, but he changed a few details. In this version, Kimberly now had only one knife. He allowed that he may have shot her three times instead of twice. In the new version, Kimberly calmed down when she was chasing him outside the house. Both went inside and Kimberly put the knife on the counter and played Nintendo for a while. Later on her temper rekindled and the knife chase was on again, Van Patten said.

From Jackson, Van Patten was taken back to Hillsdale to stand before District Judge Donald L. Sanderson. Van Patten, worried about his safety, wore Sergeant Robertson's bulletproof vest over his jail uniform. He was escorted by Robertson and another trooper who kept a watchful eye on the crowd.

The judge asked Van Patten if he would like a bond set so he could leave jail. "That would be nice," Van Patten said in his quiet, high-pitched voice. The judge set bond at 10 percent of $100,000. Relatives posted it, and Van Patten was released at 3:30 p.m.

A preliminary report from the crime lab arrived the same day, confirming that at least some of the bones in the doghouse could be human. A university anthropology professor would make the final determination.

The professor found that many of the bones were from white-tailed deer. But one four-inch piece belonged to a human female's upper right arm. Its distal end showed signs of charring because of exposure to heat or fire. Another four-inch piece of bone belonged to a woman's lower arm. Its distal end suggested that it had been cut.

The crime lab had its own grisly discovery: parts of Kimberly Knight's skin could be found on the scabbard of the chainsaw.

Hillsdale Prosecutor Michael R. Smith entered a motion to have Jeff Van Patten's bond revoked. It was rescinded at a bond hearing on September 5th, and Van Patten was moved back into the Hillsdale County Jail.

Van Patten waived a preliminary examination and was bound over to Hillsdale Circuit Court. On September 19th, he pleaded guilty to the reduced charges of manslaughter, mutilation of a corpse, and commission of a felony with a firearm.

Before Hillsdale Circuit Judge Harvey Moes, Van Patten once again recounted the story of how he killed the young waitress. Moes accepted Van Patten's guilty pleas.

Attorneys for both sides offered different reasons for the plea bargain. Van Patten's defense would have revolved around the idea of self-defense, his attorney, Thomas O'Brien, said. "I don't think it was generally understood that he was acting in self-defense," O'Brien said, shortly after Van Patten's plea was entered.

To argue self-defense, however, they would have to pit Kimberly Knight's reputation against Van Patten's. "Jeff wanted, after talking with his family, not to put the victim's family, his own family, or the community through a long gruesome trial," the defense attorney added.

Hillsdale Prosecutor Michael R. Smith said he agreed

to the plea at the wishes of the victim's relatives. "It was their desire to have it resolved in a speedy fashion. They wanted to put this tragedy behind them."

Later, the prosecutor said that Van Patten's destruction of the body prevented a murder charge. "We had no body to discount his position," he said. "Who knows whatever happened that day? He could have shot her as she lay in bed."

On October 25th, Judge Moes sentenced Jeff Van Patten to 10 to 15 years on the manslaughter charge, from 6 years, 6 months to 10 years on the mutilation of a corpse charge, and for 2 years on the felony firearms charge.

In a written opinion the judge recounted the story and concluded, "I cannot imagine a worse scenario for manslaughter."

Jeff Van Patten's lawyer later appealed the sentence, but it seems it will be a good long while before Van Patten will breathe free air again.

EDITOR'S NOTE:
Gloria Quemar and Lester Nye are not the real names of the persons so named in the foregoing story. Fictitious names have been used because there is no reason for public interest in the identities of these persons.

"THE KINKY SEX FIEND HACKED OFF LEONA'S HEAD!"

by Bob Carlsen

PIERCE COUNTY, WASHINGTON
APRIL 30, 1982

The old lady who lived next door to Leona Mae Whigham Wilson liked her. Leona was proper. She was a devoted Christian, listened to only gospel music and attended church regularly. Leona Mae didn't believe in premarital sex and never entertained men at indiscreet hours. She was the ideal neighbor. She didn't deserve to be discarded like yesterday's trash.

Leona Mae Wigham Wilson was standing in her kitchen and was cooking supper when the monster came up behind her, put the large knife to the young woman's throat, and with one swift motion, nearly severed her head.

It was over for her in seconds. Her body collapsed to the floor as her head dangled by threads of flesh. But her assailant wasn't through with her. He dragged her into the bedroom and placed her on the bed. There he allegedly raped her vaginally and rectally. However, that would never be proved in court, as the man would not face a jury.

It began on June 27, 1981. Clerks at a grocery store in a Tacoma suburb went outside to empty trash at 7:45

p.m., as they did every night. It was routine for them and, normally, the job took just a couple of minutes.

As one of them opened the lid to the dumpster the other prepared to throw garbage in. One clerk looked inside first, and noticed there was a foreign object in the dumpster. It looked like a blanket. He didn't think the store carried such merchandise and he asked his fellow employee about it.

"I didn't know we handled blankets like that," he said to the other employee. The second employee looked inside the dumpster and said that he too didn't recognize the blanket as being part of their merchandise.

The clerk who noticed the blanket reached in and tugged on it a little. "Geez, there's blood on it," he said. He opened the blanket a little more and saw that there was a body inside. That's as far as it went.

The clerks rushed inside to a telephone and called the Pierce County Sheriff's Department. Pierce County is located south of Seattle and the King County on Puget Sound. The county seat is Tacoma. The body was discovered in a well-populated area but was outside of the Tacoma city limits and was thus in the jurisdiction of the sheriff rather than the police department.

Detective Larry W. Gibbs, 34, was on duty that night. Gibbs, who had accumulated ten and a half years with the department, had been a detective for two and a half years. Before becoming a detective he was involved in field investigations as a resident deputy.

Although criminal investigations were nothing new to Gibbs, this would be his first homicide investigation and, as he was about to learn, it would be a particularly grisly one. What he was about to see was one of the most shocking and cruel crimes a detective would ever encounter.

His partner, Detective Harold Vincent "Vic" Knabel, was not new to homicide. He'd dealt with death before.

He'd been with the department since 1959 and had been a detective for 18 of his 22 years on the force.

Knabel wasn't working that night but heard the homicide chatter on his portable radio. He was just a couple of blocks from his home and when he arrived he phoned the department to find out what was up. He was told to meet Detective Gibbs and other crime scene personnel who were on their way to the store where the body had been found.

Detectives and crime scene technicians arrived on the scene, extracted the blanket and grisly cargo from the dumpster and confirmed it was the body of a nearly decapitated, naked female. She was small, and under better circumstances would have been considered petite. She seemed to be in her mid-30s and was a Negro. Other than that, there was no identifying clothing, cards, or anything at the scene. Detectives sifted through the garbage in the dumpster in the hope of finding identification cards but there was nothing. The victim obviously had been murdered elsewhere and then taken to the store parking lot and deposited in the dumpster when the assailant was certain nobody was looking.

Technicians, upon advice of Deputy Coroner Bill Barnes, a former Tacoma policeman, disturbed the body as little as possible. They merely confirmed that she was dead, saw there was nothing else in the blanket, wrapped her up in the blanket and transported her to the county morgue.

"We followed Deputy Coroner Barnes to the coroner's office," Deputy Gibbs said in an interview after the case was over. "There I received a message to contact Sergeant Bill Seewer." Detective Gibbs had no idea what Seewer might want of him but phoned department headquarters and learned that the sheriff's office had received some curious communications since the initial report of the discovered body came in.

The sheriff's office had received a telephone call from Poulsbo, Washington, a community in Kitsay County. A distraught man was on the telephone and he had told the communications officer that he thought something terrible might have happened. When asked why, the man said that he had been sent to the grocery store by his cousin and when he returned home he found blood all over the house. He panicked because he had a criminal record and he fled the home. After driving out of the county and contemplating the situation, he decided he'd better notify authorities, he told the communications officer who fielded the call.

The communications officer took the message and then tried to get directions to the man's home, but the man had trouble giving them.

"Our communications center, while talking to him, was trying to get directions from him and he had difficulty in giving correct addresses," Detective Gibbs noted afterward.

The man did not sound very educated and when asked his present location said he wasn't sure. Then he was asked to read the telephone number from the place he was calling and he said he was at a pay phone and was having trouble reading the number. The telephone operator who had relayed the call to the sheriff's office helped determine the man's location and the Pierce County Sheriff's Department contacted the Poulsbo Police Department and briefly explained the situation. A Poulsbo police sergeant was dispatched to find the man making the telephone call.

When Detective Gibbs heard the story he made several decisions while he was still at the coroner's office. At the time, they still didn't know who the woman was. However, there was a chance that she was the same one whom the man on the telephone had been talking about.

Poulsbo Police Sergeant D. Cook picked up the young man who had made the telephone call and tried to get some directions from him. The youth was gargantuan, in his late teens. The boy had thighs as large as a man's waist and was not an attractive person. Nor was he very smart.

"His addresses were very incorrect but they were finally able to arrive at a possible address," Detective Gibbs explained about the communications between Pierce County Sergeant Seewer and the Poulsbo sergeant who was talking to the boy. Once Seewer got a possible address, Gibbs told him to go there. Sergeant Sewer did as he was told and knocked on the door of the duplex. There was no answer. But an elderly lady living in the duplex adjacent to the one Seewer went to spoke to the sergeant. The elderly woman told him that earlier in the day she had heard loud yelling coming from the apartment, and that she feared something may have happened to Leona Mae Whigham Wilson, because she was not answering her phone or responding to knocks on her door.

Sergeant Seewer immediately relayed that information to Detective Gibbs who found himself in somewhat of a dilemma. He had a dead body, as yet unidentified. He had a man who said he thought something "terrible" might have happened in a certain house because he saw blood there. And he had a neighbor who was worried. If the dead woman had been murdered in that house, to send Sergeant Seewer in could jeopardize a possible case against the murderer. A smart attorney could get a hold of the fact and say that entry and search was made illegally.

On the other hand, if the body at the morgue did not belong to or come from the house in question, then maybe somebody still in that house needed help desperately and each second that ticked away meant the person was getting that much closer to death.

Detective Gibbs immediately got on the telephone and roused Deputy Prosecuting Attorney Ellsworth Connelly.

Gibbs explained the situation and asked for advice on whether he could legally send Sergeant Seewer into the house without jeopardizing a possible murder case. Connelly, a veteran prosecutor who had handled some of Pierce County's most notorious criminal cases, told Gibbs that the house could be entered but only to determine if someone needed help. Nothing else was to be examined. A search warrant for other matters would come later, he explained.

Within a matter of minutes Detective Gibbs was again talking to Sergeant Seewer and this time delivering specific instructions. The sergeant realized the sensitive situation they were in and followed orders perfectly. With the elder neighbor woman as a witness, he had to gain entry through a window. He made a brief search of the house, determined there was nobody inside and immediately left by way of the front door. He stayed at the duplex and waited for arrival of investigators.

When Detective Gibbs learned that nobody was in the house he breathed a sign of relief. He was thankful that there wasn't another corpse on his hands. Had someone been found dead in the house, or had someone died on the way to the hospital, those crucial seconds used in making a legal decision probably would have taunted the detectives for weeks, perhaps months, to come. Gibbs was thankful there had been nobody in trouble in the house.

"I contacted the prosecutor, Ellsworth Connelly, while still at the coroner's and advised him that I still needed a search warrant for the house," Detective Gibbs said after the case was over. Connelly contacted a fellow deputy prosecutor, Jerry Ackerman, who met detectives

271

at the prosecutor's office in the county-city public safety building in downtown Tacoma. While Detective Knabel met with the deputy prosecutor to get a judge to issue a search warrant, Detective Gibbs stayed at the morgue to be present during the examination of the murdered woman.

Two things about the naked woman were primarily noticed. There were very deep defensive wounds on the palms of her hands. This indicated that the assailant had come up to her from behind, put a knife to her throat. In a feeble attempt to prevent her head from being sliced off, she grabbed the blade with both hands, impulsively and futiley.

Detective Gibbs and those performing the autopsy could come up with no other explanation as to why the woman would have such deep gashes on the palms of each hand. If she had been facing her assailant while he approached, she also would have had slash marks on her forearms and the tops of her hands, the typical defense wounds one receives when defending against an assailant who is approaching from the front. There was no doubt about it then—the woman had had her back to the killer and her last effort had been a vain attempt to hold back the knife from sinking deeply into her throat.

"Her throat and neck had been hacked at by a sharp cutting instrument," Detective Gibbs noted, "to such a degree that the neck appeared to be extremely loose and the head hanging on by a couple inches of skin."

Gibbs joined Knabel and both detectives were present when the judge signed the search warrant. They proceeded to the house in which the young man had said something terrible must have happened. At that point it appeared he was indeed correct, as the house was just about one and a half miles from where the body had been found.

Accompanied by crime scene technician Don Breusaugh, the detectives entered the house to conduct a crime scene search.

It was carnage. Nothing unusual would have been noticed if someone looked in through the windows, however. Throw rugs and newspapers had been put on the living room floor to hide the puddles of blood.

The house was half of a duplex. Ms. Wilson's quarters consisted of a living room, dining area, kitchen, bath, two bedrooms and an attached garage.

Along with the blood which seemed to be everywhere, the detectives also noticed a large amount of jewelry which was scattered about the house. There was a lot of blood in the kitchen, a trail of blood that went through the living room and into one of the bedrooms.

"The kitchen area indicated Leona had been cooking when this had occurred," Detective Gibbs said afterward. There was indoor/outdoor carpet on the kitchen floor, and a large amount of blood and interior neck tissue was found on the carpet. The blood had coagulated. Although it was fairly obvious that it was interior neck tissue, the Washington State Crime Lab verified that assumption.

There were splatters of blood all over the kitchen and detectives noticed that on a dish drain rack there was a large carving knife that obviously had been recently, but carelessly, washed. There still appeared to be a trace of blood on it. That later was confirmed at the crime laboratory. The knife, along with a plethora of household items, was taken into evidence.

"The blood pattern continued from the kitchen through the dining area and a corner of the front room and into the southeast bedroom which was apparently a male's bedroom," Detective Gibbs said later. There were two large blood spots on the mattress. Detectives were curious as to why there were no sheets on the mattress.

They would soon find out the answer.

There was a rather large blood spot near the head of the mattress. This obviously had been where the woman's neck had lain while the assailant carried out what the detectives surmised was a sexual assault. That later was confirmed when the autopsy revealed the woman had been raped twice while she was dead. She was raped vaginally and was also entered anally.

A second blood spatter, actually more of a streak, was near the foot of the bed where her bloody legs had apparently been dragged across the mattress.

Detectives noticed there also was jewelry scattered in this bedroom. They searched the room thoroughly and in one of the dresser drawers they found something that was one of their major clues in the case. It was a probation order from Hattiesburg, Mississippi. The subject was a Karl Eugene Morgan.

Also found in the bedroom where the rapes had occurred was a huge pair of bloodstained trousers. They had been thrown into a closet. They apparently had been worn by the assailant because of the amount of blood on them, detectives surmised. Also they were very distinctive. Detectives figured whoever wore them had to be a huge man.

More evidence was found throughout the house. Sheets which should have been in the bedroom on the bed were found in the laundry room. They did not have any blood on them, however. Detectives figured they had been removed for cleaning earlier in the day before the attack occurred.

Found in the washing machine were other clothes. Although they had been laundered, there were still some traces of blood, obviously contaminated by that time. These also indicated the owner was a large, round man.

"Not too many people wear clothing that size," Detective Gibbs observed shortly soon afterwards.

The detectives couldn't help but wonder if the man who had telephoned from Poulsbo was the owner of the clothing. It was logical to assume so because of the size of the trousers, shirt and underwear and recalling his size. If the owner of the clothing, whom detectives were convinced was the assailant, was not the same man who had called from the Poulsbo—the same man who lived in this house—then why had the assailant left without his clothes? He certainly couldn't have put on anyone else's clothing. The killer either had to have had other clothing in the house or else had left naked. And a naked man that large certainly couldn't have slipped down the street without being noticed.

Detectives contacted the Poulsbo police and told them to take the young man who had made the telephone call into custody. They asked the arresting sergeant if the lad was of large proportions and learned such was an understatement. Sergeant Cook confirmed that the man in Poulsbo was named Karl Eugene Morgan, that he was huge, and furthermore, that a jewelry box had been found in the backseat of the car he had been driving. That was enough probable cause to hold the man for murder while detectives pieced together the rest of their case.

There was every indication that the assailant, after having sex with the nearly headless woman, went into the bathroom and showered. There also was the strong odor of disinfectant in the bathroom, as if the killer had started at that point to clean up the evidence of his terrible deed. He had apparently seen how futile that was, sleuths reasoned, and by the time he had reached other parts of the house, had decided just to throw papers and rugs over the obvious puddles of blood that could be seen from outside.

After gathering evidence, detectives then briefly talked to Sergeant Seewer and learned that the woman who lived next door in the duplex might have some crucial information regarding the case. Detectives Knabel and Gibbs talked to the old lady.

"She was an elderly lady, but she was very sharp; really had her wits about her," Detective Gibbs noted. She proved to be an excellent witness.

The lady told the detectives that it was about 5:30 p.m. that night when she heard a lot of yelling coming from the adjacent duplex. "It wasn't Leona, yelling, though," she said, claiming it sounded like a man's voice. But she couldn't be sure whose it was.

"What she heard," Detective Gibbs explained later, "was an individual, not Leona Mae, just screaming. And then she heard a faint noise from someone, probably Leona, and then there was silence."

The woman was concerned and started to walk out her back door. She was going to find out what was happening. But then she had second thoughts about it, deciding not to because it really was none of her business to stick her nose into family arguments, although she was extremely concerned.

"It's a good thing she didn't go over there at the time," Gibbs said later, "because she would have walked right into it." There is no telling what the killer would have done if an elderly woman, as incapable of defending herself as tiny Leona was, had stumbled onto the scene. If that had happened, it's possible there could have been a double homicide. It was lucky the lady had changed her mind about going to visit Leona, who by that time had been killed.

Even though she had resolved to go back into her house, that didn't mean she could not keep her eyes and ears open, the spunky old lady told detectives. Her house afforded an easy view to the backyard, and also to the front of Leona's yard and driveway. She kept a steady vigil to see who would come out of the house.

276

Detectives were impressed by the woman and queried her more about what she saw that evening. And they couldn't help thinking that if all persons were as observant as the little old lady, a lot more homicides would be solved quicker and with less gnashing of teeth.

After 5:30 p.m. she heard Leona's garage door open. Leona's car was still parked in the driveway. Then she saw Leona's cousin, a youth she knew named Karl Eugene Morgan, exit the garage, open the trunk to Leona's car, get in behind the wheel and pull it into the garage. She noted that Morgan had removed some items from the trunk but wasn't certain what those items were.

After driving the car into the garage, she heard him close the garage door.

Later she heard it open and saw him backing out of the garage. He closed the door, then left in a hurry. As he drove away, he nearly hit a stop sign, she told the detectives. He obviously was agitated.

"He looked surprised," the woman wrote in a statement later. "His eyes were big and he was looking towards the house kind of surprised . . . Unexpected, I guess you could say."

And it was very strange that he was driving the car at all, the old woman told detectives. They asked her why so and she explained that Leona had confided in her. Karl Morgan was not well educated, Leona had told her, which meant he had trouble reading, which meant he could not read street and traffic signs. Leona didn't want Karl Morgan driving her car, the elderly lady told detectives. And yet Karl drove away from the house and Leona had not yet left. She surely wouldn't have given him permission to take her car, the old lady told the investigators.

After Karl Morgan left, the old lady telephoned Leona's house and knocked on her door but received no answer. After that happened several times, she decided to call the sheriff's office. Her call came in at approximately the same time as the communications center received the telephone call from Poulsbo. It was that curious set of circumstances which enabled Sergeant Seewer in Tacoma and Sergeant Cook in Poulsbo to determine the address that the young man was talking about.

Detectives Gibbs and Knabel worked until 6:00 a.m. the next morning. As one of their last orders of business, they sat down and listened to the tape recording of the telephone conversation that Karl Morgan had placed from Poulsbo to the communication center. In that conversation Morgan said that earlier in the evening he had been at his cousin's home, whom he lived with. Her boyfriend was there and they were having a terrible argument. Both she and her boyfriend were yelling at each other. Morgan went to the store. When he returned, he found blood throughout the home. He got scared and left. That was the essence of his story. It also was the only conversation he would have with Pierce County authorities.

Detectives Knabel and Gibbs found that conversation to be very curious. Although they believed their primary suspect was Morgan, they also realized it was not impossible that the man could have been framed. Another scenario was also possible. Perhaps Morgan had been in the house at the start of an argument between Leona Mae and her boyfriend. Morgan left before the yelling got so loud as to attract the attention of the elderly witness next door.

The old lady heard the crescendo, she claimed, and then silence. The killer raped Leona and then, knowing Morgan's huge proportions, found a pair of Morgan's trousers and soaked them with blood. He also soaked Morgan's other clothing with blood and then threw those in the washer. The trousers he deliberately put in the closet, and he made a careless attempt to cover the puddles of blood with papers and rugs.

This all would then look like the careless attempt of somebody with low intelligence to hide the crime. The killer knew Morgan had little more than an elementary education. The killer also scattered jewelry about the house so it would attract detectives' attention and he put the jewelry box on the backseat of the car in the hope that when Morgan stumbled upon the crime scene he would panic because of his criminal record and would steal the car. The killer then slipped quietly out the back door, slipped along the side of the house so he couldn't be seen by the old lady, and fled.

This was not an impossible theory to believe. However, it did seem highly unlikely. But Detectives Gibbs and Knabel knew that even though a suspect was in custody, their work was far from over. If Morgan was innocent, they had a responsibility to protect his rights by finding the real killer. But if Morgan was guilty, they also had a responsibility to disprove his story, one which he would spin for jurors if the case ever went that far.

Detectives caught a few hours rest and the next day got a second search warrant for the house. The evidence inside was far greater than they had anticipated, and to take out all of the blood spattered items they wanted, they needed the second warrant which detailed what these things were.

As if it hadn't been bad enough the night before, the affair became even more grisly when investigators removed the mattress from the bedroom and discovered that the stains they had noticed the previous night had actually been ones that had soaked through the mattress. The assailant, as part of his attempt to hide evidence, had turned the mattress over after he removed

279

the body from the bed.

"In talking with neighbors we learned that Leona was a very devoted Christian," Detective Gibbs said about their activity the next day. "She was well thought of in the neighborhood, was very neat and orderly. The neighbors all around there had a high regard for her."

In talking with the old lady who lived next door and to neighbors, the detectives learned that there were two other men in her life other than her cousin, Karl Morgan. One man was her ex-husband, and the second was a friend who was in the Air Force. Although he had frequented her house, it was never late at night and neighbors weren't even sure if he could have been considered a boyfriend.

In light of Morgan's tale about another man arguing with Leona Mae before she was killed, the detectives knew they would have to check into the whereabouts of these two men at the time she was murdered.

Detective Knabel set about the task of tracking down the two men while Detective Gibbs reviewed what they had gathered in the way of evidence up to that point. An entire van load of evidence was taken from the house, he said. "We collected everything we possibly could that was connected with the case."

Of particular importance to detectives was the sentence and probation form which had been found in Karl Morgan's bedroom. The detectives checked with Mississippi authorities and learned that Morgan had been sentenced to five years in prison on a charge of committing unnatural sex acts on a one-and-a-half-year-old boy.

It was a relatively easy matter for Detective Knabel to locate the victim's ex-husband and question him about his whereabouts the evening of the murder. He said he was with another woman, and that while they were out driving, their car had broken down. He was very cooperative with the detective and gave Knabel the name of the woman he was with. Knabel checked out his story with her and she verified that he was with her at the time the murder had been committed.

"That proved without a doubt, as far as we were concerned, that he wasn't involved," Detective Gibbs explained afterward.

The matter of tracking down the second man, who neighbors said was in the United States Air Force, proved to be a little more difficult for Detective Knabel. However, after talking to the ex-husband, Knabel got a lead on the man and went to McCord Air Force Base with a name. Base authorities helped locate the man, and Detective Knabel questioned him about the evening of June 27, 1981.

The man said he had been seen with a friend, and another person, who had come over to visit him that evening. He gave Detective Knabel the names of these two other men. The friends verified the man's story. But friends have been known to do such things if it meant helping out a buddy, and so Knabel contacted the third man. The third man was not a friend of the fellow Knabel was investigating and therefore had nothing to gain by lying about matters. He too verified that the Air Force enlisted man who was Leona's friend had been on the Air Force base on the evening of June 27th.

Having two persons who verified the man's alibi left no question in the detectives' minds that Karl Eugene Morgan had been lying when he said he had left Leona Mae Whigham Wilson's house while she had been arguing with her friend from the Air Force.

By eliminating the ex-husband and the Air Force enlistee as possible suspects, the detectives had disproved Morgan's version and also verified what the elderly lady who lived next door had said. She had told them that the only one to exit Leona's house after the yelling was

Morgan.

As soon as he was arrested Morgan had refused to talk to police and demanded an attorney, which he promptly received. Other than his initial phone call to the communications center in which he accused, or at least implied, the Air Force man's involvement, he never talked to investigators.

"I never had an interview with Karl Morgan," Detective Gibbs said. "And after listening to the tape (of Morgan's conversation with the communications officer) I'm glad I didn't. We had a very good case without his confession."

Detectives learned that Leona Mae had taken Karl Morgan to a counselor earlier in the day before she was killed. Her goal was to get Karl into some type of schooling.

It was like Leona to want to help him. Karl had been in trouble in Mississippi, and because of his sexual encounter with the one-and-a-half-year-old boy, he was faced with a prison term. But relatives convinced Leona that if she would take him under her wing in Washington, he'd get a suspended sentence and could possibly get a fresh start in life. Although Leona had been hesitant to let him come live with her, she finally relented.

He got a break and had the chance at a fresh start. She wanted to get him into school. Because he had been teased relentlessly as a child about his obesity, though, he adamantly refused, and detectives surmised this is what touched off their argument that day. At what point he decided to slice her throat or why, and then have sex with her dead body, only he knew. It happened after they returned from the first day's counseling session.

After the county prosecutor filed first-degree murder charges against Morgan, the 17-year-old boy was bounced over to Western State Hospital for psychiatric exams.

"During his admission, Mr. Morgan had been alert, cooperative and oriented," the doctor's letter filed with court documents.

"No delusions or hallucinations have been noted, despite Mr. Morgan's claim that he hears voices that sound like a lot of people screaming and hollering at me and making me scared to go to sleep," the doctor wrote.

Psychiatrists pegged Morgan's I.Q. at 69, which is just borderline intelligence, and said he had only gotten up to the seventh grade. He had a spotty work record and his goal was to play football, according to information contained in the doctor's letter to the judge.

"Our diagnostic impression is borderline intelligence with sexual deviation," the doctor wrote. Psychiatrists determined Morgan was able to stand trial.

Juvenile Court Judge Thomas Saurioi determined that the 5-foot 11-inch, 245-pound youth would stand trial as an adult.

Realizing his chance of beating the charge was slim, Morgan decided it was best to plead guilty to a charge of first-degree murder if the official record would state that the murder was committed during the course of a robbery. He had taken jewelry.

The information filed in Pierce County Superior court was amended twice. The final version reflected that the murder was committed during the course of the robbery, and no mention was made of the sexual attack on the dead woman.

However, the autopsy revealed she had been raped and, also, entered in the rectum. But Morgan, it must be presumed, is innocent of that charge, until which time it is proved otherwise.

On April 30, 1982, age 18, Karl Eugene Morgan entered a plea of guilty.

"I don't have memory of what happened," Morgan wrote in his statement on a plea of guilty. "I have seen the evidence against me and discussed it with my lawyer. I believe I would be found guilty of murder at trial. I enter this plea to gain benefits of plea bargaining and because of the evidence against me and because I believe I am guilty."

Superior Court Judge D. Gary Steiner sentenced Morgan to life in prison and said that he would ask the Washington State Board of Prison Terms and Paroles to never grant parole to the man who nearly chopped off a woman's head. The crime was so vicious it staggered the imagination, the judge said.

"I really don't know what happened back at the house," the overweight sex offender said when he was sentenced.

"It is my opinion that after serving a lengthy time in prison, Morgan will be just as dangerous to the community as he is now," a probation officer who interviewed Morgan wrote in his report to the judge. "I do not see him as becoming rehabilitated while he is in prison."

Morgan had his second chance. And the woman who went out of her way to help him, to make herself responsible for him, paid dearly for it—with her life.

"CUT OFF HER FINGER TO SELL HER RING FOR CRACK!"

by Tom Basinski

It was shortly after eight o'clock in the morning on April 27, 1989, and Officer Bruce Sepanak of Michigan's Flint Police Department sat behind the wheel of his patrol car at the corner of Water and Saginaw Streets in the heart of downtown Flint.

Sepanak had just bought a cup of coffee at Halo Burgers and was looking at the sports page of the *Flint Journal*. The Tigers were hovering around last place. There was a lot of season left—plenty of time for the Tigers to take last place all to themselves.

In his rearview mirror, Sepanak saw a man running toward him at a sprinter's pace. Sepanak slid his newspaper over and got out of the car. If this guy was crazy, the officer wanted some room to maneuver.

"Officer, officer, my girlfriend," the man was yelling. "I think she's dead! Help! Please!"

Sepanak calmed down the man enough to get an address, an apartment only one block away. The beat cop radioed for assistance and followed the man, Richard Andrews, to the 800 block of Schafer Square.

It was an area of fashionable condominiums near the upscale Water Street Pavilion, a miniature mecca of trendy shops, fancy restaurants, and yuppie offices. Flint had been in decline over the years in pace with hard times for the area's biggest employer, General Motors, but now the city was on the rebound. The Pavilion and some plush residential units on Schafer Square were evidence of this comeback.

The front door of the victim's apartment was standing open. Sepanak told Andrews to wait at the door. The officer, only a few feet inside, stopped when he saw the body of a woman in the middle of the living-room floor. Blood was everywhere.

Sepanak fought his horror and proceeded to the body to confirm that the victim was dead. The victim's skin was cold in the April morning. Sepanak backed out to call for a sergeant and the homicide team.

While waiting for them, the officer learned that Richard Andrews worked the midnight shift at a large retail store. He said he had tried to call his fiancee, 29-year-old Jamese Walker, around 1:00 a.m. She had not answered.

When Andrews came to her place after work, he found her on the living-room floor. Andrews remembered seeing Officer Sepanak parked at the curb as he drove to Walker's condo, so he ran back to the parked police car to get help.

Within minutes, the homicide division of the Flint Police Department was mobilized and on the way, about a half-mile drive from headquarters.

The case would belong to Sergeant Norm Day, with assistance from Sergeant Richard Ramage. Others would help as needed, but these two sleuths would carry the ball.

Deputy Chief Jerry Dickenson also responded. Although he was firmly entrenched in administrative duties, he never really got the "hunt" out of his system. Dickenson had been such a good cop so young that he had climbed through the ranks before he had his fill of investigation.

Chief Dickenson still hung out with the detectives. In

fact, just the night before, he had played in the Fraternal Order of Police Pool Championship against Sergeant Ramage. It had been a hard-fought contest until Dickenson "slopped" in an impossible bank shot that he had actually called. Onlookers said it was the kind of shot he couldn't repeat if he was given a million chances to try.

As the officers were waiting for the lab to arrive so they could enter the condominium, Dickenson was giving Ramage a hard time about being the pool champ.

Within 30 minutes, the criminalists from the Michigan State Police post arrived and the tedious crime scene work began.

Sergeant Theresa Green was in charge of the scene and would complete a scale drawing of the premises. Sergeant Gary Elford took the measurements for this work.

The officers did a careful walk-through. They noted that the deceased was wearing a pink nightgown. She was on her back in the middle of the living room. Her right leg was bent at the knee, and there were several lacerations on her forehead.

In a bizarre twist, they noted that the victim's left ring finger had been cut off and was about 10 feet to the west of her body. Several teeth missing from her mouth were found on the floor near her body.

An autopsy would be done later, but it looked like there were stab wounds to her head, neck, and abdomen. For these crimefighters who were so used to blood and gore, this scene was still tough to take.

Sergeants Ed Clark and Gary Ruffini fanned out into the neighborhood to see if anyone saw or heard anything during the night.

Meanwhile, back at the crime scene, Ramage had heard enough about his pool championship loss and told Chief Dickenson to go back and work on a budget or something. He and Sergeant Day took a closer look at the crime scene to piece together the last minutes of Jamese

Walker's life.

They decided that the killer had gained entry through the front door without apparent force. All windows were intact and the door was fine. This probably meant that Walker knew her assailant, or had opened the door on some kind of ruse. The detectives made a note to put at least a little squeeze on Richard Andrews later.

The gray carpet had blood all over it, everywhere. Apparently, the victim had been cooking goulash in the kitchen. It was scattered all over the walls and floor. A heavy iron frying pan was found against the dining-room wall. It looked as though the goulash had been in that pan.

The victim's head was indented at the left temple. The officers believed she had been struck there by the frying pan. A broken wine bottle lay in pieces on the kitchen floor. Although Walker had been stabbed, the officers could not find a knife out of place in the house. The victim had sustained jagged slashes on her neck, probably from the wine bottle, sleuths surmised. She also had clean, uniform stab wounds, probably from a knife.

The crime scene specialists from the state police post were extremely thorough in their search. When the interior of the condo did not yield the knife, the criminalists went to the rooftop where they found a brown-handled kitchen knife with apparent bloodstains on the blade.

Ramage and Day took Richard Andrews downstairs for an in-depth interview. First, they questioned him as to anything that might be missing from the condominium.

Andrews asked them if they had checked the garage. The officers said it was empty. Walker's 1985 two-door Buick should have been there, Andrews said.

Sleuths obtained the vehicle's license number via emergency contact with the secretary of state's office. An all-points bulletin was broadcast throughout Genesee County on the Mutual Aid Radio frequency.

Andrews apparently did not know that Walker's ring finger had been amputated. He told the officers that she normally wore a diamond ring valued at $1,600. Her television was missing, he said, as was a stereo, a VCR, and a portable tape player. Her collection of blues music on compact discs was also missing.

Walker did not keep a large quantity of liquor in her place, but all of it was gone, about three bottles of medium-quality scotch.

Costume jewelry from Walker's dresser was also missing, but it was of little value. Even her blender had been stolen.

When the autopsy was performed, the pathologist, Dr. David Congdon, noted that the victim had suffered three different blows to her forehead. She had been stabbed in the head and suffered a fractured skull. In addition, her jaw had been broken, and her teeth were knocked out. Walker had two stab wounds below her neck and two stab wounds in her abdomen. One of the blows to her head had probably been dealt with the frying pan. However, there were two more blows that seemed to come from a sharp-edged instrument.

The detectives started the interview with Richard Andrews by first checking with his employer to verify that he was at work all night. Later, they would go to his workplace and examine his station to figure out if he could have slipped away for an hour or so without being noticed.

The interview lasted about two hours. The officers were not just interested in the habits of Jamese Walker. They also wanted to check out the reactions of Richard Andrews to their various questions.

Andrews, they decided, was a properly grieving boyfriend. He was helpful to the detectives and exhibited none of the telltale signs of deception that the veteran homicide investigators had been accustomed to seeing during their years of interviewing guilty people.

The sleuths asked Andrews if he'd take a polygraph test. Without hesitation Andrews said, "A polygraph? Sure. Whatever you guys want. I understand you guys got to get me out of the way first since I was closest to Jamese and all. Sure. I'll take it. Tell me when and I'll be there."

Sergeant Day told Andrews they would be in contact with him at a later date. They planned to give him the test if nothing else developed. Neither of the detectives believed Andrews to be guilty.

Sergeant Ed Clark interviewed neighbors, who told him that they heard loud noises at Walker's unit sometime between 1:30 and 2:30 in the morning. The neighbors could not be more specific. They said they had immediately rolled over and gone back to sleep.

Sergeant Gary Ruffini found a neighbor who heard noises and yelling around 2:00.

Around mid-afternoon on the 27th, Ramage and Day stopped for a famous Flint Coney Island hot dog smothered in dry chili, onions, and mustard, as they brought each other up to date on the case. Sergeant Day was a physical fitness buff who normally did not eat Coney Islands because of what went in them. But today he was hungry and in a hurry, so he ordered one. Ramage, whose physical fitness routine consisted of shooting decent pool and nearly par golf, ordered two hog dogs.

The veteran detectives believed that the killer's clean entry to the unit pointed to someone who knew Jamese Walker. They did not suspect Richard Andrews, and there was no reason for him to kill her. He had a good job and the items stolen were not worth that much. There was no other reason for Andrews to kill her either. Neither of them had any affairs going on the side, and neither of them was jealous. The two had a comfortable relationship. So Walker's death was a full-scale mystery.

While Ramage and Day were finishing their hot dogs

around 2:30, Detective Dennis Sabo was cruising in the 5500 block of Martin Luther King Boulevard on Flint's north side. Sabo worked auto theft, and the large apartment complex was a place where many stolen cars were dumped.

There it was, parked in a marked stall: the car of Jamese Walker. It still had on her license plate, 569XNE. Four people were standing around the car. Sabo drove past and did not look closely for fear of alerting the four.

Sabo parked about 100 yards from the vehicle and watched. Stealthily and with tremendous caution, he radioed headquarters for assistance. Two patrol cars were dispatched to help.

Within minutes, two of the four people Sabo saw near the car walked toward an apartment. The other two climbed into the vehicle and headed south on Martin Luther King Boulevard. The marked units were not there yet, but Sabo did not get rattled.

He followed the vehicle to Pierson Road, where it pulled into a liquor store. By the time the two occupants, a man and a woman, emerged from the liquor store, six-pack in hand, four uniformed Flint police officers were waiting for them.

The couple was taken downtown in separate vehicles to the Spartan confines of an interview room in the detective bureau.

Sergeant Day interviewed the man and Ramage the woman. The man said he had borrowed the car that morning about eight o'clock from a guy named Redwine. Day asked if that was the guy's last name. The man replied, "Heck if I know. We just call him that 'cause he drinks red wine all the time."

The man said that Redwine told him he had rented the car from a lady earlier that morning. He said Redwine was one of the people standing around the vehicle when Sabo had first seen them.

After a short time, Ramage and Day got together. The woman did not know much except that she went to the store to get some malt liquor and when she came out there were police all around.

Neither detective felt the two in custody had killed Jamese Walker. The two did not seem concerned enough. The man thought he was at the police station because he did not have car insurance.

The officers had the man wait in a cell while the woman accompanied them back to the apartment where Detective Sabo had first seen them.

Redwine was still there. Although it was only mid-afternoon, he had the glassy eyes and foul breath commonly associated with people who get their daily dose of fruit from a screw-top bottle. Nevertheless, Redwine did not seem like a guy who had earlier that day bashed a woman's head in and cut off her finger in order to steal a ring. Redwine admitted to the sleuths that he "smoked a little rock, drank a little wine, and did a little stealing — but not when the owners are around."

Redwine said he had rented the car from a woman and two men. He did not know them, but he knew someone who did.

Redwine took Ramage and Day to a house on Grand Traverse Avenue. He said the woman who lived there knew the people who rented him the car. Ramage said, "You keep saying you 'rented' the car. You mean like Avis or Hertz?"

Redwine laughed. "No officer. Nothing like that. I gave them people fifty dollars." Day asked when and how Redwine was supposed to return the car. He did not know.

The woman at the house on Grand Traverse Avenue said the names of the people who brought her the car were Rod and Angie Greenlee and some guy named John. They stayed at a place on East Lorado Avenue.

The detectives told the woman not to say they had been

292

by asking about the car. She raised her hand, ready to take an oath to guarantee her silence if necessary. As they were leaving Redwine said, "That lady sure wanted to help you boys."

Ramage laughed and said, "Redwine, my man, she was afraid we were going to search her house and find all those cocaine rocks she had. She'd sell her mother to protect their rocks."

A man named John Jackson answered the door on East Lorado Avenue. Inside were Rod and Angie Greenlee. The officers made small talk for a while and glanced around the living room.

Sergeant Ramage noticed that John Jackson had cuts on both hands. When asked, Jackson explained that he had cut them when he broke a basement window on a house about six doors west of them.

The Greenlees and Jackson agreed to accompany the investigators to the detective bureau. They were transported by uniformed officers. Before returning to the police station, Ramage checked the window on the house where Jackson said he had cut his hands. All windows were dirty—and intact.

Once at Flint Police Headquarters, the detectives let Jackson sit in the hallway. The on-duty detective was instructed to keep an eye on Jackson while Ramage and Day interviewed Rod and Angie Greenlee. Although Jackson was not under arrest, the cops did not like what those cuts on his hands insinuated about his activities in the last 24 hours.

Angie told the detectives that sometime after midnight, she drove John Jackson to a condominium near the Water Street Pavilion. She drove him in her car. Jackson left and Angie waited in the car. She heard screams, became frightened, and left.

A while later Jackson showed up at her place with the brown car. He was covered with blood. Jackson gave Rod

293

and Angie the car. When pressed, Angie said he did not really "give" them the car. He sold it for several rocks of cocaine.

When Angie was asked what happened to the bloody clothing Jackson was wearing when he returned with the car, she answered, "Oh, he burned them in our fireplace." Angie gave permission for the officers to go to the apartment and retrieve what was left of the jogging suit from the cinders.

Sergeants Ramage and Day believed they had found the killer. He was sitting, dozing upright, in a chair in the hallway. Now they had to put a cap on their adrenalin and begin the painstaking, detailed work that had to withstand the test of legal scrutiny by a defense attorney.

They brought in John Jackson and sat him in the interview room. Without giving up their entire case, they let Jackson in on the details, including their suspicions about the cuts on his hands and the jogging suit in the fireplace, to know he was doomed. They told him he could attempt to lie, and make himself look foolish, or he could tell the truth and get on with his life.

Jackson decided to be a man and own up. He explained that Richard Andrews was his uncle. He had been over to Jamese Walker's residence in the past and knew she had some nice things, including a car. He also knew his uncle worked all night and that Jamese would be alone.

Jackson went to the condominium and knocked on the door. He told Walker he had to use the phone. She let him in and showed him where the phone was. Jackson then hit her from behind and Walker went down on her knees.

Walker then stood up and Jackson smashed a wine bottle across her neck and collarbone. Walker continued to fight. Jackson grabbed the first thing he could find, a frying pan on the stove, and smashed Walker alongside the head. She went down, again.

At some point, Walker knew she was beaten. Rather

than fight, she stumbled toward the front door. Jackson chased her, catching her in front of her television stand. He tripped her. As Walker was scrambling blindly to her feet, Jackson picked up the portable television and threw it on her head.

The force of the television knocked out some of the victim's teeth and flattened the side of her head. Jackson dropped the television on Walker one more time for good measure. Finally, she lay motionless. To be on the safe side, Jackson found a knife in the kitchen and stabbed the victim. As an afterthought, he tried to remove the diamond ring from her finger. When it proved to be too tight at the knuckle, he merely cut off Walker's finger and removed the ring the back way.

Jackson admitted he had returned three times to load up the victim's car with things to be sold.

Much to their disgust and disbelief, the sleuths learned that Jackson had sold the $1,600 ring for $10. In his defense, Jackson said he had asked for $20.

Jackson also told probers the addresses of the houses where he had sold Walker's belongings. Search warrants were obtained, and the property was recovered.

John Jackson was booked, and a complaint was issued charging him with first-degree murder. Assistant Prosecutor Dan Stamos put on the case, which started on Thursday, January 11, 1990.

The case was straightforward. Jackson offered no defense. He based his chances of survival on the prosecution witnesses Rod and Angie Greenlee not showing up for court. They were there, however, and testified against him.

After a three-day trial, the jury found John Jackson guilty on the first ballot. He was sentenced to life in prison on March 6, 1990.

John Jackson, 20 years old, is currently serving his sentence in the Michigan prison system.

Sergeant Norm Day has retired from the Flint Police

Department. Sergeant Richard Ramage continues to work homicide. Deputy Chief Jerry Dickenson continues to do chief's work. But he still rolls to calls from time to time.

EDITOR'S NOTE:
Richard Andrews, Redwine, and Rod and Angie Greenlee are not the real names of the persons so named in the foregoing story. Fictitious names have been used because there is no reason for public interest in the identities of these persons.

"MURDER, MAYHEM AND MUTILATION!"

by Jerry Spangler

SALT LAKE CITY, UT
JULY 28, 1989

To the many homeless in suburban Salt Lake County, there were both good and bad about the cold February winds that whipped through the streets. The wind that numbed a transient's bones also kept discarded meat from spoiling, at least not too badly. Regardless of the cold, a homeless man needs to eat and some of the best places to find discarded food is in the garbage dumpster behind supermarkets.

Randy Whittingham, one of the many street people in Salt Lake, was only looking for something to eat when he crawled into the dumpster behind one Salt Lake supermarket on February 22, 1989. Maybe today there would be some meat in his meager diet, he hoped. But when he opened a green garbage bag, the fresh meat Randy found turned his hunger to nausea.

Even a hungry transient will not eat the flesh of two freshly severed human legs.

"He wasn't just poking through the dumpster," said veteran Salt Lake County homicide Detective Jerry Thompson. "He was really going through it, opening bags and boxes. He knew the stores sometimes bagged their food they

297

threw away and he was experienced at how to find it. Anyway, he's going through this stuff and he opens a green garbage bag and finds a leg. Then he finds another leg."

Randy Whittingham immediately reported his grisly find to the Salt Lake County Sheriff's Office. There was no question that the legs belonged to someone recently dead and detectives had no doubt they were dealing with a homicide. The severed legs were each wearing a sock. But what puzzled detectives was that the sock on the second leg was not the same color as the sock on the first leg found in the dumpster.

"We thought perhaps the legs had been surgically removed because it was such a clean cut," Thompson said. "But we had never heard of doctors or hospitals discarding human parts in dumpsters behind supermarkets. And it was unlikely a doctor would amputate a pair of legs and leave the socks on."

Detectives took the legs to experts at the Utah State Medical Examiner's Office, who confirmed the detectives' initial suspicions. The legs had been severed by someone who knew nothing about proper medical procedures for amputations. They also confirmed that such an amputation would certainly have resulted in the death of the person now missing his lower limbs.

The medical examiner also reported that both legs, which had been severed at mid-thigh, belonged to the same person, a white male 40 to 50 years old. A scar on one leg could be used for identification purposes should detectives locate a candidate, but the medical examiner could provide no further information about the victim.

Investigators carefully searched the remainder of the trash dumpster, marking most garbage items into evidence. Sleuths were uncertain what in the dumpster might be relevant to the case and what was not. In addition to empty boxes and sacks, among the items recovered were a sweater, a piece of shirt and a pair of glasses. "We took everything," Thompson recalled.

Officers also conducted thorough searches of other dumpsters in the area, but found nothing. Residents in the area were questioned, but no one had seen anything unusual.

At that point, detectives were puzzled. A check with all hospitals in the region revealed no cases of any patients having their legs amputated. Nor were any of the cadavers used at the University of Utah Medical School missing any limbs. Judging from the way the legs were severed, experts concurred that the legs probably belonged to a homicide victim.

But who? There had been no cases of missing persons anywhere in the state. "There wasn't a whole lot we could do with just a pair of legs and no one to match them to," Detective Thompson recalled. "We just went through the standard motions of a homicide investigation: Questioning people in the area, checking when the last time the dumpster had been dumped, things like that. But we weren't very optimistic."

Detectives were still going through the motions on February 23rd when they got a call from the Salt Lake City Police Department, a sister agency with jurisdiction in the downtown area. An elderly man had called to say a close relative had been missing since February 21st, the day before the legs were found. The missing man, Larry Duane White, was a freelance journalist who had recently moved to Salt Lake City from Indiana to work on a book.

A description of the missing man matched the posthumous profile given by the medical examiner. With permission of the relative (who lived with the missing man), county and city investigators began to search White's apartment. "We took the two mismatched socks with us and started going through the apartment from top to bottom," Thompson said. "The matches to both socks were in Larry White's bedroom."

The mismatched socks were not proof positive that the severed legs found in the dumpster belonged to Larry

White. Experts ran several other tests to confirm their suspicions. "Fibers found on the socks from the dumpster matched fibers on the floor of his residence, and we also matched DNA samples from the relative with those taken from the legs. There was no question they belonged to the missing Larry White."

The severed legs, meanwhile, had been sent to the FBI laboratories where forensic investigators determined they had been cut with a thin-bladed, small saw. They could not determine if it had been a power tool or an extremely sharp hand tool, like a hacksaw. Experts there could shed no further light on the case.

Now that a victim had been positively identified, detectives renewed their homicide investigation with vigor. The victim's relative was questioned in detail. When was the last time he had seen Larry White? Who were Larry's associates? What was the nature of the book Larry was working on? Where did he work? Had he and Larry argued? Had Larry ever disappeared before? Did Larry have a girlfriend?

"About the only thing the relative could tell us was that Larry was extremely shy and didn't do a lot of dating. He didn't have any brothers or sisters, no close friends and he was a churchgoing man who minded his own business. He was a total loner, but he also wasn't involved in anything remotely illegal."

The relative related to officers how on February 19th—the Sunday before Larry White had disappeared—he had joined Larry for dinner, along with a new friend Larry had invited for dinner, a man named Bill Anderson. "I even bought extra raspberries," the relative recalled. Larry had been teaching Bill Anderson how to play chess. In return, Anderson had promised to help White find a job that paid a regular paycheck. According to the victim's relative, Larry White was supposed to begin work at a Salt Lake telemarketing firm on February 28th—the same firm for which Anderson already worked.

The dinner had been uneventful. Nothing unusual was

300

said, and neither Larry White or Bill Anderson acted suspiciously. Anderson had left after playing chess. The relative said he had not seen Anderson since. Larry White had kept to his routine on Monday, February 20th, and Tuesday, February 21st, when White left the apartment in the morning. Only White never returned.

The relative knew nothing about Bill Anderson. He didn't know the name of the telemarketing firm where he worked. He didn't know where Anderson lived. He didn't have any idea whether Anderson and Larry White had been involved in anything suspicious. The only clue the victim's relative could offer was that Anderson had been driving a gold or yellow car, possibly a Plymouth.

Detectives began a search not only for a gold car registered to a Bill Anderson, they also issued an "attempt to locate" on Larry White's car, which had been missing since February 21st. The victim's car was found a few days later in Salt Lake City, but no evidence was found inside the car. It had been wiped clean of any fingerprints. Fiber evidence from the car also revealed nothing of importance.

The search for Anderson's car was not as successful. While Anderson is a common name in Utah, investigators found no gold or yellow Plymouths registered to a Bill or William Anderson. Detectives also found it odd that Anderson—if he was really such a good friend of Larry White—had not bothered to call the relative or visit to express his concern. The fact that Larry White was missing and that foul play was suspected was by now a hot item in the local media.

But Bill Anderson was missing too. Was he also a victim?

Sleuths could find no evidence anywhere that Larry White was involved in illegal activities. He had never been arrested for anything, and those who knew him described him as a solid citizen. White had a modest bank account, but it showed no unusual cash transactions. Nor were there any large cash withdrawals in the days prior to or after his disappearance.

Larry White's only pastimes were chess, working on his book and genealogy, the hobby of searching for records of one's ancestors. Detectives immediately focused on the book, a historical novel entitled *Exodu Gallioten* set during the French Revolution. Investigators found 156 pages of the manuscript and set about to determine if the clue to the victim's disappearance and murder might be in the book.

"It was a terrible book, real hard to follow," said Captain Bob Jack. "There's a little bit of politics, religion and architecture. It really bounces around. But there's nothing in it to inspire foul play."

Because witnesses told officers that White rarely, if ever, dated women, sleuths investigated the possibility that Larry White was a homosexual and had perhaps gotten involved with a violent sex cult. It would not have been the first case of that kind in Salt Lake County. But sleuths could find no evidence that Larry White had a sexual relationship with anyone, male or female. And there was certainly nothing in Larry White's personal possessions to indicate he was involved in anything kinky.

The bottom-line, the detectives realized, was that White lived a quiet, uneventful life in relative obscurity. He had lived in Salt Lake City until 1984 when his mother died. He then moved to Indiana to help a relative sell a house and returned to Salt Lake City in 1986.

"There was nothing on him. He's just not an interesting person," said one detective. "Why anyone would want him dead defies all reason. There was no motive."

The only direction the investigation pointed toward was Bill Anderson and detectives were faced with the rather formidable task of locating all Bill Andersons in the state and finding the right one. Based on the description by the victim's relative of the Bill Anderson who had come to dinner the weekend before the murder, police artists made a composite drawing of the suspect that was passed along to all patrol officers. Homicide detectives were quickly reaching a dead-end unless they could find the elusive Bill Anderson.

"We wanted to question him," Thompson said. "He was a suspect only in that he may have been the last person to see the victim alive. We didn't have anywhere else to turn."

Added homicide Lieutenant Ben Forbes at the time, "We're not saying he is a suspect, but we find it unusual that he hasn't sought to contact us or the victim's relative since all this happened.

Moreover, there had been considerable publicity on the case of the severed legs. Television and newspaper accounts had run repeated pleas by detectives for help in locating the Bill Anderson identified in the composite drawing. If anyone had recognized the drawing, they hadn't come forward yet.

There was also the probability that Bill Anderson was being intentionally elusive. Based on the relative's statement that Larry White was supposed to begin work at a telemarketing firm, officers began contacting every telemarketing firm in the region, looking for any employment records of a Bill Anderson. Detectives eventually found a telemarketing company that had hired a Bill Anderson, but Anderson had apparently stopped coming to work one day without a word to anyone. When had he last come in? February 21st, the day before the severed legs were found, lawmen were informed by the firm.

Using Social Security and employment records, one detective discovered that Bill Anderson was probably Robert Eugene Bennett. Bennett was also known to use other alias, including Joe King Bennett and Roy Anderson.

The detective filed charges in federal court against Robert Bennett for false use of a Social Security card to secure employment on June 1, 1988. The arrest warrant was simply precautionary so officers could hold Bennett for questioning on the homicide, should they ever locate him, Thompson said. "We certainly didn't have any evidence to link him to a homicide," he added.

Detectives began a thorough search into Bennett's background. Using information from job applications that

Robert Bennett had filled out, officers traced Bennett to Beaverton, Oregon. Interestingly, on February 22, 1978—exactly 11 years before—Bennett's wife, Floy Jean Bennett, had disappeared without a trace from her Beaverton home. She has never been seen nor heard from since. Police questioned Bennett at that time about her disappearance, but officers there had nothing linking him to the disappearance. Bennett disappeared from the area a short time later.

Detectives questioned Bennett's Salt Lake employer at some length about Bennett and where he might have gone. The employer at that time could not offer much information. However, a few days later, the employer called detectives from Las Vegas.

Said Thompson, "The guy that owned the telemarketing firm in Salt Lake also owned one in Las Vegas. He was down there checking out the Vegas operation when Bennett (he knew him by Anderson) shows up looking for a job."

The business owner called long distance to the Salt Lake County Sheriff's Office. "You know that Anderson guy you were asking me about? He's down here in Las Vegas," he said.

Salt Lake officers immediately called the Las Vegas Metro Police Department and requested that Anderson/Bennett be arrested on the warrant for the Social Security fraud. Upon his arrest, Anderson admitted his name was indeed Robert Eugene Bennett. Salt Lake homicide detectives immediately boarded a plane for Las Vegas.

"When he found out who we were and why we were there, he refused to answer anything we asked him," Detective Thompson recalled. "He had the same answer for everything. 'You'd better talk to my attorney about that.' He would not answer even the most basic questions, like where he had been living, or where his car was or where he had been working." Bennett was later extradited to Utah on the warrant charging him with misdemeanor Social Security violations. But still his silence continued.

Detectives remained behind in Las Vegas, convinced that

the clues to Larry White's murder were there, not in Salt Lake. In particular, they were looking for Bennett's gold or yellow car. But looking for a car in Las Vegas is harder than finding a needle in a haystack. There are literally thousands of impound lots, as well as thousands of acres of parking lots at casinos where cars could be parked for weeks at a time and not be noticed.

Utah detectives met with Las Vegas detectives, as well as investigators with the National Auto Theft Bureau, who pledged their assistance. They also met with security officers at the casinos along the famed Las Vegas Strip. And they began the tedious process of calling one impound yard after another. In each case, they came up empty.

There were other leads to follow. "We went to where he had applied for work," Thompson explained, "and they had his application for employment on file. We got a home address from that and that led us to a boardinghouse where he had lived a few days and had then moved. There wasn't anything there to help us."

Detectives asked the landlord if Bennett had been driving a car, but the landlord didn't remember a car. Bennett rode a bicycle when he lived there. The landlord also had no idea where Bennett had moved to and didn't bother to ask.

There was a considerable time lag between when Bennett had disappeared from Salt Lake and when he was spotted by his former employer. Where had he been? Had he worked elsewhere in Las Vegas? Detectives set out to canvass every telemarketing firm in Las Vegas—national capital of such companies. There are literally hundreds of telemarketing firms there.

But officers were able to focus their search on a much smaller list. When Bennett was arrested, he had in his possession a "help wanted" section from the local newspaper and several telemarketing job prospects had been circled.

One by one, the detectives began calling the companies. None had heard of Robert Bennett or Bill Anderson. Detectives later called back, trying other aliases that Bennett had been known to use in the past. "Finally, we got a hit on one of those aliases and the description they gave us over the phone matched," Thompson said.

Detectives went to the telemarketing company, which provided them with a copy of the man's job application. It listed a different home address than the one listed on the other application. However, when officers went to the address on Desert Springs Road, they found no residence at that address. In fact, that exact address didn't even exist. Detectives went inside the business establishment that came closest to the address given on the application.

"What we found was the address matched a mail drop inside that business," Thompson recalled. When Bennett was arrested, a key to a mailbox was found in his possession.

Upon questioning the owners of the business, they told probers the box had been rented in the name of Larry White and they distinctly remembered the man who had rented the box. He always rode a bicycle, they said, and he had applied for the mailbox under the name of Larry White. The owner had asked for photo identification and immediately became suspicious.

"She immediately noticed the man in the picture ID was not the man standing before her," Thompson said. "When she questioned him on it, he said, 'Oh, I work for Mr. White and I will be picking up his mail for him.' He then produced a photo identification for a Robert Eugene Bennett."

Detectives secured permission to see if the key found on Bennett's person fit the mailbox in question. It fit and inside officers found a package addressed to Larry White. But there was no clue on the package as to where Bennett was living. And sleuths were certainly no closer to finding Bennett's car.

Detectives went back to calling telemarketing firms. They eventually located three other companies that had had applications from individuals using the same mailbox address registered to Bennett. No other home address was given on the applications. Detectives also continued to check impound lots, all without luck. "There were so many of them it was an overwhelming task," Thompson said.

Despite the setbacks, detectives were able to trace Robert Bennett's movements around Las Vegas. He had applied for jobs at five different telemarketing firms on five different dates, he had rented a mailbox and he had moved into and back out of a boardinghouse. But they were no closer to finding the evidence they needed and detectives finally returned to Salt Lake City empty-handed.

"When we got back to Salt Lake we started talking about the case and what we knew about Bennett," Detective Thompson recalled. "He was looking more and more like a prime suspect in that he was using Larry White's identification, but we didn't have much more."

Sleuths got their biggest break in the case when it dawned on them that Bennett always stayed in boardinghouses, usually cheap ones. Detectives began going through the newspaper recovered from Bennett in Las Vegas and began calling the listings for boardinghouses. None of the listings were marked in the paper, but if Bennett had used the newspaper to find employment, perhaps he would have used the newspaper to find a new residence. Detectives called them all asking whether they had ever heard of Robert Bennett. Larry White? Bill Anderson?

"We called a hotel in Las Vegas and gave the guy Bennett's name and the guy there recognizes it right off," Thompson said. Bennett had paid in advance, but had never come back.

"I still have the guy's stuff here and his car is still parked out front," the hotel manager told Thompson. Detectives raced back to Las Vegas and found that a gold Plymouth was parked in front of the boardinghouse.

Armed with a search warrant, Detective Thompson and the other probers went through Bennett's belongings. In his luggage they found a loaded .38-caliber revolver, as well as Larry White's birth certificate, Social Security card, personal identification card and driver's license. They also found a letter to vital statistics requesting a copy of Larry White's birth certificate.

Sleuths also located a package of green garbage bags in the car—the same kind of bags used to wrap the victim's severed legs. But, "there was really nothing much in the car," Thompson said. "The inside had been washed thoroughly. Even the mats in the trunk had been removed and washed."

Officers put the car on a U-Haul truck to take it back to Salt Lake City for further forensic examination. They also tagged all of Bennett's belongings and booked them into evidence.

The investigators then went to the landlord and asked if Bennett had anything else. Thompson explained, "We told him we didn't care if he had taken something of value. In fact, we told him he could keep it if we didn't need it for the investigation."

The landlord hesitated, then responded. "Oh, yeah. There was something else. The guy had a microwave oven I've been using. It's on my counter."

Detectives, seeing no connection between the murder and the microwave oven, were inclined to let the man keep it. They then changed their mind and decided to take it back with them to Salt Lake. "Better safe than sorry," Thompson said, explaining their rationale.

When officers later checked the microwave oven against the other evidence collected in the case, they discovered that one item that had been removed from the dumpster was a cardboard microwave oven box. The brand and model number on the box matched the microwave that Robert Bennett had in Las Vegas.

While the car revealed no smoking gun, the officers did find a Utah and a Nevada license plate in the trunk. The Nevada plates led nowhere, but the Utah plates led to a residence in South Salt Lake. The owner of the plates said the car hadn't been registered in years, that they were still attached to a car sitting in his backyard. The officers asked him to check the car and when he did he found the plates missing.

Detectives wanted to know how Bennett had managed to get the plates. The man didn't recognize Bennett's name, but added that he owned an apartment behind his house, that maybe the people there knew something. The tenants there, when questioned by police, had never heard of Robert Bennett, nor had they seen anyone messing around with the car or its license plates.

Probers questioned the landlord further about his previous tenants and determined there had been a previous tenant named Bill Anderson. "The landlord had thought it strange because this guy had paid for the room in advance and then had never bothered to use the apartment," Thompson said. "But he was paid up and he never paid much attention to it."

Sleuths secured permission to search the apartment. They took out the drain traps, looking for flesh or hair, but found nothing. Detectives walked around the apartment. "Do you see anything unusual?" they asked the landlord.

"Nothing really. Except that there used to be flowers and grass along this fence," the landlord answered. "Now it's just dirt. And I don't recall him doing any yard work."

Detectives stuck a probe into the ground about four inches before it hit something solid and could go no further. Thinking it was solid dirt or bedrock, the officers gave up. They didn't have the equipment or the probable cause to dig deeper.

"The owner of the property got curious and started digging after we had left," explained Thompson, "and he uncovered some fresh concrete. He had never poured concrete there, so he broke out a chink. There was a garbage bag beneath the concrete. That's when he decided he had better call us back."

Homicide detectives immediately recognized the bag as the same kind of green garbage bag that the severed legs of the victim had been wrapped in—and the same kind that

309

had been recovered from Robert Bennett's car in Vegas. Upon removing the bag, detectives discovered a headless, limbless torso clad only in white undershorts. A penny, a pair of work gloves and a small neck chain were also recovered from the grave.

Investigators returned the next day with a backhoe and began unearthing different portions of the yard. Next to the house someone had planted beautiful flowers. But it wasn't the owner. "We dug down and found another portion of new concrete and below that another garbage bag," Thompson said. "We found Larry White's head inside that one."

Despite repeated excavations in the yard, detectives never discovered the victim's arms. They speculate the arms were disposed of the same way the legs were, in a dumpster. Only the arms never happened to be discovered by a transient looking for food.

"We dug up the whole countryside and we did not find those," explained Chief Deputy Charles Shepherd. "There's a possibility they may have been put in a dumpster like the legs. We don't know."

An autopsy on the torso revealed that Larry White had been shot five times and that his limbs and head had been severed after he had been shot to death. Four slugs removed from the body were matched to slugs fired from the gun found in Bennett's luggage. They were perfect matches. White had been shot twice in the back, twice in the side and once in the chest.

Robert Bennett was charged in 3rd District Court with one count of second-degree murder, a first-degree felony punishable by five years to life in prison. Detectives had wanted to charge Bennett with first-degree homicide, a capital offense, because of the gruesome nature of the crime. (Utah law allows for capital homicide charges if the murder is particularly heinous). However, the medical examiner determined that the victim was already dead when he had been dismembered. Larry White was shot to death — not legally an unusually heinous crime to warrant a death penalty.

"Still, everything was starting to fall into place," Detective Thompson said. "But we couldn't put together a motive. We never have. Larry White did not have money or anything else of value."

Thompson, like other detectives, believes Bennett may have killed a victim any time he wanted to start a new life and needed a new identity. In Bennett's possessions, lawmen found several personal identifications belonging to people they could not locate. "Are they dead? I don't know," Thompson said. "We don't know who they are."

Perhaps they, like Bennett's wife, simply disappeared without a trace. Detectives doubt they will ever find the answers. Bennett himself has refused to talk about the murder of Larry White, the disappearance of his wife or any of the other cases police want to question him about.

"We've never had any substantial information which linked Mr. Bennett to his wife's disappearance," said Beaverton Police Officer Mark Hyde. "With his arrest in Salt Lake City, it certainly sheds a bright light on our investigation up here."

While Oregon detectives were at a dead-end, Utah detectives had done their jobs well. So well, in fact, that Bennett suddenly decided to plead guilty as charged on July 28, 1989 during the middle of a preliminary hearing on the second-degree murder charge. He was immediately sentenced to five years to life in the Utah State Prison.

Today, detectives marvel that the case was ever solved. "If that transient had not opened that bag, we would never have had a homicide case. It would have been a missing person's case without a clue," Thompson said.

Added Salt Lake County Sheriff Pete Hayward, "When we started, all we had was a set of legs with different socks. If we hadn't had the legs, it would have been classified as a missing person's case. It was a tough case, they (detectives) did a good job. They just wouldn't let loose of any little piece of evidence they got. It goes back to the basics."

311

EDITOR'S NOTE:

Randy Wittingham is not the real name of the person so named in the foregoing story. A fictitious name has been used because there is no reason for public interest in the identity of this person.

"HE SLICED PAUL TO PIECES!"

by Gary Ebbels

LAS VEGAS, NV
NOVEMBER 15, 1988

Paul Wade was a dealer, and a darned good one at that, in one of the casinos that line the famous Las Vegas Strip. He worked the graveyard shift, meaning he had to be on the floor pumping cards at 3:00 a.m.

He and his girlfriend had a routine worked out whereby he could be sure to make it to the casino by 3:00 a.m. She, too, worked a graveyard shift, but she was not employed by a casino. She normally left for work at 11:00 p.m. At 2:00 p.m., she made it a point to wake up Wade with a telephone call. Wade, however, had a habit of drifting back to dreamland after the 2:00 a.m. call, so she always made another call at 2:15 a.m. to wake him up one more time. The system had worked for a long time. Wade always seemed to make it to the casino at the appointed hour.

The night of November 19, 1987, was just like any other for Wade and his girlfriend. She left his apartment for work at her usual time, and he said he would get some sleep. But before she left, there was a telephone call for Wade. She overheard part of the conversation but thought little about it. When he got off the

313

telephone, Wade kissed her goodnight and she left.

It came time for her 2:00 a.m. break at work, and she used that break to make the wake-up call as she always did. Wade answered and thanked her for calling. As her break came to an end, she made the usual 2:15 a.m. follow-up call, but this time there was no answer. Maybe Wade had stayed awake this time and was in the shower, she thought. She managed to get a few minutes more of break time at around 2:30 a.m. and called Wade again.

Still there was no answer.

Wade's girlfriend now became worried. She just knew something had to be wrong.

At 3:00 a.m., she called the casino where Wade was a dealer. The shift boss told her that Wade had never shown up this particular morning and, as an aside, the boss said he could have been used as well. The casino was full of gambling tourists, and every available dealer was needed.

The woman now knew her instincts were correct. Something was radically wrong. She asked her boss if she could leave work early to check on Wade. She explained the strange things that had happened in what should have been their normal telephone routine and she noted that according to his boss, he had never made it to the casino.

She was allowed to leave. She drove quickly to Wade's apartment and let herself in with a key. And that is when she saw something that twisted her guts—something that will live with her for the rest of her life. She saw the lifeless, blood-soaked body of Paul Wade sprawled on the floor. His flesh had been torn many times, and the blood had flowed like wine.

Wade's girlfriend quickly shook herself out of shock and reached for the telephone. She called the Las Vegas Metropolitan Police Department and reported that Wade was dead and that it didn't look like he died an accidental or natural death.

By now, the Nevada skies were starting to brighten as the daylight of November 20th began to spread itself across the Las Vegas Valley. Uniformed officers were dispatched to the Wade apartment. These officers had been patrolling in the area of the apartment and were radio-dispatched to the building. Homicide Detectives Karen Good and Al Leavitt were sent to the Wade apartment from Metro headquarters downtown.

Wade's girlfriend was asked to wait at the apartment for the officers and detectives. The uniformed officers arrived first since they had been in the area anyway. The woman briefed them on the chain of events that had brought her there after cutting her work day short.

As she briefed them, the detectives came in. One uniformed officer brought the detectives up-to-date on the woman's statement. Then the sleuths took over the questioning.

The woman said all had appeared normal when she left the apartment. True, Wade had taken a telephone call just before she left the building, but there was certainly nothing unusual about a telephone call, she said. The detectives picked up on the telephone angle, though. One sleuth asked the woman if she had overheard any of the conversation.

She said the only thing she remembered about it was that, in the course of the conversation, Wade referred to the caller as Dave. She said it seemed like a simple, innocent telephone conversation that could not have lasted more than five minutes.

One of the detectives walked to the bedroom telephone and called headquarters. A request was made for an ambulance to take the body to the morgue. It appeared to the detectives and the uniformed officers that Wade had been the victim of multiple stab wounds, but

315

an autopsy would have to be performed to make the cause of death official.

A lab team was also requested to search the apartment for any possible physical evidence.

The detectives then resumed their questioning of Wade's girlfriend who had made the grisly discovery. They asked her if she had any idea who the Dave on the telephone might have been. She said she wasn't sure. Wade had several friends, and she just couldn't remember any Daves being among them.

When the lab team and the ambulance arrived at the apartment, the sleuths left for headquarters. Here there would begin a preliminary report and try to put together the jigsaw puzzle that would hopefully end up as a picture of the knife-wielding murderer of Paul Wade. They had little to go on, but these veteran detectives had solved cases in the past with even fewer puzzle pieces in their hands.

The morning passed with little progress. The detectives were awaiting a preliminary autopsy report, as well as a report from the lab team. By mid-afternoon, they had a report on the autopsy. Paul Wade had been stabbed some 32 times, and those stab wounds were all over his body. He had even been stabbed in the head.

On top of that, the killer had left the point of his knife in what was probably the final stab wound. It had somehow broken off while the slashing took place.

No knife had been found at the crime scene. At least none that the officers and detectives had seen. The report from the lab team was still to come, though.

When it came in a bit later, it was confirmed that there was no knife in the victim's apartment. But the lab crew did bring in a notebook containing names and telephone numbers. One of the members told Detective Leavitt he had no idea why he had brought the book in. Something just told him to do it, he said.

Leavitt thumbed through the book. It had first names only, with corresponding telephone numbers on the right side. He went down the list of names and at the bottom of one page, he found a Dave. It was a longshot, but at this time it was the only lead available.

On the inter-office telephone, he notified Detective Good of the notebook that had been found in the apartment and further told him that there was a Dave listed in it.

The two detectives went to work on the book immediately. Using the services of the telephone company, they cross-referenced the number and came up with an address. It was an apartment not far from Wade's. The reason they wanted to use the address rather than call the number was to avoid spooking this Dave should he have had anything to do with the knifing. It is always better to just show up. That way, no one ever has a chance to skip out.

There was another catch. The telephone number was not registered under the name of Dave. It was a different name and that made it even more important for the detectives to simply show up completely unannounced.

When the sleuths arrived, there was no Dave at the apartment. There was another man, though, who said he was the roommate of David Riggins, a 32-year-old Las Vegan. The sleuths told him they were investigating a murder and fully expected his cooperation. The man said he wanted no trouble with the law. However, he also had no idea of how he could help them.

He related he had been with Riggins the previous night and that Riggins claimed he was running short of cash but knew where he could borrow some. He said he could borrow money from a friend who had an apartment on Bruce Street. The roommate said he drove Riggins to the apartment complex and waited outside while Riggins went in.

317

About a half hour passed, and then Riggins left the building and got into the car. He drove him back to their apartment. Riggins stayed there for a short time and then went out, saying he was going to do some good old-fashioned partying in Las Vegas now that he had been able to borrow some money.

The roommate said he had not seen him since.

On the surface there was nothing unusual about the story. But there was one coincidence that did not ring true with either detective. Wade's apartment was on Bruce Street.

The detectives returned to headquarters. Leavitt again went over the autopsy report. It was getting late, but the two detectives did not want to call it a day just yet.

In the second perusal of the report, they found that Wade also had dog bites on his legs. Yet, there had been no dog at the crime scene.

One of them made telephone contact with the victim's girlfriend. She was told knife wounds had been confirmed as the cause of death. She was also told about the dog bites.

The woman said Wade owned a dog and that the animal had probably fled the apartment during the murder. As for the bites on Wade's legs, she told them the only thing she could figure was that the dog was trying to protect his master, got confused and bit the wrong man.

That cleared up that part of the autopsy report.

But David Riggins still remained a mysterious piece of this puzzle. Had he gone to an apartment on any street but Bruce Street in his quest to borrow money, he wouldn't even be considered a piece of the puzzle. It was just too much of a coincidence.

The detectives requested that the Riggins apartment be staked out around the clock by uniformed officers. They also put out a bulletin that he was wanted for questioning.

The night passed uneventfully. The following morning, though, Riggins came back to his apartment. Uniformed officers at the scene detained him while Good and Leavitt were called to the building by radio. When they arrived, they read him his Miranda warning just in case he should turn out to be a suspect.

After telling the detectives he was the son of Marilyn Monroe and John F. Kennedy, Riggins elected to exercise his right to remain silent. He told Good and Leavitt that he had nothing to say because there was nothing to say. He declared he knew nothing of any knifing.

At this point, there was little probable cause for an arrest, but the strange behavior of David Riggins gave the sleuths enough to hold him for 48 hours while probers continued to search for clues to Wade's murder.

Riggins was handcuffed and taken to the Clark County Jail. He was booked into a cell. While uniformed officers were handling this chore, the detectives were busy conferring with Deputy District Attorney Bill Berrett. What they needed was a search warrant for the Riggins apartment. Maybe the residence would hold the key to link Riggins to the Wade slaying.

Then, again, it might hold nothing and Riggins would have to be released. In that case, the search for Wade's killer would go on, of course, but the search for Riggins would be over.

That afternoon the apartment search was conducted. A coat with blood smears was found. In one of the pockets were two snapshots. This still didn't make much of a case against Riggins if he was, indeed, Wade's murderer. The detectives kept on looking and then they found the one thing they needed. On the kitchen table was a knife. It had no blood, but it also had no tip.

The knife was placed in a plastic evidence bag. The

coat was also taken. After getting back to headquarters, the two sleuths contacted the victim's girlfriend and asked her to come downtown and check out the coat. She was at the detective bureau within the hour. Tears came to her eyes when she saw the coat. It had belonged to Wade, she said. They showed her the two photographs. She said those, too, had belonged to Wade; she had seen them several times.

The case was quickly building.

It would be up to police identification expert, Richard Good, to match up the knifepoint taken from the victim's body with the knife taken from the Riggins apartment. If he could, it would definitely seal the case. Meanwhile, the very fact that Wade's coat and pictures had been taken from the Riggins abode was enough to hold him for more than 48 hours. This would give Richard Good sufficient time to make the all-important comparison.

A charge of open murder was filed against David Riggins. No bail was set. His home would be the county jail, at least for the next several days.

The following day, Richard Good reported to detectives that their search for Wade's killer was finally over, that his murderer was already locked up tight in the county jail. Riggins' knife matched perfectly with the tip taken from the corpse. There was no doubt about it.

Back to D.A. Berrett went the detectives. They informed him of the fruits of their search of the Riggins apartment, and they told him the knife had been the one used on Paul Wade.

Berrett got the judicial ball rolling by scheduling a Justice Court arraignment and subsequent preliminary hearing. Riggins continued to be held without bail. Berrett served official notice that he was going to seek the death penalty should he obtain a first-degree murder conviction.

By now Riggins was talking to fellow inmates. He told three of them he was a heavy drug user because he had been hearing voices since the age of four. The drugs helped him drown those voices out, he said.

The inmates reported his conversations to authorities at the jail who, in turn, passed them along to Detectives Good and Leavitt. Riggins admitted killing Wade in those conversations.

He said Wade had tried to kill him by putting fiberglass in some bottled water used for mixing cocaine for injecting. He further added that Wade had AIDS, and had smeared his blood on some cocaine packets to spread the virus around town.

Riggins' court-appointed attorney got wind of these strange jailhouse conversations. He already knew his client had boasted of having a movie star and a president for parents, and that alone had had him thinking about an insanity defense. Now he had the tale of little voices and heavy drug use.

He knew the state had Riggins cold, but this might give him a way out. He decided to use an insanity defense. He spent the next year trying to put one together.

Riggins was examined by three psychiatrists. This is always the first step when insanity is the defense. But, unfortunately for Riggins, all three physicians declared him sane.

The insanity defense could still be used, of course, but just how powerful could it be with three psychiatrists saying the man was sane? Riggins had been held without bail throughout his year of trying to get somebody—anybody—to believe he was crazy.

It was not until November of 1988 that the case went to trial. A jury was assembled in the courtroom of District Judge Jim Brennan and D.A. Berrett went to work. His formal notice of seeking the death penalty still stood.

He presented the jury with the overwhelming evidence Good and Leavitt had collected. He also called the psychiatrists who testified David Riggins was not insane.

The defense then did the only thing they could do. Riggins was called to the witness stand. He told the jury of hearing voices which he believed were those of spiders. He testified he saw spirits and aliens.

D.A. Berrett was ready for the testimony. He analyzed it for the jurors during his final arguments.

"He's not crazy," argued the prosecutor. "The facts indicate he is not crazy and that it was premeditated murder. The most serious mistake Paul Wade made in his life was knowing David Riggins."

In his testimony, Riggins had also gone through the AIDS story. Berrett called Wade's girlfriend in rebuttal. She said the victim most definitely did not have AIDS.

Riggins also testified that the knifing was accidental. Then he said Wade knifed himself a couple of times and handed him the weapon, asking that he finish the job.

Berrett told the jurors that testimony was the silliest he had ever heard.

"He acted as Satan's assistant in this case and destroyed the most precious thing on earth—human life," the prosecutor argued.

The efforts of the defense fell on deaf ears in the jury box. On November 15th, the jurors found David Riggins guilty of first-degree murder. Their job was not yet over, though. They would have to sit through a penalty hearing and then set the punishment for the murderer at life in prison, with or without the possibility of parole, or death by leathal injection.

Judge Brennan scheduled that hearing for the following day. D.A. Berrett was in fine form in his quest for the death penalty. The jurors never hesitated in condemning Riggins to death. It would be a much more humane death than the one suffered by Paul Wade. Riggins' arm would take a shot of poison and he would be gone.

Just when the injection would be made was anybody's guess. Riggins could spend years on Death Row while the slow appeal process works its way through the state and federal courts. But those years would be spent in the state prison at Carson City, far from the glitter of Las Vegas that David Riggins once loved so much.

"CHOPPED HER BODY ON THE KITCHEN TABLE!"

by Philip Westwood

It was the late afternoon of Sunday, May 14, 1989. The weather outside was hot and sticky, unusually so for the time of year. But inside the police station that served the town of Wednesfield, in the heart of the industrial English Midlands, the temperature was a constant and very pleasant 70 degrees. A highly efficient air conditioning system ensured that, whatever was happening outside, the interior of the station was always comfortable and cool.

The desk sergeant's manner was extremely cool, too, as he tried to calm the anxious and agitated man who was separated from him by the width of the long wooden counter dividing the official section of the station from the area reserved for the public.

"Tell me the whole story, sir, from the start," said the sergeant, employing his best soothing voice. "And try to keep calm," he added. "Whatever it is, we'll sort it out together."

To the soothing tone of the sergeant's voice was now added the quality of reassurance. But the man on the other side of the counter was anything but reassured.

He wrung his hands together and the whiteness of his knuckles betrayed to the sergeant the high level of tension that had the man firmly in its grip. He shifted nervously from one foot to the other. The leather soles of his shoes made a harsh, grating noise on the polished tiles of the police station floor.

"Something's happened to her. I just know it has. It's been nearly a week since I've seen her. I've checked up. Nobody's seen her. She hasn't been to work. They don't know where she is. She hasn't phoned in sick. Nobody's called in to say that she's sick. I just know that something terrible has happened to her."

"Calm down, sir," said the sergeant once more. "This is getting us nowhere. Start at the beginning and tell me everything—calmly and quietly."

The man gave his name as Bob Roberts. He was 51 years old and he lived at Brownhills, a town some five miles from Wednesfield. The object of his concern was Vivienne Marshall, a 46-year-old woman with whom he shared his home.

Roberts explained to the sergeant that he had met Vivienne the previous January at a pub—the Oxley Arms, three miles to the other side of Wednesfield.

"We got to talking, and I suppose that it was love at first sight as far as I was concerned," he said. "She has a great personality and is a very caring person."

Roberts went on to say that he spent most of his evenings at the pub. The company was convivial, a fact that he appreciated greatly. Since the break-up of his marriage, he had come to understand the true meaning of loneliness.

Vivienne was bubbly and cheerful and she made him laugh. That was something he had not done in a long time. She was also very bright. Her membership in Mensa, an organization for those with an extremely high IQ, was a clear indication of Vivienne's intelligence.

But there was another side to Vivienne. She was, Roberts had learned early in their relationship, the victim of a vicious and violent husband. He would beat her unmercifully at the slightest provocation, and the woman was truly terrified of him.

"He's even had a go at me," said Roberts. "He tried to run me down with his car after he found out that I was seeing her."

Vivienne and her husband had been married for five years. Her first marriage had broken up in 1982 and she had met her current husband, Barry Marshall, Roberts told the sergeant, shortly afterward. Barry was also freshly out of the rigors of a divorce, and the couple had married more or less on the rebound. Outwardly, Barry was a solid and respectable citizen. By profession, he was a teacher. He taught mathematics at a school in the nearby town of West Bromwich. He was also a skilled chess player, potentially one of the best in the country. All of this, coupled with his softspoken, cut-glass English accent, made Barry Marshall a person whom other people respected.

But, claimed Roberts, there was a dark and sinister side to Barry's nature. He was a judo expert, not that his expertise in the sport was any indication of an illtempered disposition. If anything, the opposite applied. Practitioners of judo are usually among the most self-controlled and even-tempered people around.

Barry Marshall was, however, different. At least, according to Bob Roberts, he was different. Marshall used his judo skills to inflict pain and suffering on his wife. In fact, things had gotten so bad that Vivienne, in her quest for solace, had turned to alcohol. When Roberts first met her, she was a heavy drinker and well on her way to becoming an alcoholic.

But in the few months that they had known each

other, Vivienne's drinking had reduced dramatically.

"Many times Vivienne has said to me how wonderful it is to wake up in the morning and not feel terrified," Roberts said. "And now she's gone."

"You think that something terrible has happened to Mrs. Marshall?" the sergeant asked.

"Yes," replied Roberts.

"And that her husband is responsible?" continued the sergeant.

"Yes," came the reply.

A puzzled look came over the sergeant's face. "And just how do you think that Mr. Marshall was able to do whatever it is that you think that he's done? Did he abduct her off the street? Did he call round to your house?"

"No—nothing like that," replied Roberts.

"Then how?" the sergeant persisted.

"When she went to their home," said Roberts.

The sergeant seemed genuinely surprised. "When she went to their home?" he asked incredulously. "After the way you say that Mr. Marshall has treated her, after five years of sheer hell that turned her into a virtual alcoholic, she voluntarily goes to their home to see him?"

"Not to see him," replied Roberts. "It was the dogs."

"The dogs?" The sergeant didn't believe what he was hearing. "What dogs?"

Roberts went on to explain that Vivienne had two dogs, a German shepherd and a bloodhound.

"She loves those dogs," he told the sergeant. "But Barry wouldn't let her take them with her when she left. He wasn't particularly fond of them. But it gave him a hold over Vivienne. If she wanted to see the dogs, she would have to go back to her former home. And that's what she did."

"And how do you feel about that situation?" the sergeant wanted to know.

"I'm not happy about it, of course," replied Roberts. "But there isn't much that I can do. The one thing that I insist on is that she calls me while she's there and lets me know that she is all right. She went round on Tuesday last, and I haven't seen her since."

"Did she call you while she was there, as you had arranged?" the sergeant asked.

"Yes," answered Roberts.

"And was she all right?"

"Yes," came the reply. "She said that she was fine and that she would be home soon."

"And you haven't seen her since?" asked the sergeant, more by way of an observation than a question.

"That's right," replied Roberts anyway.

"I think you'd better have a talk with our detectives," said the sergeant, picking up a telephone and punching out a short sequence of numbers.

Half an hour later, Bob Roberts finished telling his story to two detectives who had listened to his account with great interest and more than a little sympathy. But there was one point over which they were somewhat puzzled.

"If you are as worried about Mrs. Marshall as you claim to be, why didn't you come to us earlier?" asked one of the officers. "Why did you wait for almost a week?"

"I just kept hoping that she would turn up," Roberts said. It was a pretty weak reply. One look at the detectives' faces told Roberts that they were not convinced.

"There is something else," Roberts said quietly and after a long pause. "I was worried about how you would react toward me. You see, I've got a police record."

"For what?" the officers asked.

"Assault," responded Roberts even more quietly. "I served fifteen months in prison. It was all some time ago, but I know how these things stick. They follow you around, like some dark shadow. You can never get free of it."

The detectives assured Roberts that his past record would have no bearing on their investigation. He would be treated no differently from anyone else should the initial inquiry develop into a case. If he could account for his movements at relevant times, then he would be eliminated. If he couldn't, then he would attract the same amount of attention as anyone else in a similar position. No more, and no less.

It was early evening when two detectives rang the doorbell of the small but neat house on Meadow Lane, about a mile from the center of Wednesfield. The door was opened by a tall, bespectacled man in his mid-40s. The man nodded affirmatively when the detectives asked if his name was Barry Marshall. They stood to one side as he motioned for the officers to enter.

The living room was light, airy, and decorated in a manner that magazines like to describe as "tasteful." In one corner stood a large, glass-fronted bookcase. Its obvious high-quality construction was matched by the cerebral nature of the books that packed its shelves. The detectives formed the opinion that they were dealing with a well-educated and intelligent man, an opinion reinforced by the chessboard on a small table near the window. The positions of the chess pieces showed that a game was in progress, though Marshall was alone in the house.

"A friend and I are partway through a game," he told the officers. "We shall continue tomorrow evening."

Barry Marshall seemed concerned and genuinely surprised when the detectives announced the reason for their visit.

"Vivienne was perfectly all right when I saw her last," he told the officers.

"And when was that?" the officers asked.

"Last Tuesday evening," replied Marshall. "She called round to see the dogs. I'm afraid that she had no time for me."

He went on to relate the same story of Vivienne's affection for her two dogs that the officers had already heard from Bob Roberts. The animals themselves were sitting quietly in the garden. The detectives could clearly see them through the window of the living room.

"Do you know if your wife is seeing any other men?" one of the officers asked nonchalantly and without taking his gaze off Vivienne's dogs.

Barry Marshall replied that he knew all about Bob Roberts. His wife was quite open about their relationship.

"I think she wants to marry him," Marshall told the detectives, without any trace of emotion in his voice.

"And how do you feel about that?" the policemen wanted to know.

Marshall replied that he had no strong feelings one way or the other. At first, he was not too happy about it because it came as something of a blow to his ego to think that Vivienne preferred another man to him. But he had soon gotten over that. Whatever love he had once felt for his wife was long dead. He was still fond of her, but that was all.

"So you don't feel any animosity toward Mr. Roberts?" Marshall was asked.

"No," he replied. "None at all."

"And you don't wish him any harm?" the officers

330

persisted.

"No, of course not," replied Marshall. "These things happen. It's happened to me before. You have to be civilized about it."

"Did you try to run Mr. Roberts down with your car?" asked one of the officers. It was a question that came right out of the blue, and it hit Marshall with the force of a thunderbolt. Its impact was that much greater because it was asked in a casual, and almost conversational, manner. But the effect that it had on Barry Marshall did not escape the officers' vigilant attention to detail. They watched as Marshall's face turned first white, then red, then back to white. They observed his jaw sag and then quiver as he struggled to find the words with which to answer. Eventually, he succeeded.

"No, I didn't. That's a damned lie." His previously friendly manner was fast disappearing. Marshall was getting angry. "Roberts is a troublemaker. You have to watch him. Did you know that he's got a police record?"

"Yes, we know," the officers replied. It was an answer that should've warned Marshall that nothing further on the subject of Bob Roberts' criminal record needed to be said. But it was a warning that went unheeded.

"He's done time for assault," Marshall continued.

"We know that, too," came the reply.

"Well, if you're worried about Vivienne, perhaps you should be talking to him," suggested Marshall. There was now a distinct trace of venom and hatred in his voice. It was sufficient to cast a grave doubt on his previous contention that he felt no ill will toward the new man in his wife's life.

"He's lying," said one detective to the other as they climbed into their car and headed back toward

Wednesfield.

His companion agreed. "We'd better take a closer look at Mr. Barry Marshall," he said.

That closer look began the following morning. With Marshall at work, and therefore safely out of the way, the detectives started on a round of discreet questioning of other Meadow Lane residents.

From each of those neighbors to whom they spoke, the detectives got the same story. It was a tale of a wife who was constantly abused and humiliated by her bullying husband. Barry Marshall liked to present the image of a solid and respectable citizen, but he had a violent temper. Almost nightly, the neighbors were treated to Marshall shouting and screaming at Vivienne. Sometimes she would retaliate, and then things would really heat up. The arguments would rage on for hours, though the neighbors were never able to determine what the couple was arguing about.

Occasionally, these nocturnal dramas would leave the privacy of the Marshalls' home and be played out in full public gaze in the middle of the street. And sometimes, neighbors would become so concerned for Vivienne's safety that they would call for the police to come and restore order. A check on the incident book at the Wednesfield Police Station showed that constables had twice cautioned Barry Marshall about his behavior toward his wife.

Neighbors also reported that, during the two days following Vivienne's visit to Meadow Lane on that Tuesday evening, Marshall did not appear to be at home. Milk bottles piled up on the doorstep and newspapers protruded from the letter box, just as the newsboy had left them when he made his deliveries. Curtains remained drawn across the windows.

But on Friday morning, everything seemed to be back to normal. Marshall was seen around the property, apparently busying himself with the everyday routine of running a home.

A check with the authorities at the school where Marshall worked confirmed the neighbors' story. Barry Marshall had called in sick on Wednesday morning and had remained away from work until the following Monday.

But where had he been during those two days that he was missing from his home? Detectives set to work answering this question by locating close relatives of Marshall — members of his family who might have received an unexpected visit from the chess-playing schoolteacher.

It was on the morning of Wednesday, May 17th, that a routine message received at the Wednesfield Police Station created some excitement among the officers involved in the search for Vivienne Marshall. The message had come from police in the city of York, 150 miles to the north, and had been circulated to all major police stations in the country.

The message said that a man walking through the woods outside the town of Malton, a few miles from York, had made a gruesome discovery. He had come across a large plastic rubbish bag, out of which was protruding what appeared to be a foot. At first, the man thought he had found part of a mannequin, like the ones that department stores use to display the clothes they sell. But when the man opened the bag, he discovered just how wrong he was.

The bag contained a pair of legs — human legs! The limbs had been separated from the body to which they had belonged at a point just above the knees.

Police officers who raced to the scene in answer to the man's frantic telephone call made a thorough search of the surrounding area in an effort to locate the remainder of the body. But nothing was to be found.

A pathologist quickly established that the legs had been separated from the body about a week earlier. They had belonged to a middle-aged white woman of average height, he determined. She had been dead at the time that they had been cut off. But she had not been dead long. The legs bore all the hallmarks of having belonged to a woman who had fallen victim to a killer who had gone to grisly lengths to attempt to conceal his crime. And not only was the killer a person with strong muscles and a strong stomach— dismembering a body is not a task for the weak and faint-hearted—he was also a person devoid of surgical skills. The legs had been crudely amputated with a hacksaw.

What so interested the detectives at Wednesfield about the discovery of a pair of severed legs in a wooded area 150 miles away was the fact that, during their efforts to trace Barry Marshall's close relatives, they learned that a close family member lived in York. But their attempts to contact the woman by telephone had failed. There had been no reply from her house on the city's Fountayne Street.

Immediately, the Wednesfield detectives contacted their colleagues in York and apprised them of the situation. They also asked York detectives to visit the home of Marshall's relative and find out what they could. Later that day, officers from York reported back to Wednesfield.

They had visited the house, but had been unable to get any answer to their ringing of the doorbell. Neighbors to whom they spoke reported that Marshall's relative was away on vacation and had been away for about two weeks. The house was empty, though it had been occupied for a couple of days during the previous week.

"Occupied by whom?" the detectives had asked.

They were told that a man had visited the premises. He had been seen there on a few previous occasions, and several of the neighbors knew him.

"When was he here?" the officers wanted to know.

Those questioned couldn't be certain, but they thought that he had arrived sometime during the afternoon of Wednesday, May 10th. He had left the following evening.

At the invitation of York police, Wednesfield detectives traveled north. They arrived to find that significant progress had been made in the search for the remainder of the unfortunate woman who, the officers now felt sure, was Vivienne Marshall.

In a wooded area outside the city of York, detectives had recovered the torso of a woman. Initial pathology tests indicated that the torso and the legs discovered earlier at Malton were parts of the same woman.

The affair had now taken on the gruesome aspects of a horror movie. Throughout Thursday, May 18th, bits and pieces of the woman turned up in various locations around York. An arm and a hand were discovered at a huge garbage dump in nearby Rufforth. The ring finger had been severed from the hand in a further attempt to hinder the victim's identification. Twenty officers were detailed to search through the piles of rotting household trash that covered the 125 acres of the site. A more unpleasant task is difficult to imagine, but at least it produced results. By the end of that day, police had recovered most of the woman's body. Only one part had not been recovered — her head! With the onset of darkness, it was decided to call off the search for the day and resume at first light.

Detectives from Wednesfield were more certain than

335

ever that the body parts belonged to Vivienne Marshall. All that was needed now was a positive identification. Without her head, that would be a little more difficult than usual, but not impossible.

Early next morning, the Wednesfield detectives were back at their station. After checking in, they made their way to Bob Roberts' home and told him about the happenings at York. He was suitably shocked, but was ready to help in any way he could.

The detectives explained their difficulty. They needed to ascertain whether or not the woman was Vivienne Marshall. But they didn't have her head. So they asked Roberts to describe any distinguishing marks on Vivienne's body.

"Any moles, spots, birthmarks, even bruises?" the officers asked.

They realized that it was a rather indelicate request, asking Roberts to describe things that he could only have seen while he and Vivienne had been engaged in the most intimate of activities.

But this was no time for niceties. A woman was dead, and her killer had to be caught.

Bob Roberts reeled off a list of the various marks that he had noticed on Vivienne's body. The detectives checked what he described against a checklist that had been provided for them by the pathologist. Before long, it was clear that the dead woman was indeed Vivienne Marshall. The officers called their colleagues in York and informed them that with Bob Roberts' help, a name could be put to their body.

By noon, Barry Marshall was in custody on a charge of murder. Four hours later, he appeared before a magistrate, who remanded him in custody while police inquiries continued.

Detectives paid regular visits to Marshall as he waited in prison for his trial to start. He talked freely to them, but initially he denied that he was in any way involved in Vivienne's death. As time went by, however, his denials lacked the vehemence he had originally displayed. Perhaps it was the manner in which the officers worked at demolishing Marshall's story by subtly hinting they knew he was guilty—and could prove it—that caused the accused man's resolve to crumble.

"We've found traces of blood on the kitchen table at your relative's home," they told Marshall. "It's the same blood group as that of your wife."

Blood had also been found in Marshall's car. Again, it was of the same group as that of his wife. Eventually, it all became too much for the schoolteacher. After all, he was an intelligent man. He could see that he had no chance of getting away with it. So Barry Marshall decided to make a confession.

Vivienne had called at the house on Meadow Lane on the fatal Tuesday. Marshall was feeling tense. He wanted her to come back to him. He wanted another chance. But Vivienne wasn't interested. She was happy with Bob Roberts, and she told her husband so in no uncertain terms. Marshall felt angry, but he managed to control himself. It was an effort, but he managed it. But then came the moment when Vivienne made her telephone call to Roberts.

"Don't worry, darling, I'll be home soon," Vivienne had purred into the receiver. Marshall felt the anger within him boiling up until it reached a point where he could control it no longer. As Vivienne replaced the receiver and turned toward him, Marshall struck her with his fist. It was a savage blow that caught the woman on the chin. Vivienne went out like a light and fell at her husband's feet. He looked down at her. But he felt no pity, no compassion. All he felt was rage and pure blind hatred. Marshall raised his foot and brought it down hard on the side of her face. And then again. And again.

Five or six times, Barry Marshall slammed his foot into his wife's head. He couldn't be sure exactly how many times he stamped on her. The rage was driving him on. Something inside his head told him that Vivienne's life was a continual torment and he must free her from her living hell.

After a few minutes, he stopped. He bent over Vivienne to see if she was dead. Her face was nothing but a mass of pulped flesh. But she was still breathing.

"She was limp," he told detectives, before adding in a sinister tone, "Remember I am a judo expert. I know where to put my thumbs in order to inflict the maximum damage with the minimum of effort. Obviously I intended to kill her."

When Vivienne was dead, Marshall drove her to his relative's house. He knew she was away on vacation, so the house would be empty.

He dismembered Vivienne on the kitchen table, then scattered her remains over a 25-mile area around the city of York.

"And what did you do with her head?" he was asked. Although most of the dead woman had been recovered, her head was still missing. And that was despite the efforts of a team of officers who had spent nine days meticulously combing through every waste disposal site in the area.

"I don't know," replied Marshall. "I honestly don't know." The detectives believed him.

On the advice of his lawyers, Barry Marshall pleaded not guilty to murdering Vivienne, but admitted to the lesser charge of manslaughter on the grounds of diminished responsibility. In effect, he claimed that although he intended to kill Vivienne, it was an act over which he had no control. The all-consuming anger that he had felt when he heard his wife telephoning her lover had taken him over completely, and he was unable to stop himself from killing her. It was a crime of passion.

It was a plea that the prosecution was prepared to accept. In the end, it didn't make any difference. In England, a murder conviction carries only one sentence—life imprisonment. Manslaughter can draw any sentence. But the maximum is life imprisonment, and it was the maximum for which the prosecution was aiming.

It was the early spring of 1990 before Barry Marshall stood in the dock at Stafford Crown Court to hear his fate decided.

He listened impassively as Prosecutor Anthony Palmer, Q.C., told how Marshall had driven his wife's body to his relative's house in York, where he dismembered it with a hacksaw and scattered the remains over the surrounding area. Vivienne's head, said Mr. Palmer, had still not been found.

Defense Counsel David McEvoy, Q.C., put up a spirited performance on behalf of his client. "When he heard his wife say over the phone to her lover, 'Don't worry, darling, I'll soon be home,' that triggered off in his mind a loss of self-control," McEvoy told the court. "Marshall was already in such a diminished state that he could not restrain himself from killing her."

Marshall was in his "diminished state," claimed McEvoy, because he had been humiliated by Vivienne, who had told him of her affair with Bob Roberts. The advocate went on to describe Vivienne as a neurotic and unstable woman who had tried to commit suicide on at least three occasions. He did not mention that her instability and suicide attempts may have been the result of the brutal treatment she had received at the hands of his client.

On Friday, March 16, 1990, Mr. Justice Turner was ready to pronounce sentence on Barry Marshall. "You committed an act of cold-blooded brutality," he told the chess-playing wife-killer, "and the lengths to which you went to cover up this savage crime are almost beyond belief."

Judge Turner then ordered that Marshall be jailed for seven years. The sentence was greeted with shouts of derision from Vivienne's relatives, clustered together in the public gallery. Neutral spectators looked at each other in stunned disbelief. It seemed an incredibly light punishment for such a brutal crime.

Bob Roberts summed up the feelings of many people when he told newsmen after the trial, "I think that the judge was swayed by Marshall's middle-class image. If it had been me—just an ordinary construction worker—I would probably have got life. But Marshall is a schoolteacher. He plays chess and he speaks very nicely. He comes across as a solid and respectable citizen. But in reality he is a maniac."

The detectives who investigated the case made no comment. There was nothing to say. They had seen it all before, and they would doubtless see it all again.

EDITOR'S NOTE:
Bob Roberts is not the real name of the person so named in the foregoing story. A fictitious name has been used because there is no reason for public interest in the identity of this person.

"WEIRDO CUT UP A CORPSE WITH A CHAINSAW!"

by Terrell Ecker

GAINESVILLE, FLORIDA
JANUARY 27, 1982

The 50 acres of woods known as the Foster Farm wasn't really a farm at all in the conventional sense. To the untrained eye it was just 50 acres of woods, briars and palmettos surrounding one small cleared area in which a previous owner had erected an open air "pole barn." The only other structure on the property was a vacant house trailer.

More knowledgeable eyes could see a scattered crop growing on the Foster tract in 1981, although how large it was and whether it was intended for sale or personal consumption remain matters of speculation to this day. Its existence came to the attention of authorities by chance while they were looking for the property's missing owner, Allen T. Foster III.

Foster, a 34-year-old yacht salesman, left his Gainesville, Florida home Saturday afternoon, March 28th, saying he was going to make some repairs on the house trailer, for which he had found a tenant, and add some pine straw to a mulch he was making at the farm. He loaded several green plastic bags of pine straw into the bed of his blue pickup truck, climbed into the cab with his German shepherd and headed for the farm in Fairbanks, a small community about five miles northeast of Gainesville in Alachua County.

When Foster didn't return home Saturday night his worried wife called the sheriff's office and reported him missing. It wasn't like him to come home late, let alone not come home at all, she told the police.

Saturday afternoon Mrs. Foster and a deputy sheriff made a cursory search of the farm but saw no sign of Foster or his blue truck. There was no sign of the farm's only current occupant, either, but no one thought anything of that. Mrs. Foster explained that the tent under the pole barn was the temporary home of an old friend of Foster's from Miami. She said she didn't know much about him except that he'd been down on his luck lately and Foster was letting him camp on the property, rent free, until things improved. The house trailer was vacant, but apparently a new tenant was supposed to be moving into it soon.

By Monday afternoon Mrs. Foster was thoroughly alarmed, and Foster's friends and co-workers had become worried as well. Missing work was no more like Allen Foster than was his unexplained absence from home.

Sheriff Lu Hinderey agreed that a thorough search of the Foster farm seemed in order, but using the manpower on duty would stretch the county's regular patrol coverage too thin. For that reason the sheriff authorized a search by his highly trained Special Emergency Response Team (SERT), Alachua County's version of the well-known SWAT, under the command of Lieutenant Jerry Hansen. Fifteen of Foster's friends and co-workers joined the seven SERT officers, making a total of 22 men who began a systematic search of the Foster property at 3:00 p.m. Monday, March 30th.

The plan was literally to comb the entire 50 acres in a series of sweeps. The searchers spread out at arms' length in the southeastern corner of the tract and walked northward side by side, examining every briar patch and palmetto thicket in their path. By the time they reached the northern boundary it was raining heavily. They shifted westward and started southward on the second sweep.

The search party had advanced several yards on the second sweep when it came upon an odd pile of brush. It was too big, for one thing, a little larger than a vehicle, and too neatly rectangular. In fact, the brush pile, which included a few small trees, was shaped roughly like a pickup truck. Peering into the brush at close range, searchers could see the blue sheet metal. They had found Allen Foster's truck.

Because the poorly hidden truck could be a crime scene, it was left covered as found, with only enough brush removed to allow a closer look. The bed appeared to be empty except for a length of nylon rope, and the only thing visible in the cab was a chainsaw.

About ten yards south of the truck, searchers found the body of a black German Shepherd. Leaving one SERT officer to watch the truck and the dog's body, the other 21 men reformed their line and continued south through thickening underbrush and driving rain.

About 50 yards father south, Deputy Daniel Pascucci's attention was captured by a bare plant stalk lying in a heavy palmetto thicket. To the evidence

343

technician's trained eyes, it looked suspiciously like the stripped stalk of a harvested marijuana plant. Walking toward it through the thick palmettos, Pascucci tripped on something but kept his balance and thought nothing of it since whatever it was didn't bite him. Picking up the suspicious looking stalk for a close look, he saw that it was indeed a fully grown and carefully stripped marijuana stalk with its dirt-laden roots intact. It had not been touched.

Deputy Pascucci looked around for a hole from which the plant might have been pulled. Not seeing one, he started walking around among the palmettos and promptly tripped again. Still no bite, and this time it occurred to the deputy that he could have tripped on the stump of another marijuana plant. He reached down and got hold of something, then bent down for a close look.

He had a bone in his hand.

Pascucci brushed some pine straw from around the bone and saw that it seemed to be protruding from a buried green plastic garbage bag. He tugged on the plastic enough to open it slightly and saw what looked like human flesh adorned by fine, scattered dark hairs. Peering closer with the aid of his flashlight, the deputy saw what appeared to be blue denim. Foster had left home Saturday wearing blue jeans, a cowboy shirt and moccasins.

Pascucci's discovery brought a halt to the search and precipitated a host of new and considerably more grim activities. For starters, the civilians were removed from the property and the entire tract secured as a crime scene. Sheriff Hinderey himself was soon on the scene along with his chief of detectives, Captain B.E. "Bubba" Roundtree, and a growing army of investigators, evidence experts and medical people.

The buried plastic garbage bag obviously contained

a human corpse, apparently dismembered and buried in a more or less upright position. The poorly hidden pickup truck and the dead German shepherd were strong indications that the human corpse was that of Allen Foster, but positive identification could be a problem under the circumstance. The detectives were not yet sure whether they even had a complete body. The only thing they knew for sure was that they had an uncommonly grisly murder on their hands and they didn't want to risk losing evidence through improper procedures. The thing to do was shut the scene down for the night and come back Tuesday morning with a search warrant and the best technical help available.

The state crime lab in Jacksonville agreed to send a team of experts with a portable lab, housed in a van, first thing Tuesday morning. The sheriff also requested and got help from a resource closer to home: the University of Florida's archeology department. Dr. William Ross Maples, who has dug up and studied dismembered bodies around the world, said he too would have a team on the scene Tuesday morning. And with that the crime scene was shut down, undisturbed and heavily guarded, for the night. But the investigation wasn't.

While the search had been going on, Captain Roundtree's investigators had been questioning such neighbors of the Foster property as could be found at home. Virtually all of them knew Allen Foster in a very casual way, but none knew him well or had any idea where he might be. After all, Foster didn't live among them, just owned some property that he visited occasionally. Most of the neighbors were much more familiar with the guy who lived on the property, although no one had seen him that day. A tall, skinny "weirdo" named Tim Burgess who lived in a tent, the man had no visible means of support and walked around the property wearing guns much of the time.

As the afternoon struggled on through the rain toward darkness, and more neighbors began arriving home from work with bits and pieces of information about Tim Burgess, the detectives' interest in his background and current whereabouts increased sharply. In the first place, the body could be his; it wouldn't be identified until Tuesday morning, if then. In the second place, if the body was that of Allen Foster, as suspected, Burgess would have to be an automatic suspect until cleared, if only because he lived in a tent less than 100 yards from the buried corpse.

It was late evening when Sergeant Kenny Mack obtained, thus far, the most startling bit of information about the mysterious Mr. Burgess. A 14-year-old neighbor told Mack that he had had a curious conversation with Burgess on Friday, March 27th, but hadn't really thought much about it because, he said, all conversations with Burgess were curious.

The boy said that Burgess, high on marijuana as usual, had bragged in gory detail about how he was going to murder Allen Foster, with whom he was terribly upset for some reason. Burgess had said he was going to ambush Foster with a shotgun, dismember his body, bury the pieces and cover them with lime. Burgess had seemed to relish the prospect, but the boy hadn't taken it seriously because Burgess was always carrying on about the horrible things he intended to do to whomever he happened to be angry with at the time.

Sergeant Mack took it seriously, however, especially when conversations with officers who had discovered the body confirmed that the remains and immediate

346

surrounding area appeared to have been sprinkled with a lime-like substance of an extremely corrosive nature.

Tuesday morning brought welcome sunshine and a three-pronged attack on the bizarre case. One group of detectives and uniformed deputies cooperated with the state crime lab technicians and the University of Florida archeologists charged with digging up and identifying the mutilated corpse. As Dan Pascucci recalled later, "It took quite a while. They did it with teaspoons and brushes, and what have you. It was a very, very slow process. They documented it all the way down."

What they ended up documenting was the body of Allen Foster, killed by three shotgun blasts, its legs severed and its head scalped after death, the entire mess buried head downward in a plastic garbage bag, sprinkled with lime and covered with pine straw.

A second group of deputies, armed with a search warrant, began a painstaking three-day search of the entire Foster tract with special attention to Burgess's apparently abandoned home. It looked more like a garbage dump than a campsite, and nothing of particular interest was obvious. One thing the searchers did find of interest was a substantial marijuana crop growing here and there about the property.

A third group of detectives concentrated on the missing Mr. Burgess. They had no luck at all in finding him, but each new bit of information they obtained strengthened their determination to do so.

It turned out that Burgess was on probation from Washington, D.C., and a bit of routine checking into that interesting fact revealed a fascinating story.

On October 6, 1979, the White House was under even more scrutinization than usual by both the public and the police as President Jimmy Carter awaited the imminent arrival of Pope John Paul II. Across the street in Lafayette Park, police eyes were attracted to a tall, skinny redhead leading a Great Dane around on a leash. The huge dog was enough to attract attention but no cause for alarm. But having noticed the guy, the police couldn't help noticing the heavy vest he wore—much too heavy for the warm weather.

As officers moved closer and watched the man with professional curiosity, the dog started getting frisky and jumping playfully at its master. One jump knocked the guy off balance and opened his vest— revealing three .45-caliber semi-automatic pistols and two big knives. Their curiosity now thoroughly aroused, the officers wrestled the man to the ground for a closer examination and found 200 rounds of ammunition for the three fully loaded pistols.

In the interest of presidential and papal safety, the officers took the precaution of hauling Timothy Robert Burgess off to jail.

Charged with carrying the concealed weapons, ammunition and three marijuana cigarettes, Burgess, then 35, pled not guilty and explained that he was just trying to draw a little attention to himself in order to publicize a problem he was having with the Veterans Administration. Something about having been injured in a motorcycle accident while in the Navy and being unable to get any financial help from the VA.

Naturally, before the case could proceed any further, Burgess's competency to stand trial had to be established, so he was turned over to the mental health unit of the D.C. Department of Human Resources. Eventually one of the unit's 18 part-time psychiatrists reported to Superior Court Judge Robert M. Scott that the suspect's competency couldn't be determined because Burgess wouldn't talk. But the doctor said he had the "impression" that Burgess was suffering from a mental illness of psychotic proportions.

Judge Scott allowed Burgess to plead guilty to one count of carrying a pistol without a license, gave him a one-year suspended sentence and three years probation.

Now, with Burgess possibly in trouble again, a spokesman for the D.C. mental health unit said they couldn't ethically discuss the case, and anyway they were too busy trying to determine John Hinckley's competency to stand trial for the attempted murder of President Reagan.

While that information was being digested, Deputy Gregory Weeks was following a lead to Burgess's possible current whereabouts. The lead came from the proprietor of a mom and pop type grocery store near the Foster property.

The grocer told Deputy Weeks that he last had seen Burgess about 9 o'clock the previous morning, Monday, and knew where he might be now. He said Burgess had come into the store carrying a large canvas duffle bag and said he needed a place to stay. He'd said his landlord was missing and the police probably would blame him because of some trouble he'd had in the past. Actually, he'd said, his landlord was probably just off with a woman somewhere having a good time.

The grocer said he knew that old Harvey Hanks, who lives down the road a ways, sometimes takes in roomers, so he had taken Burgess down there and left him. That had been about 10:00 a.m. or so. He hadn't seen or heard from Burgess since then.

It was 11:45 a.m. Tuesday when Deputy Weeks found and questioned Harvey Hanks at his house.

349

Hanks confirmed that Burgess had spent Monday night there, but said he didn't know where he was now. Hanks said Burgess had behaved very strangely and had given Hanks the impression that he was running from the police. Then, this morning, Hanks had heard on the radio that a body had been discovered in the Fairbanks area. After thinking that over for a few seconds he had told Burgess he'd have to leave. So Burgess had left, and Hanks said he hadn't seen him since about 9:00 a.m. and didn't know where he might have gone.

Others heard the news on the radio, too, and the expected flood of phone calls started. As is usual in such cases, most of the calls were useless, but all were listened to carefully and a few proved to be of genuine value. One in particular proved to be of great value. One caller named Ginny Burnside said she had Tim Burgess's sawed-off shotgun if an officer would like to drop by her office and pick it up.

Detective Martin Snook promptly dropped by Miss Burnside's office and was given, from the trunk of her car, a sawed-off Stephens 16-gauge pump action repeating shotgun in a green plastic garbage bag. She said Burgess had left it with her Sunday morning—the last time she'd seen him. She and her boyfriend had let him out at that little grocery store in Fairbanks after he'd accompanied them on a grocery shopping trip into Gainesville. Miss Burnside's boyfriend, Greg Thompson, verified her story and added some very interesting details, including a possible motive for murder.

Thompson said there had been a dispute between Allen Foster and Tim Burgess over the use of the house trailer on the property. It was not exactly a landlord-tenant dispute because Burgess wasn't a paying tenant, just an old friend down on his luck whom Foster allowed to camp on the property. Burgess didn't see any reason why he shouldn't live in the trailer and simply moved in—without Foster's permission. Foster explained that he had rented the trailer to a paying tenant who would be moving in in a few days, and ordered Burgess to move out. Not off of the property, just out of the trailer. That was on Tuesday, March 24th. Foster told Burgess to be out of the trailer by the following morning, then had carefully cleaned up Burgess's mess while Burgess watched, silent and pouting.

Later Foster had told Thompson about the incident, Thompson said. Foster was concerned about Burgess's welfare, of course, and had done the best he could for the guy. Burgess had electricity in his tent, after all, through a long extension cord from the trailer. He cooked with electricity and had television. He had no bathroom, of course, but no one ever brought that subject up.

But Foster was also worried about Burgess's effect on the new tenant. Burgess was a weird looking dude, six feet four and 150 pounds, unkempt red hair and ragged clothes, walking around armed to the teeth. He usually wore a pair of .357-magnum revolvers and carried a sawed-off shotgun. Moreover, Burgess said if his probation officer ever showed up he'd blow her away. No one else really took him seriously, though. Burgess just liked to talk that way.

Thompson said he had seen Burgess three times since that incident. Friday night, March 27th, Burgess came to Thompson's trailer, located very near the Foster property, for a cookout. Saturday night Thompson heard that Foster was missing and went over to Burgess's camp to see if Foster was there. He wasn't, but Burgess said he apparently had been there during the afternoon while Burgess was away and had left some fertilizer.

Then, about 8:30 Sunday morning, Burgess had accompanied Thompson and Ginny Burnside into Gainesville to do some food shopping. Burgess had worn his guns into town, which was unusual, and wouldn't get out of the car. He just waited in the car while they shopped. When they let him out later in Fairbanks, he left the shotgun with Ginny.

Thompson said he hadn't seen Burgess since then.

In the meantime, the press had gathered in force about the perimeter of the Foster property, but wasn't allowed onto the property itself and was given virtually no information beyond the fact that Allen Foster's body had been found. One enterprising reporter managed to gather a few odds and ends of information and misinformation, including the non fact that the victim's head as well as the legs had been severed from the body, and something about a chainsaw being found, and wrote an interesting if not accurate story for the Wednesday morning paper. From that point on the case was known, to the eventual embarrassment of the press, as the "Chainsaw Murder."

Actually, by then the University of Florida's Dr. William Maples had determined that the legs had been chopped off with considerable effort, while the lifeless body lay face down on the ground. There had been no chainsaw involved, although one had been found in the cab of Foster's pickup truck.

Also by then, a new witness had come forth with some intriguing information. Bill Herring, another Fairbanks trailer dweller, arrived at the sheriff's office in Gainesville accompanied by his lawyer after the lawyer had arranged a meeting with detectives. Herring had taken that precaution because, he said, he knew so much that he was worried about his own vulnerability to possible criminal charges.

Herring said he met Tim Burgess in October 1979. At the time, Foster was living in his trailer on the "farm" and he and Herring were neighbors and friends. Burgess lived in a tiny trailer on property adjacent to Foster's with a big dog, a Great Dane. About a week after Herring had met him, Burgess got himself arrested in Washington, D.C., and wasn't seen locally for several months.

Foster bought a home in Gainesville and moved into it, Herring continued, but made frequent trips to his farm property and usually stopped by to visit Herring. In the spring of 1980 Foster asked Herring if he'd like to go partners on a marijuana crop. Herring told Foster he would consider it, he said, and was considering seriously when, in the early summer, Tim Burgess showed up again, broke and homeless — and on probation for a weapons conviction.

Herring said that when he asked Foster about Burgess, Foster said that Burgess would be camping on the farm rent free and would be helpful in the marijuana project, but that it was understood there were to be no guns on the property. Well, okay, Herring said he told Foster, but the proposed pot crop deal was off, period. Herring wasn't about to get mixed up in any kind of operation that included Tim Burgess.

Herring said he did get pretty well acquainted with Burgess, however, and as the year wore on it became obvious that Foster and Burgess were cultivating a marijuana crop. They didn't try to hide that fact from Herring, and occasionally discussed the crop's progress in his presence.

Then the trouble started. One day late in the summer Burgess came to Herring's trailer and said 30 marijuana plants had been stolen. Later the same day, Foster told Herring that he suspected Burgess of having stolen the plants himself. A few days later Burgess showed Herring a .22-caliber rifle he had bought. Burgess said he also had a sawed-off shotgun, but Herring didn't see it. Still later, Burgess showed Herring a pair of .357-magnum revolvers.

Herring said that at that point he started getting paranoid about Burgess and talked to Foster about the guns. Foster said not to worry, that he could handle Tim Burgess.

Not reassured at all, Herring considered trying to contact Burgess's parole officer but decided that would just invite revenge from Burgess. He said, "I was extremely skeptical of the state's system of supervising such a dangerous person because I had witnessed the complete lack of supervision of what I thought was a demonstrably dangerous person."

In a December, 1980, conversation, Herring said, Burgess stated he was at the end of his rope. He had decided to go to town and blow up the parole office—take a can of gas, spread the gas around and light it, then shoot the secretary, janitor, anyone who got in the way.

Then, Herring said, "He started describing the glory of death, of watching people die, the sensuality of that death look as they knew they were dying, experiencing physical agony and emotional stress at the moment of death.

"I talked to him about twenty minutes on that occasion, turning the conversation to suggesting that he commit suicide rather than kill all those people if he was that distraught over his life and the uselessness and pain of it all.

"He said he wanted to go out in a blaze of glory. He told me at that point he had killed six or seven policemen and had never been caught, that he particularly liked to kill policemen and that he wanted to kill as many as he could before he died.

"At that point I was afraid for my own life and maneuvered myself out of the situation. I got in my truck and drove to a phone, called Allen Foster and talked to him at length. Allen said he would go out and talk to Tim and find out what the situation was."

Herring said Foster told him in a later conversation that he had tried repeatedly to contact Burgess's parole officer but couldn't get any response.

Herring said he then removed himself from the frightening situation by simply moving and avoiding any further contact with Burgess. When he heard what had happened to Allen Foster he felt obligated to tell the police what he knew. But he was worried enough about his own legal position that he contacted them through his lawyer.

Wednesday, April Fool's Day, brought an intensified search for Timothy Burgess. But the 37-year-old suspect, normally so conspicuous, seemed to have evaporated. Press coverage was intensified as well as the "Chainsaw Murder" label spread through the journalism community.

The break came late Wednesday afternoon with a phone call from Harvey Hanks, who had evicted Burgess from his home after one night. Hanks said Burgess had simply moved into the woods behind the house, pitched a tent and apparently had been there the whole time. Anyway, Burgess was again in Hanks's house, and Hanks was out of it for the duration.

At 6 o'clock Lieutenant Hansen and his SER Team, armed with an arrest warrant among other things, secured the Hanks house. Hansen yelled for Burgess to come out and surrender. Burgess yelled that he wanted Deputy Gary Buchanan. He said he knew and trusted Buchanan, who lived in the Fairbanks area. Hansen yelled that he had a warrant for Burgess's arrest and demanded that he give up. Burgess yelled that he wasn't going to surrender to anyone but Gary Buchanan.

Hansen then left the scene to fetch Buchanan, leaving Sergeant Curtis O'Quinn in charge at the scene. During Hansen's absence, O'Quinn and Burgess exchanged shouts, mostly concerning treatment of prisoners. At one point Burgess shouted that the killing had been in self-defense. O'Quinn quickly changed the subject and they shouted about other things. "Just whatever I could think of," O'Quinn recalled later.

Gary Buchanan, it turned out, didn't even know Burgess and could not remember ever having seen him. But he must have seen him sometime, somewhere, or at least *been seen by* Burgess. In any event, he was glad to be of service. He called Burgess on Hanks's telephone.

"Tim," Buchanan said, "this is Gary Buchanan. I understand that you wanted to talk with me and give up to me."

"Yes, I feel like I can trust you," Burgess replied.

Buchanan said, "Well, you know, I'll do my best to uphold that confidence in me."

"But you think you can get me something to eat?" Burgess asked. "My ulcers are really bad."

"Well, I'm sure we can find you something to eat," Buchanan assured him.

"Cigarettes?"

"Yes."

"Okay."

"Now, Tim," Buchanan said, "when I approach the house I'm going to tell you who I am and at that time I want you to come out the front door with your hands straight in the air and with no shirt on."

The arrest was accomplished without incident and Buchanan drove Burgess to the sheriff's office in Gainesville where he was given a hamburger, a coke and a pack of cigarettes.

"It was pretty gory, wasn't it?" Burgess said as he consumed his goodies. "This is the first food I've been able to hold down since I got rid of him."

After finishing his hamburger, Burgess asked for a lawyer. "I want to get my story straight before I talk to you about what happened," he explained.

In the meantime, however, he was perfectly willing to talk about his unsuccessful trip to Washington. He told Sergeant William "Bear" Bryan that he had gone to Washington intending to shoot President Carter, and would have pulled it off if his dog hadn't screwed up. Then maybe the VA would have listened to his complaints.

After talking to a lawyer Burgess decided that he wasn't guilty of the Foster murder or possession of a short-barreled shotgun and so pled on April 2nd.

Burgess's arrest brought a new round of publicity about his 1979 Washington adventure, and it occurred to some reporters that perhaps a would-be presidential assassin ought to have been under Secret Service surveillance. All a Secret Service spokesman would say on the subject was, "Let's just say we have been very much aware of Mr. Burgess."

On January 27, 1982, Timothy Robert Burgess, then 38, went to trial before a capital jury of seven men and five women. The trial didn't last long. The jury heard detailed testimony about the death of Allen Foster, then was shown photographs of his dismembered body. Watching the jurors' reactions to the grisly photographs, Burgess decided to call it off and plead guilty.

Circuit Judge John J. Crews immediately sentenced Burgess to life in prison with a mandatory minimum of 25 years before parole eligibility.

EDITOR'S NOTE:
Harvey Hanks, Ginny Burnside, Greg Thompson, and Bill Herring are not the real names of the persons so named in the foregoing story. Fictitious names have been used because there is no reason for public interest in the identities of these persons.

358

"HEINOUS MUTILATION OF THE SPRY WIDOW"

by Bruce Stockdale

FAIRFAX COUNTY, VA
JULY 7, 1987

It was typically sweltering in Fairfax County, Virginia, that Monday, July 28, 1980. A bedroom suburb of the nation's capital, Fairfax County shares the ungodly heat and humidity for which Washington, D.C., is notorious in the summer. And this was one reason why a relative of 62-year-old Phoebe Parsons was most disturbed by the failure of the spry widow to beat the heat and keep a date for a nice air-conditioned movie at nearby Tysons Corners Mall. It was just not like Phoebe Parsons to stand somebody up without calling in an explanation.

After waiting an hour for Phoebe to show, the worried relative decided that the situation demanded investigation. It took only a few minutes to drive from Tysons Corners to the small white frame house on Lisle Avenue, a neighborhood of modest homes nestled in the Pimmitt Hills section of the county just inside the Capital Beltway. Phoebe Parsons had lived here for 30 years and raised a family here.

Entering the front door, which to her surprise was unlocked, the relative called out. No response. But when she entered the bedroom, it became readily apparent why Phoebe Parsons had been unable to keep her date that day. For lying beneath a pile of clothes on the floor beside the bed was Phoebe's bloody, nude body.

The Fairfax County uniformed officer who responded to the 911 call took one look at the gruesome sight and called for the assistance of the Major Crime Squad. Responding to the scene were Detectives Jesse Sutherland and Andy Johnson, each of whom had more than 100 murder investigations to their credit.

But even these two case-hardened lawmen found themselves shocked by the carnage with which they were now confronted. Examination of the body revealed the presence of bruise marks around the neck, which gave mute testimony to the work of a merciless strangler who, not content with strangling his victim, had apparently cut her throat at the jugular vein as well. But this was not all. Umbrellas had been jammed into both her rectal and vaginal cavities.

By now the two detectives had been joined by criminalistics personnel. All the lawmen on the scene — detectives, uniformed officers, and civilian criminalists — combined their efforts to come up with an answer to a question both simple and complex: What happened to Phoebe Parsons?

Their first order of business was a painstaking search of the house for evidence. The sleuths noted that the entire house bore signs of a ransacking. Drawers had been pulled out and their contents spilled out over the floor; desks, cabinets, and closets had been rifled.

Apparently, the killer had been looking for something.

Just inside the front door, the lawmen found a mass of dried blood, indicating that the victim had been attacked and killed at that spot and her body dragged into the bedroom. In addition, the police found a typewriter ribbon (which could have been used to strangle the victim), a link from a man's watchband (found near the front door) and a man's necklace (found near the body).

As the criminalists busied themselves with the processing of the interior crime scene, Detective Sutherland and a detail of uniformed officers conducted a door-to-door canvass of the neighborhood in order to come up with somebody who might know something helpful to the investigation.

But this proved to be a fruitless endeavor. It seemed that no one in the neighborhood had seen or heard anything suspicious at the Parsons place prior to the discovery of the body.

However, during their canvass, the officers did glean an impression of the type of person Phoebe Parsons had been in life. Apparently, she had been much loved in the neighborhood. "She could have been a role model for Aunt Bee," one householder told Detective Sutherland, in reference to Sheriff Andy Taylor's doting aunt in the television show "Mayberry R.F.D." Another resident recalled Parsons as "a really good woman, a church woman, and a mother."

So why would anyone do such a terrible thing to her? wondered Detective Jesse Sutherland.

One possible motive—robbery—was indicated by the fact that the victim's car, usually parked on the street, was nowhere to be found in the neighborhood. Also, the victim's wallet, containing cash and credit cards, was missing from the location where it was usually kept — a hook in the kitchen.

Hearing this, Sutherland issued a BOLO for the car, a 1978 Volkswagen Rabbit, which he figured the perpetrator had used for his getaway.

After the discouraging neighborhood canvass, Detective Sutherland's spirits were buoyed by a positive note struck by the fingerprint technicians assigned to the investigation. They had found a plethora of fingerprints, both inky and bloody, throughout the crime scene. "I'll bet my paycheck that some belong to the perp," averred one technician.

After several hours of work, the crime scene was sealed and the body of the unfortunate woman was removed to the office of the Virginia medical examiner for a postmortem examination.

As practitioners of the "point of the circle" method of homicide investigation, Detectives Sutherland and Johnson would begin their field investigation by conducting exhaustive interviews with members of the victim's immediate family.

It was during one of these interviews that the name Richard Whitley emerged. The family member related that there was a person whom Phoebe Parsons had expressed fear of in the past, her next-door neighbor, Richard Whitley. It seemed the man was the type of person who was continually experiencing difficulty of one sort or another in life. During the few months that Richard Whitley and his family had lived next door, Parsons had tried to help them. She had loaned them kitchen utensils for example, and had even placed Richard Whitley on her prayer list.

With this, Jesse Sutherland decided to have a little talk with Richard Whitley. He and Detective Johnson headed back to Pimmitt Hills.

When repeated knocks at the small frame house

located next door to the crime scene failed to bring any response, the two detectives queried neighbors in an effort to get a line on Richard Whitley. But no one had seen the man for the past several days. As for his family, they had moved out some weeks before after what appeared to have been a violent quarrel.

Further checking on Richard Lee Whitley, w/m/33, disclosed that the part-time housepainter and handyman was currently wanted by neighboring Arlington County as the perpetrator of the sexual assault and robbery of a hitchhiker. Arlington County Detective Pete Tyler advised his Fairfax County counterpart that his investigation had disclosed a considerable criminal record for Whitley, with prior arrests noted for thefts, burglaries, and even an attempted murder.

By now, the sleuths were convinced they had a viable suspect to focus their attention on in the Phoebe Parsons case. As a result, an all-points bulletin was issued for Richard Lee Whitley as "Wanted For Questioning" in the murder of Phoebe Parsons.

However, this was promptly revised to "Wanted For Murder" when the fingerprint technicians reported that the bloody and inky prints lifted at the crime scene matched those on file in Arlington County in the name of Richard Lee Whitley.

With this, the manhunt for the now formally accused man shifted into high gear, with all available detectives joining the search. But as time passed it became apparent that Whitley, using his victim's car and credit cards, had evaded the dragnet. With no fresh leads to pursue, Detective Sutherland and his colleagues turned their attention to other cases and hoped for a break in the Parsons case. If the fugitive was not apprehended within 60 days of being charged, the FBI would enter the case on a federal charge—interstate flight to avoid prosecution.

As it turned out, the FBI's help would not be needed. On September 10, 1980, Jesse Sutherland took a call from the Tampa, Florida, police. It was the break he had been praying for. It seemed that Richard Lee Whitley had been picked up as a suspect in a triple homicide in Tampa. While the suspect had been cleared of involvement in that case, he had still been identified as a fugitive from Fairfax County, Virginia.

Detectives Sutherland and Johnson wasted no time in boarding a flight to Tampa, Florida, where they were met by Sergeant Jerry Feltman of the Tampa police. Feltman arranged for the Virginia lawmen to interrogate Whitley in an interview room at the Tampa Police Department lockup.

From the start, the investigating officers were taken aback by the genial, friendly demeanor of a man they were convinced had committed the most brutal crime they had ever investigated. He was quick to admit that he killed Phoebe Parsons although he denied any mutilation of the body with umbrellas.

He related that he had gone to the victim's home early in the evening on Friday, July 22, 1980, to use her telephone to call his employer. His car was disabled and there was no way for him to get to work, he explained. But his employer was not there. When two hours had passed, he returned to Parsons' house to call his employer again.

At the time, he had been on a two-week drug and alcohol binge resulting from a quarrel with family members who had left him. As he started to leave Mrs. Parsons' house, she stopped him and said she wanted to tell him about Jesus and how everything would be all right if he would give his heart to Him.

"The next thing I knew she was dead," Whitley said.

When Whitley went on to recount details of the crime scene known only to the police, Detective Sutherland knew that he was not dealing with a wacko who was confessing to a heinous crime just to become famous. Whitley even remembered which credit cards belonging to the victim he had used to get to Florida, and where the victim's car could be found by Tampa police. Finally, when Whitley identified the watchband link and necklace found at the crime scene as his, Detective Sutherland knew that he had an airtight case against the outwardly genial and unconcerned housepainter.

As for the actual murder, Whitley admitted he had choked Parsons with his hands, strangled her with a ligature (the typewriter ribbon), and cut her jugular vein with a Boy Scout pocketknife as she prayed. But he could not be budged from his denial of any sexual assaults with umbrellas.

With Whitley's confession reduced to writing, signed and witnessed, the lawmen were ready to return to Virginia. The smiling, ever-obliging suspect smoothed their path by waiving extradition proceedings. The Virginia lawmen returned to Fairfax County with Whitley in tow and referred their findings to Prosecutor Robert F. Horan.

The accused killer was soon to learn that he had picked a particularly poor jurisdiction in which to commit his atrocious crime because Prosecutor Horan had a solid reputation as an ace crime-fighter with an excellent record in prosecuting murder cases. In his opinion, Virginia's death penalty was designed for criminals like Richard Lee Whitley and he served notice on the accused killer's lawyer, Warren MacLane,

365

that he would seek the death penalty against his client.

Nor would there be any plea-bargain arrangement entertained.

The defendant pleaded not guilty and asked for a jury trial. It took the jury only a short while to bring in a verdict of guilty as charged of first-degree murder. It took an even shorter time (15 minutes) for the jury of eight women and four men to vote the death penalty for Whitley.

Unlike some states, which may have death penalty laws on the books but never carry them out, the state of Virginia, with its cherished tradition of no-nonsense treatment of the criminal, has actually carried out a number of executions since the Supreme Court legalized them under certain guidelines in 1977. However, like every state, Virginia has those who are opposed to the death penalty as a matter of principle. As a result, the next seven years were to see Richard Whitley's case become a focal point for those opposing views.

Appeals on Whitley's behalf were taken through the court system all the way to the U.S. Supreme Court. These portrayed Whitley as a mentally and emotionally disturbed individual who had problems that started in childhood. He had an unhappy childhood and dropped out of school in the eighth grade.

A psychiatrist report done when Whitley was in an Illinois prison at age 19 indicated his academic performance was so poor that he had to repeat the sixth and seventh grades.

According to a family member, he had been struck by a train at the age of 16 and was never the same after that. It was further believed that he was homosexually raped in prison and had relationships with both men and women since then.

The Illinois psychiatric report concluded that Whitley's "judgment is nil and he is intellectually and emotionally crippled."

In 1984, a psychologist and a psychiatrist who examined Whitley for the purpose of his appeal suspected he was brain-damaged from liquor or blows to the head or both. They concluded that he also had an antisocial personality. The combination of brain damage and personality disorder left him dangerous to society and in need of institutionalization because he would be unable to control his behavior, they advised.

As Whitley's case made its tortuous way through the court system, appellate judges repeatedly held that while Whitley's background was indeed unfortunate, it did not constitute a legal defense to murder or affect the legality of the death sentence against him.

Richard Whitley would have to keep his date with the electric chair.

One July 7, 1987, at 7:10 p.m., Whitley's final appeal was laid to rest when the U.S. Supreme Court refused to block his execution. But Governor Gerald Baliles, who had rejected a clemency bid on July 4th, remained in his office at the statehouse and kept a telephone line open to the penitentiary in the event of an unexpected development.

Prisoners scheduled to die must spend their last 15 days in a basement cell next to the room housing the electric chair. Whitley had been there twice before, but appeals had stayed those executions.

But how would he leave this, the third time?

For his part, Whitley remained calm in the face of impending doom, telling a Richmond television station: "I'm ready to die! I know they're going to kill me."

This was buttressed by a death penalty protestor who told a *Washington Times* reporter: "The one thing I can tell you is that he (Whitley) is with God, and he believes that, and that's very helpful and strengthens him a lot."

However, despite the brave face shown by the prisoner, Virginia Penitentiary officials were wondering, based on statements to the media, whether Whitley might not present problems with the execution that could only be resolved by the use of force.

In an interview with the *Alexandria Journal* he had said: "It's not going to be easy for them to get me in there (the chair). I'm not just going to walk to it and say, 'Yeah, here I am. It's me.' 'Course, (laughs) it depends on how big they are when they come in. The only way I'd walk to it is if they blindfolded me. Other than that, I ain't going to walk to it."

Whitley also had repeatedly said he did not want to wear the helmet-like mask placed over the face of a prisoner being executed. The mask is designed in part to keep the witnesses to the execution from becoming uncomfortable. Wearing the mask is mandatory, however.

Finally, with all appeals exhausted and the governor having made it clear he would not intervene by granting last-minute clemency, the awesome death-work began.

Whitley was given a last meal of steak, salad, pie a la mode and coffee. At 11 p.m., he was led to the electric chair without incident and without making a final statement. The current was applied and he was pronounced dead at 11:07 p.m.

Everyone connected with the execution was relieved

he had gone to his death without making a fuss. And, as in past executions, rival crowds of protesters showed up outside the brick-walled prison. On one side were about 100 anti-death penalty demonstrators. On the other was a like number who jeered at the death penalty opponents.

"AN OHIO WOMAN WAS CHOPPED INTO 100 PIECES!"

by J. L. Jacobs

Cold and gray, the Maumee River flows through Toledo, Ohio, separating the east side from the rest of the city. Once the waterway of Indian canoes, now it carries ocean and lake freighters during the busy shipping season. Sometimes, however, the dirty Maumee carries a much more grisly cargo.

The riverbanks and bridges attract fishermen, gulls, suicides, and, of course, boys who live nearby. Curiosity is a large part of any lad's make-up, so it is not surprising that curiosity was rampant among three young South Toledo friends that day.

It was Friday, March 25, 1988. Sometime earlier in the day an acquaintance of one of the boys claimed he had seen part of a human leg along the shore of the river. Now the three teens were excitedly discussing it. They didn't really believe him, of course, but they wondered if they should they go take a look. After daring each other to go, they finally decided to band together for a search of the area. It was about seven o'clock in the evening and darkness comes early in March. One of the boys obtained a flashlight and the three adventurers bravely set off on their mission.

The part of the riverbank they were headed for was not the neat, clean shoreline found in the downtown area. The boys' destination, rocky and weedy, strewn with trash, was home to less-than-desirable wildlife. And it was in these gloomy surroundings that a pleasurable adventure turned into an unforgettable nightmare for the young trio.

The oldest boy, investigating a torn brown plastic garbage bag, yelled to his companions. It is hard to imagine what their feelings must have been as they grouped around their find on that dark, chill shore. For caught in the beam of the flashlight were bits and pieces of a human body. When this grim reality finally sank in, panic and fright put wings on their feet and they fled to the nearest houses.

Their frustration mounting, they went from one house to another but could find no one who would believe their story. At about the fifth house they went to, the person they talked to was a block parent. This person calmed them as much as possible and advised them to go to one of their parents to report their discovery.

Later, the mother of one of the teens said, "When they came in here, they were just white." That parent was convinced the boys were telling the truth and she quickly telephoned the Toledo Police Department.

A patrol car was dispatched to the location pinpointed by the boys. When it was verified that what the youngsters had found was indeed a bag full of human body parts, a call was radioed through to the Toledo Homicide Unit. Responding to the call was a crew under the direction of Lieutenant Dave Roberts.

It would be Lieutenant Roberts' responsibility to organize and coordinate the investigation.

Over the next hour or so, officers hunting along the rocky shore recovered other plastic bags containing more pieces of the unknown victim. Soon it was too dark to continue the search. Plans were made to continue looking along the river the following morning. The bags and body parts already found were taken to the coroner's morgue, where there would be an autopsy the next day in hopes of establishing I.D.

Detective John Tharp, an 18-year-veteran of the Toledo PD, was named to head the investigation. A very pleasant, easy-spoken man, Detective Tharp had been with the narcotics squad for 13 years. He was now in his fifth year with homicide, which is a part of the Crimes Against Persons Unit headed by Captain Kenneth Koperski.

On Saturday morning, March 26th, Detective Tharp and his fellow officers returned to the shores of the Maumee River. With daylight, the men were now able to greatly expand the area of the search. Starting at the point of the original discovery, they worked their way in both directions along the shoreline. Before they were done, they had recovered even more pieces of the body. These, too, were parceled off to the coroner's morgue.

Satisfied that there was nothing more to be found along the river, Detective Tharp returned to police headquarters to begin the task of identifying the victim and apprehending the person or persons who had committed such a gruesome crime.

Detective Tharp certainly had very little to work with. Other than body parts, the plastic bags had yielded no other clues—no weapons, no clothing, and nothing in the way of identification. There was no person reported missing who fit the description of the victim.

As of Saturday afternoon, it was still uncertain whether the plastic bags had been discarded where they were found, or if they had been thrown into the river elsewhere and had then washed ashore.

At an autopsy on the parts which had been located the night before, the deputy coroner had at least 70 body pieces, most of which were pieces of skin. However, a very important part, the decapitated head, was among the lot. It was determined by X-ray that the victim had been shot once in the head and that the bullet was still embedded in the head and could be recovered. It was not yet known if the gunshot was the cause of death.

The victim remained unidentified. The city's only newspaper and the other news media were given a sketchy description: the victim was a heavyset white female who wore dentures and had shoulder-length reddish-brown hair. The deputy coroner stated that her age could have been as young as 40 to as old as 70 years. The head was made as presentable as possible and then photographed. This photograph would later be recognized and the victim's identity would finally be established.

It was now Saturday evening. A beauty salon on Starr Avenue in East Toledo had closed for the day. The owner, Kevin Parker, and his helper were busy cleaning up. A small television set was tuned to the evening news, and the newscaster had just given the known details and description of the mutilated body.

At once Kevin was reminded of one of his regular customers. She not only regularly got her hair done, her wigs styled, and her nails polished, but she was also an almost daily visitor, stopping in just to chat with Kevin and any of the customers she happened to know.

Kevin had had a growing concern about her. He knew her health was not good and it had been about a week since she had last been in for a visit. Kevin had even tried telephoning her at home to see if she was all right.

"I think I know who that is!" he exclaimed. "I wonder if I should call the police?"

His helper tried to dissuade him, telling him he was probably wrong in thinking that he knew the victim and that the description given wasn't really detailed enough. Kevin partially agreed. No one expects a friend to be involved in serious crime, let along such a horrendous one. But Kevin's feelings were so strong that, foolish or not, he decided to make the call.

When connected with homicide, Kevin identified himself and explained why he was calling. The detective taking the call was interested — the description of Kevin's "missing" friend seemed to match. He was especially interested to learn Kevin was the lady's hairdresser.

The investigator knew several things about the victim, details that Kevin could either confirm or refute. This could go a long way toward a positive identification of the body.

In addition to her approximate height, weight and age, Kevin was asked questions about her hair — was it permed? Had it been colored? He was also asked about the condition of her fingernails. Finally, Kevin was asked where he could be located. He said he was calling from his shop and gave the address. He was told someone would be out shortly to see him.

Detectives quickly made the two-mile trip to Kevin's shop. They presented him with a photograph of the victim's head. Quickly, unhesitatingly, Kevin told Detective Tharp that he recognized it.

Her name was Cecilia D. Arthur, Kevin said. He was able to furnish her home address and a little background information. She was married to a truck driver. A man had been renting a room from the Arthurs, Kevin said, but there was no one else living at her address. That was all he knew about her.

This almost unbelievable break gave investigators a firm starting point in their probe. It was barely 24 hours after the first bag of body parts had been discovered, and already they were on to something. Detective Tharp smiled thinly. Satisfaction is a fleeting thing for a big-city cop, and the detective was not yet satisfied. Sure, the victim had been identified. A lucky break. How many more lucky breaks could he count on? Maybe none.

And what about Cecilia's killer? He was still on the loose, wasn't he? Was he satisfied? Would he strike again? Not very comforting thoughts.

By Sunday, March 27th, 100 pieces of Cecilia Arthur's body had been recovered. A coroner's investigator said it was now believed that the brown plastic bags containing the body parts had been thrown into the river at some other point and had washed up along the shore as the bags had been torn open on the rocks and debris littering the shoreline. Authorities said the bags had been recovered from a 350-yard stretch of riverbank.

On Sunday, several lines of inquiry were initiated. Cecilia Arthur's husband was an independent long-haul truck driver. It would be necessary to locate him. He would need to be informed of what had happened. They also wanted to locate the couple's boarder.

Detective Tharp, accompanied by a team from the

Scientific Investigation Unit, drove to the Arthur home in the 800 block of Greenwood Avenue, a quiet residential street. The address turned out to be a small one-story house covered in imitation red-brick shingles. It looked a bit rundown and shabby compared to the many nicer homes surrounding it. However, the little place proved to be an Aladdin's cave of treasure, for the detectives.

Detective Tharp described what happened: "We knocked several times. No one responded, at which time we talked to some of the neighbors. We showed neighbors the photograph of the victim's head and it was again identified (as Cecilia D. Arthur). We did a visual check of the house. We could see through every window, and were able to view the entire residence."

After determining that the house was unoccupied, the probers obtained search warrants for the house and a car parked on the property. They returned to Greenwood Avenue and entered the house at about five o'clock on Sunday evening.

Although some items would need to be verified by forensic experts, the investigators felt certain that the Arthur home was the scene of the murder and the dismemberment of the body. According to Detective Tharp, whoever had been responsible "had done a pretty good job of cleaning up the crime scene, although there were bloody footprints in the bathroom, the kitchen, throughout the crime scene where he had walked in the victim's blood and tracked it through the house."

Members of the Scientific Investigation Unit photographed the interior of the house and the evidence found there. The evidence was substantial: blood samples from a hallway wall and floor, water from the shower track, a mop, carpet samples from the kitchen, sink water, a towel, a rug, and a washrag.

Officers also found some saws on the back porch, a knife in the kitchen, a bloody hacksaw and ax in a back room, and a .25-caliber automatic pistol and a box of .25-caliber ammunition in a dresser drawer.

On Monday, ballistic tests were run on the .25-caliber pistol. Dr. James Patrick, the Lucas County Coroner, said that the bullet removed from the victim's head was similar to a .25-caliber, and that he felt Mrs. Arthur probably died of the gunshot wound. It was confirmed that the gun found at the residence was the weapon used to fire the fatal shot.

Dr. Patrick also said that he was interested in what was used to dismember the body, and that some of the bones displayed saw marks. "This task didn't take a short period of time," Dr. Patrick remarked. "There's no way I could have done that in an hour." This statement was later proven to be only too correct.

In another development on Monday, Toledo authorities were contacted by Northwood, Ohio police. Northwood is a suburban community adjacent to East Toledo. Investigating an unrelated case, a Northwood detective was searching an abandoned trailer loaded with scrap lumber which had been left on property owned by Conrail. During his search, this officer came across evidence he believed to be linked to the Cecilia Arthur homicide.

When Toledo police arrived at the site of the trailer, according to Sergeant Robert A. Maxwell, they found a golf-ball-sized piece of flesh, some clothing, and an identification card connected to Mrs. Arthur.

At this point, Mrs. Arthur's husband had still not been located, but was believed headed for New York State. He was supposedly due to arrive at a Buffalo truck stop on Wednesday evening. Toledo authorities contacted police in New York State and asked that they try to get in touch with him upon his arrival at the Buffalo stopover.

Investigators were also continuing their attempts to find Ronald Allen Scott, the 55-year-old man who had been renting a room in the Arthur home.

Scott was spotted in the downtown area on Tuesday afternoon. He was picked up and taken to the Safety Building. There he was interviewed for about three hours.

Captain Kenneth Koperski said later that police were trying to verify the information Scott had given them. He had been asked when he'd last seen the victim, and where he had been since the previous Friday.

Captain Koperski explained, "He's not very clear on dates and times. All we can do is check out a few of the things he told us." Before Scott left the building on Tuesday he was asked to return to the Safety Building the following morning to take a lie-detector test.

Wednesday brought two important developments in the case. First, the husband made a long-distance call to a relative and was finally told of his wife's brutal murder. When he learned that the police had been trying to locate him, he called headquarters. He stated that he was calling from somewhere in Pennsylvania. Because of the load he was hauling, he couldn't return to Toledo immediately, but he thought he would be able to get back by Thursday evening. The request to New York authorities to assist in locating the husband was cancelled.

Some of the Arthurs' neighbors claimed that they had seen the husband around home during the previous week. A relative said he thought that the victim's husband had been on the road since sometime in February.

378

When asked if the husband had ever been under suspicion, Detective Tharp replied, "In a homicide everyone and anyone is a suspect."

He went on to explain that the neighbors had been mistaken. It was actually Ronald Scott they had seen. Most hadn't known Scott was staying in the Arthur home and took it for granted that the man they saw was the husband.

Regarding the husband, Detective Tharp said, "He was a long-haul truck driver and he had a log of stops he'd made. I was able to verify his whereabouts from that."

In the second development, Ronald Scott failed to show up for his lie-detector test. It was late in the day before detectives were able to locate him and return him to the Safety Building.

He was advised of his rights several times. He was given a lie-detector test that evening. After failing the test, and after again being given his rights, Ronald Allen Scott made a voluntary statement in which he confessed to the shooting and dismemberment of 50-year-old Cecilia D. Arthur.

Scott was then placed under arrest and booked into Lucas County Jail. He was arraigned in Toledo Municipal Court the following morning.

Captain Koperski said that a great deal of the investigation centered around Mrs. Arthur herself: ". . . her lifestyle more or less, because we don't have a real clear picture of what her life was like."

Through a door-to-door canvass of her neighbors and interviews with other acquaintances, it was found that Cecilia had been born in Baltimore, Maryland. She had been married once before, and had been married to her current husband for about six years.

Her husband was away for extended periods of time.

379

Because of heart and diabetes problems, Cecilia was not able to work. She was often lonely, but she was an outgoing person who liked getting out to visit in the neighborhood.

Stunned neighbors of the murdered woman described her as a person with time on her hands: a warm, friendly person who roamed the neighborhood visiting people, often buying small trifles for the neighborhood children.

And almost daily she would walk the few blocks to a nearby business district on Starr Avenue. In addition to the beauty salon, one of her regular stops along the avenue was an antique-filled inn, the type of place where most of the customers know each other, and where there is a lot of good-natured conversation at about any time of day.

Cecilia would always take the same end barstool, sip a few diet sodas, and enjoy the opportunity to chat with the other patrons. The day barmaid had also wondered what had happened to Cecilia when several days passed without a visit from her.

The barmaid later said, "She drank nothing but diet Coke . . . she never gave me any problems."

Not long before her death, Cecilia had been back east to visit her family. The visit to her old home had stirred up some homesickness. In her last weeks she often talked about moving back to the Baltimore area.

And what was known of Ronald Allen Scott? Al Scott, as his friends knew him, was an "eastsider" and had been a member of a winning football team during his high school days. He'd begun to patronize the same tavern on Starr Avenue several years earlier. He came in with the after-work crowd, well-dressed, well-spoken, very sociable, and was quickly accepted by the

380

other regular customers.

And then, for no apparent reason, he dropped out of sight. It was some time before he was seen in the tavern again.

One evening, an acquaintance noticed him sitting quietly by himself at the bar. He looked thin and a bit bedraggled.

"Al, how are you?" the friend inquired. And, taking note of his appearance, "Have you been ill?"

Scott mentioned that he had suffered a sad series of losses. His mother had died, his wife had divorced him. He had lost his home, his car, and his business.

Although these events may have really happened to him, the true explanation for his disappearance from the social scene was something quite different. He had been serving a jail term for being involved in an alleged arson case.

It wasn't long after this that the same friend was talking with Cecilia Arthur and was surprised to learn that Al was renting a room in Cecilia's home.

"How did that come about?" the friend inquired.

Cecilia replied, "I heard Al say that he had no place to stay and I said, 'Well, you do now,' and I took him home with me." Later, when asked how the arrangement was working out, Cecilia smiled and said it was working out fine. She was glad that Al and her husband "hit it off so good."

Thus it was that Cecilia and Al met, and she eventually extended a helping hand to the man who would later become her murderer.

Is it fate, kismet, destiny? As Agatha Christie put it in one of her novels, the murder is the end result. It can begin years before with the persons involved slowly converging "Towards Zero"—murder being the zero hour. That seems especially apt in Cecilia Arthur's case: from Baltimore to Toledo to the bar where she met Ronald Allen Scott, all the time headed toward her zero hour.

And when that hour arrived on the night of Monday, March 21, 1988, according to Ronald Scott's taped statement, this is what happened . . .

Scott, who was unemployed, had been out drinking that day. "I came home. I was highly intoxicated. Cecilia started in on me about the rent money I owed."

Claiming that Cecilia slapped and kicked him, Scott said he slapped her back and got out his .25-caliber pistol to scare her. She had already thrown some of his clothing into the yard, and she told Scott that she was going to throw out the rest of his things. "That's when I raised the gun and shot her," Scott confessed on tape.

He stayed in the house with the body, leaving only to go to the liquor store. On Wednesday, March 23rd, he decided he had to do something about the corpse. Calmly, he told the police, "I figured I had to dispose of the body, so I started cutting it up." He began the dismemberment at four o'clock on Wednesday afternoon and worked throughout the night.

It was Thursday morning before he finished his gruesome task. He then drove to Northwood and dumped the clothes and the other items that were later found in the abandoned trailer. He returned to the house to wait for nightfall to complete his disposal of the remains.

On Thursday night, after loading the bags of body parts into the car, he drove to the heavily-traveled Craig Bridge, which carries the I-280 expressway traffic across the Maumee River. There, in the middle of the bridge in full view of passing cars, he threw the bags into the river.

The bags would drift and float through the downtown area and beyond, a distance of some three miles, before they would finally wash up along that 350-yard stretch of riverbank where they were found the following night.

Scott was out drinking all day Friday and stayed in the house that night, and again Saturday night. He left on Sunday morning. When he returned to Greenwood Avenue he saw police cars outside the house. Not wanting to confront the officers, he went to another part of town and registered into a transient hotel. It was later determined that he'd registered under a phony name.

It was two days later, on Tuesday, that police first interviewed him. They gave him the lie-detector test and arrested him on Wednesday.

On the following July 11th, the taped-recording of Ronald Scott's confession was played in Lucas County Common Pleas Court. Scott's defense attorney had requested the hearing in an attempt to bar use of the tape as evidence during the trial. The attorney also contended that the confession was improperly obtained, that Scott had not slept or eaten for three days, and that he had been drinking before being questioned. Scott claimed he'd been coerced into giving the confession, and had done so under threat of bodily harm.

Ronald Allen Scott had been given his rights several times, he had given his statement voluntarily, and he was not arrested until after he had confessed. In other words, he had been given every chance and consideration suspects always receive.

The hearing was continued until July 28th with the trial date set for September 6th.

However, with postponements, it wasn't until the

middle of September that the judge finally denied the motion to bar use of the taped confession during the trial. The trial date was rescheduled for Monday, September 26, 1988. The charge against Ronald Allen Scott was murder and the abuse of a corpse.

The day of the trial arrived and jury selection was about to begin. In a surprise move, Ronald Scott decided to plead no contest to the charges against him.

Although it is rarely used, the state of Ohio does have an electric chair. If Ronald Allen Scott's case had gone before the jury, there was a strong possibility he would have been the next resident on Death Row. By pleading no contest he was not actually admitting his guilt, but was putting himself at the mercy of the court.

Judge Charles Abood of the Lucas County Common Pleas Court sentenced Ronald Scott to the maximum time allowed by law: 15 years to life on the charge of murder, 3 years for the use of a gun in committing the homicide, and 18 months for abuse of the corpse. According to the law, Scott must serve a minimum of 18 years before being considered for parole.

Ronald Allen Scott went to a prison in Ohio to serve out his time.

Detective John Tharp, who started with 100 pieces of an unknown, incomplete body, successfully closed the case in five short days, left the force and went on to tackle the problem of drug abuse in the city schools.

Earlier in the year, on Saturday, April 16th, friends paid a final farewell to Cecilia at a memorial service in Toledo, and Cecilia D. Arthur finally went home to a private family service in Baltimore, Maryland.

"NO WAY TO BURY THE HATCHET!"

by Gary C. King

The street lights flickered on and mixed with the dregs of day as 20-year-old Daniel William Pierce left his home, located in the 2500 block of Southwest 23rd Circle in Troutdale, Oregon, and headed for his job as assistant manager at the Pizza Hut outlet in nearby Gresham. Although the winter of 1985 had mellowed into the bright, colorful spring of 1986, the evening air was still crisp, which prompted Pierce to turn his car's heater on full blast as soon as the engine became warm enough.

Fifteen minutes later, with circles of fatigue beneath tired, uncertain eyes, Pierce walked into the pizza parlor, as ready as ever for yet another shift, innocently unaware that it would be his last.

A young, bright-eyed man, Pierce was described by friends, co-workers, and relatives as a marvel of organized efficiency, an ambitious man who didn't feel right unless he was constantly moving forward, going somewhere with his life. At times he burned the candle at both ends, but he seemed to have two wicks to burn in his aspiration to move upward. He was an amiable young man with a perpetual smile and, despite his ambitious nature, he was still boyishly benign, utterly harmless to anyone. That's what made it so difficult for nearly everyone close to the case to understand why anyone would want to kill him.

It had been a typically slow Monday at the pizza shop, which allowed Pierce to get the restaurant cleaned up, the cash tills balanced, and the deposit made, enabling him to go home early to the house he'd moved into barely two weeks before and shared with two roommates. After the short drive from the pizza shop, he pulled carefully into the driveway to a spot near his roommates' vehicles and, after he parked and locked his own car, Pierce let himself into the rented, split-level two-story house, located on the north side of a cul-de-sac, and walked quietly up the stairs to his room.

Pierce had apparently just finished readying himself for bed and had just laid down when the attack occurred — he probably never even knew what had hit him. Even though the precise details of the attack are not known, one thing is certain: the killer's blood lust was at fever pitch as he raised the sharp hatchet over his sleeping victim's head.

Pierce's head must have erupted in blinding white pain as the hatchet fell, bringing with it a moment of extreme horror as he realized something terrible had happened to him. With each successive blow colors likely exploded in his brain, bringing with them unconsciousness and death moments later.

The following day one of Pierce's roommates, a young woman named Sally, who occupied the downstairs bedroom, noticed Pierce's absence but thought little of it at the time, thinking that perhaps he'd spent the night somewhere else. After all, Pierce was good looking, she thought, and women were naturally attracted to him. Since he worked in a public place, it was not an unreasonable assumption for Sally to consider that he'd met a young lady and had gone home with her. But when Pierce failed to return home by early Tuesday evening,

Sally became concerned and decided to check his room.

She knocked softly on the door to Pierce's bedroom and gently called out his name. Not receiving a response, she turned the knob and entered. She turned on the light, and the illumination was accompanied by an unanticipated exhalation of breath when she saw the blood. A sudden, inexplicable chill overcame her, and goose bumps appeared on her arms. Terror, she soon realized, had stuck its icy finger to her heart. She also felt somewhat sickened by the awful confrontation and its dreadful implications.

Sally rushed out of the room and ran for her other roommate's bedroom. However, he wasn't there, either, she soon learned, and the thought of being all alone in the immense house, where she knew something horrible had occurred, terrified her even more and prompted her to run to a neighbor's house.

The neighbor, Cynthia Fuller, was having dinner when Sally frantically rang her front doorbell. She recognized Sally and, after seeing that she was upset about something, let her inside and asked what was wrong. Sally said she wasn't sure, but insisted that Cynthia accompany her to her house to look at Pierce's upstairs bedroom.

"Do you see anything unusual?" Sally asked as she led Cynthia into the bedroom.

The neighbor stopped in mid-stride, cold dread clawing at her insides as she observed the pools of blood on Pierce's water bed and headboard. She turned to Sally and told her to call the police.

A short time later, Troutdale Police Chief Douglas Dorsey and an officer arrived at the Southwest 23rd Circle residence. He took a statement from Sally and Cynthia, viewed Pierce's bedroom, then sealed the home. He notified the Multnomah County Sheriff's Department that possible foul play had occurred at the residence and requested their help. He also asked for the assistance of the Oregon State Police (OSP) crime lab, and subsequently informed Pierce's relatives of the suspicious circumstances.

By the time Pierce's relatives arrived at the house, so had Multnomah County sheriff Fred Pearce (pronounced *purse*) and detectives from his department, as well as a deputy district attorney. Even though they were unsure what they were dealing with at this point, the usual officials had been called to the scene and the situation was treated as a possible crime of violence.

Troutdale Police Chief Dorsey told eager reporters, who received word of the suspicious circumstances over the police radios they routinely monitored, that there was evidence of foul play at the home, but he would not elaborate. However, another person at the house provided the reporters with a few details.

"There were bloodstains on the boards that were used in the water bed," said one person at the scene. "One board was broken. One bloodstain was eight or ten inches in diameter. Another was in the shape of an arc, about three feet long." The blood, observed one source close to the investigation, was like the after-image of a half-remembered nightmare . . . except this was very real.

The relatives told detectives they hadn't seen Pierce for a few days, and that he hadn't contacted them by telephone, either. Not enough time had elapsed for them to become concerned, and they said they assumed he had just been busy with his job. Sally, on the other hand, told the investigators she had last seen Pierce on Monday, March 10th, and hadn't become concerned about his well-being until Tuesday evening.

Because of the large amount of blood and the shape of the bloodstains, crime lab technicians processed the house in the usual manner by collecting blood samples, latent fingerprints, and trace evidence, concentrating their efforts in Pierce's bedroom. Although they worked throughout much of the night, no one associated with the case would reveal if anything that could lead to Pierce's whereabouts was obtained.

Over the next few hours detectives contacted people who were close to Pierce. They began with his co-workers, and learned that he had worked a full shift on Monday night, the last time anyone at the pizza parlor had seen him. Nothing unusual had occurred during the evening; it had simply been a typical, slow Monday night.

Like his co-workers, Pierce's friends and acquaintances, as well as other relatives, had not seen him recently. Nothing had been troubling him, said one person, except that he was having a dispute over his bank account that he said he had hoped to resolve. When pressed for details about the bank account, investigators were told that the bank's figures didn't match the balance in his checkbook, and Pierce couldn't understand why. On another occasion, said the witness, Pierce attempted to shift money from his savings account to his checking account but found there was no money left in his savings account.

Although the case was quickly taking on Rubik's Cube complexity, particularly since no one had seen Pierce after he left work Monday night and because of the unexplained blood in his room, investigators had little choice but to write it up as a missing-person investigation at this point, with a notation that extreme violence may have occurred. Although no one close to the case really expected Pierce to turn up alive, his photograph was nonetheless made available to all law enforcement agencies in the area, just in case.

They didn't have to wait long for a new development in the case. Detectives received a call at Pierce's home from a person who declined to identify himself. The investigators would not comment on the significance of the call, which was placed early Thursday morning, March 13th. However, Troutdale Police Chief Douglas Dorsey said that his department, working with the Multnomah County sheriff's detectives, were able to develop a lead involving a stolen car that was possibly connected to the case.

The car, they learned, had been stolen recently from Renton, Washington, near Seattle, and was recovered at a location in Tualatin, Oregon, a small community located a few miles south of Portland. Unsure of what role the car played at this point, Dorsey and Multnomah County detectives contacted the Tualatin Police Department for assistance. They didn't waste any time getting to the site of the abandoned stolen vehicle, unaware, but at the same time hopeful, that it would supply them with the next piece to their complex puzzle.

As the detectives and officers walked casually around the car, they made a cursory examination of its interior and engaged in light conversation with each other. Finding little of significance in the front part of the car, they turned their attention to the trunk. When they gained entry to the trunk and saw the horrible body parts, their conversation stopped in mid-sentence. One of the officers retched with nausea and another turned pale and nearly fainted at the bloody, grisly sight.

The car and surrounding area was quickly cordoned off, and all the usual authorities were promptly notified that a homicide victim had been found. Everyone associated with the case knew they were really behind the eight ball on this one, and that they could leave no stone unturned to solve this case.

"During a subsequent search of the vehicle, identifiable parts of a victim's body were found in the trunk," said Chief Dorsey when word of the gruesome discovery leaked out to the press. He said there was no way to immediately determine the cause of death.

No one on the case would reveal just what anatomical parts were found inside the car's trunk. However, one person said there was only a small percentage of a human body, but it would be enough for anyone familiar with the victim to make a positive identification.

As soon as the car and its unwholesome contents were photographed and processed, the body parts were bagged, tagged, and sent to the Multnomah County Morgue in Portland. A short time later, according to Dr. Larry Lewman, acting State Medical Examiner, the dismembered body parts were identified as Daniel W. Pierce. The positive identification, he said, was made by a sheriff's deputy who was an acquaintance of the family.

Following an autopsy the next day, Dr. Karen Gunson, deputy medical examiner, said that the small percentage of the body that had been recovered enabled her to confirm "who it was and that was about it." Although she could not determine the actual cause of death because not enough of the body was available to examine, Gunson could confidently say Pierce died of homicidal violence.

"I drew my conclusions that I'd never see (Daniel) again," said one of Pierce's relatives, struggling with tears. He said that when he went to Pierce's house the night he was reported missing, it was very definite and obvious from the blood that Pierce was dead. "But until parts of his body were found I couldn't make that statement to anybody but my own heart. I kept up the facade of hope."

Pierce's murder brought an already skyrocketing homicide rate in Portland even higher, causing concern for law enforcement personnel and citizens alike.

"Part of the reason for the increase is because the city has grown, and we've annexed more areas," said Lieutenant Al Dean of the Portland Police Bureau. "But another reason, and this is only my opinion, is there's just less respect for each other as humans . . . I think we all get anesthetized by television and movies where someone is shot. There might be a little bit of blood, but I think that death looks too easy. They don't show what really happens when someone is shot in the side of the head (or cut up into pieces). It doesn't happen all the time, but we've had suspects allude to the fact that the murder was different than what they thought it would be."

In the meantime sheriff's deputies continued searching for other of Pierce's remains and sought additional information on the case. According to Sergeant James A. Davis, spokesman for the sheriff's department, there was just no rhyme or reason for Pierce's brutal murder based on the limited information they had so far developed. He stressed, however, that detectives from his department would work around the clock if necessary to develop new leads.

Chief Dorsey, likewise, stressed that his department would do everything possible to bring out a speedy resolution to the case, and he pleaded publicly for the anonymous tipster who called Pierce's home early Thursday morning to contact the authorities. Chief Dorsey said it was possible the individual could have information important to the case but might not know it, and he assured that the person could call his office or the Multnomah County sheriff's department in confidence.

The next day authorities made yet another public plea for assistance, this time for help in the search for more of Pierce's body parts. Sergeant Davis of the sheriff's department announced that detectives had installed a confidential telephone line with a recorder, and that anyone seeking to help could call and have information recorded. The effort would eventually pay off, they reasoned, but they didn't know how long it would take.

The detectives in this case were dealing with a "trunk murder," a name which is commonly used to describe a murder in which the perpetrator places the body of the victim inside a trunk, chest, large suitcase, box, or other similar container in an attempt to dispose of the corpse. Even though a portion of Pierce's body was concealed in the trunk of a car, the term still fit the crime in this case, perhaps even more so. The body in a trunk murder, it is interesting to note, is commonly cut up into several parts, as was the case here, but even more commonly the victim is placed inside a sack or is covered with a blanket, tarpaulin, or articles of clothing.

The detectives knew from training and experience that the dismemberment of a body is either a defensive or an offensive act. While the offensive act is often associated with passion, sometimes regarded as a form of sadism when the victim is female or, as in some cases, a homosexual male, the defensive act, on the other hand, is utilized by the murderer who wishes to conceal the victim's body or make it unrecognizable to aid him in his attempts to elude detection. Since Pierce was a young man and because there was no evidence that he'd ever been involved in a homosexual relationship, the detectives theorized that the dismemberment of his body fell into the defensive classification. It was readily apparent that Pierce's murderer intended to make identification of the body difficult by concealing parts of it at different places, likely spread out over a considerable area. Where he made his mistake, the detectives reasoned, was by leaving an identifiable part of the body in the stolen car's trunk. They further reasoned that the killer must have been attempting to dispose of the parts in the trunk but instead had left the car in a panic, perhaps frightened away by someone.

If the identifiable part of Pierce's body hadn't been found so quickly, it would have been a much more difficult case for the investigators.

But the rapid discovery of a body part that enabled identification of the victim provided the sleuths in the Pierce case with a solid starting point.

Meanwhile, detectives stepped up their efforts in locating more of Pierce's body parts. Although detectives remained tight-lipped about the case, sources close to the investigation revealed that the confidential telephone line, installed shortly after the mysterious phone call to Pierce's residence, seemed to be working. The investigators apparently developed enough information to lead searchers from the Multnomah County Sheriff's Department and the Troutdale Police Department to a heavily wooded area off Oregon highway 35, approximately 25 miles south of Hood River.

"Everything we have so far points to that direction," said Sergeant Jim Davis, without being more specific. He said a search party had been organized, and they would begin the endeavor the next day.

The searchers got off to an early start, shortly before dawn. As they drove through the Columbia River Gorge, they met the orange rays of the sun head-on as it made its way into the eastern sky. It was a beautiful sunrise as they entered the town called Hood River, well-known for its wonderful apples, and before they turned onto Oregon 35, they passed row after row of apple trees, the orchards being a major source of income for many in the area. The trees were budding beautifully, their delicate, pretty blossoms only a week or two away from making their first appearance, but unfortunately the lawmen weren't there on a sightseeing trip.

The searchers soon found themselves in the deep shade of the heavily wooded area in the Mount Hood

National Forest, making the morning chill all the more noticeable. A short time later they reached the area they wanted to search, and parked their vehicles and climbed out, some shivering in the cool morning air.

The giant fir trees stretched tall against the sky as they made their way into the forest. Nearby a pebbled brook chattered with cold water as it relentlessly polished its stones, and the twitter of birds still waking could be hard in every direction. One of the searchers pointed out a lone eagle that soared majestically overhead, and as they walked along they were occasionally distracted by ravens gliding by their nests on the sides of nearby cliffs. It was a captivating morning in an enchanting area, much too beautiful to be out there searching for some poor soul's body parts.

A short time later one of the searchers spotted a shape in the foreground, in itself frightening, considering what they were looking for. But as the deputy came closer to it, he could see that it was a trap. He called out to his co-searchers that he'd found something.

It was wet in the forest and there were slugs galore, the slimy things were so thickly concentrated that the searchers actually had to watch where they stepped. But they pushed on and in minutes reached the trap.

Even before they reached the trap the despicable odor told them they had found what they came looking for, at least part of it. With handkerchiefs over their noses, the searchers gazed at the trap in stunned disbelief, none wanting to remove the covering and expose what was beneath it. But they knew they must, and when one of the searchers pulled the tarp to one side, all of the deputies and officers stared in awe and horror as they watched the maggots helping themselves to the body parts that lay on the ground. The sight was so horrible that it unbraided something inside every one present, enough so that it left a scar on their souls. It was a sight they would relive for the rest of their days.

Because of the delicate nature of what they were dealing with, no one attempted to immediately move the parts. Instead, one of the deputies was sent back to his car to radio the gruesome discovery to his dispatcher, fighting to keep his voice steady as he described what they'd found.

Because the body parts required delicate handling from the beginning, handling and examination of the parts was left to the crime lab experts. When the technicians arrived at the remote site a short time later, they immediately examined the wrapping for dirt, dust, and anything else that could indicate what had been wrapped in the tarp before using it for the body pieces. They also examined the tarp and the human segments for fingerprints, hair, and other traces of the perpetrator. However, they delayed using any development media in their search for fingerprints until after the parts had been removed from the site and the laboratory experts had completed their examination to avoid contaminating the specimens. Despite their efforts, there was nothing from the extensive examination to point the investigators toward a suspect.

In the meantime detectives were still trying to locate Pierce's other roommate, whom they identified as Socrates Edward Ladner, 27, for questioning. Ladner, also known as Dan Brown, the sleuths learned, had met Pierce at the Pizza Hut restaurant in Gresham where they both worked. They lived together in Gresham for several weeks prior to finding Sally to share the house they rented in Troutdale.

Because of their strong interest in Ladner the detectives initiated a thorough background check on the subject. They learned that he was born in the Panama Canal Zone on March 22, 1959, and had relatives in Texas, but they were unable to learn when he came to the United States.

The background check provided an abundance of information on Ladner and enabled investigators to develop a number of significant leads to run down. Sheriff's detectives and Troutdale police traced Ladner to New Mexico, Colorado, Minnesota, Washington and, finally, Oregon, and learned that their subject had outstanding warrants for his arrest in New Mexico on accusations of forgery, in Colorado on accusations of forgery and fraud, in Washington on charges of forgery, and in Texas on charges of parole violation and car theft.

According to Sergeant Davis of the sheriff's department, Ladner had used at least 17 aliases including Eduardo Socrates Ladner, Louis Socrates Ladner, Louis S. Ladner, Ed Ladner, Louis Ladner, Ed Landier, Edward S. Landier, Socrates E. Osario, Virgilio Mario Stevens, Michael Stevens, Gary Freeman, Robert Linhart, David Canchola, Delbert Owen Thomas, Scott Thomas, and Dan Brown. The detectives strongly suspected there may have been other aliases, but they were unable to immediately confirm those suspicions.

Further investigating revealed that the *modus operandi* (M.O.) of the suspect involved in the forgery and fraud cases typically shared a room with a victim for a period of time, took the victim's blank checks, credit and bank cards, and through forgery and fraud, withdrew funds from the victim's bank account and made charges on the credit cards. Often a car was stolen, driven to another state, and the process started all over again. Authorities believe the crime spree began in Texas in June 1985.

Because of the warrants on forgery and fraud in multiple states, as well as the M.O. that also fit in Pierce's case, the detectives theorized that Pierce was murdered because he had found out about Ladner's past and, because of the missing funds from his own bank account, had put two and two together. The detectives speculated that Pierce confronted Ladner at some point, thinking he could handle the situation, but soon was out of his depth.

An APB was immediately issued for Ladner's arrest, and he was taken into custody at an undisclosed location a short time later on the outstanding warrants from Texas. He was lodged in the Justice Center Jail in downtown Portland, and an additional charge of murder was leveled against him.

Wearing a gray jacket and black-framed glasses at his first court appearance on the murder charge, Ladner told Multnomah County District Court Judge William J. Keys that he could not afford an attorney. Keys subsequently appointed attorney Tommy Hawk to take his case.

After agreeing to talk, the detectives and Ladner squabbled for an hour in one of the interrogation rooms before they got down to brass tacks, the major problem being that Ladner had agreed to talk but wasn't giving them any useful information. His constant smile seemed to be a red herring to keep them from knowing his real intentions, but after a few more hours of interrogation, Ladner spilled the beans about Pierce's murder. He refused, however, to discuss the motive.

In an unusual move, knowing that it would take two Philadelphia lawyers and a million bucks to get him out of this one, not to mention the horrendous fear of being indicted by a grand jury on a charge of aggravated murder (the legal theory being that Pierce was killed to conceal other crimes such as forgery and theft), which could bring the death penalty, Ladner appeared before Judge Lee Johnson and pleaded guilty to the murder charge before the grand jury had time to convene.

"We did this obviously to avoid a death penalty or a

30-year mandatory minimum sentence," said Defense Attorney Hawk. During the brief appearance Ladner admitted that he intentionally killed Pierce by striking him with a sharp object. When Judge Johnson asked what the sharp object was, Ladner told him it was a hatchet.

Ladner appeared before Judge Philip J. Roth on Tuesday, June 3, 1986, for sentencing. Although Ladner never admitted the motive for the killing, Deputy District Attorney Marilyn A. Curry said that Pierce was killed because he'd apparently made Ladner aware of what he knew with regard to his past and the forgeries made on Pierce's accounts. She added that it would have been "uncharacteristic for Pierce to confront anyone in a violent manner or to have made any threats."

Prior to sentencing, Judge Roth described the confessed hatchet killer as a "predatory animal for a good period of time." He also said that Pierce's murder was a "brutal slaying of a person who had befriended Ladner." The judge then asked Ladner if he had anything to say before sentencing.

"I know something terrible was committed," said Ladner in a low voice. "That's an understatement. I am not asking anyone to feel sorry for me because I am getting what I deserve." Ladner said he was sorry for the killing.

Judge Roth then threw the book at Ladner and sentenced him to life in prison, and setting a minimum term of 25 years before he could become eligible for parole. Roth added that Ladner was "very fortunate he's only facing a life sentence" and that he would be "derelict not to impose the maximum sentence" available under Oregon law. Ladner is now serving that sentence at Oregon State Penitentiary.

"HE CAME, HE SAWED, HE DISMEMBERED!"

by Philip Westwood

Harry Godfrey swung the wheel to the left and steered his car into the rest area by the side of the rushing main highway. A line of trees and bushes screened out the traffic, and Harry felt an immediate sense of relaxation. He followed the curve around until the trees thinned out and the highway became visible once more. Twenty yards ahead of him, the pull-in for the rest area rejoined the main road. Harry's foot shifted to the brake and the car came to a halt.

Harry switched off the engine and looked out the window. Warm sunshine bathed the surrounding countryside. Small birds, their beaks stuffed full of dry grass and twigs, flitted in and out of the bushes before darting off across the fields to their nesting sites. On the trees, the leaves were beginning to burst out of their buds. It was the afternoon of Wednesday, March 21, 1990, and spring was in the air.

Harry yawned, stretched, and looked at his watch. It was 10 minutes after one. Time for lunch. He smiled contentedly to himself, and reached over for the sandwich box and the flask of coffee that lay concealed under the topcoat draped across the backseat.

Harry had earned his lunch that day. Being a salesman can be hard work. It can bring frustration and disappointment. But on a good day, it can be very rewarding. And for Harry Godfrey, this was looking like a really good day.

During the morning Harry had closed a deal with a company in the town of Tredegar in the South Wales county of Gwent. It was a deal that would prove lucrative for his employers, and, when the commissions were paid out, for himself. That afternoon, he had an appointment with a company in the nearby town of Newport. Harry had high hopes that his afternoon appointment would prove equally profitable. After that, it was back to his home on the outskirts of the city of Bristol, across the English border.

The hands on Harry's watch had moved around to 1:45. Harry had finished his sandwiches and had just poured himself a second cup of coffee. He sipped carefully at the steaming liquid as he stared through the windshield at the world passing by. The highway, empty of lunching travelers, was quieter now.

Harry watched each car as it came into view on the highway and he kept on watching until they disappeared behind the tress that lined his hiding place. He started to count them as they passed. One, two, three, four, five . . .

But car number five was different. It didn't pass by. Instead, it pulled over to the side of the highway. The driver got out and looked all around. He couldn't see Harry behind the trees of the pull-in, but Harry could see him. He put down his coffee cup and gave the man his undivided attention.

Satisfied that no one was around, the man went to the trunk of his car and opened it. Harry could not see what the man was doing because he was concealed by the open trunk lid. But when the man emerged from behind the lid, Harry could see that he was carrying a large green plastic bag. Still looking all round him, the man made his way toward the shoulder. One last look around, and then the man balanced himself carefully and raised the plastic bag above his head.

Summoning all of his strength, the man suddenly threw the plastic bag as far as he could toward the fields at the side of the highway. Harry watched in horror as the bag arched through the air and fell to the ground, hitting the shoulder and rolling away down the grassy back into a ditch.

Harry Godfrey was amazed. He was a concerned environmentalist, and polluting the countryside in this manner was something that deeply offended his strongly held principles. He felt that he should say something to the man, point out the error of his ways in disposing of trash in such a thoughtless and uncaring way.

But Harry had not gotten over his initial amazement before the man did it again. A second green plastic bag followed the first on its short journey from the trunk of the man's car to its resting place in the ditch at the side of the highway.

Harry felt he had to do something. He thought he should remonstrate with the man. But by the time Harry had untangled himself from the confines of his seat belt, gotten out of the driving seat, and sprinted the short distance to the highway, the man was back in his car and speeding off down the road in the direction of Newport, about three miles away.

Harry thought of getting back into his car and chasing after the man, but he knew that would be useless. He stood no chance of catching him. At least he had managed to get a good look at the man. He felt like reporting him to the police. After all, depositing litter like that was a crime. The man should be punished.

Harry thought for a moment. Maybe he should take a

look in the bags that the man had been so anxious to get rid of before he reported the matter to the police. After all, he wanted to make sure there was something worth reporting. He didn't want to waste the time of already overworked officers on some trivial matter that he could quite easily deal with himself.

But if the truth be told, it was the satisfying of his own natural curiosity as much as his concern for the environment that triggered in Harry the desire to check out the contents of the bags. What was it about the bags and their contents, Harry wondered, that had prompted the man to drive out of town and deposit them at the side of the highway instead of simply taking them to the city dump?

Harry crossed the road to the place where the man's car had been parked. He walked slowly and carefully along the grassy bank from which the man had hurled the bags. The plastic bundles were quite easy to see in the ditch below. Harry went down the bank and into the ditch. It was only a matter of seconds before he was standing over the two bright green objects.

Almost immediately, Harry was struck by the silence. He was about 15 feet below road level, though it was as if the highway didn't exist. There was no traffic noise down there, nothing but the humming of insects and the occasional call of a bird.

Harry prodded the bags with his foot. One, he deduced, contained three or four long and somewhat thick objects, while the other was occupied by a single square-shaped hulk that defied all of Harry's powers of reasoning as to its identity. There was only one way to find out. Harry would have to look inside.

The bags were tied at their tops with thick string that had been knotted several times. But the knots succumbed easily to Harry's nimble fingers and it was not long before he had one bag opened.

Immediately, Harry's nostrils were assailed by a strong, pungent odor. It was a sickly, nauseating smell, so strong that it caused Harry to drop the bag and start gasping for air. The bag hit the sloping ground of the side of the ditch, overturned, and spilled its contents out onto the grass.

It was at that moment that Harry Godfrey saw a vision of sheer hell. On the grass in front of him, was a decomposing human torso. The arms, legs, and head had all been crudely hacked off. Only round red patches marked the places where they had once been attached. Slivers of bone, from which dangled obscene-looking strings of rotting flesh, protruded from the joints of the arms and legs. The head had been more cleanly removed. The neck joint was smooth.

It was the team of detectives who rushed to the scene in answer to Harry's frantic telephone call who were faced with the unenviable task of opening the second bag.

Harry's first impression of the contents, as he prodded it with his foot, was that the objects inside the bag might be the branches of a small tree. Harry couldn't have been more wrong.

The detectives who opened the bag were greeted by the sight of two severed human arms and two severed human legs. The hands were missing from both of the arms.

It was a reasonable supposition that the contents of the bags were the remains of one person. The person had been a man, and, detectives concluded, a young man. The skin showed no signs of the wrinkling that advancing years inevitably produce, though the victim had reached physical maturity. He was probably in his 20s or early 30s. But more than that could not be deduced from an initial examination. There were no distinguishing marks on the skin, such as tattoos or natural blemishes, and no clothing or other possessions that would provide a clue as to his identity. A search of the surrounding area failed to turn up any trace of the man's missing head and hands.

Establishing the man's identity was of paramount importance. But that would require a special kind of skill not possessed by ordinary law enforcement officers.

Dr. Stephen Leadbetter had worked as a pathologist for many years. In that time, he had seen the results of most of the cruel and savage acts that one human being can perpetrate on another. Piecing together the dismembered remains of a body was nothing new to him. Leadbetter was quickly able to establish that, whoever the murderer was, he was not a man who had received any medical training. He was also sure that the killer was not a butcher or anyone who might be acquainted with the practices of the slaughterhouse. The dismemberment had been perpetrated in a crude and unskilled manner. It had been carried out with a rough-toothed saw of the type used for cutting logs. And it had been carried out very quickly.

"The body could have been cut up and placed in the bags ready for disposal in about an hour," Dr. Leadbetter told detectives.

But there was little else that the pathologist could report. The body was that of a young man between 20 and 25 years of age. He had been in perfect health up to the moment when the killer struck, and that moment had been only about 12 hours before the body was discovered. It was highly unlikely that the records of missing persons would provide the answer to the question of the dead man's identity, but they were checked out anyway. The results were negative.

Doctor Leadbetter was unable to say how the man had been killed. He was dead when the dismemberment commenced, and the body parts recovered bore no knife or gunshot wounds or any other signs of what might have caused the death of such a healthy young man.

"He must have been killed by a blow to the head," the pathologist told detectives. "That's the only part of him missing that would have been able to sustain an injury serious enough to prove fatal. It's essential that it is found, and found quickly before decomposition makes any postmortem examination impossible."

So teams of officers were assigned to the task of scouring the countryside for a human head. The investigation was rapidly taking on the aspects of a scenario for a horror movie rather than a murder inquiry. But results were not long in coming.

On the morning of Sunday, March 25th, four days after Harry Godfrey's lunch was so rudely interrupted — shepherd Jack Neames was on his way to tend his flock of sheep in a field on the outskirts of the village of St. Brides.

Jack was unaware of the grisly discovery that had been made only 10 miles away from where his sheep were peacefully grazing. He took no interest in such matters. In fact, old Jack took no interest in anything that happened outside of his own village. He had been born there and he would die there. It was his whole world. Anywhere else, especially somewhere as far away as 10 miles, might as well be on the moon. But on that quiet Sunday morning, all of that was about to change.

It was while Jack was opening the gate that led into the field that he noticed the object lying half-concealed in the ditch. He took a closer look and saw that it was a large green plastic bag.

Muttering to himself about inconsiderate townsfolk

dumping their trash in the countryside with no regard for the consequences, Jack made his way into the ditch and over to the bag. His intention was to retrieve it and dispose of it properly. Why didn't people think before they simply threw their rubbish anywhere? Jack wondered.

It was at that point that Jack's curiosity got the better of him. He had recovered the bag from the tangle of vegetation and found that it was quite heavy. He shook it and was aware of a bulky object rolling around in the bottom of the bag. What could it be? Carefully, Jack loosened the string fastened around the top of the bag and looked inside.

Jack Neames was sitting on the grassy bank of the ditch, still in a state of shock, when detectives and forensics experts arrived on the scene a little while later. They had been summoned by the farmer for whom Jack worked when he had become concerned because the old shepherd had not arrived to tend the sheep. He had found Jack, still standing in the ditch, and still holding the bag. The farmer had taken the bag from Jack and had looked inside. Then he called the police.

The bag contained the missing head and hands for which detectives had been searching for four days. Dr. Stephen Leadbetter was informed of the find and was soon back at work.

From his examination of the head, Dr. Leadbetter was able to determine the cause of death. The victim had suffered multiple skull fractures as a consequence of being battered about the head 12 times with a hammer. The resulting brain damage was colossal.

Meanwhile, fingerprint expert Kenneth Hobbs was putting the plastic bag through his routine albeit meticulous examination. Similar treatment of the bag containing the torso had revealed nothing. But with the bag that contained the victim's head, Hobbs was having better luck. Near the top of the bag, he was able to isolate a clear print of a right forefinger.

It was quickly established that the print had not been made by the victim. It was also established within a short space of time that the print was on file at the Criminal Records Office in London. The contents of the file were transmitted by fax to detectives in South Wales.

The print had been made by a man named Malcolm Green. There was only one conviction against Green's name, but it was a conviction that caused great interest among the Welsh detectives: Green had served time for murder. In 1971, he had been jailed for life for killing prostitute Glenys Johnson in his hometown of Cardiff, the Welsh capital.

But "life" rarely means *life*. And in Green's case, it didn't. The file showed that he had spent the last few years at the low security Leyhill Open Prison outside Bristol from where he had been released in October 1989—just five months previously.

A killer released from a life sentence in Great Britain is never really free. He is only out on license. He has to keep police informed on a regular basis of his address of any employment that he might be able to obtain. According to the file, Malcolm Green lived in an apartment in the Easton district of Bristol. He worked as a heating engineer, installing and servicing heating systems in commercial premises.

Welsh detectives informed their colleagues in Bristol of these new developments and asked them to check out the situation. Two Bristol detectives were immediately dispatched to the address shown on Green's file. Green had not returned from work, so the detectives decided to wait. While they were waiting, they thought it might prove useful to talk to the neighbors. It usually does.

This occasion was no exception.

Neighbors reported that Green had lived in the apartment for about four months. He kept pretty much to himself and didn't say much to anyone. But he did have one friend with whom he seemed particularly close. That was the young man in the next apartment to Green's. He was a pleasant, friendly person by the name of Clive Tully, a New Zealander who had come to Britain to seek out relatives who lived in the area.

None of the neighbors to whom the detectives spoke could remember seeing Tully around for a few days. But nobody thought that was unusual. It was merely assumed that Tully had succeeded in tracing his relatives and was staying with them. The detectives did not share the neighbors' views on the reason for Tully's apparent disappearance.

So the building supervisor was contacted and requested to open up both Tully's and Green's apartments. Forensics experts were summoned, and before long, the normally quiet apartment block was a hive of police activity.

Tully's apartment showed no signs of disturbance. Everything was neat and tidy, except in the kitchen where the unwashed crockery and cutlery of a finished meal were stacked by the sink. They appeared to have been there for several days. The remains of food on the plates had congealed, and a thin film of fungus was starting to form. Forensics technicians carefully scraped the remains into a variety of small plastic bags, tagged them, and sealed them. They would be taken to the laboratory for analysis and comparison with the undigested remains of a meal that Dr. Leadbetter had found in the dismembered victim's stomach. Fingerprints were lifted from the crockery and the cutlery, and from a range of items in the apartment. These would be compared with the prints of the severed hands that Jack Neames had discovered, to see if the dead man was, as detectives suspected, the apartment's tenant, Clive Tully.

Wherever Tully had gone, it did not seem to be a planned trip. His clothes were still hanging in the wardrobe. Drawers were stacked with ties, socks, and underwear, and a set of empty luggage stood in one corner of the bedroom.

Green's apartment was similarly tidy. There was nothing unusual about it, except that in the kitchen, the table and the floor appeared to have been subjected to a recent, and thorough, cleaning. The tiles on the table top had been scrubbed so severely that, in parts, it had been scraped away. Forensics experts were in the middle of examining the table when Malcolm Green arrived home from work.

"What's going on here?" Green demanded. It was a reasonable question, so the detectives answered it.

"When did you last see Mr. Tully?" they wanted to know.

"Four or five days ago," replied Green. "I don't remember exactly. He said he was going to stay with relatives somewhere in South Wales."

Detectives looked the 44-year-old heating engineer up and down. Well spoken and slightly built, Green didn't look like he would have either the nerve or the strength to batter to death and then dismember another human being. But appearances can be deceptive. Detectives investigating the murder of Glenys Johnson 19 years earlier had probably thought exactly the same thing when confronted by the skinny suspect with the soft Welsh accent.

A search through Green's bedroom turned up a pair of shoes which, on their uppers, had a number of tiny, almost imperceptible, speckles of a substance that

411

looked remarkably like blood. Asked for an explanation of the marks, Green could offer none. So the detectives took him along to their local station and contacted their colleagues in South Wales. By the next morning, Green had been taken across the border and was facing Welsh detectives at the Newport Police Station. The officers' questions brought little response. In fact, they brought no response at all. Green refused to speak, except to say that he was the victim of a frame-up.

But the evidence against Malcolm Green was beginning to build up. Forensic and medical tests confirmed that the dead man was 45-year-old Clive Tully. They also confirmed that the substance on Green's shoes was blood and that the blood was of the same group as that of Tully.

Traces of blood of the same group were also found on the table and the floor of Green's kitchen. Detectives were now certain that Clive Tully had been killed in Green's kitchen, but they didn't know why. From their question of the residents of the apartment block in which the two men had lived, the officers could find no motive for the killing. Green and Tully had not argued. They got on extremely well. In the days prior to his disappearance, Tully had seemed cheerful and carefree. He had not spoken of a rift in his friendship with Green. In fact, he had not spoken of Green at all.

As the days passed, more and more evidence against Malcolm Green began to emerge. Dr. Leadbetter had concluded that the dismemberment of Tully had been performed with a rough-toothed saw. Such a saw was found in Green's toolbox. He said he used it for cutting through copper pipes during the course of his work.

When the saw was scientifically examined, the teeth were found to be impregnated with traces of copper and other metals. But there were also traces of another substance. Apparently, an attempt had been made to clean the saw, but in spite of that, the forensics team was able to detect microscopic particles of human flesh still clinging to the saw's teeth. When asked for an explanation of how human flesh came to be on the saw, Green again refused to speak. He also refused to account for how his fingerprint came to be on the plastic bag that had been used to dispose of some of Tully's remains.

But the detectives were not particularly concerned by their suspect's silence. They didn't need a confession. They had sufficient forensic and medical evidence to put Green away for a very long time. There remained just one final thing to be done.

Harry Godfrey, the man whose inquisitiveness into the contents of two discarded plastic bags had sparked off the investigation, had stated that he would be able to recognize the man he had seen dumping them. Detectives decided to put Green into a lineup, and see if Harry's faith in his powers of recollection were justified.

In the basement at the police station, Green, along with eight men picked at random because they bore a passing resemblance to the suspect, stood side-by-side on a raised platform. Above their heads were a series of boards bearing the numbers 1 to 9. From behind a glass panel, Harry surveyed the men.

"Just take your time," an officer advised Harry. "Have a good look at each man and if you see one whom you recognize, just refer to him by the number on the board above his head."

Harry did as he was told. He looked at each man in turn. He took a long, hard look. Finally, he spoke.

"It's Number Four," he said to the officer at his side. "That's the man I saw dumping the plastic bags."

"Are you sure?" asked the officer.

"Absolutely certain," replied Harry. "It's Number

413

Four. That's the man."

In the lineup, none of the men could hear what was being said on the other side of the glass panel. Each man stood motionless, staring ahead. Malcolm Green's face registered no expression. He appeared to be totally disinterested in what was taking place. Above his head was a board bearing the number "4".

Malcolm Green was formally charged with the murder of Clive Tully. It was one of the rare occasions on which he chose to speak.

"I didn't do it," he said when the charge was put to him. "It's a frame-up."

The following morning, Malcolm Green appeared before local magistrates who remanded him in custody to await trial at Bristol Crown Court.

It was a long wait. Not until the early part of October 1991 were the authorities ready to put the case against him before the court.

In the intervening period, investigators had been seeking, without success, a motive for the killing. But they were not too surprised. Detectives who had investigated Green's murder of Glenys Johnson had also been unable to find any reason for that killing. It seemed that something inside of Green just snapped, and when it did, he killed. There was no logical explanation for it.

The jury at Bristol Crown Court had no idea that the man before them in the dock had already served time for murder. Under British law, no details of an accused person's past crimes, however serious or however trivial, can be mentioned at his trial. They cannot even be hinted at, or any intimation made that the accused person may have a past that is somewhat on the shady side.

The jury listened attentively as the prosecutor, Paul Chadd, Q.C., detailed the evidence.

Clive Tully had spent some time in Britain, seeking

414

out relatives. He had managed to find quite a few and had visited them on several occasions. But he was not due to see any of his relatives at the time of his disappearance.

Tully had died as a result of being struck over the head 12 times with a hammer. He had been struck from behind, indicating that he had no idea that he was about to be attacked. The attack had taken place in the kitchen of Green's apartment and had continued as Tully lay, definitely unconscious and probably dead, on the floor. The number of the blows, and the force with which they were inflicted, gave a clear indication that there was a deliberate intent to kill. This was not merely an assault that had gone too far.

After he had been killed, Tully was dismembered on Green's kitchen table. Forensics experts had found traces of blood and flesh embedded in the table, along with scratches that they were able to prove had been made by the saw in Green's toolbox. There was also blood on the floor and on a pair of Green's shoes. More traces of blood were found on two towels in Green's bathroom.

After dismemberment, the body parts were put into two plastic bags. The bags were of a common type, readily available at any hardware store. A number of bags of the same type had been found in a cupboard of Green's kitchen.

Malcolm Green listened to the case against him with the same disinterest that he had shown throughout the investigation. The only words he spoke during the trial were "Not guilty" when the charge was read to him. He elected not to go into the witness box to give evidence on his own behalf.

Faced with such overwhelming evidence, it was not really surprising that the jury required only a short deliberation before finding Green guilty as charged.

"You are intelligent, cold-blooded, sadistic, and a liar," the judge, Mr. Justice Rose, told the murderous heating engineer. It seemed a pretty fair assessment. Green was sentenced to life imprisonment—again—and the judge ordered that he serve at least 25 years before parole be considered.

In reality, Malcolm Green will probably never be released from prison. He had already been let out from one life sentence when he killed Clive Tully. In retrospect, to have released Green back in October 1989 was a mistake. And the authorities are keen not to make the same mistake twice.

EDITOR'S NOTE:
Harry Godfrey and Jack Neames are not the real names of the persons so named in the foregoing story. Fictitious names have been used because there is no reason for public interest in the identities of these persons.

"SMOTHERED, THEN CHOPPED INTO BITS!"

by Bill Kelly

It was time to go. On April 5, 1992, Mary Louise Asbury, 59, helped her companion, 79-year-old Lillian Shepherd, down the steps of their single-wide mobile home and into the car. Mary pulled out of the mobile home park on Third Avenue. Even in the dim light, "Pretty," Lillian's black cat, was visibly nervous and meowing in anticipation of another one of Lillian's all too familiar trips.

According to Mary, the last words her roommate Lillian said were, "Take good care of Pretty."

It wasn't unusual that Lillian, who hobbled with a cane following abdominal surgery, would go off on treks without telling anyone. Joe Moss, a neighbor who would have coffee and donuts with the two ladies every Wednesday morning, said he never knew when he would show up for their weekly date only to be informed by Mary that "Miss Lillian got itchy feet and took off for a while."

Residents in the mobile home complex affectionately referred to Lillian Shepherd as "Miss Lillian."

Joe Moss remembered when Mary drove Lillian to

the airport several months earlier so she could visit some out-of-state friends.

"We didn't hear from Miss Lillian for several weeks until she called Mary to tell her to pick her up at the airport," he said.

Mary Asbury had been Lillian's constant companion for three years now, ever since Lillian's husband had died and the grieving Lillian asked her long-time friend to look after her. Mary quit a good job in Northern California to come to San Diego County. The mere room and board, plus the $100-a-week salary, was immaterial.

But on this day, Mary drove Lillian to Pomona for a visit with one of Lillian's relatives, and no one ever heard from Lillian again. Lillian Shepherd, to everyone's astonishment, had apparently vanished.

According to the missing person's report, when the two Chula Vista women arrived in Pomona, the relative wasn't home. Lillian's thoughts were strictly devoted to her black cat. She instructed Mary to go back home immediately so that Pretty wouldn't be lonely.

"Don't worry about me," Lillian reportedly told Mary. "If my [relative] doesn't show up, I'll take a taxi home."

Even after she hadn't heard from Lillian for two weeks, Mary didn't fret or worry. Neither did the neighbors in the mobile home park—although in light of events that were forthcoming, they all had good cause to worry.

A relative of Lillian's from Montana was the first to open the can of worms. She called two weeks after Lillian was last seen and was told by Mary that she had dropped her off on April 5th at a relative's place in Pomona. The Montana relative called the family member in Pomona. She said Lillian had never arrived at her house. When informed of this, Mary called the Chula Vista police to report Lillian Shepherd missing.

That night, the little single-wide mobile home just inside the gate of the ranch-style mobile home plaza was packed with sympathizers trying to calm Mary Asbury down.

"If anything happened to her, I blame myself," Mary said apologetically to neighbors. "I never should have left her alone. But she was so worried about Pretty. She wanted me to get back here as soon as I could to take care of her precious cat."

Neighbors assembling at the Shepherd trailer cast a sympathetic eye toward Pretty. The shiny black cat was sitting on the windowsill, peering out the window, meowing. It was an eerie, ghostly yowl, almost as if Pretty were trying to tell them something horrible.

"It was almost as if the animal had caught the scent of death," one neighbor would later recall.

"It was spooky," another neighbor said. "I'm convinced that cat knew something terrible had happened to Miss Lillian."

Shepherd's sudden disappearance had an unprecedented effect among the close-knit community of the mobile home park. While neighbors held prayer meetings for Shepherd, the baffled Chula Vista police launched a search for the missing woman.

Chief Bill Winters called on the state police, the Boy Scouts, and various other organizations to join in a massive effort to find Lillian Shepherd. Aided by low-flying helicopters, the police took to the outlying wastelands to concentrate their search.

But the short, slight Lillian had disappeared. Three weeks passed without a word from Lillian Shepherd.

All of Lillian's family members promised to let the

authorities know if they saw or heard from her.

Although Chief Winters didn't want to alarm Mary, or anyone else for that matter, he had grown increasingly concerned for the elderly woman's safety. He was well aware that Shepherd was wearing expensive jewelry when she disappeared and was easy prey for those who roam the streets at night.

The city of Chula Vista has a population of about 84,000. Although crime is not unknown to the city's residents, the sudden disappearance of Lillian Shepherd had people, especially residents of the mobile home park, feeling more concerned than usual.

"It's beginning to look bad," a neighbor across the street said, shaking his head. "Looks to me like one of them drug addicts got hold of her. Those dopers will kill anybody for enough money to get their next fix."

Articles in the hometown newspaper, the *Star-News*, reported that mobile home residents evidently held little hope of finding their neighbor alive. This further intensified the fears of people living in the areas of Chula Vista, neighboring National City, Bonita, and Imperial Beach.

It was almost dark and unusually hot even for Southern California on the Friday evening of May 1st as the pedestrian walking his dog off Miramar Road peered into the pit of a 25-foot-deep canyon. He became increasingly nervous as he cautiously made his way down the side, half-sliding, half-stumbling. Curiosity had gotten the best of him and he was easing toward what looked to him like a large overripe melon that had busted open.

When the dog-walker realized it was a dead body, he went scrambling back up the hill faster than he went down with his mutt right behind him. From the nearest pay phone, the man dialed 911 and was transferred

420

to the San Diego County Homicide Department.

In a flash, a team of homicide detectives arrived on the heels of several road deputies. They were met by the man who had discovered the body, and, although he was in an agitated state, he took lawmen to the canyon verging on the Miramar Naval Air Station and explained how he had discovered the corpse.

The detectives couldn't immediately determine how the victim had died. But one thing was certain: since the victim's face was twisted into a repulsive grimace, it would be safe to assume that whoever the unfortunate creature was had died a terrifying death.

Since this was obviously a homicide, one of the detectives put in a call for the county medical examiner.

By morning, police obtained confirmation that the body in the morgue was *not* that of the missing Lillian Shepherd. Apparently, the victim was a male, Robert Raymond Evans, former owner of a Northern California gold mine. Evans' homicide remains unsolved at this writing.

As word spread about this latest killing, the phone at police headquarters rang unceasingly. People wondered if the person who had tossed Evans' body in the canyon might have also kidnapped or killed Lillian Shepherd. Police beefed up their search for the missing Chula Vista woman. Every law enforcement officer in the immediate vicinity worked long and hard on the search. Many off-duty lawmen returned to work on their own time.

For two Coronado residents, getting up at 5:00 a.m. and jogging around Spreckels Park in the 500 block of C Street was a welcome respite from their routine. On April 30th, however, when the two men were trotting down C Street toward the park, a sickening odor hit their nostrils. There, on a corner lawn facing the park,

421

not 10 feet from the asphalt, was a brown garbage bag.

As the two men jogged past the foul-smelling garbage bag, one cursed the litterbug who had tossed the bag on a neighbor's lawn in the respectable neighborhood. More annoying was that the repugnant litter was only two blocks from the Coronado police station.

By mid-afternoon, the glaring sun had bulged the bag, bursting it at the seams. People on their way to the park could see a bloody flesh protruding from the sack. A steady stream of flies was buzzing above the sun-hardened lawn. The stench was unbearable. Finally, someone called the animal control board about a dead dog lying on a lawn that was stinking up the entire neighborhood.

Arriving animal control officers were shocked by the sight. Inside the garbage bag was not the carcass of a dog, but parts of a human body that had apparently been crudely sawed into pieces. The humane society officials notified the Coronado Police Department (CPD).

As every law enforcement officer knows, processing an outdoor crime scene is considerably more labor intensive than an interior probe for evidence. Although these specific CPD officers were reasonably renowned for their finesse in this area, they searched the neighborhood for over three hours but found no evidence.

By evening, the sleuths had expanded the area of the search clear down to Fifth Street several blocks away. Still they found no weapon or any other clue that would point them toward the person who had left the bag of body parts on the lawn of the house adjacent to Spreckels Park.

Pathologists at San Diego's forensic science laboratory reassembled the body parts that had been recovered from the lawn of the Coronado home. Still missing were the head, arms, and legs. However, transparencies of the spinal cord showed, in addition to identifying surgical scars—one from a mastectomy and another from abdominal surgery—indisputable correspondence between the unknown woman's torso and that of the missing Lillian Shepherd.

It was sultry and uncomfortable in the mobile home park as word spread about Miss Lillian's grisly death. Teary-eyed neighbors gathered at Mary Asbury's single-wide trailer to offer their condolences.

Joe Moss remembered how he had always looked forward to their Wednesday morning coffee-and-donut get-togethers. Mary Asbury was totally devastated by the atrocity that had befallen her loyal companion. And Pretty, the victim's devoted black cat, seemed to take the news hardest of all.

"That cat just yowled the eeriest sounds," Moss later told investigators. "The cries kept up during the dead of night until even Lillian's closest friends complained to the management."

Since no suspect and no motive had been established, both Sergeant Manny Castillo of the Sheriff's Department and Sergeant Jeffery C. Hutchins of the Coronado Police Department declined to discuss the fate of those body parts of Shepherd's that were still missing.

Likewise, authorized personnel at the county coroner's office refused to give out any information concerning the case, including the time and date of death. They explained to media members who had flocked into the area from as far away as Lake Elsinore and Carlsbad, that those details were part of the ongoing investigation.

For those who had known and loved Lillian Shepherd, the wait was unbearable. The thought that a killer was lurking in their midst was terrifying and almost incomprehensible. While Sergeant Jeffery Hutchins and various Coronado sleuths huddled at headquarters in an effort to reconstruct possible scenarios for the murder, an incessant flow of phone calls from both print and electronic journals as well as from bewildered citizens flooded the switchboards. It also set off an unusual number of the type of rumors that usually accompany such horrible crimes—and those rumors were checked out by the authorities.

Said one neighbor, "I'm not blaming Mary because I don't know what I would have done. I'd like to think that I would have seen to it that Miss Lillian got safely into her [relative's] house. But Mary said she wasn't too worried after two weeks. She told me. 'Well, I'm not going to worry yet.' We all figured maybe it was somebody who wanted to rob Miss Lillian that killed her."

"I feel sorry for Mary," another neighbor said. "Miss Lillian was her entire life. I don't know what she will do now."

Still another neighbor confided, "If you saw Miss Lillian, you saw Mary helping her up and down the stairs, helping her in and out of the car. She took Miss Lillian everywhere. She looked out after her."

As the lawmen continued questioning family members and friends of the deceased woman, they ferreted out important information that pointed to an unlikely suspect.

"Mary told us that Miss Lillian asked to be dropped off at the parking lot of a family restaurant in Pomona and later called and told her to send her a suitcase of clothes there. She said that Lillian was wearing all her jewelry and gave her no address to send the suitcase," a neighbor confided to police. "We were beginning to think that Miss Lillian had flipped her lid."

So Mary Asbury's conflicting stories, first about having dropped Miss Lillian off at her relative's house and later about dropping her off in the restaurant parking lot, immediately aroused suspicions among crafty lawmen working on the case.

There is an old adage among investigators that any homicide case begins by looking "close to home" for potential suspects. Now, Sergeant Castillo was convinced that he had to look no further than Mary Asbury to find Lillian Shepherd's killer. Armed with a search warrant, Castillo and a crew of laboratory technicians drove into the circled mobile home park in Chula Vista and rapped on Mary's door.

"We want to offer you the opportunity to explain the discrepancies in your stories," Sergeant Castillo told the woman. "Do you want to talk about it?"

Mary indicated she did; she was immediately advised of her rights. Meanwhile, fast-moving forensic technicians began sifting through the tiny trailer for clues. Out back, in the toolshed, they found spatters of blood.

They also found Pretty curled up among miscellaneous debris in the toolshed. The cat was meowing eerily for her departed mistress.

Subsequently, on May 5, 1992, with this and other incriminating information, Mary Asbury was placed under arrest and taken to the Chula Vista police station for questioning. After Asbury's interrogation, in which she staunchly maintained her innocence, she was taken to the Las Colinas Woman's Detention Facility in Santee, where she was held without bail pending an arraignment.

The news of Mary Asbury's arrest swept through the

communities of Coronado and neighboring Chula Vista like a tornado.

"Everybody here feels sick over it," said one resident who had lived in the 500 block of C Avenue since 1963. "It's just not something that we're used to in Coronado, and this is a very quiet street."

Meanwhile, back in Chula Vista, the sparks were flying upwards.

"They got along well," said a neighbor who lived next to the Shepherd trailer. "Sure they squabbled once in a while, but who doesn't. Two old women living together like that . . . Lillian once told me, 'I think Mary deserves what I got because she has taken good care of me.' She said she was leaving everything she owned to Mary."

The woman added, "If Mary did do it, I hope she gets punished for it. But I just don't see how she could have done it. It's unbelievable."

At her May 7th arraignment, Asbury pleaded innocent to a charge of murdering her beloved friend and employer. But Deputy District Attorney Lori Koster produced a videotape, in which a rambling Mary Asbury said she killed Miss Lillian because she treated her "like a dog." Then she changed her mind and said she killed the victim because she feared her job was in jeopardy and that she would be fired and would have no money to live on.

Judge Harvey Hiber ordered Mary Asbury held in lieu of $1 million bail and set a preliminary hearing for May 20th.

At the May 20th hearing, Public Defender Deborah Carson asked for more time to prepare her case. The judge postponed the trial until July 1st. When that date arrived, the judge allowed another defense request for more time and set a new pretrial date for July

30th.

An anonymous source at the district attorney's office confirmed what the news media had already printed. If convicted of murder, Asbury could be sentenced to no more than 25 years to life behind bars because in the state of California, there is no additional punishment for dismemberment of a body unless it can be proven that the act caused death.

On the day of her rescheduled preliminary hearing, Mary Louise Asbury told D.A. Koster that she wanted to make a statement. Outside the courtroom, Asbury calmly gave the prosecuting attorney two reasons for killing and dismembering the woman she had lived with for three years.

With her hair neatly coiffed, looking more like a grandmother than a cold-blooded killer, Asbury pleaded "guilty" when Municipal Court Judge Joan Weber asked her how she wanted to plead to a second-degree murder charge. The first-degree murder charge against her was dismissed moments before, in light of her confession to the district attorney.

Judge Weber set sentencing for August 24th.

The courtroom was packed with the victim's relatives and friends. Some came from as far away as Montana. D.A. Koster told Judge Weber that her office was flooded with phone calls from Shepherd's neighbors, asking for the most stringent sentence allowable by law.

"I don't think second-degree murder is a good disposition of the case," Koster told the judge. "Our intention is to keep her in custody forever."

A neighbor who lived across from Asbury and Shepherd told the court that she had adopted the victim's black cat mostly because it was keeping everybody in the court awake at nights with its yowling.

"Pretty would stand in the room in the middle of the night, making these awful odd noises," the woman said.

According to Asbury's own statement, Pretty had begun her wailing while she was sawing through Miss Lillian's bones in the toolshed, and she continued wailing for three weeks.

According to another resident of the mobile home park, Asbury showed not one iota of remorse for killing Miss Lillian.

"On the Sunday before they arrested her, she came over and said she had reservations to an expensive restaurant which she and Miss Lillian had never canceled," the witness said, adding that throughout dinner, Asbury never once showed any concern about the disappearance of her devoted friend and employer.

Asbury's version of the murder was even more sadistic. At first she said she killed the victim because Shepherd was grieving for her husband and, Asbury asserted, she wanted to "join them in heaven." Then Asbury changed her mind and said she killed the victim because she thought her job was in jeopardy and she would be out on the street with no money.

Asked how she killed Shepherd, Asbury replied matter-of-factly, "I went into Lillian Shepherd's bedroom Sunday morning to wake her up for church, and she was laying so peaceful. I took a pillow and smothered her for no apparent reason."

Like any killer who is faced with disposing of the body, Asbury said she couldn't lift the corpse, so she dragged it to the toolshed and cut Lillian into pieces with a hacksaw. The plastic bags containing the grisly body parts remained on her front porch for three weeks, Asbury testified, while she pondered what to do with them.

Asked if anyone noticed an odor, Asbury shrugged her shoulders and replied matter-of-factly, "Apparently not."

Neighbors who came by frequently to visit her walked right past the hacked-up pieces of Miss Lillian's remains. Ironically, so did police officers who periodically stopped by to question Asbury about Shepherd's disappearance.

One officer told the court that Asbury chuckled when she told him he walked right past Lillian's remains on the front porch.

Responding to questions from Judge Weber, Asbury said she decided to dump the bag containing the victim's head, arms, and legs in a Dumpster in back of a supermarket. Those body parts were never recovered.

Picking up the story from there, Asbury said she placed the second bag of body parts in the trunk of her car and drove across the Coronado Bridge. After cruising around for a while, she decided to drop the last of Miss Lillian in Spreckels Parks. But she noticed some people jogging around the park, so she dumped the bag on a lawn opposite the park, then drove back home and had a cup of tea.

Public Defender Deborah Carson begged the judge to be lenient with Asbury, citing the fact that although she had access to Lillian's bank and safety deposit box, she only spent enough money to pay the rent and other necessities after she killed her. Furthermore, Carson said, at Asbury's age, anything other than a minimal sentence would be a death sentence.

If anyone expected Mary Asbury to break into tears as Judge Weber sentenced her to 15 years to life, they were sadly disappointed. Mary Louise Asbury sat emotionless and never batted an eye as Judge Weber berated her. "It is my sincere hope that this should be a life sentence," the judge said. "This was a particularly brutal and heinous crime against a defenseless seventy-nine-year-old woman."

Nor did the murderess show any remorse as she was being placed in a Chula Vista prison van and whisked away to the Las Colinas Woman's Detention Facility in Santee.

In interviews following the sentence, various neighbors of the victim said they would begin a letter-writing campaign targeting attorneys, judges, and the entire legal system. Friends and family members of the victim said they were outraged by the plea-bargain agreement that had reduced Asbury's sentence to second-degree murder, thereby enabling the murderess to apply for parole in 10 years.

"The prosecutors were too lenient with Mary," said one of several family members of the victim who had been in attendance throughout the proceedings. "Mary didn't have to stay with Lillian. She could have moved. Cold-blooded killing is too much. Mary could have had a life with Lillian as long as she wanted. Lillian left her everything she owned."

As for Pretty, the black cat who witnessed the brutal murder, a detective remarked, "If only that cat could talk, what an eerie story she could tell."

EDITOR'S NOTE:
Joe Moss is not the real name of the person so named in the foregoing story. A fictitious name has been used because there is no reason for public interest in the identity of this person.

430

APPENDIX
The Mutilators

"He Dismembered 52, Then Ate Their Organs!" *True Detective,* June, 1993.

"Bloody Money Solved Dena's Decapitation!" *Front Page Detective,* June, 1986.

"Bisexual Thrill-Killer Was a Mutilation Freak!" *Official Detective,* October, 1991.

"Cuffed and Hacked By a 400-Pound Nude!" *True Detective,* May, 1991.

"Jeffrey Dahmer: The Butcher of Milwaukee's Human Slaughterhouse," *True Detective,* December, 1991.

"Hammered Knives into Stephanie!" *Official Detective,* August, 1992.

"The Barfly Lost Her Head to a Ninja Nut!" *True Detective,* November, 1990.

"Butchered Nude in the Bathtub!" *Front Page Detective,* October, 1986.

431

"He Left Julie Hacked Up and 'Heart-less'!" *Official Detective,* November, 1991.

"He Sawed Off Her Pelvis and Buttocks!" *Inside Detective,* March, 1992.

"Carol Was Cut Up into 200 Pieces—Ground Up, Then Cooked!" *Official Detective,* October, 1992.

"Wolfman's Bizarre Mutilation of 3 Gays!" *Front Page Detective,* April, 1988.

"Blonde's Body Washed Ashore—Bit by Bit!" *Inside Detective,* January, 1985.

"Shot, Chainsawed, Cremated, and Fed to the Dogs!" *Official Detective,* June, 1992.

"The Kinky Sex Fiend Hacked Off Leona's Head!" *Front Page Detective,* October, 1983.

"Cut Off Her Finger to Sell Her Ring for Crack!" *Official Detective,* December, 1993.

"Murder, Mayhem, and Mutilation!" *Front Page Detective,* May, 1990.

"He Sliced Paul to Pieces!" *Inside Detective,* May, 1989.

"Chopped Her Body on the Kitchen Table!" *True Detective,* January, 1991.

"Weirdo Cut Up a Corpse with a Chainsaw!" *Inside Detective,* October, 1983.

"Heinous Mutilation of the Spry Widow," *Inside Detec-*

tive, January, 1988.

"An Ohio Woman Was Chopped into 100 Pieces!" *True Detective,* May, 1990.

"No Way to Bury the Hatchet!" *Official Detective,* July, 1988.

"He Came, He Sawed, He Dismembered!" *Official Detective,* June, 1992.

"Smothered, then Chopped into Bits!" *Master Detective,* July, 1993.

GRUESOME REAL LIFE EVENTS FROM PINNACLE TRUE CRIME

BEYOND ALL REASON   (0-7860-0292-1, $5.99)
My Life with Susan Smith
By David Smith with Carol Calef
On a fall evening in 1994, David Smith began every father's worst nightmare when he learned his two young sons had been kidnapped. Nine days later, his wife, Susan Smith, confessed that the kidnapping had been a hoax, a cruel lie. The truth would be even crueler: 3-year-old Michael and 14-month-old Alex Smith were dead, slain by their mother's own hand.

BLOOD CRIMES   (0-7860-0314-6, $5.99)
The Pennsylvania Skinhead Murders
By Fred Rosen
On February 26, 1995, in a quiet suburb of Allentown, Pennsylvania, 17-year-old Bryan Freeman and his 15-year-old brother David slit their father's throat, stabbed their mother numerous times, and smashed the skull of their 12-year-old brother Erik with a baseball bat. Their hideous mass slaughter led to something even more frightening: the Nazi skinhead movement in America.

LOBSTER BOY   (0-7860-0133-X, $4.99)
The Bizarre Life and Brutal Death of Grady Stiles, Jr.
By Fred Rosen
Descended from a notorious carny family, Grady Stiles, Jr. led an unusual life. With a deformity that gave his hands and feet the appearance of lobster claws, he achieved fame and fortune as "Lobster Boy." But beneath Stiles's grotesque sideshow persona lurked a violent man who secretly abused his family for years. Until his wife and stepson decided to do something about it—by entering a conspiracy to kill.

HORROR FROM HAUTALA

SHADES OF NIGHT (0-8217-5097-6, $4.99)
Stalked by a madman, Lara DeSalvo is unaware that she is most in danger in the one place she thinks she is safe—home.

TWILIGHT TIME (0-8217-4713-4, $4.99)
Jeff Wagner comes home for his sister's funeral and uncovers long-buried memories of childhood sexual abuse and murder.

DARK SILENCE (0-8217-3923-9, $5.99)
Dianne Fraser fights for her family—and her sanity—against the evil forces that haunt an abandoned mill.

COLD WHISPER (0-8217-3464-4, $5.95)
Tully can make Sarah's wishes come true, but Sarah lives in terror because Tully doesn't understand that some wishes aren't meant to come true.

LITTLE BROTHERS (0-8217-4020-2, $4.50)
Kip saw the "little brothers" kill his mother five years ago. Now they have returned, and this time there will be no escape.

MOONBOG (0-8217-3356-7, $4.95)
Someone—or some*thing*—is killing the children in the little town of Holland, Maine.

Available wherever paperbacks are sold, or order direct from the Publisher. Send cover price plus 50¢ per copy for mailing and handling to Penguin USA, P.O. Box 999, c/o Dept. 17109, Bergenfield, NJ 07621. Residents of New York and Tennessee must include sales tax. DO NOT SEND CASH.